Applications of Artificial Intelligence

Contents

Chapter 1

Applications of artificial intelligence

Artificial intelligence has been used in a wide range of fields including medical diagnosis, stock trading, robot control, law, remote sensing, scientific discovery and toys. However, due to the AI effect, many AI applications are not perceived as AI: "A lot of cutting edge AI has filtered into general applications, often without being called AI because once something becomes useful enough and common enough it's not labeled AI anymore," Nick Bostrom reports.[1] "Many thousands of AI applications are deeply embedded in the infrastructure of every industry."[2] In the late 90s and early 21st century, AI technology became widely used as elements of larger systems,[2][3] but the field is rarely credited for these successes.

1.1 Computer science

AI researchers have created many tools to solve the most difficult problems in computer science. Many of their inventions have been adopted by mainstream computer science and are no longer considered a part of AI. (See AI effect). According to Russell & Norvig (2003, p. 15), all of the following were originally developed in AI laboratories: time sharing, interactive interpreters, graphical user interfaces and the computer mouse, rapid development environments, the linked list data structure, automatic storage management, symbolic programming, functional programming, dynamic programming and object-oriented programming.

1.2 Finance

Use of AI in banking can be tracked back to 1987 when Security Pacific National Bank in USA set-up a Fraud Prevention Task force to counter the unauthorised use of debit cards. Apps like Kasisito and Moneystream are using AI in financial services[4] Banks use artificial intelligence systems to organize operations, invest in stocks, and manage properties. In August 2001, robots beat humans in a simulated financial trading competition.[5]

Financial institutions have long used artificial neural network systems to detect charges or claims outside of the norm, flagging these for human investigation.

1.3 Hospitals and medicine

A medical clinic can use artificial intelligence systems to organize bed schedules, make a staff rotation, and provide medical information and other important tasks.

Artificial neural networks are used as clinical decision support systems for medical diagnosis, such as in Concept Processing technology in EMR software.

Other tasks in medicine that can potentially be performed by artificial intelligence include:

- Computer-aided interpretation of medical images. Such systems help scan digital images, *e.g.* from computed tomography, for typical appearances and to highlight conspicuous sections, such as possible diseases. A typical application is the detection of a tumor.

- Heart sound analysis[6]

- Watson project is another use of AI in this field, a Q/A program that suggest for doctor's of cancer patients.

1.4 Heavy industry

Robots have become common in many industries. They are often given jobs that are considered dangerous to humans. Robots have proven effective in jobs that are very repetitive which may lead to mistakes or accidents due to a lapse in concentration and other jobs which humans may find degrading. Japan is the leader in using and producing robots in the world. In 1999, 1,700,000 robots were in use worldwide.

1.5 Online and telephone customer service

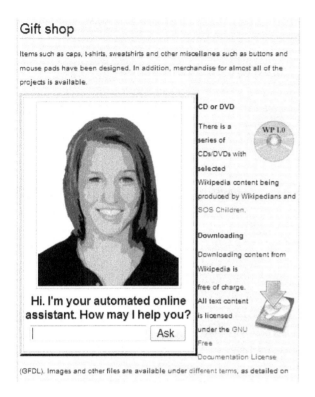

An automated online assistant providing customer service on a web page.

Artificial intelligence is implemented in automated online assistants that can be seen as avatars on web pages.[7] It can avail for enterprises to reduce their operation and training cost.[7] A major underlying technology to such systems is natural language processing.[7]

Similar techniques may be used in answering machines of call centres, such as speech recognition software to allow computers to handle first level of customer support, text mining and natural language processing to allow better customer handling, agent training by automatic mining of best practices from past interactions, support automation and many other technologies to improve agent productivity and customer satisfaction.[8]

1.6 Transportation

Fuzzy logic controllers have been developed for automatic gearboxes in automobiles. For example, the 2006 Audi TT, VW Toureg and VW Caravell feature the DSP transmission which utilizes Fuzzy Logic. A number of Škoda variants (Škoda Fabia) also currently include a Fuzzy Logic-based

controller.

1.7 Telecommunications maintenance

Many telecommunications companies make use of heuristic search in the management of their workforces, for example BT Group has deployed heuristic search[9] in a scheduling application that provides the work schedules of 20,000 engineers.

1.8 Toys and games

The 1990s saw some of the first attempts to mass-produce domestically aimed types of basic Artificial Intelligence for education, or leisure. This prospered greatly with the Digital Revolution, and helped introduce people, especially children, to a life of dealing with various types of Artificial Intelligence, specifically in the form of Tamagotchis and Giga Pets, iPod Touch, the Internet (example: basic search engine interfaces are one simple form), and the first widely released robot, Furby. A mere year later an improved type of domestic robot was released in the form of Aibo, a robotic dog with intelligent features and autonomy.

AI has also been applied to video games, for example video game bots, which are designed to stand in as opponents where humans aren't available or desired; or the AI Director from Left 4 Dead, which decides where enemies spawn and how maps are laid out to be more or less challenging at various points of play.

1.9 Music

The evolution of music has always been affected by technology. With AI, scientists are trying to make the computer emulate the activities of the skillful musician. Composition, performance, music theory, sound processing are some of the major areas on which research in Music and Artificial Intelligence are focusing. Among these efforts, Melomics seems to be ahead by powering computer-composers that learn to compose the way humans do.[10]

1.10 Aviation

The Air Operations Division (AOD) uses AI for the rule based expert systems. The AOD has use for artificial intelligence for surrogate operators for combat and training simulators, mission management aids, support systems for tactical decision making, and post processing of the simulator data into symbolic summaries.

The use of artificial intelligence in simulators is proving to be very useful for the AOD. Airplane simulators are using artificial intelligence in order to process the data taken from simulated flights. Other than simulated flying, there is also simulated aircraft warfare. The computers are able to come up with the best success scenarios in these situations. The computers can also create strategies based on the placement, size, speed and strength of the forces and counter forces. Pilots may be given assistance in the air during combat by computers. The artificial intelligent programs can sort the information and provide the pilot with the best possible maneuvers, not to mention getting rid of certain maneuvers that would be impossible for a human being to perform. Multiple aircraft are needed to get good approximations for some calculations so computer simulated pilots are used to gather data. These computer simulated pilots are also used to train future air traffic controllers.

The system used by the AOD in order to measure performance was the Interactive Fault Diagnosis and Isolation System, or IFDIS. It is a rule based expert system put together by collecting information from TF-30 documents and the expert advice from mechanics that work on the TF-30. This system was designed to be used for the development of the TF-30 for the RAAF F-111C. The performance system was also used to replace specialized workers. The system allowed the regular workers to communicate with the system and avoid mistakes, miscalculations, or having to speak to one of the specialized workers.

The AOD also uses artificial intelligence in speech recognition software. The air traffic controllers are giving directions to the artificial pilots and the AOD wants to the pilots to respond to the ATC's with simple responses. The programs that incorporate the speech software must be trained, which means they use neural networks. The program used, the Verbex 7000, is still a very early program that has plenty of room for improvement. The improvements are imperative because ATCs use very specific dialog and the software needs to be able to communicate correctly and promptly every time.

The Artificial Intelligence supported Design of Aircraft,[11] or AIDA, is used to help designers in the process of creating conceptual designs of aircraft. This program allows the designers to focus more on the design itself and less on the design process. The software also allows the user to focus less on the software tools. The AIDA uses rule based systems to compute its data. This is a diagram of the arrangement of the AIDA modules. Although simple, the program is proving effective.

In 2003, NASA's Dryden Flight Research Center, and many other companies, created software that could enable a damaged aircraft to continue flight until a safe landing zone can be reached. The software compensates for all the damaged components by relying on the undamaged components. The neural network used in the software proved to be effective and marked a triumph for artificial intelligence.

The Integrated Vehicle Health Management system, also used by NASA, on board an aircraft must process and interpret data taken from the various sensors on the aircraft. The system needs to be able to determine the structural integrity of the aircraft. The system also needs to implement protocols in case of any damage taken the vehicle.

1.11 News, publishing and writing

The company Narrative Science makes computer generated news and reports commercially available, including summarizing team sporting events based on statistical data from the game in English. It also creates financial reports and real estate analyses.[12]

The company Automated Insights generates personalized recaps and previews for Yahoo Sports Fantasy Football.[13] The company is projected to generate one billion stories in 2014, up from 350 million in 2013.[14]

Another company, called Yseop, uses artificial intelligence to turn structured data into intelligent comments and recommendations in natural language. Yseop is able to write financial reports, executive summaries, personalized sales or marketing documents and more at a speed of thousands of pages per second and in multiple languages including English, Spanish, French & German.[15]

1.12 Other

Various tools of artificial intelligence are also being widely deployed in homeland security, speech and text recognition, data mining, and e-mail spam filtering. Applications are also being developed for gesture recognition (understanding of sign language by machines), individual voice recognition, global voice recognition (from a variety of people in a noisy room), facial expression recognition for interpretation of emotion and non verbal cues. Other applications are robot navigation, obstacle avoidance, and object recognition.

1.13 List of applications

Typical problems to which AI methods are applied

Other fields in which AI methods are implemented

1.14 See also

- List of artificial intelligence projects
- Progress in artificial intelligence

1.15 Notes

[1] AI set to exceed human brain power CNN.com (July 26, 2006)

[2] Kurzweil 2005, p. 264.

[3] NRC 1999, "Artificial Intelligence in the 90s".

[4] ICICIbank.com

[5] Robots Beat Humans in Trading Battle. BBC.com (August 8, 2001)

[6] Reed, T. R.; Reed, N. E.; Fritzson, P. (2004). "Heart sound analysis for symptom detection and computer-aided diagnosis". *Simulation Modelling Practice and Theory* **12** (2): 129. doi:10.1016/j.simpat.2003.11.005.

[7] Implementing an online help desk system based on conversational agent Authors: Alisa Kongthon, Chatchawal Sangkeettrakarn, Sarawoot Kongyoung and Choochart Haruechaiyasak. Published by ACM 2009 Article, Bibliometrics Data Bibliometrics. Published in: Proceeding, MEDES '09 Proceedings of the International Conference on Management of Emergent Digital EcoSystems, ACM New York, NY, USA. ISBN 978-1-60558-829-2, doi:10.1145/1643823.1643908

[8] L Venkata Subramaniam (February 1, 2008). "Call Centers of the Future" (PDF). i.t. magazine. pp. 48–51. Retrieved 2008-05-29.

[9] Success Stories.

[10] Ball, Philip (8 August 2014). "Artificial music: The computers that create melodies". BBC Future.

[11] AIDA Homepage. Kbs.twi.tudelft.nl (April 17, 1997). Retrieved on 2013-07-21.

[12] business intelligence solutions. Narrative Science. Retrieved on 2013-07-21.

[13] Eule, Alexander. "Big Data and Yahoo's Quest for Mass Personalization". *Barron's*.

[14] Kirkland, Sam. "'Robot' to write 1 billion stories in 2014 — but will you know it when you see it?". *Poynter*.

[15] http://yseop.com/EN/solutions.html

1.16 External links

- AI applications at aitopics.org

1.17 References

- Russell, Stuart J.; Norvig, Peter (2003). *Artificial Intelligence: A Modern Approach* (2nd ed.). Upper Saddle River, New Jersey: Prentice Hall. ISBN 0-13-790395-2

- Kurzweil, Ray (2005). *The Singularity is Near: When Humans Transcend Biology*. New York: Viking. ISBN 978-0-670-03384-3

- National Research Council (1999). "Developments in Artificial Intelligence". *Funding a Revolution: Government Support for Computing Research*. National Academy Press. ISBN 0-309-06278-0. OCLC 246584055.

- Moghaddam, M. J., M. R. Soleymani, and M. A. Farsi. "Sequence planning for stamping operations in progressive dies." Journal of Intelligent Manufacturing(2013): 1-11.

Chapter 2

Activity recognition

Activity recognition aims to recognize the actions and goals of one or more agents from a series of observations on the agents' actions and the environmental conditions. Since the 1980s, this research field has captured the attention of several computer science communities due to its strength in providing personalized support for many different applications and its connection to many different fields of study such as medicine, human-computer interaction, or sociology.

To understand activity recognition better, consider the following scenario. An elderly man wakes up at dawn in his small studio apartment, where he stays alone. He lights the stove to make a pot of tea, switches on the toaster oven, and takes some bread and jelly from the cupboard. After he takes his morning medication, a computer-generated voice gently reminds him to turn off the toaster. Later that day, his daughter accesses a secure website where she scans a check-list, which was created by a sensor network in her father's apartment. She finds that her father is eating normally, taking his medicine on schedule, and continuing to manage his daily life on his own. That information puts her mind at ease.

Many different applications have been studied by researchers in activity recognition; examples include assisting the sick and disabled. For example, Pollack et al.[1] show that by automatically monitoring human activities, home-based rehabilitation can be provided for people suffering from traumatic brain injuries. One can find applications ranging from security-related applications and logistics support to location-based services. Due to its many-faceted nature, different fields may refer to activity recognition as plan recognition, goal recognition, intent recognition, behavior recognition, location estimation and location-based services.

2.1 Types of activity recognition

2.1.1 Sensor-based, single-user activity recognition

Sensor-based activity recognition integrates the emerging area of sensor networks with novel data mining and machine learning techniques to model a wide range of human activities.[2][3] Mobile devices (e.g. smart phones) provide sufficient sensor data and calculation power to enable physical activity recognition to provide an estimation of the energy consumption during everyday life. Sensor-based activity recognition researchers believe that by empowering ubiquitous computers and sensors to monitor the behavior of agents (under consent), these computers will be better suited to act on our behalf.

Levels of sensor-based activity recognition

Sensor-based activity recognition is a challenging task due to the inherent noisy nature of the input. Thus, statistical modeling has been the main thrust in this direction in layers, where the recognition at several intermediate levels is conducted and connected. At the lowest level where the sensor data are collected, statistical learning concerns how to find the detailed locations of agents from the received signal data. At an intermediate level, statistical inference may be concerned about how to recognize individuals' activities from the inferred location sequences and environmental conditions at the lower levels. Furthermore, at the highest level a major concern is to find out the overall goal or subgoals of an agent from the activity sequences through a mixture of logical and statistical reasoning. Scientific conferences where activity recognition work from wearable and environmental often appears are ISWC and UbiComp.

2.1.2 Sensor-based, multi-user activity recognition

Recognizing activities for multiple users using on-body sensors first appeared in the work by ORL using active badge systems[4] in the early 90's. Other sensor technology such as acceleration sensors were used for identifying group activity patterns during office scenarios.[5] Activities of Multiple Users in intelligent environments are addressed in Gu et al.[6] In this work, they investigate the fundamental problem of recognizing activities for multiple users from sensor readings in a home environment, and propose a novel pattern mining approach to recognize both single-user and multi-user activities in a unified solution.

2.1.3 Sensor-based group activity recognition

Recognition of group activities is fundamentally different from single, or multi-user activity recognition in that the goal is to recognize the behavior of the group as an entity, rather than the activities of the individual members within it.[7] Group behavior is emergent in nature, meaning that the properties of the behavior of the group are fundamentally different then the properties of the behavior of the individuals within it, or any sum of that behavior.[8] The main challenges are in modeling the behavior of the individual group members, as well as the roles of the individual within the group dynamic [9] and their relationship to emergent behavior of the group in parallel.[10] Challenges which must still be addressed include quantification of the behavior and roles of individuals who join the group, integration of explicit models for role description into inference algorithms, and scalability evaluations for very large groups and crowds. Group activity recognition has applications for crowd management and response in emergency situations, as well as for social networking and Quantified Self applications.[11]

2.1.4 Vision-based activity recognition

It is a very important and challenging problem to track and understand the behavior of agents through videos taken by various cameras. The primary technique employed is computer vision. Vision-based activity recognition has found many applications such as human-computer interaction, user interface design, robot learning, and surveillance, among others. Scientific conferences where vision based activity recognition work often appears are ICCV and CVPR.

In vision-based activity recognition, a great deal of work has been done. Researchers have attempted a number of methods such as optical flow, Kalman filtering, Hidden Markov models, etc., under different modalities such as single camera, stereo, and infrared. In addition, researchers have considered multiple aspects on this topic, including single pedestrian tracking, group tracking, and detecting dropped objects.

Recently some researchers have used RGBD cameras like Microsoft Kinect to detect human activities. Depth cameras add extra dimension i.e. depth which normal 2d camera fails to provide. Sensory information from these depth cameras have been used to generate real-time skeleton model of humans with different body positions. These skeleton information provides meaningful information that researchers have to used to model human activities which are trained and later used to recognize unknown activities.[12]

Levels of vision-based activity recognition

In vision-based activity recognition, the computational process is often divided into four steps, namely human detection, human tracking, human activity recognition and then a high-level activity evaluation.

Automatic gait recognition

Main article: Gait recognition

One way to identify specific people is by how they walk. Gait-recognition software can be used to record a person's gait or gait profile in a database for the purpose of recognizing that person later, even if they are wearing a disguise.

2.2 Approaches of activity recognition

2.2.1 Activity recognition through logic and reasoning

Logic-based approaches keep track of all logically consistent explanations of the observed actions. Thus, all possible and consistent plans or goals must be considered. Kautz[13] provided a formal theory of plan recognition. He described plan recognition as a logical inference process of circumscription. All actions, plans are uniformly referred to as goals, and a recognizer's knowledge is represented by a set of first-order statements called event hierarchy encoded in first-order logic, which defines abstraction, decomposition and functional relationships between types of events.

Kautz's general framework for plan recognition has an exponential time complexity in worst case, measured in the size of input hierarchy. Lesh and Etzioni[14] went one step further and presented methods in scaling up goal recognition to scale up his work computationally. In contrast to Kautz's approach where the plan library is explicitly represented, Lesh and Etzioni's approach enables automatic plan-library construction from domain primitives. Furthermore, they introduced compact representations and efficient algorithms for goal recognition on large plan libraries.

Inconsistent plans and goals are repeatedly pruned when new actions arrive. Besides, they also presented methods for adapting a goal recognizer to handle individual idiosyncratic behavior given a sample of an individual's recent behavior. Pollack et al. described a direct argumentation model that can know about the relative strength of several kinds of arguments for belief and intention description.

A serious problem of logic-based approaches is their inability or inherent infeasibility to represent uncertainty. They offer no mechanism for preferring one consistent approach to another and incapable of deciding whether one particular plan is more likely than another, as long as both of them can be consistent enough to explain the actions observed. There is also a lack of learning ability associated with logic based methods.

Another approach to logic-based activity recognition is to use stream reasoning based on Answer Set Programming,[15] and has been applied to recognising activities for health-related applications,[16] which uses weak constraints to model a degree of ambiguity/uncertainty.

2.2.2 Activity recognition through probabilistic reasoning

Probability theory and statistical learning models are more recently applied in activity recognition to reason about actions, plans and goals.

Plan recognition can be done as a process of reasoning under uncertainty, which is convincingly argued by Charniak and Goldman.[17] They argued that any model that does not incorporate some theory of uncertainty reasoning cannot be adequate. In the literature, there have been several approaches which explicitly represent uncertainty in reasoning about an agent's plans and goals.

Using sensor data as input, Hodges and Pollack designed machine learning-based systems for identifying individuals as they perform routine daily activities such as making coffee.[18] Intel Research (Seattle) Lab and University of Washington at Seattle have done some important works on using sensors to detect human plans.[19][20][21][22] Some of these works infer user transportation modes from readings of radio-frequency identifiers (RFID) and global positioning systems (GPS).

The use of temporal probabilistic models has been shown to perform well in activity recognition and generally outperform non-temporal models.[23] Generative models such as the hidden Markov model (HMM) and the more generally

formulated dynamic Bayesian networks (DBN) are popular choices in modeling activities from sensor data.[24][25][26] Discriminative models such as Conditional Random Fields (CRF) are also commonly applied and also give good performance in activity recognition.[27][28]

Generative and discriminative models both have their pros and cons and the ideal choice depends on their area of application. A dataset together with implementations of a number of popular models (HMM, CRF) for activity recognition can be found here.

Conventional temporal probabilistic models such as the hidden Markov model (HMM) and conditional random fields (CRF) model directly model the correlations between the activities and the observed sensor data. In recent years, increasing evidence has supported the use of hierarchical models which take into account the rich hierarchical structure that exists in human behavioral data.[24][29][30] The core idea here is that the model does not directly correlate the activities with the sensor data, but instead breaks the activity into sub-activities (sometimes referred to as actions) and models the underlying correlations accordingly. An example could be the activity of preparing spaghetti, which can be broken down into the subactivities or actions of cutting vegetables, frying the vegetables in a pan and serving it on a plate. Examples of such a hierarchical model are Layered Hidden Markov Models (LHMMs)[29] and the hierarchical hidden Markov model (HHMM), which have been shown to significantly outperform its non-hierarchical counterpart in activity recognition.[24]

2.2.3 Wi-Fi-based activity recognition

When activity recognition is performed indoors and in cities using the widely available Wi-Fi signals and 802.11 access points, there is much noise and uncertainty. These uncertainties are modeled using a dynamic Bayesian network model by Yin et al.[31] A multiple goal model that can reason about user's interleaving goals is presented by Chai and Yang,[32] where a deterministic state transition model is applied. A better model that models the concurrent and interleaving activities in a probabilistic approach is proposed by Hu and Yang.[33] A user action discovery model is presented by Yin et al.,[34] where the Wi-Fi signals are segmented to produce possible actions.

A fundamental problem in Wi-Fi-based activity recognition is to estimate the user locations. Two important issues are how to reduce the human labelling effort and how to cope with the changing signal profiles when the environment changes. Yin et al.[35] dealt with the second issue by transferring the labelled knowledge between time periods. Chai and Yang[36] proposed a hidden Markov model-based method to extend labelled knowledge by leveraging the unlabelled user traces. J. Pan et al.[37] propose to perform location estimation through online co-localization, and S. Pan et al.[38] proposed to apply multi-view learning for migrating the labelled data to a new time period.

2.2.4 Data mining based approach to activity recognition

Different from traditional machine learning approaches, an approach based on data mining has been recently proposed. In the work of Gu et al.,[39] the problem of activity recognition is formulated as a pattern-based classification problem. They proposed a data mining approach based on discriminative patterns which describe significant changes between any two activity classes of data to recognize sequential, interleaved and concurrent activities in a unified solution. Gilbert *et al.*[40] use 2D corners in both space and time. These are grouped spatially and temporally using a hierarchical process, with an increasing search area. At each stage of the hierarchy, the most distinctive and descriptive features are learned efficiently through data mining (Apriori rule).

2.3 Labs in the world

- Wireless Sensor Data Mining Lab at Fordham University
- Martha Pollack's research group
- Prof Qiang Yang's research group
- RSE Lab @ University of Washington, leading by Dieter Fox
- Fraunhofer IGD Lab for Ambient Intelligence
- Tao Gu's Advanced Network System Lab at University of Southern Denmark
- Jeffrey Junfeng Pan's Sensor-based Localization and Tracking Project
- Prof. Helal's mobile and pervasive computing lab at University of Florida
- Ajou University CUSLAB Vision-based Activity Awareness
- Tanzeem Choudhury's People-Aware Computing (PAC) Group
- Computer Vision and Multimodal Computing Group at MPI INF
- Wearable Computing Lab at ETH Zurich

- The BehaviorScope Project at ENALAB - Yale
- The Embedded Sensing Systems group at TU Darmstadt
- The Embedded Systems group at the University of Freiburg
- WSU CASAS Smart Home Project
- DLR Institute for Communications and Navigation Activity Recognition Project
- Activity Analysis Research Group of Leeds University, UK
- Laboratoire d'Intelligence Ambiante pour la Reconnaissance de l'Activité (LIARA), Canada
- Pervasive Computing Systems / TecO Lab at Karlsruhe Institute of Technology, Germany
- Department of Intelligent System at Jožef Stefan Institute
- SmartLab of Mobile Multimedia Information Systems Group at University of Rostock, Germany
- Imagine Research group at LIRIS laboratory, Lyon, France
- Digital Interaction Group at Culture Lab, Newcastle University, UK
- Bio-imaging Lab at Kyung Hee University, Republic of Korea

2.4 Related conferences

- AAAI
- CVPR
- ICCV
- IJCAI
- NIPS
- PERVASIVE
- Ubicomp
- PerCom
- ISWC
- ICAPS

2.5 See also

online lectures on activity recognition

- Introduction to Activity Recognition lecture at ESS, Darmstadt

related articles

- AI effect

- Applications of artificial intelligence

- Conditional random field

- Hidden Markov model

- Naive Bayes classifier

- Planning

- Support vector machines

Lists

- List of emerging technologies

- Outline of artificial intelligence

2.6 References

[1] Pollack, M.E., and et al., L. E. B. 2003. "Autominder: an intelligent cognitive orthotic system for people with memory impairment". *Robotics and Autonomous Systems* 44(3-4):273–282.

[2] Tanzeem Choudhury, Gaetano Borriello, et al. The Mobile Sensing Platform: An Embedded System for Activity Recognition. Appears in the IEEE Pervasive Magazine - Special Issue on Activity-Based Computing, April 2008.

[3] Nishkam Ravi, Nikhil Dandekar, Preetham Mysore, Michael Littman. Activity Recognition from Accelerometer Data. Proceedings of the Seventeenth Conference on Innovative Applications of Artificial Intelligence (IAAI/AAAI 2005).

[4] Want R., Hopper A., Falcao V., Gibbons J.: The Active Badge Location System, ACM Transactions on Information, Systems, Vol. 40, No. 1, pp. 91-102, January 1992

[5] Bieber G., Kirste T., Untersuchung des gruppendynamischen Aktivitaetsverhaltes im Office-Umfeld, 7. Berliner Werkstatt Mensch-Maschine-Systeme, Berlin, Germany, 2007

[6] Tao Gu, Zhanqing Wu, Liang Wang, Xianping Tao, and Jian Lu. Mining Emerging Patterns for Recognizing Activities of Multiple Users in Pervasive Computing. In Proc. of the 6th International Conference on Mobile and Ubiquitous Systems: Computing, Networking and Services (MobiQuitous '09), Toronto, Canada, July 13–16, 2009.

[7] Dawud Gordon, Jan-Hendrik Hanne, Martin Berchtold, Ali Asghar Nazari Shirehjini, Michael Beigl: Towards Collaborative Group Activity Recognition Using Mobile Devices, Mobile Networks and Applications 18(3), 2013, p. 326-340

[8] Lewin, K. Field theory in social science: selected theoretical papers. Social science paperbacks. Harper, New York, 1951.

[9] Hirano, T., and Maekawa, T. A hybrid unsupervised/supervised model for group activity recognition. In Proceedings of the 2013 International Symposium on Wearable Computers, ISWC '13, ACM (New York, NY, USA, 2013), 21–24

[10] Brdiczka, O., Maisonnasse, J., Reignier, P., and Crowley, J. L. Detecting small group activities from multimodal observations. Applied Intelligence 30, 1 (July 2007), 47–57.

[11] Dawud Gordon, Group Activity Recognition Using Wearable Sensing Devices, Dissertation, Karlsruhe Institute of Technology, 2014

[12] Piyathilaka, L.; Kodagoda, S., "Gaussian mixture based HMM for human daily activity recognition using 3D skeleton features," Industrial Electronics and Applications (ICIEA), 2013 8th IEEE Conference on , vol., no., pp.567,572, 19–21 June 2013 URL: http://ieeexplore.ieee.org/stamp/stamp.jsp?tp=&arnumber=6566433&isnumber=6566328

[13] H. Kautz. "A formal theory of plan recognition". In PhD thesis, University of Rochester, 1987.

[14] N. Lesh and O. Etzioni. "A sound and fast goal recognizer". In *Proceedings of the International Joint Conference on Artificial Intelligence*, 1995.

[15] Do, Thang; Seng W. Loke; Fei Liu (2011). "Answer Set Programming for Stream Reasoning". *Advances in Artificial Intelligence, Lecture Notes in Computer Science* **6657**: 104–109.

[16] Do, Thang; Seng W. Loke; Fei Liu (2012). "HealthyLife: an Activity Recognition System with Smartphone using Logic-Based Stream Reasoning" (PDF). *Proceedings of the 9th International Conference on Mobile and Ubiquitous Systems: Computing, Networking and Services, (Mobiquitous 2012)*.

[17] E. Charniak and R.P. Goldman. "A Bayesian model of plan recognition". *Artificial Intelligence*, 64:53–79, 1993.

[18] M.R. Hodges and M.E. Pollack. "An 'object-use fingerprint': The use of electronic sensors for human identification". In *Proceedings of the 9th International Conference on Ubiquitous Computing*, 2007.

[19] Mike Perkowitz, Matthai Philipose, Donald J. Patterson, and Kenneth P. Fishkin. "Mining models of human activities from the web". In *Proceedings of the Thirteenth International World Wide Web Conference (WWW 2004), pages 573–582, May 2004.*

[20] Matthai Philipose, Kenneth P. Fishkin, Mike Perkowitz, Donald J. Patterson, Dieter Fox, Henry Kautz, and Dirk Hähnel. "Inferring activities from interactions with objects". In *IEEE Pervasive Computing*, pages 50–57, October 2004.

[21] Dieter Fox Lin Liao, Donald J. Patterson and Henry A. Kautz. "Learning and inferring transportation routines". *Artif. Intell.*, 171(5-6):311–331, 2007.

[22] Piyathilaka, L.; Kodagoda, S., "Gaussian mixture based HMM for human daily activity recognition using 3D skeleton features," Industrial Electronics and Applications (ICIEA), 2013 8th IEEE Conference on , vol., no., pp.567,572, 19–21 June 2013

[23] TLM van Kasteren, Gwenn Englebienne, BJA Kröse. "Human activity recognition from wireless sensor network data: Benchmark and software." Activity Recognition in Pervasive Intelligent Environments, 165-186, Atlantis Press

[24] TLM van Kasteren, Gwenn Englebienne, Ben Kröse"Hierarchical Activity Recognition Using Automatically Clustered Actions", 2011, ,Ambient Intelligence, 82-91, Springer Berlin/Heidelberg

[25] Daniel Wilson and Chris Atkeson. Simultaneous tracking and activityrecognition (star) using many anonymous binary sensors. In Proceedings of the 3rd international conference on Pervasive Computing, Pervasive, pages 62–79, Munich , Germany, 2005.

[26] Nuria Oliver, Barbara Rosario and Alex Pentland "A Bayesian Computer Vision System for Modeling Human Interactions" Appears in PAMI Special Issue on Visual Surveillance and Monitoring, Aug 00

[27] TLM Van Kasteren, Athanasios Noulas, Gwenn Englebienne, Ben Kröse"Accurate activity recognition in a home setting", 2008/9/21, Proceedings of the 10th international conference on Ubiquitous computing, 1-9, ACM

[28] Derek Hao Hu, Sinno Jialin Pan, Vincent Wenchen Zheng, Nathan NanLiu, and Qiang Yang. Real world activity recognition with multiple goals.In Proceedings of the 10th international conference on Ubiquitous computing,Ubicomp, pages 30–39, New York, NY, USA, 2008. ACM.

[29] Nuria Oliver, Ashutosh Garg, and Eric Horvitz. Layered representations for learning and inferring office activity from multiple sensory channels. Comput. Vis. Image Underst., 96(2):163–180, 2004.

[30] Amarnag Subramanya, Alvin Raj, Jeff Bilmes, and Dieter Fox. Hierarchical models for activity recognition. In Proceedings of the international conference on Multimedia Signal Processing, MMSP, Victoria, CA, October 2006.

[31] Jie Yin, Xiaoyong Chai and Qiang Yang, "High-level Goal Recognition in a Wireless LAN". In *Proceedings of the Nineteenth National Conference on Artificial Intelligence* (AAAI-04), San Jose, CA USA, July 2004. Pages 578-584

[32] Xiaoyong Chai and Qiang Yang, "Multiple-Goal Recognition From Low-level Signals". *Proceedings of the Twentieth National Conference on Artificial Intelligence* (AAAI 2005), Pittsburg, PA USA, July 2005. Pages 3-8.

[33] Derek Hao Hu, Qiang Yang. "CIGAR: Concurrent and Interleaving Goal and Activity Recognition", to appear in AAAI 2008

[34] Jie Yin, Dou Shen, Qiang Yang and Ze-nian Li "Activity Recognition through Goal-Based Segmentation". *Proceedings of the Twentieth National Conference on Artificial Intelligence* (AAAI 2005), Pittsburg, PA USA, July 2005. Pages 28-33.

[35] Jie Yin, Qiang Yang and Lionel Ni. "Adaptive Temporal Radio Maps for Indoor Location Estimation". In *Proceedings of the 3rd Annual IEEE International Conference on Pervasive Computing and Communications* (IEEE PerCom 2005), Kauai Island, Hawaii, March, 2005. Pages 85-94.

[36] Xiaoyong Chai and Qiang Yang. "Reducing the Calibration Effort for Location Estimation Using Unlabeled Samples". In *Proceedings of the 3rd Annual IEEE International Conference on Pervasive Computing and Communications*, (IEEE PerCom 2005) Kauai Island, Hawaii, March 2005. Pages 95-—104.

[37] Jeffrey Junfeng Pan, Qiang Yang and Sinno Jialin Pan. "Online Co-Localization in Indoor Wireless Networks". In *Proceedings of the 22nd AAAI Conference on Artificial Intelligence* (AAAI'07) Vancouver, British Columbia, Canada. July 2007. 1102-1107

[38] Sinno Jialin Pan, James T. Kwok, Qiang Yang, Jeffrey Junfeng Pan. "Adaptive localization in a dynamic WiFi environment through multi-view learning". In *Proceedings of the 22nd AAAI Conference on Artificial Intelligence* (AAAI'07) Vancouver, British Columbia, Canada. July 2007. 1108-1113

[39] Tao Gu, Zhanqing Wu, Xianping Tao, Hung Keng Pung, and Jian Lu. epSICAR: An Emerging Patterns based Approach to Sequential, Interleaved and Concurrent Activity Recognition. In Proc. of the 7th Annual IEEE International Conference on Pervasive Computing and Communications (Percom '09), Galveston, Texas, March 9–13, 2009.

[40] Gilbert A, Illingworth J, Bowden R. Action Recognition using Mined Hierarchical Compound Features. IEEE Trans Pattern Analysis and Machine Learning

Chapter 3

AForge.NET

AForge.NET is a computer vision and artificial intelligence library originally developed by Andrew Kirillov for the .NET Framework.

The source code and binaries of the project are available under the terms of the Lesser GPL and the GPL (GNU General Public License).

Another (unaffiliated) project named **Accord.NET** extends the features of the original **AForge.NET** library.

3.1   Features

The framework's API includes support for:

- Computer vision, image processing and video processing
  - Including a comprehensive image filter library
- Neural networks
- Genetic programming
- Fuzzy logic
- Machine learning
- and libraries for a select set of robotics kits
  - Lego Mindstorms NXT and RCX kits
  - TeRK Qwerk kit
  - Surveyor SRV-1 and SVS kits

Complete list of features is available on the features page of the project.

The framework is provided not only with different libraries and their sources, but with many sample applications, which demonstrate the use of this framework, and with documentation help files, which are provided in HTML Help format. The documentation is also available on-line.

3.2   See also

- OpenCV - A popular C++ computer vision library.
- VXL - Another C++ computer vision library.
- CVIPtools - A complete GUI based computer vision and image processing software environment.
- OpenNN - An open source C++ neural networks library.

3.3   References

[1] End of free public support, April 1, 2012, AForge.NET

[2] http://aforgenet.com/news/2011.12.21.five_years_framework.html

3.4   External links

- Official website
- Google Code project home
- Accord.NET Website

Chapter 4

Akinator

Akinator, the Web Genie (formerly *Akinator, the web Genius*) is an internet game and mobile app based on Twenty Questions that can attempt to determine which character the player is thinking of by asking them a series of questions. It is an artificial intelligence program that can find and learn the best questions to be asked to the player. Created by three French programmers in 2007, it became worldwide-popular in November 2008, according to Google Trends. In Europe popularity peak was reached in 2009 and Japan in 2010 with the launch of mobile apps by French mobile company SCIMOB,[1] reaching highest ranks on app store[2]. While playing "Akinator" the questions are asked by a cartoon genie.

4.1 Gameplay

In order to begin the questionnaire, the user must hit the play button and think of a popular character (musician, athlete, political personality, actor, fictional film/TV character, YouTuber, Viner etc.). Then, it begins asking a series of questions (as much as he needed), with "Yes", "No", "Probably", "Probably not" and "Don't know" as possible answers, in order to narrow down the potential character that the user is thinking of.[3][4] If the answer is narrowed down to a single likely option before 25 questions are asked, the program will automatically ask if the character it chose is correct. If the character is guessed wrong three times in a row, then the program will prompt the user to input the character's name, in order to expand its database of choices.[5] It predicts the answer based on the tree match algorithm. You can get AKI AWARDS by guessing a new Character. After a new update, the user is able to purchase accessories for the genie with money obtained in-game.

4.2 Critical reception

L'Express rated Akinator a 5 out of 5 on their list of iPhone Apps of the Week for September 9, 2009.[6] *Excite France*

stated that Akinator "is just that interactive. It is revolutionary, attractive, and entertaining."[7]

4.3 References

[1] Akinator Mobile Apps | SCIMOB (10/09/2009)

[2] Akinator - Daily Ranks | App Annie (10/05/2011)

[3] Jen Chaney (August 3, 2010). "Summer time waster: Stumping the Akinator". *The Washington Post*. Retrieved June 23, 2011.

[4] "Akinator, el genio que leerá tu mente". *Medio Tiempo* (in Spanish). October 19, 2010. Retrieved June 23, 2011.

[5] "⬚⬚⬚⬚⬚⬚⬚⬚⬚Akinator⬚⬚⬚⬚⬚⬚⬚⬚⬚⬚⬚⬚". *Asahi Shimbun* (in Japanese). July 21, 2010. Retrieved June 23, 2011.

[6] "Paybuddy, Stand o'food et Akinator". *L'Express* (in French). September 9, 2009. Retrieved June 23, 2011.

[7] "Akinator, vraiment le plus fort!". *Excite France* (in French). November 23, 2008. Retrieved June 23, 2011.

4.4 External links

- English site

Chapter 5

Artificial imagination

Artificial imagination (**AIm**), also called **Synthetic imagination** or **machine imagination** is defined as artificial simulation of human imagination by general or special purpose computers or artificial neural networks.

The term artificial imagination is also used to describe a property of machines or programs: Among some of the traits that researchers hope to simulate using machines include creativity, vision, digital art, humor, satire, etc.

Artificial imagination research uses tools and insights from many fields, including computer science, Rhetoric, psychology, creative arts, philosophy, neuroscience, affective computing, Artificial Intelligence, Artificial intuition, cognitive science, linguistics, operations research, creative writing, probability and logic.

The various practitioners in the field are researching various aspects of Artificial imagination, such as Artificial (visual) imagination,[1] Artificial (aural) Imagination,[2] modeling/filtering content based on human emotions[3] and Interactive Search.[4] Some articles on the topic speculate on how artificial imagination may evolve to create an artificial world which people may not want to leave at all. [5]

Some researchers in the field, such as G. Schleis and M. Rizki, Dept. of Comput. Sci., Wayne State Univ. have focused on using artificial neural networks for simulating artificial imagination.[6]

The topic of artificial imagination has gotten interest from scholars outside the computer science domain, such as noted communications scholar Ernest Bormann, who came up with the Symbolic Convergence Theory and has worked on a project to develop artificial imagination in computer systems.[7]

How to Build a Mind: Toward Machines with Imagination by Igor Aleksander is a good academic book on the topic. *Artificial Imagination*,[8] a roman à clef, is a good non-academic book supposedly written by an Artificial imagination system.

5.1 References

[1] *Visual Information Retrieval Using Synthesized Imagery* http://portal.acm.org/ft_gateway.cfm?id=1282303&type=pdf

[2] *AUDIO CONTENT TRANSMISSION* by Xavier Amatriain & Perfecto Herrera, http://www.iua.upf.es/mtg/publications/dafx2001-xamat.pdf

[3] *Is It Out There? The Perspectives of Emotional Information Retrieval from the Internet Resources* by R. Rzepka, K. Araki, and K. Tochinai (Japan), 2007 http://actapress.com/PDFViewer.aspx?paperId=25600

[4] *An Artificial Imagination for Interactive Search. ICCV-HCI, 4796: 19-28, 2007* by Bart Thomee, Mark J. Huiskes, Erwin M. Bakker and Michael Lew http://dblp.uni-trier.de/db/conf/iccv/iccv-hci2007.html#ThomeeHBL07

[5] *Hypertext and "the Hyperreal"* by Stuart Moulthrop, Yale University http://portal.acm.org/citation.cfm?doid=74224.74246

[6] *Learning from a random player using the reference neuron model* in the *Proceedings of the 2002 Congress on Evolutionary Computation, 2002. http://ieeexplore.ieee.org/xpl/freeabs_all.jsp?arnumber=1007019*

[7] *Twentieth-Century Roots of Rhetorical Studies, by Jim A. Kuypers and Andrew King, 2001. published by Praeger/Greenwood, page 225.*

[8] *Artificial Imagination* http://www.amazon.com/Artificial-Imagination-Special-Photostory-Washington/dp/098147621X

Chapter 6

Artificial Intelligence Applications Institute

AIAI Logo

The **Artificial Intelligence Applications Institute** (AIAI) at the School of Informatics at the University of Edinburgh is a non-profit technology transfer organisation that promotes the benefits of the application of Artificial Intelligence research to commercial, industrial, and government organisations worldwide.

6.1 History

AIAI was created in July 1983, and received it formal charter from the University of Edinburgh in July 1984. It joined the School of Informatics when this was created from a number of departments and research institutes in 1998. The Director of AIAI is Austin Tate.

6.2 Activities

AIAI specialises in Intelligent and Knowledge-based systems, including:

- Ontology development and knowledge engineering;

- Case-based reasoning: a technique for utilising past experiences and existing corporate resources such as databases to guide diagnosis and fault finding;

- Genetic algorithms: an adaptive search technique with very broad applicability in scheduling, optimization, and model adaptation;

- Planning and workflow: the modelling, task setting, planning, execution, monitoring and coordination of activities;

- Data mining: the identification and extraction of useful general patterns from data.

6.3 External links

- AIAI website

- AIAI projects

- AIAI people

- AIAI2 - AIAI in Second Life

Chapter 7

Artificial intuition

Artificial intuition is the capacity of an artificial object or software to function with intuition, or a machine-based system that has some capacity to function analogous to the human intuition.

7.1 Comparison

Conventional human intuition is a function of the human mind, defined particularly by the psychologist and psychiatrist Carl Jung. Psychologist Jean Piaget showed that intuitive functioning within the normally developing human child at the *Intuitive Thought Substage* of the preoperational stage occurred at from four to seven years of age.[1][2] In Carl Jung's concept of synchronicity, the concept of "intuitive intelligence" is described as something like a capacity that transcends ordinary-level functioning to a point where information is understood with a greater depth than is available in more simple rationally-thinking entities.[3][4][5][6][7]

Artificial intuition is theoretically (or otherwise) a sophisticated function of an artifice that is able to interpret data with depth and locate hidden factors functioning in Gestalt psychology,[8][9] and that intuition in the artificial mind would, in the context described here, be a bottom-up process upon a macroscopic scale identifying something like the archetypal.[10](see τύπος [11]).

To create artificial intuition supposes the possibility of the re-creation of a higher functioning of the human mind, with capabilities such as what might be found in semantic memory and learning.[12][13][14] The transferral of the functioning of a biological system to synthetic functioning is based upon modeling of functioning from knowledge of cognition and the brain,[15][16] for instance as applications of models of artificial neural networks from the research done within the discipline of Computational neuroscience.[17]

7.2 Application software

The notion of a process of a data-interpretative synthesis has already been found in a computational-linguistic software application that has been created for use in an internal security context.[18][19] The software integrates computed data based specifically on objectives incorporating a paradigm described as "religious intuitive" [20](hermeneutic [21][22]),[23] functional to a degree that represents advances upon the performance of *generic lexical* data mining.[24][25]

7.3 Discussion

Should the definition of artificial intuition be considered with regard to a completely functioning artificial consciousness, then the earlier literary workings of artificial life found in *Frankenstein* provide a possible starting place, sufficiently human (or humanoid) to exhibit intuition. Representations in cinema of artificial intelligence (such as *The Terminator*, by James Cameron, Gale Anne Hurd, William Wisher, Jr. and *Star trek*, written by Gene Roddenberry), are still a long way from being the reality today, possibly due to limitations in the replication of functioning with artificial materials.[26] Although the creatures of *Blade Runner*[27] (Hampton Fancher & David Peoples) in some way strictly artificial are conceivably possible, full cloning of *Homo sapiens* is impermissible.[28][29]

7.4 See also

- Artificial Imagination

- Artificial intelligence

- Intuitionistic logic

- Intuition (philosophy)

- Analogy (biology)

- Animism
- Concept-mapping and mind-mapping
- Connectionism
- Cybernetics
- information theory
- List of concept- and mind-mapping software
- Natural language processing
- Dreyfus's criticism of A.I.
- Usability
- Panayiotis Zavos[30]

7.5 References

[1] Psychology: The Science of Mind and Behaviour, Richard Gross ISBN 978-1-4441-0831-6 see: Jean Piaget

[2] Santrock, John W. (2004). Life-Span Development (9th Ed.). Boston, MA: McGraw-Hill College - Chapter 8 *from* Piaget's theory of cognitive development

[3] worldcat retrieved 11:03(GMT) 26.10.201

[4] *Farlex* retrieved 11:08(GMT) 26.10.2011

[5] Jung, C.G. ([1921] 1971). Psychological Types, Collected Works, Volume 6, Princeton, N.J.: Princeton University Press. ISBN 0-691-01813-8.

[6] Jung, Carl (2006). The Undiscovered Self: The Problem of the Individual in Modern Society. (*introduction*) ISBN 0-451-21860-4. see also : *the Unconscious mind*

[7] The Essential Jung:Selected Writings (with an introduction by Anthony Storr) ISBN 0-00-653065-6

[8] Herbert Simon. Artificial intelligence as a framework for understanding intuition by Roger Frantz doi:10.1016/S0167-4870(02)00207-6 retrieved 11:03(UTC) 27.10.2011 see also: Herbert A. Simon

[9] *Gestalt psychology*:Christian von Ehrenfels, Kurt Koffka & Wolfgang Köhler

[10] ISBN 0-691-01813-8

[11] Henry George Liddell, Robert Scott, A Greek-English Lexicon retrieved 11:21(UTC) 27.10.2011

[12] Fuzzy Information and Engineering Volume 1 Chapter titled *Crime pattern study and fuzzy Information Analysis* (Springer, 2008) By Bing-Yuan Cao 19:17(GMT) 25.10.2011 *see also*:Fuzzy logic

[13] Monica Anderson (research company website) retrieved 12:23(GMT) 26.10.2011

[14] website by Gunther Sonnenfeld retrieved 19:36(GMT) 25.10.2011

[15] sulcus.berkeley.edu retrieved 20:57(GMT) 25.10.2011

[16] ITP retrieved 20:52(GMT) 25.10.2011

[17] Schwartz, Eric (1990). Computational neuroscience. Cambridge, Mass: MIT Press. ISBN 0-262-19291-8.

[18] Video lecturer: Shmuel Bar, CEO and Founder (secondary source) retrieved 19:26(GMT) 25.10.2011

[19] "Artificial Intuition" Technology for Security and Defense Applications, Israel Uploaded by TAUVOD on 25 Sep 2011 (secondary source) retrieved 19:30(GMT) 25.10.2011

[20] Roland Faber : Professor of Systematic Theology at the University of Vienna, from *Process Studies*, pp.195-211, Vol. 28, Number 3-4, Fall-Winter, 1999(secondary source) (*in situ*) 12:21(UTC)27.10.2011

[21] ISBN 978-0-8014-8564-0, 27.10.2011 see also: Martin Heidegger and Richard Polt

[22] Ramberg, Bjørn and Gjesdal, Kristin, "Hermeneutics", The Stanford Encyclopedia of Philosophy (Summer 2009 Edition), Edward N. Zalta (ed.) (secondary source) 09:50(UTC) 27.10.2011

[23] (primary source)© Copyright 2011 Smiths Detection. A Part of Smiths Group plc. All Rights Reserved retrieved 09:12(UTC) 27.10.2011

[24] company website (primary source) retrieved 19:41(GMT) 25.10.2011

[25] Nathan Hodge October 31, 2008 retrieved 19:31(GMT) 25.10.2011

[26] *Abstract of a paper written by* Mark Zilbermann retrieved 19:45(GMT) 25.10.2011 see also: algorithms

[27] BR.movie website 13:56(UTC) 26.10.2011 [from previous]

[28] Codification Division, Office of Legal Affairs, United Nations (18 May 2005). "Ad Hoc Committee on an International Convention against the Reproductive Cloning of Human Beings". United Nations. retrieved 21:14(UTC) 26.10.2011(2007-01-28).

[29] dictionary.cambridge.org (tertiary source) retrieved 12:32(UTC) 26.10.2011

[30] *BBC News* report of the 4th of February retrieved 20:12(UTC)26.10.2011

7.6 External links

- image/drawing showing meta-map 19:49(GMT)

- Academia © 2011 retrieved 19:38(GMT) 25.10.2011 (People who have Artificial Intuition as a research subject)

- transcript of conversation (2) retrieved 19:57(UTC) 26.10.2011 (a discussion held within *The Intuition Network* website showing a discussion between John McCarthy (primarily credited amongst others with introducing the idea of artificial intelligence (Dartmouth Conferences) and J.Mishlove.

Chapter 8

Artificial Solutions

Artificial Solutions is a multinational software company that develops and sells natural language interaction products for enterprise and consumer use.[1] The company's natural language solutions have been deployed in a wide range of industries including finance,[2][3][4] telecoms,[5][6] the public sector,[7][8] retail[9] and travel.[10]

8.1 History

Artificial Solutions was founded in Stockholm in 2001 by friends Johan Åhlund, Johan Gustavsson and Michael Söderström to create interactive web assistants using a combination of artificial intelligence and natural language processing. Though Åhlund initially took some persuading, he thought it sounded ridiculous to be talking to a virtual agent on the internet.[11]

The company expanded with the development of online customer service optimization products and by 2005 it had several offices throughout Europe supporting the development and sales of its online virtual assistants.[12] Artificial Solutions was placed as visionary in the latest Gartner Magic Quadrant for CRM Web Customer Service Applications.[13]

In 2006 Artificial Solutions acquired Kiwilogic, a German software house creating its own virtual assistants.[14] Elbot, Artificial Solutions' test-bed to explore the psychology of human-machine communication, won the Loebner Prize in 2008 and is the closest contestant of the annual competition based on the Turing Test to reach the 30% threshold by fooling 25% of the human judges.[15][16][17]

With a change in management in 2010 the company started to focus the basis of its technology on Natural Language Interaction and launched the Teneo Platform, which allows people to hold humanlike, intelligent conversations with applications and services running on electronic devices.[18][19][20] In 2013 Artificial Solutions launched Indigo, a mobile personal assistant that is able to operate and remember the context of the conversation across differ-

ent platforms and operating systems.[21][22][23] A new round of funding was announced in June 2013. The $9.4m will be used to support expansion in the US market.[24]

In February 2014 Artificial Solutions announced the Teneo Network of Knowledge, a patented intelligent framework that enables users to interact using natural language with private, shared and public ecosystem of devices, also known as the Internet of Things.[25]

8.2 References

[1] Ion, Florence (2013-06-05). "Review: Indigo wants to bring Siri-like conversation to the Android platform". Ars Technica. Retrieved 2013-09-08.

[2] Thompson, Scott. "Agria working with Artificial Solutions". *FStech*. Perspective Publishing. Retrieved 12 September 2013.

[3] Savvas, Antony. "Co-operative Bank uses Mia to speed up contact centre calls". *Computerworld UK*. IDG. Retrieved 12 September 2013.

[4] Thompson, Scott. "2012 FStech Awards: winners announced". *FStech*. Perspective Publishing. Retrieved 12 September 2013.

[5] Westerholm, Joel. "Telenors elektroniska kundtjänst pressar kostnaderna". *ComputerSweden*. IDG. Retrieved 12 September 2013.

[6] "Artificial Solutions Powers Online IVA for Vodafone". *LangTechNews*. Retrieved 12 September 2013.

[7] Brax, Sofia. "Digitala kolleger alltid till tjänst". *Publik*. Fackforbundet ST. Retrieved 12 September 2013.

[8] Nilsson, Orjan. "Cyber-damene husker deg". *Nettavisen*. iBergen.

[9] Aaron Travis (2013-01-05). "In Defense Of The Humble App Walkthrough". TechCrunch. Retrieved 2013-09-08.

[10] Fox, Linda. "CWT brings virtual face to mobile service". *Tnooz*. Retrieved 12 September 2013.

[11] "Löjlig affärside vinstlott för Artificial Solutions". IT24. Retrieved 2013-09-08.

[12] "Al grano". Elnuevolunes.es. Retrieved 2013-09-08.

[13] Barry Levine. "Gartner MQ for CRM Web Customer Service: Kana, Moxie Software, Oracle-RightNow Among Leaders". Cmswire.com. Retrieved 2013-09-08.

[14] "Venture Capital: KIWILOGIC.COM AG". Earlybird. Retrieved 2013-09-08.

[15] Loebner Prize

[16] "UK | England | Berkshire | Test explores if robots can think". BBC News. 2008-10-13. Retrieved 2013-09-08.

[17] Robson, David. "Almost human: Interview with a chatbot". *New Scientist*. Reed Business Information Ltd.

[18] Mike Elgan (2013-03-09). "Smart apps think (so you don't have to)". Computerworld. Retrieved 2013-09-08.

[19] "Artificial Solutions Unveils a Software Toolkit for Adding Speech to Mobile Apps". SpeechTechMag.com. 2012-01-17. Retrieved 2013-09-08.

[20] "Så effektiv er Ikeas chat-robot: Har været på 'efteruddannelse' - Computerworld". Computerworld.dk. Retrieved 2013-09-08.

[21] Hoyle, Andrew (2013-02-24). "Indigo brings Siri-like assistance to Android for free (hands-on) | Mobile World Congress - CNET Reviews". Reviews.cnet.com. Retrieved 2013-09-08.

[22] "Indigo Wants to Be Your Personal Assistant Across Devices". Lifehacker.com. Retrieved 2013-09-08.

[23] Wollman, Dana (2013-02-26). "Indigo is a cloud-based, cross-platform personal assistant for Android and Windows Phone 8 (hands-on)". Engadget.com. Retrieved 2013-09-08.

[24] "Artificial Solutions raises $9.4m in Scope-led round for US expansion | AltAssets Private Equity News". Altassets.net. 2013-06-25. Retrieved 2013-09-08.

[25] Trenholm, Rich. "Next generation of personal assistant takes a step towards 'Her'-style super-Siri". *Cnet*. CBS Interactive.

8.3 External links

- Indigo

- Elbot

Chapter 9

Automatic image annotation

Automatic image annotation (also known as automatic image tagging or linguistic indexing) is the process by which a computer system automatically assigns metadata in the form of captioning or keywords to a digital image. This application of computer vision techniques is used in image retrieval systems to organize and locate images of interest from a database.

This method can be regarded as a type of multi-class image classification with a very large number of classes - as large as the vocabulary size. Typically, image analysis in the form of extracted feature vectors and the training annotation words are used by machine learning techniques to attempt to automatically apply annotations to new images. The first methods learned the correlations between image features and training annotations, then techniques were developed using machine translation to try to translate the textual vocabulary with the 'visual vocabulary', or clustered regions known as *blobs*. Work following these efforts have included classification approaches, relevance models and so on.

The advantages of automatic image annotation versus content-based image retrieval (CBIR) are that queries can be more naturally specified by the user . CBIR generally (at present) requires users to search by image concepts such as color and texture, or finding example queries. Certain image features in example images may override the concept that the user is really focusing on. The traditional methods of image retrieval such as those used by libraries have relied on manually annotated images, which is expensive and time-consuming, especially given the large and constantly growing image databases in existence.

Some annotation engines are online, including the ALIPR.com real-time tagging engine developed by Pennsylvania State University researchers, and Behold.

9.1   Some major work

- Word co-occurrence model

Y Mori, H Takahashi, and R Oka (1999). "Image-to-word transformation based on dividing and vector quantizing images with words.". *Proceedings of the International Workshop on Multimedia Intelligent Storage and Retrieval Management.*

- Annotation as machine translation

P Duygulu, K Barnard, N de Fretias, and D Forsyth (2002). "Object recognition as machine translation: Learning a lexicon for a fixed image vocabulary". *Proceedings of the European Conference on Computer Vision.* pp. 97–112.

- Statistical models

J Li and J Z Wang (2006). "Real-time Computerized Annotation of Pictures". *Proc. ACM Multimedia.* pp. 911–920.

J Z Wang and J Li (2002). "Learning-Based Linguistic Indexing of Pictures with 2-D MHMMs". *Proc. ACM Multimedia.* pp. 436–445.

- Automatic linguistic indexing of pictures

J Li and J Z Wang (2008). "Real-time Computerized Annotation of Pictures". *IEEE Trans. on Pattern Analysis and Machine Intelligence.*

J Li and J Z Wang (2003). "Automatic Linguistic Indexing of Pictures by a Statistical Modeling Approach". *IEEE Trans. on Pattern Analysis and Machine Intelligence.* pp. 1075–1088.

- Hierarchical Aspect Cluster Model

K Barnard, D A Forsyth (2001). "Learning the Semantics of Words and Pictures". *Proceedings of International Conference on Computer Vision.* pp. 408–415.

- Latent Dirichlet Allocation model

  D Blei, A Ng, and M Jordan (2003). "Latent Dirichlet allocation" (PDF). *Journal of Machine Learning Research*. pp. 3:993–1022.

- Supervised multiclass labeling

  G Carneiro, A B Chan, P Moreno, and N Vasconcelos (2006). "Supervised Learning of Semantic Classes for Image Annotation and Retrieval" (PDF). *IEEE Trans. on Pattern Analysis and Machine Intelligence*. pp. 394–410.

- Texture similarity

  R W Picard and T P Minka (1995). "Vision Texture for Annotation". *Multimedia Systems*.

- Support Vector Machines

  C Cusano, G Ciocca, and R Scettini (2004). "Image Annotation Using SVM". *Proceedings of Internet Imaging IV*.

- Ensemble of Decision Trees and Random Subwindows

  R Maree, P Geurts, J Piater, and L Wehenkel (2005). "Random Subwindows for Robust Image Classification". *Proceedings of the IEEE International Conference on Computer Vision and Pattern Recognition*. pp. 1:34–30.

- Maximum Entropy

  J Jeon, R Manmatha (2004). "Using Maximum Entropy for Automatic Image Annotation" (PDF). *Int'l Conf on Image and Video Retrieval (CIVR 2004)*. pp. 24–32.

- Relevance models

  J Jeon, V Lavrenko, and R Manmatha (2003). "Automatic image annotation and retrieval using cross-media relevance models" (PDF). *Proceedings of the ACM SIGIR Conference on Research and Development in Information Retrieval*. pp. 119–126.

- Relevance models using continuous probability density functions

  V Lavrenko, R Manmatha, and J Jeon (2003). "A model for learning the semantics of pictures" (PDF). *Proceedings of the 16th Conference on Advances in Neural Information Processing Systems NIPS*.

- Coherent Language Model

  R Jin, J Y Chai, L Si (2004). "Effective Automatic Image Annotation via A Coherent Language Model and Active Learning" (PDF). *Proceedings of MM'04*.

- Inference networks

  D Metzler and R Manmatha (2004). "An inference network approach to image retrieval" (PDF). *Proceedings of the International Conference on Image and Video Retrieval*. pp. 42–50.

- Multiple Bernoulli distribution

  S Feng, R Manmatha, and V Lavrenko (2004). "Multiple Bernoulli relevance models for image and video annotation" (PDF). *IEEE Conference on Computer Vision and Pattern Recognition*. pp. 1002–1009.

- Multiple design alternatives

  J Y Pan, H-J Yang, P Duygulu and C Faloutsos (2004). "Automatic Image Captioning" (PDF). *Proceedings of the 2004 IEEE International Conference on Multimedia and Expo (ICME'04)*.

- Natural scene annotation

  J Fan, Y Gao, H Luo and G Xu (2004). "Automatic Image Annotation by Using Concept-Sensitive Salient Objects for Image Content Representation". *Proceedings of the 27th annual international conference on Research and development in information retrieval*. pp. 361–368.

- Relevant low-level global filters

  A Oliva and A Torralba (2001). "Modeling the shape of the scene: a holistic representation of the spatial envelope" (PDF). *International Journal of Computer Vision*. pp. 42:145–175.

- Global image features and nonparametric density estimation

  A Yavlinsky, E Schofield and S Rüger (2005). "Automated Image Annotation Using Global Features and Robust Nonparametric Density Estimation" (PDF). *Int'l Conf on Image and Video Retrieval (CIVR, Singapore, Jul 2005)*.

- Video semantics

  N Vasconcelos and A Lippman (2001). "Statistical Models of Video Structure for Content Analysis and Characterization" (PDF). *IEEE Transactions on Image Processing*. pp. 1–17.

  Ilaria Bartolini, Marco Patella, and Corrado Romani (2010). "Shiatsu: Semantic-based Hierarchical Automatic Tagging of Videos by Segmentation Using Cuts". *3rd ACM International Multimedia Workshop on Automated Information Extraction in Media Production (AIEMPro10)*.

- Image Annotation Refinement

  Yohan Jin, Latifur Khan, Lei Wang, and Mamoun Awad (2005). "Image annotations by combining multiple evidence & wordNet". *13th Annual ACM International Conference on Multimedia (MM 05)*. pp. 706–715.

  Changhu Wang, Feng Jing, Lei Zhang, and Hong-Jiang Zhang (2006). "Image annotation refinement using random walk with restarts". *14th Annual ACM International Conference on Multimedia (MM 06)*.

  Changhu Wang, Feng Jing, Lei Zhang, and Hong-Jiang Zhang (2007). "content-based image annotation refinement". *IEEE Conference on Computer Vision and Pattern Recognition (CVPR 07)*.

  Ilaria Bartolini and Paolo Ciaccia (2007). "Imagination: Exploiting Link Analysis for Accurate Image Annotation". *Springer Adaptive Multimedia Retrieval*.

  Ilaria Bartolini and Paolo Ciaccia (2010). "Multi-dimensional Keyword-based Image Annotation and Search". *2nd ACM International Workshop on Keyword Search on Structured Data (KEYS 2010)*.

- Automatic Image Annotation by Ensemble of Visual Descriptors

  Emre Akbas and Fatos Y. Vural (2007). "Automatic Image Annotation by Ensemble of Visual Descriptors". *Intl. Conf. on Computer Vision (CVPR) 2007, Workshop on Semantic Learning Applications in Multimedia*.

- A New Baseline for Image Annotation

  Ameesh Makadia and Vladimir Pavlovic and Sanjiv Kumar (2008). "A New Baseline for Image Annotation" (PDF). *European Conference on Computer Vision (ECCV)*.

- Simultaneous Image Classification and Annotation

  Chong Wang and David Blei and Li Fei-Fei (2009). "Simultaneous Image Classification and Annotation" (PDF). *Conf. on Computer Vision and Pattern Recognition (CVPR)*.

- TagProp: Discriminative Metric Learning in Nearest Neighbor Models for Image Auto-Annotation

  Matthieu Guillaumin and Thomas Mensink and Jakob Verbeek and Cordelia Schmid (2009). "TagProp: Discriminative Metric Learning in Nearest Neighbor Models for Image Auto-Annotation" (PDF). *Intl. Conf. on Computer Vision (ICCV)*.

- Image Annotation Using Metric Learning in Semantic Neighbourhoods

  Yashaswi Verma and C. V. Jawahar (2012). "Image Annotation Using Metric Learning in Semantic Neighbourhoods" (PDF). *European Conference on Computer Vision (ECCV)*.

9.2   See also

- Pattern recognition
- Image retrieval
- Content-based image retrieval

9.3   References

- Datta, Ritendra; Dhiraj Joshi; Jia Li; James Z. Wang (2008). "Image Retrieval: Ideas, Influences, and Trends of the New Age". *ACM Computing Surveys* **40** (2): 1–60. doi:10.1145/1348246.1348248.

- Nicolas Hervé; Nozha Boujemaa (2007). "Image annotation : which approach for realistic databases ?" (PDF). *ACM International Conference on Image and Video Retrieval.*

- M Inoue (2004). "On the need for annotation-based image retrieval" (PDF). *Workshop on Information Retrieval in Context.* pp. 44–46.

9.4 External links

- ALIPR.com - Real-time automatic tagging engine developed by Penn State researchers.

- Behold Image Search - An image search engine that indexes over 1 million Flickr images using automatically generated tags.

- SpiritTagger Global Photograph Annotation - Annotation system from UCSB on 1.4 million images that predicts where a photo was taken and suggests tags.

- Akiwi - Semi automatic image tagging - Image Annotation with user interaction

Chapter 10

Automatic number plate recognition

The system must be able to deal with different styles of license plates

Automatic number plate recognition (**ANPR**; see also other names below) is a mass surveillance method that uses optical character recognition on images to read vehicle registration plates. They can use existing closed-circuit television or road-rule enforcement cameras, or ones specifically designed for the task. They are used by various police forces and as a method of electronic toll collection on pay-per-use roads and cataloging the movements of traffic or individuals.

ANPR can be used to store the images captured by the cameras as well as the text from the license plate, with some configurable to store a photograph of the driver. Systems commonly use infrared lighting to allow the camera to take the picture at any time of the day.[1][2][3] ANPR technology tends to be region-specific, owing to plate variation from place to place.

Concerns about these systems have centered on privacy

License-plate recognition process

fears of government tracking citizens' movements, misidentification, high error rates, and increased government spending.

10.1 Etymology

ANPR is sometimes known by various other terms:

- **Automatic license-plate recognition** (ALPR)

- **Automatic license-plate reader** (ALPR)

- **Automatic vehicle identification** (AVI)

- **Car plate recognition** (CPR)

- **License-plate recognition** (LPR)

- **Lecture automatique de plaques d'immatriculation** (LAPI)

- **Mobile license-plate reader** (MLPR)

- **Vehicle license-plate recognition** (VLPR)

10.2 Development history

ANPR was invented in 1976 at the Police Scientific Development Branch in the UK. Prototype systems were working by 1979, and contracts were let to produce industrial systems, first at EMI Electronics, and then at Computer Recognition Systems (CRS) in Wokingham, UK. Early trial systems were deployed on the A1 road and at the Dartford Tunnel. However it did not become widely used until new developments in cheaper and easier to use software was pioneered during the 1990s. The first arrest through detection of a stolen car was made in 1981 and the first documented case of ANPR in helping solve a murder occurred in November 2005 after the murder of Sharon Beshenivsky, in which City of Bradford based ANPR played a vital role in locating and subsequently convicting her killers.[4]

10.3 Components

The software aspect of the system runs on standard home computer hardware and can be linked to other applications or databases. It first uses a series of image manipulation techniques to detect, normalize and enhance the image of the number plate, and then optical character recognition (OCR) to extract the alphanumerics of the license plate. ANPR systems are generally deployed in one of two basic approaches: one allows for the entire process to be performed at the lane location in real-time, and the other transmits all the images from many lanes to a remote computer location and performs the OCR process there at some later point in time. When done at the lane site, the information

captured of the plate alphanumeric, date-time, lane identification, and any other information required is completed in approximately 250 milliseconds. This information can easily be transmitted to a remote computer for further processing if necessary, or stored at the lane for later retrieval. In the other arrangement, there are typically large numbers of PCs used in a server farm to handle high workloads, such as those found in the London congestion charge project. Often in such systems, there is a requirement to forward images to the remote server, and this can require larger bandwidth transmission media.

10.4 Technology

The font on Dutch plates was changed to improve plate recognition.

ANPR uses optical character recognition (OCR) on images taken by cameras. When Dutch vehicle registration plates switched to a different style in 2002, one of the changes made was to the font, introducing small gaps in some letters (such as *P* and *R*) to make them more distinct and therefore more legible to such systems. Some license plate arrangements use variations in font sizes and positioning—ANPR systems must be able to cope with such differences in order to be truly effective. More complicated systems can cope with international variants, though many programs are individually tailored to each country.

The cameras used can include existing road-rule enforcement or closed-circuit television cameras, as well as mobile units, which are usually attached to vehicles. Some systems use infrared cameras to take a clearer image of the plates.[5][6][7][8][9] [10] [11][12][13][14]

10.4.1 ANPR in mobile systems

During the 1990s, significant advances in technology took automatic number plate recognition (ANPR) systems from

The Dubai police use ANPR cameras to monitor vehicles in front and either side of the patrol car

A Merseyside Police car equipped with mobile ANPR.

limited expensive, hard to set up, fixed based applications to simple "point and shoot" mobile ones. This was made possible by the creation of software that ran on cheaper PC based, non-specialist hardware that also no longer needed to be given the pre-defined angles, direction, size and speed in which the plates would be passing the cameras field of view. Further scaled-down components at more cost-effective price points led to a record number of deployments by law enforcement agencies around the world. Smaller cameras with the ability to read license plates at higher speeds, along with smaller, more durable processors that fit in the trunks of police vehicles, allowed law enforcement officers to patrol daily with the benefit of license plate reading in real time, when they can interdict immediately.

Despite their effectiveness, there are noteworthy challenges related with mobile ANPRs. One of the biggest is that the processor and the cameras must work fast enough to accommodate relative speeds of more than 100 mph (160 km/h), a likely scenario in the case of oncoming traffic. This equipment must also be very efficient since the power source is the vehicle battery, and equipment must be small to minimize the space it requires.

Relative speed is only one issue that affects the camera's ability to actually read a license plate. Algorithms must be able to compensate for all the variables that can affect the ANPR's ability to produce an accurate read, such as time of day, weather and angles between the cameras and the license plates. A system's illumination wavelengths can also have a direct impact on the resolution and accuracy of a read in these conditions.

Installing ANPR cameras on law enforcement vehicles requires careful consideration of the juxtaposition of the cameras to the license plates they are to read. Using the right number of cameras and positioning them accurately for optimal results can prove challenging, given the various missions and environments at hand. Highway patrol requires forward-looking cameras that span multiple lanes and are able to read license plates at very high speeds. City patrol needs shorter range, lower focal length cameras for capturing plates on parked cars. Parking lots with perpendicularly parked cars often require a specialized camera with a very short focal length. Most technically advanced systems are flexible and can be configured with a number of cameras ranging from one to four which can easily be repositioned as needed. States with rear-only license plates have an additional challenge since a forward-looking camera is ineffective with oncoming traffic. In this case one camera may be turned backwards.

10.5   Algorithms

Steps 2, 3 and 4: The license plate is normalized for brightness and contrast, and then the characters are segmented to be ready for OCR.

There are seven primary algorithms that the software requires for identifying a license plate:

1. Plate localization – responsible for finding and isolat-

ing the plate on the picture.

2. Plate orientation and sizing – compensates for the skew of the plate and adjusts the dimensions to the required size.

3. Normalization – adjusts the brightness and contrast of the image.

4. Character segmentation – finds the individual characters on the plates.

5. Optical character recognition.

6. Syntactical/Geometrical analysis – check characters and positions against country-specific rules.

7. The averaging of the recognised value over multiple fields/images to produce a more reliable or confident result. Especially since any single image may contain a reflected light flare, be partially obscured or other temporary effect.

The complexity of each of these subsections of the program determines the accuracy of the system. During the third phase (normalization), some systems use edge detection techniques to increase the picture difference between the letters and the plate backing. A median filter may also be used to reduce the visual noise on the image.

10.6 Difficulties

Early ANPR systems were unable to read white or silver lettering on black background, as permitted on UK vehicles built prior to 1973.

Swedish license plate

There are a number of possible difficulties that the software must be able to cope with. These include:

- Poor file resolution, usually because the plate is too far away but sometimes resulting from the use of a low-quality camera.

Must be able to recognize international license plates as such.

- Blurry images, particularly motion blur.

- Poor lighting and low contrast due to overexposure, reflection or shadows.

- An object obscuring (part of) the plate, quite often a tow bar, or dirt on the plate.

- Read license plates that are different at the front and the back because of towed trailers, campers, etc.

- Vehicle lane change in the camera's angle of view during license plate reading.

- A different font, popular for vanity plates (some countries do not allow such plates, eliminating the problem).

- Circumvention techniques.

- Lack of coordination between countries or states. Two cars from different countries or states can have the same number but different design of the plate.

While some of these problems can be corrected within the software, it is primarily left to the hardware side of the system to work out solutions to these difficulties. Increasing the height of the camera may avoid problems with objects (such as other vehicles) obscuring the plate but introduces and increases other problems, such as the adjusting for the increased skew of the plate.

On some cars, tow bars may obscure one or two characters of the license plate. Bikes on bike racks can also obscure the number plate, though in some countries and jurisdictions, such as Victoria, Australia, "bike plates" are supposed to be fitted. Some small-scale systems allow for some errors in the license plate. When used for giving specific vehicles access to a barricaded area, the decision may be made to have an acceptable error rate of one character. This is because the likelihood of an unauthorized car having such a similar license plate is seen as quite small. However, this level of inaccuracy would not be acceptable in most applications of an ANPR system.

10.7   Imaging hardware

At the front end of any ANPR system is the imaging hardware which captures the image of the license plates. The initial image capture forms a critically important part of the ANPR system which, in accordance to the garbage in, garbage out principle of computing, will often determine the overall performance.

License plate capture is typically performed by specialized cameras designed specifically for the task, although new software techniques are being implemented that support any I.P.-based surveillance camera and increase the utility of ANPR for perimeter security applications. Factors which pose difficulty for license plate imaging cameras include the speed of the vehicles being recorded, varying level of ambient light, headlight glare and harsh environmental conditions. Most dedicated license plate capture cameras will incorporate infrared illumination in order to solve the problems of lighting and plate reflectivity.

Portable traffic enforcement system used by the Hungarian police. The rows of infrared LEDs are visible on the right.

Many countries now use license plates that are retroreflective.[15] This returns the light back to the source and thus improves the contrast of the image. In some countries, the characters on the plate are not reflective, giving a high level of contrast with the reflective background in any lighting conditions. A camera that makes use of active infrared imaging (with a normal colour filter over the lens and an infrared illuminator next to it) benefits greatly from this as the infrared waves are reflected back from the plate. This is only possible on dedicated ANPR cameras, however, and so cameras used for other purposes must rely more heavily on the software capabilities. Further, when a full-colour image is required as well as use of the ANPR-retrieved details, it is necessary to have one infrared-enabled camera and one normal (colour) camera working together.

To avoid blurring it is ideal to have the shutter speed of a dedicated camera set to 1/1000 of a second. It is also important that the camera uses a global shutter, as op-

posed to rolling shutter, to assure that the taken images are distortion-free. Because the car is moving, slower shutter speeds could result in an image which is too blurred to read using the OCR software, especially if the camera is much higher up than the vehicle. In slow-moving traffic, or when the camera is at a lower level and the vehicle is at an angle approaching the camera, the shutter speed does not need to be so fast. Shutter speeds of 1/500 of a second can cope with traffic moving up to 40 mph (64 km/h) and 1/250 of a second up to 5 mph (8 km/h). License plate capture cameras can produce usable images from vehicles traveling at 120 mph (190 km/h).

To maximize the chances of effective license plate capture, installers should carefully consider the positioning of the camera relative to the target capture area. Exceeding threshold angles of incidence between camera lens and license plate will greatly reduce the probability of obtaining usable images due to distortion. Manufacturers have developed tools to help eliminate errors from the physical installation of license plate capture cameras.

10.8   Circumvention techniques

Vehicle owners have used a variety of techniques in an attempt to evade ANPR systems and road-rule enforcement cameras in general. One method increases the reflective properties of the lettering and makes it more likely that the system will be unable to locate the plate or produce a high enough level of contrast to be able to read it. This is typically done by using a plate cover or a spray, though claims regarding the effectiveness of the latter are disputed. In most jurisdictions, the covers are illegal and covered under existing laws, while in most countries there is no law to disallow the use of the sprays.[16][17] Other users have attempted to smear their license plate with dirt or utilize covers to mask the plate.

Novelty frames around Texas license plates were made illegal in Texas on 1 September 2003 by Texas Senate Bill 439 because they caused problems with ANPR devices. That law made it a Class C misdemeanor (punishable by a fine of up to US $200), or Class B (punishable by a fine of up to US $2,000 and 180 days in jail) if it can be proven that the owner did it to deliberately obscure their plates.[18] The law was later clarified in 2007 to allow Novelty frames.

If an ANPR system cannot read the plate, it can flag the image for attention, with the human operators looking to see if they are able to identify the alphanumerics.

In order to avoid surveillance or penalty charges, there has been an upsurge in car cloning. This is usually achieved by copying registration plates from another car of a similar model and age. This can be difficult to detect, especially as cloners may change the registration plates and travel behavior to hinder investigations.

In 2013 researchers at Sunflex Zone Ltd created a privacy license plate frame that uses near infrared light to make the license plate unreadable to license plate recognition systems.[19]

10.9 Police enforcement

Mobile ANPR cameras fitted to a New South Wales Police Force Highway Patrol vehicle.

Closed-circuit television cameras such as these can be used to take the images scanned by automatic number plate recognition systems

10.9.1 Australia

Several State Police Forces, and the Department of Justice (Victoria)[20] use both fixed and mobile ANPR systems. The New South Wales Police Force Highway Patrol were the first to trial and use a fixed ANPR camera system in Australia in 2005. In 2009 they began a roll-out of a mobile ANPR system (known officially as MANPR)[21] with three infrared cameras fitted to its Highway Patrol fleet.[22] The system identifies unregistered and stolen vehicles as well as disqualified or suspended drivers as well as other 'persons of interest' such as persons having outstanding warrants.[23]

10.9.2 Belgium

The city of Mechelen uses an ANPR system since September 2011 to scan all cars crossing the city limits (inbound and outbound). Cars listed on 'black lists' (no insurance, stolen, etc.) generate an alarm in the dispatching room, so they can be intercepted by a patrol. As of early 2012, 1 million cars per week are automatically checked in this way.[24]

10.9.3 Denmark

The technique is tested by the Danish police. It will be in permanent use from the end of 2015.[25]

10.9.4 France

180 gantries over major roads have been built throughout the country. These together with a further 250 fixed cameras is to enable a levy of an eco tax on lorries over 3.5 tonnes. The system is currently being opposed and whilst they may be collecting data on vehicles passing the cameras, no eco tax is being charged.[26]

10.9.5 Germany

On 11 March 2008, the Federal Constitutional Court of Germany ruled that some areas of the laws permitting the use of automated number plate recognition systems in Germany violated the right to privacy.[27] More specifically, the court found that the retention of any sort of information (i.e., number plate data) which was not for any predestined use (e.g., for use tracking suspected terrorists or for enforcement of speeding laws) was in violation of German law. These systems were provided by Jenoptik Robot GmbH, and called TraffiCapture.[28]

10.9.6 Hungary

In 2012 a state consortium was formed among the Hungarian Ministry of Interior, the National Police Headquarters and the Central Commission of Public Administration and Electronic Services with the aim to install and operate a

Road gantry traffic enforcement and data point on the M7 highway at Érd, Hungary

unified intelligent transportation system (*ITS*) with nationwide coverage by the end of 2015.[29] Within the system, 160 portable traffic enforcement and data-gathering units and 365 permanent gantry installations were brought online with ANPR, speed detection, imaging and statistical capabilities. Since all the data points are connected to a centrally located ITS, each member of the consortium is able to separately utilize its range of administrative and enforcement activities, such as remote vehicle registration and insurance verification, speed, lane and traffic light enforcement and wanted or stolen vehicle interception among others.

Several Hungarian auxiliary police units also use a system called Matrix Police[30] in cooperation with the police. It consists of a portable computer equipped with a web camera that scans the stolen car database using automatic number plate recognition. The system is installed on the dashboard of selected patrol vehicles (PDA-based hand-held versions also exist) and is mainly used to control the license plate of parking cars. As the Auxiliary Police do not have the authority to order moving vehicles to stop, if a stolen car is found, the formal police is informed.

10.9.7   Turkey

Several cities have tested—and some have put into service—the "City Security Administration System", i.e., capital Ankara, has debuted KGYS- "Kent Guvenlik Yonetim Sistemi" which consists of a registration plate number recognition system on the main arteries and city exits.[31] The system has been used with two cameras per lane, one for plate recognition, one for speed detection. Now the system has been widened to network all the registration number cameras together, and enforcing average speed over preset distances. Some arteries have 70Kmh limit, and some 50 kmh, and photo evidence with date-time details are posted to registration address if speed violation is detected. As of 2012, the fine for exceeding the speed limit for more than 30% is approximately US$175.

10.9.8   Ukraine

The project of system integration «OLLI Technology» and the Ministry of Internal Affairs of Ukraine Department of State Traffic Inspection (STI) experiments on the introduction of a modern technical complex which is capable to locate stolen cars, drivers deprived of driving licenses and other problem cars in real time. The Ukrainian complex "Video control"[32] working by a principle of video fixing of the car with recognition of license plates with check under data base.

10.9.9   United Kingdom

An ANPR Equipped Vectra of the Greater Manchester Police force

Main article: Police-enforced ANPR in the UK

The UK has an extensive (ANPR) automatic number plate recognition CCTV network. Effectively, the police and security services track all car movements around the country and are able to track any car in close to real time. Vehicle movements are stored for 2 years in the National ANPR Data Center to be analyzed for intelligence and to be used as evidence.

In 1997 a system of one hundred ANPR cameras, codenamed GLUTTON, was installed to feed into the automated British Military Intelligence Systems in Northern Ireland. Further cameras were also installed on the British mainland, including unspecified ports on the east and west coasts.

10.9.10   United States

In the United States, ANPR systems are more commonly referred to as ALPR (Automatic License Plate Reader/Recognition) technology, due to differences in lan-

A City of Alexandria police car equipped with mobile ALPR.

ANPR cameras in operation on the Brooklyn Bridge in New York.

guage (i.e., "number plates" are referred to as "license plates" in American English)

Mobile ANPR use is widespread among US law enforcement agencies at the city, county, state and federal level. According to a 2012 report by the Police Executive Research Forum, approximately 71% of all US police departments use some form of ANPR.[33] Mobile ANPR is becoming a significant component of municipal predictive policing strategies and intelligence gathering,[34] as well as for recovery of stolen vehicles, identification of wanted felons, and revenue collection from individuals who are delinquent on city or state taxes or fines, or monitoring for "Amber Alerts". Successfully recognized plates may be matched against databases including "wanted person", "protection order", missing person, gang member, known and suspected terrorist, supervised release, immigration violator, and National Sex Offender lists.[35] In addition to the real-time processing of license plate numbers, ALPR systems in the US collect (and can indefinitely store) data from each license plate capture. Images, dates, times and GPS

coordinates can be stockpiled and can help place a suspect at a scene, aid in witness identification, pattern recognition or the tracking of individuals.

An early, private sector mobile ANPR application has been applications for vehicle repossession and recovery[36]), although the application of ANPR by private companies to collect information from privately owned vehicles or collected from private property (for example, driveways) has become an issue of sensitivity and public debate.[37] Other ALPR uses include parking enforcement, and revenue collection from individuals who are delinquent on city or state taxes or fines. The technology is often featured in the reality TV show *Parking Wars* featured on A&E Network. In the show, tow truck drivers and booting teams use the ALPR to find delinquent vehicles with high amounts of unpaid parking fines.

10.9.11 Saudi Arabia

Vehicle registration plates in Saudi Arabia use white background, but several vehicle types may have a different background. United States diplomatic plates have the letters 'USD', which in Arabic reads 'DSU' when read from right to left in the direction of Arabic script. There are only 17 Arabic letters used on the registration plates.[38] A Challenge for plates recognition in Saudi Arabia is the size of the digits. Some plates use both Eastern Arabic numerals and the 'Western Arabic' equivalents. A research with source code is available for APNR Arabic digits.[39]

10.9.12 Sweden

The technique is tested by the Swedish police at nine different places in Sweden.[40]

10.10 Average-speed cameras

Main article: Speed limit enforcement

ANPR is used for speed limit enforcement in Australia, Austria,[41] Belgium,[42] Dubai (UAE), France, Italy,[43] The Netherlands,[44] Spain,[45] and the UK.[46]

This works by tracking vehicles' travel time between two fixed points, and calculating the average speed. These cameras are claimed to have an advantage over traditional speed cameras in maintaining steady legal speeds over extended distances, rather than encouraging heavy braking on approach to specific camera locations and subsequent acceleration back to illegal speeds.[47]

10.10.1 Italy

In Italian Highways has developed a monitoring system named Tutor covering more than 2500 km (2012). The Tutor system is also able to intercept cars while changing lanes.[48]

10.10.2 The Netherlands

Average speed cameras (*trajectcontrole*) are in place in the Netherlands since 2002. As of July 2009, 12 cameras were operational, mostly in the west of the country and along the A12.[47] Some of these are divided in several "sections" to allow for cars leaving and entering the motorway.

A first experimental system was tested on a short stretch of the A2 in 1997 and was deemed a big success by the police, reducing overspeeding to 0.66%, compared to 5 to 6% when regular speed cameras were used at the same location.[49] The first permanent average speed cameras were installed on the A13 in 2002, shortly after the speed limit was reduced to 80 km/h to limit noise and air pollution in the area.[50] In 2007, average speed cameras resulted in 1.7 million fines for overspeeding out of a total of 9.7 millions. According to the Dutch Attorney General, the average number of violation of the speed limits on motorway sections equipped with average speed cameras is between 1 and 2%, compared to 10 to 15% elsewhere.[51]

10.10.3 UK

See also: Road speed limit enforcement in the United Kingdom

One of the most notable stretches of average speed cameras in the UK is found on the A77 road in Scotland, with 32 miles (51 km) being monitored between Glasgow and Ayr.[52] In 2006 it was confirmed that speeding tickets could potentially be avoided from the 'SPECS' cameras by changing lanes and the RAC Foundation feared that people may play "Russian Roulette" changing from one lane to another to lessen their odds of being caught.[46] However, in 2007 the system was upgraded for multi-lane use and in 2008 the manufacturer described the "myth" as "categorically untrue".[53] There exists evidence that implementation of systems such as SPECS has a considerable effect on the volume of drivers travelling at excessive speeds; on the stretch of road mentioned above (A77 Between Glasgow and Ayr) there has been noted a "huge drop" in speeding violations since the introduction of a SPECS system.[52]

10.11 Crime deterrent

Recent innovations have contributed to the adoption of ANPR for perimeter security and access control applications at government facilities. Within the US, "homeland security" efforts to protect against alleged "acts of terrorism" have resulted in adoption of ANPR for sensitive facilities such as embassies, schools, airports, maritime ports, military and federal buildings, law enforcement and government facilities, and transportation centers. ANPR is marketed as able to be implemented through networks of IP based surveillance cameras that perform "double duty" alongside facial recognition, object tracking, and recording systems for the purpose of monitoring suspicious or anomalous behavior, improving access control, and matching against watch lists. ANPR systems are most commonly installed at points of significant sensitivity, ingress or egress. Major US agencies such as the Department of Homeland Security, the Department of Justice, the Department of Transportation and the Department of Defense have purchased ANPR for perimeter security applications.[54] Large networks of ANPR systems are being installed by cities such as Boston, London and New York City to provide city-wide protection against acts of terrorism, and to provide support for public gatherings and public spaces.[55]

10.12 Enterprise security and services

In addition to government facilities, many private sector industries with facility security concerns are beginning to implement ANPR solutions. Examples include casinos, hospitals, museums, parking facilities, and resorts.[56] In the US, private facilities typically cannot access government or police watch lists, but may develop and match against their own databases for customers, VIPs, critical personnel or "banned person" lists. In addition to providing perimeter security, private ANPR has service applications for valet / recognized customer and VIP recognition, logistics and key personnel tracking, sales and advertising, parking management, and logistics (vendor and support vehicle tracking).

10.13 Traffic control

Many cities and districts have developed traffic control systems to help monitor the movement and flow of vehicles around the road network. This had typically involved looking at historical data, estimates, observations and statistics, such as:

Video tolling at Schönberg, Austria

- Car park usage
- Pedestrian crossing usage
- Number of vehicles along a road
- Areas of low and high congestion
- Frequency, location and cause of road works

CCTV cameras can be used to help traffic control centres by giving them live data, allowing for traffic management decisions to be made in real-time. By using ANPR on this footage it is possible to monitor the travel of individual vehicles, automatically providing information about the speed and flow of various routes. These details can highlight problem areas as and when they occur and help the centre to make informed incident management decisions.

Some counties of the United Kingdom have worked with Siemens Traffic to develop traffic monitoring systems for their own control centres and for the public.[57] Projects such as Hampshire County Council's ROMANSE provide an interactive and real-time web site showing details about traffic in the city. The site shows information about car parks, ongoing road works, special events and footage taken from CCTV cameras. ANPR systems can be used to provide average point-to-point journey times along particular routes, which can be displayed on a variable-message sign(VMS) giving drivers the ability to plan their route. ROMANSE also allows travellers to see the current situation using a mobile device with an Internet connection (such as WAP, GPRS or 3G), allowing them to view mobile device CCTV images within the Hampshire road network.

The UK company Trafficmaster has used ANPR since 1998 to estimate average traffic speeds on non-motorway roads without the results being skewed by local fluctuations caused by traffic lights and similar. The company now operates a network of over 4000 ANPR cameras, but claims

that only the four most central digits are identified, and no numberplate data is retained.[58][59][60]

- IEEE transactions on Intelligent Transportation Systems(IEEE Intelligent Transportation Systems Society) published some papers on the plate number recognition technologies and applications.

10.14 Electronic toll collection

10.14.1 Toll roads

The FasTrak system in Orange County uses ANPR and radio transponders

Film showing the approach to and passing of a toll station in Italy, using a Telepass OBU. Note the yellow Telepass lane signs and road markings and the sound emitted by the OBU when passing the lane

Ontario's 407 ETR highway uses a combination of ANPR and radio transponders to toll vehicles entering and exiting the road. Radio antennas are located at each junction and detect the transponders, logging the unique identity of each vehicle in much the same way as the ANPR system does.

Without ANPR as a second system it would not be possible
to monitor all the traffic. Drivers who opt to rent a transpon-
der for C$2.55 per month are not charged the "Video Toll
Charge" of C$3.60 for using the road, with heavy vehicles
(those with a gross weight of over 5,000 kg) being required
to use one. Using either system, users of the highway are
notified of the usage charges by post.

There are numerous other electronic toll collection networks which use this combination of Radio frequency identification and ANPR. These include:

- The Golden Gate Bridge in San Francisco, California,
  began using an all-electronic tolling system combining
  Fastrak and ANPR on March 27, 2013.[61]

- NC Quick Pass for the Interstate 540 (North Carolina)
  Triangle Expressway in Wake County, North Carolina

- Bridge Pass[62] for the Saint John Harbour Bridge in
  Saint John, New Brunswick

- Quickpass[63] at the Golden Ears Bridge, crossing the
  Fraser River between Langley and Maple Ridge

- CityLink & Eastlink in Melbourne, Australia

- Gateway Motorway and Logan Motorway, Brisbane,
  Australia

- FasTrak in California, United States

- Highway 6 in Israel

- Tunnels in Hong Kong

- Autopista Central[64] in Santiago, Chile (site in Spanish)

- E-ZPass in New York, New Jersey, Massachusetts (as
  Fast Lane until 2012), Virginia (formerly Smart Tag),
  and other states. Maryland Route 200 uses a combination of E-ZPass and ANPR.

- TollTag in North Texas and EZ-Tag in Houston,
  Texas.

- I-Pass in Illinois

- Pike Pass in Oklahoma

- Peach Pass I-85 Atlanta, GA Gwinnett County

- OGS (Otomatik Geçiş Sistemi) used at Bosphorus
  Bridge, Fatih Sultan Mehmet Bridge, and Trans European Motorway entry points in İstanbul, Turkey

- M50 Westlink Toll in Dublin, Ireland

- Hi-pass in South Korea

- Northern Gateway, SH 1, Auckland, New Zealand

- Evergreen Point Floating Bridge, Seattle, and
  Washington State Route 167 HOT-lanes in western
  Washington

- ETC[65] in Taiwan

10.14.2   Portugal

Portuguese roads have old highways with toll station where
drivers can pay with cards and also lanes where there are
electronic collection systems. However most new highways
only have the option of electronic toll collection system.
The electronic toll collection system comprises three different structures: ANPR which works with infrared cameras and reads license plates from every vehicle Lasers to
measure the volumetry of the vehicle to confirm whether
it is a regular car or if it is a SUV or truck as charges are
very different RFID-like to read smart tags that cars can
have installed. When the smart tag is installed, the car is
quickly identified and owners bank account is automatically
deducted. This process is realized at any speed up to over
250 km per hour. If the car does not have the smart tag, the
driver is required to go to a pay station to pay the tolls between 3rd and 5th day after with a surplus charge. If he fails
to do so, the owner is sent a letter home with a heavy fine.
If this is not paid, it increases five-fold and after that, the
car is inserted into a police database for vehicle impound-
ing. This system is also used in some limited access areas
of main cities to allow only entry from pre-registered resi-
dents. It is planned to be implemented both in more roads
and in city entrance toll collection/access restriction. The
efficacy of the system is considered to be so high that it is
almost impossible for the driver to complain.

See also: List of electronic toll collection systems

10.14.3   Charge zones – the London conges-
          tion charge

The London congestion charge is an example of a system
that charges motorists entering a payment area. Transport
for London (TfL) uses ANPR systems and charges motorists a daily fee of £10 paid before 10pm if they enter,
leave or move around within the congestion charge zone
between 7 a.m. and 6:00 p.m., Monday to Friday. A reduced fee of £9 is paid by vehicle owners who sign up for
the automatic deduction scheme. Fines for traveling within
the zone without paying the charge are £60 per infraction
if paid before the deadline, doubling to £120 per infraction
thereafter.

There are currently 1,500 cameras which use automatic

The London congestion charge scheme uses 230 cameras and ANPR to help monitor vehicles in the charging zone

number plate recognition (ANPR) technology.[66] There are also a number of mobile camera units which may be deployed anywhere in the zone.

It is estimated that around 98% of vehicles moving within the zone are caught on camera. The video streams are transmitted to a data centre located in central London where the ANPR software deduces the registration plate of the vehicle. A second data centre provides a backup location for image data.

Both front and back number plates are being captured, on vehicles going both in and out – this gives up to four chances to capture the number plates of a vehicle entering and exiting the zone. This list is then compared with a list of cars whose owners/operators have paid to enter the zone – those that have not paid are fined. The registered owner of such a vehicle is looked up in a database provided by the DVLA.[67]

10.14.4   Sweden

In Stockholm, Sweden, ANPR is used for the Stockholm congestion tax, owners of cars driving into or out of the inner city must pay a charge, depending on the time of the day. From 2013, also for the Gothenburg congestion tax, which also includes vehicles passing the city on the main highways.

10.15   Usage

Several UK companies and agencies use ANPR systems. These include Vehicle and Operator Services Agency (VOSA),[68] Driver and Vehicle Licensing Agency (DVLA)[69] and Transport for London.[70]

10.16   Challenges

10.16.1   Controversy

The introduction of ANPR systems has led to fears of misidentification and the furthering of *1984*-style surveillance.[71] In the United States, some such as Gregg Easterbrook oppose what they call "machines that issue speeding tickets and red-light tickets" as the beginning of a slippery slope towards an automated justice system:

> "A machine classifies a person as an offender, and you can't confront your accuser because there is no accuser... can it be wise to establish a principle that when a machine says you did something illegal, you are presumed guilty?"[72]

Similar criticisms have been raised in other countries. Easterbrook also argues that this technology is employed to maximize revenue for the state, rather than to promote safety.[72] The electronic surveillance system produces tickets which in the US are often in excess of $100, and are virtually impossible for a citizen to contest in court without the help of an attorney. The revenues generated by these machines are shared generously with the private corporation that builds and operates them, creating a strong incentive to tweak the system to generate as many tickets as possible.

Older systems had been notably unreliable; in the UK this has been known to lead to charges being made incorrectly with the vehicle owner having to pay £10 in order to be issued with proof (or not) of the offense. Improvements in technology have drastically decreased error rates, but false accusations are still frequent enough to be a problem.

Perhaps the best known incident involving the abuse of an ANPR database in North America is the case of *Edmonton Sun* reporter Kerry Diotte in 2004. Diotte wrote an article critical of Edmonton police use of traffic cameras for revenue enhancement, and in retaliation was added to an ANPR database of "high-risk drivers" in an attempt to monitor his habits and create an opportunity to arrest him.[73][74][75] The police chief and several officers were fired as a result, and The Office of the Privacy Commissioner of Canada expressed public concern over the "growing police use of technology to spy on motorists."[76]

Other concerns include the storage of information that could be used to identify people and store details about their driving habits and daily life, contravening the Data Protection Act along with similar legislation (see personally identifiable information). The laws in the UK are strict for any system that uses CCTV footage and can identify individuals.[77][77][78][79][80][81][82][83][84]

Also of concern is the safety of the data once it is mined, following the discovery of police surveillance records lost in a gutter.[85][86]

There is also a case in the UK for saying that use of ANPR cameras is against the law under the Regulation of Investigatory Powers Act 2000.[87] The breach exists, some say, in the fact that ANPR is used to monitor the activities of law-abiding citizens and treats everyone like the suspected criminals intended to be surveyed under the act. The police themselves have been known to refer to the system of ANPR as a "24/7 traffic movement database" which is a diversion from its intended purpose of identifying vehicles involved in criminal activities.[88] The opposing viewpoint is that where the plates have been cloned, a 'read' of an innocent motorist's vehicle will allow the elimination of that vehicle from an investigation by visual examination of the images stored. Likewise, stolen vehicles are read by ANPR systems between the time of theft and report to the Police, assisting in the investigation.

The *Associated Press* reported in August 2011 that New York Police Department cars and license plate tracking equipment purchased with federal HIDTA (High Intensity Drug Trafficking Area) funds were used to spy on Muslims at mosques, and to track the license plate numbers of worshipers. [89] Police in unmarked cars outfitted with electronic license plate readers would drive down the street and automatically catalog the plates of everyone parked near the mosque, amassing a covert database that would be distributed among officers and used to profile Muslims in public.[90]

In 2013 the American Civil Liberties Union released 26,000 pages of data about ANPR systems obtained from local, state, and federal agencies through freedom of information laws. "The documents paint a startling picture of a technology deployed with too few rules that is becoming a tool for mass routine location tracking and surveillance" wrote the ACLU. The ACLU reported that in many locations the devices were being used to store location information on vehicles which were not suspected of any particular offense. "Private companies are also using license plate readers and sharing the information they collect with police with little or no oversight or privacy protections. A lack of regulation means that policies governing how long our location data is kept vary widely," the ACLU said.[91] In 2012 the ACLU filed suit against the Department of Homeland Security, which funds many local and state ANPR programs through grants, after the agency failed to provide access to records the ACLU had requested under the Freedom of Information Act about the programs.[92]

10.16.2 Plate inconsistency and jurisdictional differences

Many ANPR systems claim accuracy when trained to match plates from a single jurisdiction or region, but can fail when trying to recognize plates from other jurisdictions due to variations in format, font, color, layout, and other plate features.[93] Some jurisdictions offer vanity or affinity plates (particularly in the US), which can create many variations within a single jurisdiction.[94]

From time to time, US states will make significant changes in their license plate protocol that will affect OCR accuracy. They may add a character or add a new license plate design. ALPR systems must adapt to these changes quickly in order to be effective. Another challenge with ALPR systems is that some states have the same license plate protocol. For example, more than one state uses the standard three letters followed by four numbers. So each time the ALPR systems alarms, it is the user's responsibility to make sure that the plate which caused the alarm matches the state associated with the license plate listed on the in-car computer. For maximum effectiveness, an ANPR system should be able to recognize plates from any jurisdiction, and the jurisdiction to which they are associated, but these many variables make such tasks difficult.

Currently at least one US ANPR provider (PlateSmart) claims their system has been independently reviewed as able to accurately recognize the US state jurisdiction of license plates, and one European ANPR provider claims their system can differentiate all EU plate jurisdictions.[95][96]

10.16.3 Accuracy and measurement of ANPR system performance

A 2008 article in *Parking Trend International* discussed a disparity in claimed vs. experienced license plate recognition read rates, with manufacturers claiming that their recognition engines can correctly report 98% of the time, although customers experience only 90% to 94% success, even with new equipment under perfect conditions. Early systems were reportedly only 60% to 80% reliable.[97]

True system error rate is the product of its subsystem error rates (image capture, license plate image extraction, LP image interpretation); slight increases in subsystem error rates can produce dramatic reductions of read rates. The effects of real-world interfering factors on read rate are not uniformly specified or tested by manufacturers. The article states "there is a need for the industry to adopt a standard performance measurement protocol to enable potential customers assess the best fit for their particular requirements."[97]

10.17 Other uses

ANPR systems may also be used for/by:

- Section control, to measure average vehicle speed over longer distances.[98]

- Border crossings

- Automobile repossessions[36][99]

- petrol stations to log when a motorist drives away without paying for their fuel.

- A marketing tool to log patterns of use

- Targeted advertising, a-la "Minority Report"-style billboards.[100][101]

- Traffic management systems, which determine traffic flow using the time it takes vehicles to pass two ANPR sites[102]

- Analyses of travel behaviour (route choice, origin-destination etc.) for transport planning purposes[103][104]

- Drive Through Customer Recognition, to automatically recognize customers based on their license plate and offer them the items they ordered the last time they used the service.

- To assist visitor management systems in recognizing guest vehicles.

- Police and Auxiliary Police

- Car parking companies

- Hotels

10.18 Related research society

- IEEE Intelligent Transportation Systems Society

10.19 See also

- AI effect

- Applications of artificial intelligence

- Closed circuit television

- Facial recognition system

- Parking lot

- Road Policing Unit

- SPECS (speed camera)

- Vehicle location data

Lists

- List of emerging technologies

- Outline of artificial intelligence

10.20 References

[1] "ANPR Tutorial". ANPR Tutorial. 15 August 2006. Retrieved 2012-01-24.

[2] "Shan Du ; IntelliView Technol., Inc., Calgary, AB, Canada ; Ibrahim, M. ; Shehata, M. ; Badawy, Wael; Automatic License Plate Recognition (ALPR): A State-of-the-Art Review". IEEE. 1 Feb 2013. Retrieved 2014-01-09.

[3] "An introduction to ANPR". Cctv-information.co.uk. Retrieved 2012-01-24.

[4] "CCTV network tracks 'getaway' car". BBC News. 21 November 2005. Retrieved 2013-08-12.

[5] "Plate Recognition". PhotoCop.com.

[6] "Algorithm for License Plate Recognition". VISL, Technion. 2002.

[7] "A Real-time vehicle License Plate Recognition (LPR)". VISL, Technion, 2003

[8] "An Approach To License Plate Recognition" (PDF). University of Calgary. 1996. Retrieved 2012-01-24.

[9] Draghici, Sorin (1997). "A neural network based artificial vision system for license plate recognition" (PDF). Dept. of Computer Science, Wayne State University. Retrieved 2012-01-24.

[10] "License Plate Recognition in Turkey (Plaka Okuma Sistemi)". Grimedia.com. Retrieved 2012-01-24.

[11] Kwaśnicka, Halina; Wawrzyniak, Bartosz (2002), "License plate localization and recognition in camera pictures" (PDF), *AI-METH 2002 – Artificial Intelligence Methods November 13–15* (Gliwice, Poland), retrieved 2014-01-13

[12] Kahraman, Fatih; Gokmen, Muhittin (2003). "License Plate Character Segmentation Based on the Gabor Transform and Vector Quantization" (PDF). Archived from the original (PDF) on 2006-05-24. Retrieved 2012-01-24.

[13] Ondrej Martinsky (2007). "Algorithmic and mathematical principles of automatic number plate recognition systems" (PDF). Brno University of Technology. Retrieved 2012-01-24.

[14] "A License Plate Recognition algorithm for Intelligent Transportation System applications". University of the Aegean and National Technical University of Athens. 2006. Archived from the original on 2008-04-20. Retrieved 2012-01-24.

[15] "Automatic Number Plate Recognition". Cctv-information.co.uk. Retrieved 2012-01-24.

[16] Sexton, Steve (3 July 2003). "License-plate spray foils traffic cameras". *Washington Times*. Retrieved 2013-07-02.

[17] Sexton, Steve (3 July 2003). "License-plate spray foils traffic cameras". *Washington Times*. Retrieved 2013-07-02.

[18] Wentworth, Jeff. "Obscured license plate could be motorists' ticket to fine". Texas State Senate. Archived from the original on 24 March 2005. Retrieved 5 April 2005.

[19] http://www.sunflexzone.com/product/ stealth-anti-tracking-ir-infrared-license-plate-blocker-privacy-frame-section-4-040 .VVrj2kbEnrg

[20]

[21] "eTendering - Contract Award Notice Detail View - 01092010RFT". Tenders.nsw.gov.au. Retrieved 2014-04-23.

[22] http://www.police.nsw.gov.au/__data/assets/pdf_file/ 0008/184886/Annual_Report_-_Year_in_Review.pdf

[23] Hoctor, Michelle (2012-06-06). "Mass surveillance system nicks drivers". Illawarra Mercury. Retrieved 2014-04-23.

[24] "ANPR in Mechelen". Belgium.

[25] "Politiet vil tjekke millioner af danske nummerplader". Denmark: B.dk.

[26] "Portiques écotaxe. Ils copient la plaque d'immatriculation de Hollande". *OuestFrance*. OuestFrance. Retrieved 21 Feb 2014.

[27] "Das Bundesverfassungsgericht" (in German). Bverfg.de. 3 November 2008. Retrieved 2009-02-16.

[28] "TraffiCapture". Jenoptic.com.

[29] "VÉDA Közúti Intelligens Kamerahálózat" (in Hungarian). Országos Rendőr-főkapitányság. Retrieved 2015-09-02.

[30] "Matrix Police". Hungary. Retrieved 2012-01-24.

[31] "Turk Telekom deploys traffic surveillance service in Ankara". Telecompaper. 2010-12-09. Retrieved 2012-08-03.

[32] "Video control". Ukraine: Ollie.com.ua.

[33] "How are Innovations in Technology Transforming Policing?" (PDF). *Police Executive Research Forum*. January 2012.

[34] "Cameras for insurance verification considered". *Tulsa World*. 29 November 2009.

[35] "License Plate Reader Technology Enhances the Identification, Recovery of Stolen Vehicles". *FBI*. September 2011.

[36] Belson, Ken (28 February 2010). "The Wired Repo Man: He's Not 'As Seen on TV'". *New York Times*. Retrieved 2012-01-24.

[37] "License plate data not just for cops: Private companies are tracking your car". *NBC News*. 19 July 2013.

[38] Vehicle registration plates of Saudi Arabia

[39] "Arabic Licence Plate Recognition". Sourceforge.

[40] "Polisens nya vapen: "Terminator"-teknik". Sweden: Expressen.se.

[41] "Section Control: 24.000 Raser angezeigt" (in German). Austria: ORF.at. 7 June 2010.

[42] "Flitsers.net".

[43] "Ecco come funziona il Tutor in autostrada - Notizie brevi - News - Informazione - A.S.A.P.S. Il Portale della Sicurezza Stradale". Asaps.it. Retrieved 2012-08-03.

[44] "Description of the system" (in Dutch). Dutch Attorney General. 31 December 2009. Retrieved 2012-01-24.

[45] "Llegan los radares de velocidad media a España" (in Spanish). Noticias.coches.com. 23 September 2009. Retrieved 2012-01-24.

[46] "Speeding tickets can potentially be avoided by changing lanes". *The Daily Mail* (London). 15 October 2006. Retrieved 2012-01-24. The Home Office admitted last night that drivers can avoid being caught the by hi-tech 'SPECS' cameras which calculate a car's average speed over a long distance.

[47] "Frequently Asked Question over Trajectcontrole" (in Dutch). Dutch Attorney General. Retrieved 2012-01-24.

[48] "Autostrade S.p.A" (in Italian). Autostrade.it. 2008-05-25. Retrieved 2012-08-03.

[49] "Niemand rijdt meer te hard op de A2" (in Dutch). *Trouw*. 18 October 1997. Retrieved 2012-01-24.

[50] "Nummerborden lezen op de A13" (in Dutch). *Trouw*. 6 May 2002. Retrieved 2012-01-24.

[51] Kreling, Tom (28 August 2008). "Een duur foutje van de computer" (in Dutch). *NRC Handelsblad*. Retrieved 2012-01-24.

[52] "SPECS - average speed cameras on SPECS". A77safetygroup.com. 14 July 2005. Retrieved 2012-01-24.

[53] "Jeremy Clarkson tilts at windmills – Speed camera avoidance is an urban myth". *The Register*. 21 July 2008. Retrieved 23 January 2012.

[54] base-security-and-investigations/ "US Navy Selects PlateSmart® Exclusively to Help with Base Security and Investigations" Check |url= scheme (help). *Defense Procurement News*. 4 March 2013.

[55] "After Boston: The pros and cons of surveillance cameras". *CNN Tech*. 26 April 2013.

[56] "License Plate Recognition, Tribal Casinos, and Banned Persons" (PDF). *Indiangaming.com*. February 2011.

[57] "Recognising a new way to keep traffic moving". Siemenstraffic.com. Retrieved 2012-01-24.

[58] "PIPS supplies Journey Time Measurement Systems to Trafficmaster". PIPS Technology. Archived from the original on 2009-01-24. Retrieved 2012-01-24.

[59] "BLURA License Plate Recognition Engine". Blura.com. Retrieved 2012-01-24.

[60] "Trunk Roads – PTFM". Trafficmaster.co.uk. Retrieved 2012-01-24.

[61] Hansen, Megan and Will Jason (27 Mar 2013). "Golden Gate Bridge sees smooth transition to all-electronic tolls". *Marin Independent Journal*. Retrieved 17 May 2013.

[62] "HugeDomains.com - SaintjohnHarbourBridge.com is for Sale". Saintjohn Harbour Bridge. Retrieved 2014-04-23.

[63] http://www.translink.ca/en/Driving/Golden-Ears-Bridge.aspx

[64] "autopistacentral.cl". autopistacentral.cl. 2014-01-22. Retrieved 2014-04-23.

[65] "中港通". Fetc.net.tw. 2006-02-10. Retrieved 2014-04-23.

[66] "Met given real time c-charge data". *BBC*. 17 July 2007. Archived from the original on 13 September 2007. Retrieved 2007-09-20.

[67] "Transport for London". Cclondon.com. 17 July 2011. Retrieved 2012-01-24.

[68] vosa.gov.uk

[69] https://www.gov.uk/government/organisations/driver-and-vehicle-licensing-agency

[70] cclondon.com

[71] Mathieson, SA (19 June 2003). "Keeping 1984 in the past". *The Guardian* (UK).

[72] Easterbrook, Gregg (28 February 2005). "Daily Express - Lights, Camera, Action". *The New Republic Online*. Archived from the original on 2005-09-03.(subscription required)

[73] "Edmonton officer reprimanded for checking up on newspaper columnist". CBC News. 14 November 2005.

[74] "CBC Edmonton - Features - Edmonton Police". CBC News. Archived from the original on 2007-10-23. Retrieved 2 July 2013.

[75] "Officer faces suspension for Overtime sting". Edmonton Police Watch. 6 September 2008. Retrieved 2012-01-24.

[76] "Canada: Privacy Commissioner Concerned Over License Plate Spying". Thenewspaper.com. 3 July 2007. Retrieved 2012-01-24.

[77] Lettice, John (21 February 2003). "The London charge zone, the DP Act, and MS .NET". London: The Register. Retrieved 2012-01-24.

[78] "ANPR Strategy for the Police Service 2005/2006". ACPO (Association of Chief Police Officers) ANPR Steering Group. 17 March 2005. Archived from the original on 2010-03-31. Retrieved 2012-01-24.

[79] "Driving crime down" (PDF). London: UK Government Home Office. 22 October 2004. Archived from the original (PDF) on 2007-01-08. Retrieved 2013-07-02.

[80] Constant, Mike. "ANPR". CCTV Information. Archived from the original on 21 March 2005. Retrieved 30 March 2005.

[81] Hofman, Yoram. "License Plate Recognition – A Tutorial". Archived from the original on 24 March 2005. Retrieved 28 March 2005.

[82] Lucena, Raul (24 August 2006). "Automatic Number Plate Recognition Tutorial". ANPR-tutorial.com.

[83] Lettice, John (24 March 2005). "No hiding place? UK number plate cameras go national". The Register. Archived from the original on 28 March 2005. Retrieved 28 March 2005.

[84] "Recognizing a new way to keep traffic moving". Siemens Traffic. Archived from the original on 17 April 2005. Retrieved 3 April 2005.

[85] "UK: Traffic Camera Data Dropped in Gutter". thenewspaper.com. Retrieved 2012-01-24.

[86] Clements, Jon (11 March 2008). "A police memory stick containing secret data is found in gutter". *The Mirror (UK)*. Retrieved 2013-07-02.

[87] "Regulation of Investigatory Powers Act 2000". *legislation.gov.uk*. The National Archives. 2000. Retrieved 2012-01-24.

[88] "Police number plate cameras may breach RIPA - Commissioner". TheRegister.com. 17 July 2006. Retrieved 2012-01-24.

[89] "Money for nothing: the drug war and the war on Muslims".

[90] Green, Jonah (24 February 2012). "NYPD Defends Tactics Over Mosque Spying; Records Reveal New Details On Muslim Surveillance". *Huffington Post.*

[91] "ACLU raises privacy concerns about police technology tracking drivers - CNN.com". *CNN.* 18 July 2013.

[92] Klein, Allison (26 September 2012). "ACLU files suit over info on license plate readers". *The Washington Post.*

[93] "Automated License Plate Recognition Systems: Policy and Operational Guidance for Law Enforcement" (PDF). *U.S. Department of Justice, National Institute of Justice.* 2012.

[94] "New Developments In ALPR". *Police Technology Magazine.* 15 February 2011.

[95]

[96] the license plate recognition company (2004-10-20). "License Plate Recognition Algorithms and Technology". Platerecognition.info. Retrieved 2014-04-23.

[97] "Measuring ANPR System Performance" (PDF). *Parking Trend International.* June 2008. Retrieved 2012-01-24.

[98] "Section control". Verkeershandhaving Dossiers. Archived from the original on 2006-05-12. Retrieved 2012-01-24.

[99] "High-Tech System Helps Repo Man Find Cars". WFTV. November 11, 2009.

[100] "UK Billboards Equipped with License Plate Spy Cameras". TheNewspaper.com. 25 September 2009. Retrieved 2013-07-02.

[101] "UK Billboards Equipped with License Plate Spy Cameras". 25 September 2009. Retrieved 2013-07-02.

[102] "Extreme CCTV Announces Contract for Stockholm Traffic Cameras" (PDF). Extremecctv.com. 22 April 2004. Archived from the original (PDF) on 2008-04-09. Retrieved 2012-01-24.

[103] Friedrich, Markus; Jehlicka, Prokop; Schlaich, Johannes (2008). "Automatic number plate recognition for the observance of travel behavior". Universität Stuttgart Institut für Straßen und Verkehrswesen. Retrieved 2013-07-02.

[104] Friedrich, Markus; Jehlicka, Prokop; Schlaich, Johannes (2008). "Automatic number plate recognition for the observance of travel behavior" (PDF). *8th International Conference on Survey Methods in Transport: Harmonisation and Data Comparability, May 2008, Annecy, France.* Universität Stuttgart Institut für Straßen und Verkehrswesen. Retrieved 2013-07-02.

Chapter 11

Big mechanism

Big Mechanism is a $45 million DARPA research program, begun in 2014, aimed at developing software that will read cancer research papers, integrate them into a cancer model and frame new hypotheses by the end of 2017.[1]

11.1 Ras gene

The program focuses on mutations in the Ras gene family, which underlie some one-third of human cancers. Currently, a rough road map shows interaction sequences among proteins affecting cell replication and death. However, the causal relations are poorly understood.[1]

11.2 Plan

The program is to occur in three stages. The first is to read literature and convert it into formal representations. Second is to integrate the knowledge into computational models. Third is to produce experimentally testable explanations and predictions. Research teams are developing four separate systems targeting all three tasks.[1]

In February 2015 an evaluation meeting reviewed progress on the first stage. Multiple tasks were considered. One was extraction of experimental procedure details and evaluating statements such as "we demonstrate" and "we suggest." Another worked to map sentence meaning and relationships. The best machine-reading system extracted 40% of relevant information from a small corpus and correctly determined how each passage related to the model.[1]

The second stage is to become active in summer 2015, when members attempt to produce a single reference model. The third stage is the most challenging, because the artificial intelligence community has had limited success at developing hypothesis generators. Molecular biology may be more amenable, because most domain knowledge is technical and available in written form.[1]

11.3 References

[1] You, J. (2015). "DARPA sets out to automate research". *Science* **347** (6221): 465. doi:10.1126/science.347.6221.465.

11.4 External links

- Official website

Chapter 12

Braina

Braina is an intelligent personal assistant application for Microsoft Windows developed by Brainasoft.[1][2] Braina uses natural language interface[3] and speech recognition[4] to interact with its users and allows users to use English language sentences to perform various tasks on their computer. The application can find information from the internet, play songs and videos of user's choice, take dictation, find and open files, set alarms and reminders, performs math calculations, controls windows and programs etc.[2][5] Braina's Android app can be used to interact with the system remotely over a Wi-Fi network.[1]

The name Braina is a short form of Brain Artificial.[6] The software adapts to the user's behavior over time to better anticipate needs.[2] The software also allows users to type commands using keyboard instead of saying them. Braina comes in both free and paid version.

Future plc's TechRadar recognized Braina as one of the top 10 free essential software for 2015.[2]

12.1 References

[1] Rasika Anera, Utkarsh Mehta, Sharangdhar Vaze, G. Hrishikesh. "Personal Assistant to Facilitate User Task Automation" (PDF). *International Journal of Computer Trends and Technology (IJCTT) ISSN 2231-2803* (Seventh Sense Research Group) **15** (4): 155–156. External link in |work= (help)

[2] Nick Peers. "Best free software for 2015: 10 essential downloads for the year ahead". Future plc. Retrieved 2015-01-10.

[3] Vladimir A. Fomichov, Alexander A. Razorenov. "The Design of A Natural Language Interface for File System Operations on the basis of a Structured Meanings Model" (PDF). *Procedia Computer Science* (Elsevier) **31** (2014): 1005–1011. doi:10.1016/j.procs.2014.05.353. Retrieved 2015-01-10.

[4] "Braina Speech Recognition Software". Retrieved 2015-04-04.

[5] Joel Lee. "Windows 10 Transformation Pack Gives a Facelift to Windows 7 & 8". MakeUseOf. Retrieved 2015-06-28.

[6] "Braina Homepage". Retrieved 2015-01-10.

Chapter 13

Chinese speech synthesis

Chinese speech synthesis is the application of speech synthesis to the Chinese language (usually Standard Chinese). It poses additional difficulties due to the Chinese characters (which frequently have different pronunciations in different contexts), the complex prosody, which is essential to convey the meaning of words, and sometimes the difficulty in obtaining agreement among native speakers concerning what the correct pronunciation is of certain phonemes.

13.1 Approaches taken

13.1.1 Corpus-based

Anhui USTC iFlyTek Co., Ltd (iFlyTek) published a W3C paper in which they adapted Speech Synthesis Markup Language to produce a mark-up language called Chinese Speech Synthesis Markup Language (CSSML) which can include additional markup to clarify the pronunciation of characters and to add some prosody information.[1] Their synthesiser takes a "corpus-based" approach, which means it can sound very natural in most cases but can err in dealing with unusual phrases if they can't be matched with the corpus. The amount of data involved is not disclosed by iFlyTek but can be seen from the commercial products that iFlyTek have licensed their technology to; for example, Bider's SpeechPlus is a 1.3 Gigabyte download, 1.2 Gigabytes of which is used for the highly compressed data for a single Chinese voice. iFlyTek's synthesiser can also synthesise mixed Chinese and English text with the same voice (e.g. Chinese sentences containing some English words); they claim their English synthesis to be "average".

The iFlyTek corpus appears to be heavily dependent on Chinese characters, and it is not possible to synthesize from pinyin alone. It is sometimes possible by means of CSSML to add pinyin to the characters to disambiguate between multiple possible pronunciations, but this does not always work.

A corpus-based approach is also taken by Tsinghua University's SinoSonic, with the Harbin voice data taking 800 Megabytes. As of 2007 (and 2011), the download link for SinoSonic has not yet been activated. (Vapourware?)

13.1.2 Concatenation (KeyTip)

A less complex approach is taken by cjkware.com's KeyTip Putonghua Reader, which contains 120 Megabytes of sound recordings (GSM-compressed to 40 Megabytes in the evaluation version), comprising 10,000 multi-syllable dictionary words plus single-syllable recordings in 6 different prosodies (4 tones, neutral tone, and an extra third-tone recording for use at the end of a phrase). These recordings can be concatenated in any desired combination, but the joins sound forced (as is usual for simple concatenation-based speech synthesis) and this can severely affect prosody; the synthesizer is also inflexible in terms of speed and expression. However, because this synthesizer does not rely on a corpus, there is no noticeable degradation in performance when it is given more unusual or awkward phrases.

13.1.3 eSpeak

The lightweight open-source speech project eSpeak, which has its own approach to synthesis, has started experimenting with Chinese synthesis. It was used by Google Translate from May 2010[2] until December 2010.[3]

13.1.4 Ekho

Ekho is another open source TTS, which simply concatenates sampled syllables. It currently supports Cantonese, Mandarin, and Korean. Some of the Mandarin syllables have been pitched-normalised in Praat. A modified version of these is used in Gradint's "synthesis from partials".

43

13.2   Online Demos and Bell Labs

There is an online interactive demonstration for NeoSpeech speech synthesis,[4] which accepts Chinese characters and also pinyin if it's enclosed in their proprietary "VTML" markup.[5]

iFlyTek has two demos available online.[6][7]

Bell Labs have an online Mandarin text-to-speech demo[8] dated 1997, but it is now non-functional (the server that the query is to be submitted to does not exist in the DNS) and the contact email is no longer valid. However, their approach was described in a monograph "Multilingual Text-to-Speech Synthesis: The Bell Labs Approach" (Springer, October 31, 1997, ISBN 978-0-7923-8027-6), and the former employee who was responsible for the project, Chilin Shih (who now works at the University of Illinois), has some notes about her methods on her website.[9]

13.3   Mac OS

Mac OS had Chinese speech synthesizers available up to version 9. This was removed in 10.0 and reinstated in 10.7 (Lion).[10]

13.4   See also

- Speech synthesis

13.5   References

[1] http://www.w3.org/2005/08/SSML/Papers/iFLYTech.pdf

[2] http://googletranslate.blogspot.com/2010/05/giving-voice-to-more-languages-on.html

[3] http://googletranslate.blogspot.com/2010/12/listen-to-us-now.html

[4] http://www.neospeech.com/

[5] for example <vtml_phoneme alphabet="x-pinyin" ph="ni3hao3"></vtml_phoneme>; see pages 7 and 25-27 of https://ondemand.neospeech.com/vt_eng-Engine-VTML-v3.9.0-3.pdf

[6] Anhui USTC iFlyTek Co., Ltd Demo

[7] Anhui USTC iFlyTek Co., Ltd Beta 1.0

[8] Mandarin TTS

[9] Home Page: Chilin Shih

[10] Voice packs are automatically downloaded as needed when selected in System Preferences, Speech Settings, Text to Speech, System Voice, Customize. Three Chinese female voices are available in the system. One each for Mainland China, Hong Kong and Taiwan.

13.6   External links

- Anhui USTC iFlyTek Co., Ltd homepage

Chapter 14

Cleverbot

Cleverbot is a web application that uses an artificial intelligence algorithm to have conversations with humans. It was created by the British AI scientist Rollo Carpenter, who also created Jabberwacky, a similar web application. It is unique in the sense that it learns from humans, remembering words within its AI. In its first decade Cleverbot held several thousand conversations with Carpenter and his associates. Since launching on the web in 1997, the number of conversations held has exceeded 200 million. Cleverbot is also now an iOS, Android and Windows phone app.[2]

14.1 Operation

Unlike other chatterbots, Cleverbot's responses are not programmed. Instead, it "learns" from human input; Humans type into the box below the Cleverbot logo and the system finds all keywords or an exact phrase matching the input. After searching through its saved conversations, it responds to the input by finding how a human responded to that input when it was asked, in part or in full, by Cleverbot.[3][4]

Cleverbot participated in a formal Turing test at the 2011 Techniche festival at the Indian Institute of Technology Guwahati on September 3, 2011. Out of the 334 votes cast, Cleverbot was judged to be 59.3% human, compared to the rating of 63.3% human achieved by human participants. A score of 50.05% or higher is often considered to be a passing grade.[5] The software running for the event had to handle just 1 or 2 simultaneous requests, whereas online Cleverbot is usually talking to around 80,000 people at once.

14.2 Developments

Cleverbot is constantly "learning", growing in data size, and perhaps also in the degree of "intelligence" it appears to display. Updates to the software have been mostly behind the scenes. In 2014 Cleverbot was upgraded to use GPU serving techniques.[6] The program chooses how to respond to users fuzzily, and contextually, the whole of the conversation being compared to the millions that have taken place before. The Cleverbot database now has over 265 million rows, using several Big Data techniques and more recently with Machine Learning.

A significant part of the engine behind Cleverbot, and an API for access to serving, has been made available to developers in the form of Cleverscript.

An app that uses the Cleverscript engine to play a game of 20 Questions, has been launched under the name *Clevernator*. Unlike other such games, the player asks the questions and it is the role of the AI to understand, and answer factually. An app that allows owners to create and talk to their own small Cleverbot-like AI has been launched, called *Cleverme!* for Apple products.[7]

14.3 See also

- List of chatterbots

14.4 References

[1] "Cleverbot.com Site Info". Alexa Internet. Retrieved 2014-04-01.

[2] "Cleverbot". Cleverbot.com. Retrieved 14 January 2013.

[3] Saenz, Aaron (2010-01-13). "Cleverbot Chat Engine Is Learning From The Internet To Talk Like A Human". *Singularity Hub*. Retrieved 2011-06-06.

[4] "Rollo Carpenter". *Technische*. Indian Institute of Technology Guwahati. Retrieved 13 November 2011.

[5] Aron, Jacob (6 September 2011). "Software tricks people into thinking it is human". *New Scientist*. Retrieved 13 November 2011.

[6] "Parallel Processing on Graphics Cards - Existor.com - Cleverbot". Existor.com. 2014-02-05. Retrieved 2014-06-09.

[7] "Cleverme! on the App Store on iTunes". *iTunes*. Retrieved
      24 March 2014.

14.5   External links

- Official website

- Cleverscript website

Chapter 15

Clinical decision support system

A **clinical decision support system** (**CDSS**) is a health information technology system that is designed to provide physicians and other health professionals with **clinical decision support** (**CDS**), that is, assistance with clinical decision-making tasks. A working definition has been proposed by Robert Hayward of the Centre for Health Evidence: "Clinical Decision Support systems link health observations with health knowledge to influence health choices by clinicians for improved health care". CDSSs constitute a major topic in artificial intelligence in medicine.

15.1 Effectiveness

The evidence of the effectiveness of CDSS is mixed. A 2014 systematic review did not find a benefit in terms of risk of death when the CDSS was combined with the electronic health record.[1] There may be some benefits, however, in terms of other outcomes.[1]

A 2005 systematic review concluded that CDSSs improved practitioner performance in 64% of the studies. The CDSSs improved patient outcomes in 13% of the studies. Sustainable CDSSs features associated with improved practitioner performance include the following:

- automatic electronic prompts rather than requiring user activation of the system

Both the number and the methodological quality of studies of CDSSs increased from 1973 through 2004.[2]

Another 2005 systematic review found... *"Decision support systems significantly improved clinical practice in 68% of trials."* The CDSS features associated with success include the following:[3]

- the CDSS is integrated into the clinical workflow rather than as a separate log-in or screen.
- the CDSS is electronic rather than paper-based templates.

- the CDSS provides decision support at the time and location of care rather than prior to or after the patient encounter.
- the CDSS provides (active voice) recommendations for care, not just assessments.

However, other systematic reviews are less optimistic about the effects of CDS, with one from 2011 stating *"There is a large gap between the postulated and empirically demonstrated benefits of [CDSS and other] eHealth technologies ... their cost-effectiveness has yet to be demonstrated".*[4]

A 5 year evaluation of the effectiveness of a CDSS in implementing rational treatment of bacterial infections published in 2014; according to the authors it was the first long term study of a CDSS.[5]

15.2 Characteristics

A clinical decision support system has been defined as an "active knowledge systems, which use two or more items of patient data to generate case-specific advice."[6] This implies that a CDSS is simply a decision support system that is focused on using knowledge management in such a way to achieve clinical advice for patient care based on multiple items of patient data.

15.2.1 Purpose

The main purpose of modern CDSS is to assist clinicians at the point of care.[7] This means that clinicians interact with a CDSS to help to analyse, and reach a diagnosis based on, patient data.

In the early days, CDSSs were conceived of as being used to literally make decisions for the clinician. The clinician would input the information and wait for the CDSS to output the "right" choice and the clinician would simply act on that output. However, the modern methodology of using

CDSSs to assist means that the clinician interacts with the CDSS, utilizing both their own knowledge and the CDSS, to make a better analysis of the patient's data than either human or CDSS could make on their own. Typically, a CDSS makes suggestions for the clinician to look through, and the clinician is expected to pick out useful information from the presented results and discount erroneous CDSS suggestions.[6]

There are two main types of CDSS:[7]

- Knowledge-based

- Non-knowledge-based

as detailed below.

An example of how a CDSS might be used by a clinician is a specific type of Clinical Decision Support System, a DDSS (Diagnosis Decision Support Systems). A DDSS requests some of the patients data and in response, proposes a set of appropriate diagnoses. The doctor then takes the output of the DDSS and determines which diagnoses might be relevant and which are not,[7] and if necessary orders further tests to narrow down the diagnosis.

Another important classification of a CDSS is based on the timing of its use. Doctors use these systems at point of care to help them as they are dealing with a patient, with the timing of use being either pre-diagnosis, during diagnosis, or post diagnosis. Pre-diagnosis CDSS systems are used to help the physician prepare the diagnoses. CDSS used during diagnosis help review and filter the physician's preliminary diagnostic choices to improve their final results. Post-diagnosis CDSS systems are used to mine data to derive connections between patients and their past medical history and clinical research to predict future events.[7] It has been claimed that decision support will begin to replace clinicians in common tasks in the future.[8]

Another approach, used by the National Health Service in England, is to use a DDSS (either, in the past, operated by the patient, or, today, by a phone operative who is not medically-trained) to triage medical conditions out of hours by suggesting a suitable next step to the patient (e.g. call an ambulance, or see a general practitioner on the next working day). The suggestion, which may be disregarded by either the patient or the phone operative if common sense or caution suggests otherwise, is based on the known information and an implicit conclusion about what the *worst-case* diagnosis is likely to be (which is not always revealed to the patient, because it might well be incorrect and is not based on a medically-trained person's opinion - it is only used for initial triage purposes).

15.2.2 Knowledge-based CDSS

Most CDSSs consist of three parts: the knowledge base, an inference engine, and a mechanism to communicate. The knowledge base contains the rules and associations of compiled data which most often take the form of IF-THEN rules. If this was a system for determining drug interactions, then a rule might be that IF drug X is taken AND drug Y is taken THEN alert user. Using another interface, an advanced user could edit the knowledge base to keep it up to date with new drugs. The inference engine combines the rules from the knowledge base with the patient's data. The communication mechanism allows the system to show the results to the user as well as have input into the system.[6][7]

15.2.3 Non-knowledge-based CDSS

CDSSs that do not use a knowledge base use a form of artificial intelligence called machine learning,[9] which allow computers to learn from past experiences and/or find patterns in clinical data. This eliminates the need for writing rules and for expert input. However, since systems based on machine learning cannot *explain* the reasons for their conclusions (they are so-called "black boxes", because no meaningful information about how they work can be discerned by human inspection), most clinicians do not use them directly for diagnoses, for reliability and accountability reasons.[6][7] Nevertheless, they can be useful as postdiagnostic systems, for suggesting patterns for clinicians to look into in more depth.

Three types of non-knowledge-based systems are support vector machines, artificial neural networks and genetic algorithms.[10]

Artificial neural networks use nodesBased and weighted connections between them to analyse the patterns found in patient data to derive associations between symptoms and a diagnosis.

Genetic Algorithms are based on simplified evolutionary processes using directed selection to achieve optimal CDSS results. The selection algorithms evaluate components of random sets of solutions to a problem. The solutions that come out on top are then recombined and mutated and run through the process again. This happens over and over until the proper solution is discovered. They are functionally similar to neural networks in that they are also "black boxes" that attempt to derive knowledge from patient data.

Non-knowledge-based networks often focus on a narrow list of symptoms, such as symptoms for a single disease, as opposed to the knowledge based approach which cover the diagnosis of many different diseases.[6][7]

15.3 Regulations

15.3.1 United States

With the enactment of the American Recovery and Reinvestment Act of 2009 (ARRA), there is a push for widespread adoption of health information technology through the Health Information Technology for Economic and Clinical Health Act (HITECH). Through these initiatives, more hospitals and clinics are integrating Electronic Medical Records (EMRs) and Computerized physician order entry (CPOE) within their health information processing and storage. Consequently, the Institute of Medicine (IOM) promoted usage of health information technology including Clinical Decision Support Systems to advance quality of patient care. The IOM had published a report in 1999, *To Err Is Human*, which focused on the patient safety crisis in the United States, pointing to the incredibly high number of deaths. This statistic attracted great attention to the quality of patient care.

With the enactment of the HITECH Act included in the ARRA, encouraging the adoption of health IT, more detailed case laws for CDSS and EMRs are still being defined by the Office of National Coordinator for Health Information Technology (ONC) and approved by Department of Health and Human Services (HHS). A definition of "Meaningful use" is yet to be polished.

Despite the absence of laws, the CDSS vendors would almost certainly be viewed as having a legal duty of care to both the patients who may adversely be affected due to CDSS usage and the clinicians who may use the technology for patient care. However, duties of care legal regulations are not explicitly defined yet.

With recent effective legislations related to performance shift payment incentives, CDSS are becoming more attractive.

15.4 Challenges to adoption

15.4.1 Clinical challenges

Much effort has been put forth by many medical institutions and software companies to produce viable CDSSs to support all aspects of clinical tasks. However, with the complexity of clinical workflows and the demands on staff time high, care must be taken by the institution deploying the support system to ensure that the system becomes a fluid and integral part of the clinical workflow. Some CDSSs have met with varying amounts of success, while others have suffered from common problems preventing or reducing successful adoption and acceptance.

Two sectors of the healthcare domain in which CDSSs have had a large impact are the pharmacy and billing sectors. There are commonly used pharmacy and prescription ordering systems that now perform batch-based checking of orders for negative drug interactions and report warnings to the ordering professional. Another sector of success for CDSS is in billing and claims filing. Since many hospitals rely on Medicare reimbursements to stay in operation, systems have been created to help examine both a proposed treatment plan and the current rules of Medicare in order to suggest a plan that attempts to address both the care of the patient and the financial needs of the institution.

Other CDSSs that are aimed at diagnostic tasks have found success, but are often very limited in deployment and scope. The Leeds Abdominal Pain System went operational in 1971 for the University of Leeds hospital, and was reported to have produced a correct diagnosis in 91.8% of cases, compared to the clinicians' success rate of 79.6%.

Despite the wide range of efforts by institutions to produce and use these systems, widespread adoption and acceptance has still not yet been achieved for most offerings. One large roadblock to acceptance has historically been workflow integration. A tendency to focus only on the functional decision making core of the CDSS existed, causing a deficiency in planning for how the clinician will actually use the product in situ. Often CDSSs were stand-alone applications, requiring the clinician to cease working on their current system, switch to the CDSS, input the necessary data (even if it had already been inputted into another system), and examine the results produced. The additional steps break the flow from the clinician's perspective and cost precious time.

15.4.2 Technical challenges and barriers to implementation

Clinical decision support systems face steep technical challenges in a number of areas. Biological systems are profoundly complicated, and a clinical decision may utilize an enormous range of potentially relevant data. For example, an electronic evidence-based medicine system may potentially consider a patient's symptoms, medical history, family history and genetics, as well as historical and geographical trends of disease occurrence, and published clinical data on medicinal effectiveness when recommending a patient's course of treatment.

Clinically, a large deterrent to CDSS acceptance is workflow integration, as mentioned above.

Another source of contention with many medical support systems is that they produce a massive number of alerts. When systems produce high volume of warnings (especially those that do not require escalation), aside from the annoyance, clinicians may pay less attention to warnings, causing potentially critical alerts to be missed.

15.4.3   Maintenance

One of the core challenges facing CDSS is difficulty in incorporating the extensive quantity of clinical research being published on an ongoing basis. In a given year, tens of thousands of clinical trials are published.[11] Currently, each one of these studies must be manually read, evaluated for scientific legitimacy, and incorporated into the CDSS in an accurate way. In 2004, it was stated that the process of gathering clinical data and medical knowledge and putting them into a form that computers can manipulate to assist in clinical decision-support is "still in its infancy".[12]

Nevertheless, it is more feasible for a business to do this centrally, even if incompletely, than for each individual doctor to try to keep up with all the research being published.

In addition to being laborious, integration of new data can sometimes be difficult to quantify or incorporate into the existing decision support schema, particularly in instances where different clinical papers may appear conflicting. Properly resolving these sorts of discrepancies is often the subject of clinical papers itself (see meta-analysis), which often take months to complete.

15.4.4   Evaluation

In order for a CDSS to offer value, it must demonstrably improve clinical workflow or outcome. Evaluation of CDSS is the process of quantifying its value to improve a system's quality and measure its effectiveness. Because different CDSSs serve different purposes, there is no generic metric which applies to all such systems; however, attributes such as consistency (with itself, and with experts) often apply across a wide spectrum of systems.[13]

The evaluation benchmark for a CDSS depends on the system's goal: for example, a diagnostic decision support system may be rated based upon the consistency and accuracy of its classification of disease (as compared to physicians or other decision support systems). An evidence-based medicine system might be rated based upon a high incidence of patient improvement, or higher financial reimbursement for care providers.

15.5   Combining CDSS with Electronic Health Records

Implementing Electronic Health Records (EHR) was an inevitable challenge. The reasons behind this challenge are that it is a relatively uncharted area, and there are many issues and complications during the implementation phase of an EHR. This can be seen in the numerous studies that have been undertaken. However, challenges in implementing electronic health records (EHRs) have received some attention, but less is known about the process of transitioning from legacy EHRs to newer systems.[14]

With all of that said, electronic health records are the way of the future for healthcare industry. They are a way to capture and utilise real-time data to provide high-quality patient care, ensuring efficiency and effective use of time and resources. Incorporating EHR and CDSS together into the process of medicine has the potential to change the way medicine has been taught and practiced.[15] It has been said that "the highest level of EHR is a CDSS".[16]

Since "clinical decision support systems (CDSS) are computer systems designed to impact clinician decision making about individual patients at the point in time that these decisions are made",[15] it is clear that it would be beneficial to have a fully integrated CDSS and EHR.

Even though the benefits can be seen, to fully implement a CDSS that is integrated with an EHR has historically required significant planning by the healthcare facility/organisation, in order for the purpose of the CDSS to be successful and effective. The success and effectiveness can be measured by the increase in patient care being delivered and reduced adverse events occurring. In addition to this, there would be a saving of time and resources, and benefits in terms of autonomy and financial benefits to the healthcare facility/organisation.[17]

15.5.1   Benefits of CDSS combined with EHR

A successful CDSS/EHR integration will allow the provision of best practice, high quality care to the patient, which is the ultimate goal of healthcare.

Errors have always occurred in healthcare, so trying to minimise them as much as possible is important in order to provide quality patient care. Three areas that can be addressed with the implementation of CDSS and Electronic Health Records (EHRs), are:

1. Medication prescription errors

2. Adverse drug events

3. Other medical errors

CDSSs will be most beneficial in the future when healthcare facilities are "100% electronic" in terms of real-time patient information, thus simplifying the number of modifications that have to occur to ensure that all the systems are up to date with each other.

The measurable benefits of clinical decision support systems on physician performance and patient outcomes remain the subject of ongoing research, as noted in the "Effectiveness" section above.

15.5.2 Barriers to CDSS combined with EHR

Implementing electronic health records (EHR) in healthcare settings incurs challenges; none more important than maintaining efficiency and safety during rollout,[18] but in order for the implementation process to be effective, an understanding of the EHR users' perspectives is key to the success of EHR implementation projects.[19] In addition to this, adoption needs to be actively fostered through a bottom-up, clinical-needs-first approach.[20] The same can be said for CDSS.

The main areas of concern with moving into a fully integrated EHR/CDSS system are:

1. Privacy
2. Confidentiality
3. User-friendliness
4. Document accuracy and completeness
5. Integration
6. Uniformity
7. Acceptance
8. Alert desensitisation

[21] as well as the key aspects of data entry that need to be addressed when implementing a CDSS to avoid potential adverse events from occurring. These aspects include whether:

- correct data is being used

- all the data has been entered into the system

- current best practice is being followed

- the data is evidence-based

A Service oriented architecture has been proposed as a technical means to address some of these barriers.[22]

15.5.3 Status in Australia

As of July 2015, the planned transition to EHRs in Australia is facing difficulties. The majority of healthcare facilities are still running completely paper-based systems, and some are in a transition phase of scanned EHRs, or are moving towards such a transition phase.

Victoria has attempted to implement EHR across the state with its HealthSMART program, but due to unexpectedly high costs it has cancelled the project.[23]

South Australia (SA) however is slightly more successful than Victoria in the implementation of an EHR. This may be due to all public healthcare organisations in SA being centrally run. (However, on the other hand, the UK's National Health Service is also centrally administered, and its National Programme for IT in the 2000s, which included EHRs in its remit, was an expensive disaster.)

SA is in the process of implementing "Enterprise patient administration system (EPAS)". This system is the foundation for all public hospitals and health care sites for an EHR within SA and it was expected that by the end of 2014 all facilities in SA will be connected to it. This would allow for successful integration of CDSS into SA and increase the benefits of the EHR.[24] By July 2015 it was reported that only 3 out of 75 indented health care facilities implemented EPAS.[25]

15.6 See also

- Clinical Informatics
- Gello Expression Language
- International Health Terminology Standards Development Organisation
- Personal Health Information Protection Act (a law in force in Ontario)

15.7 References

[1] Moja, L; Kwag, KH; Lytras, T; Bertizzolo, L; Brandt, L; Pecoraro, V; Rigon, G; Vaona, A; Ruggiero, F; Mangia, M; Iorio, A; Kunnamo, I; Bonovas, S (December 2014). "Effectiveness of computerized decision support systems linked to electronic health records: a systematic review and meta-analysis.". *American journal of public health* **104** (12): e12–22. doi:10.2105/ajph.2014.302164. PMID 25322302.

[2] Garg AX, Adhikari NK, McDonald H, Rosas-Arellano MP, Devereaux PJ, Beyene J; et al. (2005). "Effects of computerized clinical decision support systems on practitioner

performance and patient outcomes: a systematic review.".
JAMA **293** (10): 1223–38. doi:10.1001/jama.293.10.1223.
PMID 15755945.

[3] Kensaku Kawamoto, Caitlin A Houlihan, E Andrew Balas,
David F Lobach. (2005). "Improving clinical practice us-
ing clinical decision support systems: a systematic review
of trials to identify features critical to success." (PDF).
BMJ **330** (7494): 765. doi:10.1136/bmj.38398.500764.8F.
PMC 555881. PMID 15767266.

[4] Black, A.D., J. Car, C. Pagliari, C. Anandan, K. Cress-
well, T. Bokun, B. McKinstry, R. Procter, A. Ma-
jeed, and A. Sheikh. (2011). "The impact of ehealth
on the quality and safety of health care: A systematic overview.". *PLoS Medicine* **8** (1): e1000387.
doi:10.1371/journal.pmed.1000387.

[5] Nachtigall I, Tafelski S, Deja M, et al. BMJ Open. 2014;
4(12): e005370. http://bmjopen.bmj.com/content/4/12/
e005370.full

[6] "Decision support systems ." 26 July 2005. 17 Feb. 2009
<http://www.openclinical.org/dss.html>.

[7] Berner, Eta S., ed. Clinical Decision Support Systems. New
York, NY: Springer, 2007.

[8] Khosla, Vinod (4 December 2012). "Technology will replace 80% of what doctors do". *CNN*. Retrieved 25 April
2013.

[9] "Tanveer Syeda-Mahmood plenary talk: The Role of Machine Learning in Clinical Decision Support". *SPIE News-
room*. March 2015. doi:10.1117/2.3201503.29.

[10] Wagholikar, Kavishwar; V. Sundararajan; Ashok Desh-
pande (2012). "Modeling Paradigms for Medical Diagnostic
Decision Support: A Survey and Future Directions". *Journal of Medical Systems* (Journal of Medical Systems) **36**:
3029–3049. doi:10.1007/s10916-011-9780-4.

[11] Gluud C, Nikolova D (2007). "Likely country of origin
in publications on randomised controlled trials and controlled clinical trials during the last 60 years.". *Trials* **8**:
7. doi:10.1186/1745-6215-8-7. PMC 1808475. PMID
17326823.

[12] Gardner, Reed M (April 2004). "Computerized Clinical
Decision-Support in Respiratory Care". *Respiratory Care*
49: 378–388.

[13] Wagholikar, K; Kathy L. MacLaughlin; Thomas M Kastner;
Petra M Casey; Michael Henry; Robert A Greenes; Hong-
fang Liu; Rajeev Chaudhry (2013). "Formative evaluation
of the accuracy of a clinical decision support system for cer-
vical cancer screening". *Journal of the American Medical
Informatics Association* (Journal of American Medical Informatics Association) **20**: 747–759. doi:10.1136/amiajnl-
2013-001613.

[14] Zandieh, Stephanie O.; Kahyun Yoon-Flannery; Gilad J.
Kuperman; Daniel J. Langsam; Daniel Hyman; Rainu
Kaushal (2008). "Challenges to EHR Implementation in
Electronic- Versus Paper-based Office Practices". *Journal
of Global Information Management*: 755–761.

[15] Berner, Eta S.; Tonya J.La Lande (2007). "1". *Clinical Decision Support Systems: Theory and Practice* (2 ed.). New
York: Springer Science and Business Media. pp. 3–22.

[16] Rothman, Brian; Joan. C. Leonard; Michael. M. Vigoda
(2012). "Future of electronic health records: implications
for decision support". *Mount Sinai Journal of Medicine* **79**
(6): 757–768. doi:10.1002/msj.21351.

[17] Sambasivan, Murali; Pouyan Esmaeilzadeh; Naresh Kumar;
Hossein Nezakati (2012). "Intention to adopt clinical decision support systems in a developing country: effect of
Physician's perceived professional autonomy, involvement
and belief: a cross-sectional study". *BMC Medical Informatics and Decision Making* **12**: 142–150. doi:10.1186/1472-
6947-12-142.

[18] Spellman Kennebeck, Stephanie; Nathan Timm; Michael
K Farrell; S Andrew Spooner (2012). "Impact of electronic health record implementation on patient flow metrics in a pediatric emergency department". *Journal of
the American Medical Informatics Association*: 443–447.
doi:10.1136/amiajnl-2011-000462.

[19] McGinn, Carrie A; Marie-Pierre Gagnon; Nicola Shaw;
Claude Sicotte; Luc Mathieu; Yvan Leduc; Sonya Gre-
nier; Julie Duplantie; Anis B Abdeljelil; France Légaré
(2012). "Users' perspectives of key factors to implementing electronic health records in Canada: a Delphi study".
BMC Medical Informatics & Decision Making **12**: 105–118.
doi:10.1186/1472-6947-12-105.

[20] Rozenblum, Ronen; Yeona Jang; Eyal Zimlichman; Clau-
dia Salzberg; Melissa Tamblyn; David Buckeridge; Alan
Forster; David W. Bates and Robyn Tamblyn (2011). "A
qualitative study of Canada's experience with the implementation of electronic health information technology". *Canadian Medical Association Journal*: 281–288.

[21] Berner, Eta S.; Tonya J.La Lande (2007). "4". *Clinical Decision Support Systems: Theory and Practice* (2 ed.). New
York: Springer Science and Business Media. pp. 64–98.

[22] Loya, S. R.; Kawamoto, K; Chatwin, C; Huser, V (2014).
"Service oriented architecture for clinical decision support:
A systematic review and future directions". *Journal of Med-
ical Systems* **38** (12): 140. doi:10.1007/s10916-014-0140-z.
PMID 25325996.

[23] Charette, Robert N. "Troubled HealthSMART System Finally Cancelled in Victoria Australia". Retrieved 18 May
2013.

[24] South Australian Health. "EPAS program update". South
Australian Health. Retrieved 15 May 2013.

[25] http://www.abc.net.au/news/2015-07-01/
hospital-beds-closure-epas-electronic-records-delay/
6586492 as accessed on 26.07.2015

15.8 External links

- Decision support chapter from Coiera's Guide to Health Informatics

- OpenClinical maintains an extensive archive of Artificial Intelligence systems in routine clinical use.

- Robert Trowbridge/ Scott Weingarten. Chapter 53. Clinical Decision Support Systems

- Stanford CDSS

Chapter 16

Concept mining

Concept mining is an activity that results in the extraction of concepts from artifacts. Solutions to the task typically involve aspects of artificial intelligence and statistics, such as data mining and text mining.[1] Because artifacts are typically a loosely structured sequence of words and other symbols (rather than concepts), the problem is nontrivial, but it can provide powerful insights into the meaning, provenance and similarity of documents.

16.1 Methods

Traditionally, the conversion of words to concepts has been performed using a thesaurus,[2] and for computational techniques the tendency is to do the same. The thesauri used are either specially created for the task, or a pre-existing language model, usually related to Princeton's WordNet.

The mappings of words to concepts[3] are often ambiguous. Typically each word in a given language will relate to several possible concepts. Humans use context to disambiguate the various meanings of a given piece of text, where available machine translation systems cannot easily infer context.

For the purposes of concept mining however, these ambiguities tend to be less important than they are with machine translation, for in large documents the ambiguities tend to even out, much as is the case with text mining.

There are many techniques for disambiguation that may be used. Examples are linguistic analysis of the text and the use of word and concept association frequency information that may be inferred from large text corpora. Recently, techniques that base on semantic similarity between the possible concepts and the context have appeared and gained interest in the scientific community.

16.2 Applications

16.2.1 Detecting and indexing similar documents in large corpora

One of the spin-offs of calculating document statistics in the concept domain, rather than the word domain, is that concepts form natural tree structures based on hypernymy and meronymy. These structures can be used to produce simple tree membership statistics, that can be used to locate any document in a Euclidean concept space. If the size of a document is also considered as another dimension of this space then an extremely efficient indexing system can be created. This technique is currently in commercial use locating similar legal documents in a 2.5 million document corpus.

16.2.2 Clustering documents by topic

Standard numeric clustering techniques may be used in "concept space" as described above to locate and index documents by the inferred topic. These are numerically far more efficient than their text mining cousins, and tend to behave more intuitively, in that they map better to the similarity measures a human would generate.

16.3 See also

- Formal concept analysis
- Information extraction
- Compound term processing

16.4 References

[1] Yuen-Hsien Tseng, Chun-Yen Chang, Shu-Nu Chang Rundgren, and Carl-Johan Rundgren, " Mining Concept Maps from News Stories for Measuring Civic Scientific Literacy in Media", Computers and Education, Vol. 55, No. 1, August 2010, pp. 165-177.

[2] Yuen-Hsien Tseng, " Automatic Thesaurus Generation for Chinese Documents", Journal of the American Society for Information Science and Technology, Vol. 53, No. 13, Nov. 2002, pp. 1130-1138.

[3] Yuen-Hsien Tseng, " Generic Title Labeling for Clustered Documents", Expert Systems With Applications, Vol. 37, No. 3, 15 March 2010, pp. 2247-2254 .

Chapter 17

Content-based image retrieval

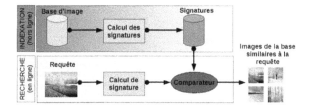

General scheme of content-based image retrieval

Content-based image retrieval (**CBIR**), also known as **query by image content** (**QBIC**) and **content-based visual information retrieval** (**CBVIR**) is the application of computer vision techniques to the image retrieval problem, that is, the problem of searching for digital images in large databases (see this survey[1] for a recent scientific overview of the CBIR field). Content-based image retrieval is opposed to traditional **concept-based approaches** (see **Concept-based image indexing**).

"Content-based" means that the search analyzes the contents of the image rather than the metadata such as keywords, tags, or descriptions associated with the image. The term "content" in this context might refer to colors, shapes, textures, or any other information that can be derived from the image itself. CBIR is desirable because searches that rely purely on metadata are dependent on annotation quality and completeness. Having humans manually annotate images by entering keywords or metadata in a large database can be time consuming and may not capture the keywords desired to describe the image. The evaluation of the effectiveness of keyword image search is subjective and has not been well-defined. In the same regard, CBIR systems have similar challenges in defining success.[2]

17.1   History

The term "content-based image retrieval" seems to have originated in 1992 when it was used by T. Kato to describe experiments into automatic retrieval of images from a database, based on the colors and shapes present.[2] Since then, the term has been used to describe the process of retrieving desired images from a large collection on the basis of syntactical image features. The techniques, tools, and algorithms that are used originate from fields such as statistics, pattern recognition, signal processing, and computer vision[1]

The earliest commercial CBIR system was developed by IBM and was called QBIC (Query by Image Content).[3]

17.2   Technical progress

The interest in CBIR has grown because of the limitations inherent in metadata-based systems, as well as the large range of possible uses for efficient image retrieval. Textual information about images can be easily searched using existing technology, but this requires humans to manually describe each image in the database. This can be impractical for very large databases or for images that are generated automatically, e.g. those from surveillance cameras. It is also possible to miss images that use different synonyms in their descriptions. Systems based on categorizing images in semantic classes like "cat" as a subclass of "animal" can avoid the miscategorization problem, but will require more effort by a user to find images that might be "cats", but are only classified as an "animal". Many standards have been developed to categorize images, but all still face scaling and miscategorization issues.[2]

Initial CBIR systems were developed to search databases based on image color, texture, and shape properties. After these systems were developed, the need for user-friendly interfaces became apparent. Therefore, efforts in the CBIR field started to include human-centered design that tried to meet the needs of the user performing the search. This typically means inclusion of: query methods that may allow descriptive semantics, queries that may involve user feedback, systems that may include machine learning, and systems that may understand user satisfaction levels.[1]

17.3 CBIR techniques

Many CBIR systems have been developed, but the problem of retrieving images on the basis of their pixel content remains largely unsolved.[1]

17.3.1 Query techniques

Different implementations of CBIR make use of different types of user queries.

Query by example is a query technique that involves providing the CBIR system with an example image that it will then base its search upon. The underlying search algorithms may vary depending on the application, but result images should all share common elements with the provided example.[4]

See also: Reverse image search

Options for providing example images to the system include:

- A preexisting image may be supplied by the user or chosen from a random set.

- The user draws a rough approximation of the image they are looking for, for example with blobs of color or general shapes.[4]

This query technique removes the difficulties that can arise when trying to describe images with words.

Semantic retrieval

Semantic retrieval starts with a user making a request like "find pictures of Abraham Lincoln". This type of open-ended task is very difficult for computers to perform - Lincoln may not always be facing the camera or in the same pose. Many CBIR systems therefore generally make use of lower-level features like texture, color, and shape. These features are either used in combination with interfaces that allow easier input of the criteria or with databases that have already been trained to match features (such as faces, fingerprints, or shape matching). However, in general, image retrieval requires human feedback in order to identify higher-level concepts.[3]

Relevance Feedback (Human Interaction)

Combining CBIR search techniques available with the wide range of potential users and their intent can be a difficult task. An aspect of making CBIR successful relies entirely on the ability to understand the user intent.[5] CBIR systems can make use of *relevance feedback*, where the user progressively refines the search results by marking images in the results as "relevant", "not relevant", or "neutral" to the search query, then repeating the search with the new information. Examples of this type of interface have been developed.[6]

Iterative/Machine Learning

Machine learning and application of iterative techniques are becoming more common in CBIR.[7]

Other query methods

Other query methods include browsing for example images, navigating customized/hierarchical categories, querying by image region (rather than the entire image), querying by multiple example images, querying by visual sketch, querying by direct specification of image features, and multimodal queries (e.g. combining touch, voice, etc.)[8]

17.3.2 Content comparison using image distance measures

The most common method for comparing two images in content-based image retrieval (typically an example image and an image from the database) is using an image distance measure. An image distance measure compares the similarity of two images in various dimensions such as color, texture, shape, and others. For example a distance of 0 signifies an exact match with the query, with respect to the dimensions that were considered. As one may intuitively gather, a value greater than 0 indicates various degrees of similarities between the images. Search results then can be sorted based on their distance to the queried image.[4] Many measures of image distance (Similarity Models) have been developed.[9]

Color

Computing distance measures based on color similarity is achieved by computing a color histogram for each image that identifies the proportion of pixels within an image holding specific values.[2] Examining images based on the colors they contain is one of the most widely used techniques because it can be completed without regard to image size or orientation.[3] However, research has also attempted to segment color proportion by region and by spatial relationship among several color regions.[8]

Texture

Texture measures look for visual patterns in images and how they are spatially defined. Textures are represented by texels which are then placed into a number of sets, depending on how many textures are detected in the image. These sets not only define the texture, but also where in the image the texture is located.[4]

Texture is a difficult concept to represent. The identification of specific textures in an image is achieved primarily by modeling texture as a two-dimensional gray level variation. The relative brightness of pairs of pixels is computed such that degree of contrast, regularity, coarseness and directionality may be estimated.[3][10] The problem is in identifying patterns of co-pixel variation and associating them with particular classes of textures such as *silky*, or *rough*.

Other methods of classifying textures include:

- Co-occurrence matrix

- Laws texture energy

- Wavelet Transform

- Orthogonal Transforms (Discrete Tchebichef moments)

Shape

Shape does not refer to the shape of an image but to the shape of a particular region that is being sought out. Shapes will often be determined first applying segmentation or edge detection to an image. Other methods use shape filters to identify given shapes of an image.[11] Shape descriptors may also need to be invariant to translation, rotation, and scale.[3]

Some shape descriptors include:[3]

- Fourier transform

- Moment Invariant

17.3.3   Image Retrieval Evaluation

Measures of image retrieval can be defined in terms of precision and recall. However, there are other methods being considered.[12]

17.4   Applications

Potential uses for CBIR include:[2]

- Architectural and engineering design

- Art collections

- Crime prevention

- Geographical information and remote sensing systems

- Intellectual property

- Medical diagnosis

- Military

- Photograph archives

- Retail catalogs

- Nudity-detection filters[13]

- Face Finding

- Textiles Industry[6]

Commercial Systems that have been developed include:[2]

- IBM's QBIC

- Virage's VIR Image Engine

- Excalibur's Image RetrievalWare

- VisualSEEk and WebSEEk

- Netra

- MARS

- Vhoto

- Pixolution

Experimental Systems include:[2]

- MIT's Photobook

- Columbia University's WebSEEk

- Carnegie-Mellon University's Informedia

- iSearch - PICT

17.5   See also

- MPEG-7

- Document classification

- GazoPa

- Image retrieval

- List of CBIR engines

- Macroglossa Visual Search

- Multimedia Information Retrieval

- Multiple-instance learning

- Nearest neighbor search

17.6   References

[1] *Content-based Multimedia Information Retrieval: State of the Art and Challenges*, Michael Lew, et al., ACM Transactions on Multimedia Computing, Communications, and Applications, pp. 1–19, 2006.

[2] Eakins, John; Graham,Margaret. "Content-based Image Retrieval". University of Northumbria at Newcastle. Retrieved 2014-03-10.

[3] Rui, Yong; Thomas S. Huang; Shih-Fu Chang (1999). "Image Retrieval: Current Techniques, Promising Directions, and Open Issues".

[4] Shapiro, Linda; George Stockman (2001). *Computer Vision*. Upper Saddle River, NJ: Prentice Hall. ISBN 0-13-030796-3.

[5] Datta, Ritendra; Dhiraj Joshi; Jia Li; James Z. Wang (2008). "Image Retrieval: Ideas, Influences, and Trends of the New Age". *ACM Computing Surveys* **40** (2): 1–60. doi:10.1145/1348246.1348248.

[6] Bird, C.L.; P.J. Elliott, Griffiths (1996). "User interfaces for content-based image retrieval".

[7] Cardoso, Douglas; et al. "Iterative Technique for Content-Based Image Retrieval using Multiple SVM Ensembles" (PDF). Federal University of Parana(Brazil). Retrieved 2014-03-11.

[8] Liam M. Mayron. "Image Retrieval Using Visual Attention" (PDF). Mayron.net. Retrieved 2012-10-18.

[9] Eidenberger, Horst (2011). "Fundamental Media Understanding", atpress. ISBN 978-3-8423-7917-6.

[10] Tamura, Hideyuki; Mori, Shunji; Yamawaki, Takashi (1978). "Textural Features Corresponding to Visual Perception". *Systems, Man and Cybernetics, IEEE Transactions on* **8** (6): 460, 473. doi:10.1109/tsmc.1978.4309999.

[11] Tushabe, F.; M.H.F. Wilkinson (2008). "Content-based Image Retrieval Using Combined 2D Attribute Pattern Spectra". *Springer Lecture Notes in Computer Science.*

[12] Deselaers, Thomas; Keysers, Daniel; Ney, Hermann (2007). "Features for Image Retrieval: An Experimental Comparison" (PDF). RWTH Aachen University. Retrieved 11 March 2014.

[13] Wang, James Ze; Jia Li; Gio Wiederhold; Oscar Firschein (1998). "System for Screening Objectionable Images". *Computer Communications* **21** (15): 1355–1360. doi:10.1016/s0140-3664(98)00203-5.

17.7   Further reading

Relevant research papers

- *Query by Image and Video Content: The QBIC System*, (Flickner, 1995)

- *Finding Naked People* (Fleck et al., 1996)

- *Virage Video Engine*, (Hampapur, 1997)

- *Library-based Coding: a Representation for Efficient Video Compression and Retrieval*, (Vasconcelos & Lippman, 1997)

- *System for Screening Objectionable Images* (Wang et al., 1998)

- *Content-based Image Retrieval* (JISC Technology Applications Programme Report 39) (Eakins & Graham 1999)

- *Windsurf: Region-Based Image Retrieval Using Wavelets* (Ardizzoni, Bartolini, and Patella, 1999)

- *A Probabilistic Architecture for Content-based Image Retrieval*, (Vasconcelos & Lippman, 2000)

- *A Unifying View of Image Similarity*, (Vasconcelos & Lippman, 2000)

- *Next Generation Web Searches for Visual Content*, (Lew, 2000)

- *Image Indexing with Mixture Hierarchies*, (Vasconcelos, 2001)

- *SIMPLIcity: Semantics-Sensitive Integrated Matching for Picture Libraries* (Wang, Li, and Wiederhold, 2001)

- *A Conceptual Approach to Web Image Retrieval* (Popescu and Grefenstette, 2008)

- *FACERET: An Interactive Face Retrieval System Based on Self-Organizing Maps* (Ruiz-del-Solar et al., 2002)

- *Automatic Linguistic Indexing of Pictures by a Statistical Modeling Approach* (Li and Wang, 2003)

- *Video google: A text retrieval approach to object matching in videos* (Sivic & Zisserman, 2003)

- *Minimum Probability of Error Image Retrieval* (Vasconcelos, 2004)

- *On the Efficient Evaluation of Probabilistic Similarity Functions for Image Retrieval* (Vasconcelos, 2004)

- *Extending image retrieval systems with a thesaurus for shapes* (Hove, 2004)

- *Names and Faces in the News* (Berg et al., 2004)

- *Cortina: a system for large-scale, content-based web image retrieval* (Quack et al., 2004)

- *A new perspective on Visual Information Retrieval* (Eidenberger 2004)

- *Language-based Querying of Image Collections on the basis of an Extensible Ontology* (Town and Sinclair, 2004)

- *The PIBE Personalizable Image Browsing Engine* (Bartolini, Ciaccia, and Patella, 2004)

- *Costume: A New Feature for Automatic Video Content Indexing* (Jaffre 2005)

- *Automatic Face Recognition for Film Character Retrieval in Feature-Length Films* (Arandjelovic & Zisserman, 2005)

- *Meaningful Image Spaces* (Rouw, 2005)

- *Content-based Multimedia Information Retrieval: State of the Art and Challenges* (Lew *et al.* 2006)

- *Adaptively Browsing Image Databases with PIBE* (Bartolini, Ciaccia, and Patella, 2006)

- *Algorithm on which Retrievr (Flickr search) and imgSeek is based on* (Jacobs, Finkelstein, Salesin)

- *Imagination: Exploiting Link Analysis for Accurate Image Annotation* (Bartolini and Ciaccia, 2007)

- *Evaluating Use of Interfaces for Visual Query Specification.* (Hove, 2007)

- *From Pixels to Semantic Spaces: Advances in Content-Based Image Retrieval* (Vasconcelos, 2007)

- *Content-based Image Retrieval by Indexing Random Subwindows with Randomized Trees* (Maree et al., 2007)

- *Image Retrieval: Ideas, Influences, and Trends of the New Age* (Datta et al., 2008)

- *Real-Time Computerized Annotation of Pictures* (Li and Wang, 2008)

- *Query Processing Issues in Region-based Image Databases* (Bartolini, Ciaccia, and Patella, 2010)

- *Shiatsu: Semantic-based Hierarchical Automatic Tagging of Videos by Segmentation Using Cuts* (Bartolini, Patella, and Romani, 2010)

- *Efficient and Effective Similarity-based Video Retrieval* (Bartolini and Romani, 2010)

- *Multi-dimensional Keyword-based Image Annotation and Search* (Bartolini and Ciaccia, 2010)

- *The Windsurf Library for the Efficient Retrieval of Multimedia Hierarchical Data* (Bartolini, Patella, and Stromei, 2011)

- "Pl@ntNet: Interactive plant identification based on social image data" (Joly, Alexis et al.)

- *Superimage: Packing Semantic-Relevant Images for Indexing and Retrieval* (Luo, Zhang, Huang, Gao, Tian, 2014)

- *Indexing and searching 100M images with Map-Reduce* (Moise, Shestakov, Gudmundsson, and Amsaleg, 2013)

17.8   External links

- cbir.info CBIR-related articles

- Search by Drawing

- Demonstration of an visual search engine for images. (Search by example image or colors)

Chapter 18

Context-sensitive user interface

A **context sensitive user interface** is one which can automatically choose from a multiplicity of options based on the current or previous state(s) of the program operation.[1] *Context sensitivity* is almost ubiquitous in current graphical user interfaces, usually in the form of context menus. Context sensitivity, when operating correctly, should be practically transparent to the user.

For example:

Clicking on a text document automatically opens the document in a word processing environment. The user does not have to specify what type of program opens the file under standard conditions.

The same methodology applies to other file types e.g.:

- Video files (.mpg .mov .avi etc.) open in a video player without the user having to select a specific program.

- Photographic and other image files (.jpg .png etc.) will open in a photo viewer automatically.

- Program files and their shortcuts (i.e. .exe files) are automatically run by the operating system.

The user-interface may also provide *Context sensitive* feedback, such as changing the appearance of the mouse pointer or cursor, changing the menu color, or with applicable auditory or tactile feedback.

18.1 Reasoning and advantages of context sensitivity

The primary reason for introducing context sensitivity is to simplify the user interface. Advantages include :

- Reduced number of commands required to be known to the user for a given level of productivity.

- Reduced number of clicks or keystrokes required to carry out a given operation.

- Allows consistent behaviour to be pre-programmed or altered by the user.

- Reduces the number of options to be on screen at one time (i.e. "clutter").

18.1.1 Disadvantages

Context sensitive actions may be perceived as dumbing down of the user interface - leaving the operator at a loss as to what to do when the computer decides to perform an unwanted action. Additionally non-automatic procedures may be hidden or obscured by the context sensitive interface causing an increase in user workload for operations the designers did not foresee.

A poor implementation can be more annoying than helpful - a classic example of this is Office assistant.

18.2 Implementation

At the simplest level each possible action is reduced to a single most likely action - The action performed is based on a single variable (such as file extension). In more complicated implementations multiple factors can be assessed such as the users previous actions, the size of the file, the programs in current use, metadata[2] etc.

The method is not only limited to the response to imperative button presses and mouse clicks - pop up menus can be pruned and/or altered, or a web search can prune results based on previous searches.

At higher levels of implementation *context sensitive* actions require either larger amounts of meta-data, extensive case analysis based programming, or other artificial intelligence algorithms.

18.2.1   In computer and video games

Context sensitivity is important in video games - especially those controlled by a gamepad, joystick or computer mouse in which the number of buttons available is limited. It is primarily applied when the player is in a certain place and is used to interact with a person or object. For example, if the player is standing next to an NPC, an option may come up allowing the player to talk with him/her.

Implementations range from the embryonic 'Quick Time Event' to context sensitive sword combat in which the attack used depends on the position and orientation of both the player and opponent, as well as the virtual surroundings. A similar range of use is found in the 'action button' which dependent on the in game position of the player's character may cause the avatar to pick something up, open a door, grab a rope, punch a monster or opponent, or smash an object.[3]

The response does not have to be player activated - an on-screen device may only be shown in certain circumstances, e.g. 'targeting' cross hairs in a flight combat game may indicate the player should fire. An alternative implementation is to monitor the input from the player (e.g. level of button pressing activity) and use that to control the pace of the game in an attempt to maximize enjoyment or to control the excitement or ambiance.[4]

The method has become increasingly important as more complex games are designed for machines with few buttons (keyboard-less consoles). Bennet Ring commented (in 2006) that "*Context-sensitive* is the new lens flare".[5]

18.2.2   Context-sensitive help

Main article: Context-sensitive help

Context sensitive help is a common implementation of context sensitivity, a single help button is actioned and the help page or menu will open a specific page or topic related [6]

18.3   See also

- Semantics

- Autocomplete

- Autofill

- Autotype

- Combo box

- DWIM "Do What I Mean"

- Principle of least astonishment (PLA/POLA)

- Quick time event (QTE)

18.4   References

[1] Webopedia : context sensitive

[2] Alan Dix, Tiziana Catarci, Benjamin Habegger, Yannis Ioannidis, Azrina Kamaruddin, Akrivi Katifori, Giorgos Lepouras, Antonella Poggi, Devina Ramduny-Ellis. "intelligent context-sensitive interactions on desktop and the web" (PDF).

[3] Assassin's Creed E3 Preview

[4] Next Generation User Interfaces (A MIT Computer Science Masters Thesis by Eitan Glinert)

[5] Gears of War review - Now this is what next-gen gaming is all about

[6] Webopedia : Help

18.5   Sources

- Dix, Alan; Catarci, Tiziana; Habegger, Benjamin; Ioannidis, Yannis; Kamaruddin, Azrina; Katifori, Akrivi; Lepouras, Giorgos; Poggi, Antonella et al. (2006). "Intelligent context-sensitive interactions on desktop and the web" (PDF). Association for Computing Machinery.

- Glinert, Eitan (2008). "**The Human Controller: Usability and Accessibility in Video Game Interfaces.** Chapter 4.2 Next Generation User Interfaces:context sensitivity." (PDF).

- William Abner (2007-07-27). "Assassin's Creed E3 Preview". gameshark.com.

- "context sensitive". *webopedia*. Retrieved 1996-09-01. Check date values in: |accessdate= (help)

- Bennet Ring (2006-11-12). "Gears of War review - Now this is what next-gen gaming is all about.". Yahoo!.

- "Help". *webopedia*. Retrieved 2004-09-20.

Chapter 19

DialogOS

DialogOS is a graphical programming environment to design computer system which can converse through voice with the user. Dialogs are clicked together in a Flowchart. DialogOS includes bindings to control Lego Mindstorms robots with the voice.

DialogOS is used in computer science courses in schools and universities to teach programming and to introduce beginners in the basic principles of human/computer interaction and dialog design.

19.1 Bindings to Lego Minstorn NXT

DialogOS can control the LEGO Mindstorms NXT Series. It uses sensor-nodes to obtain values for the following sensors:

- noise sensor
- ultrasonic sensor
- touch sensor
- luminosity sensor

19.2 External links

- Official website

Chapter 20

Document capture software

Document Capture Software refers to applications that provide the ability and feature set to automate the process of scanning paper documents. Most scanning hardware, both scanners and copiers, provides the basic ability to scan to any number of image file formats, including: PDF, TIFF, JPG, BMP, etc. This basic functionality is augmented by document capture software, which can add efficiency and standardization to the process.

20.1 Typical features

Typical features of Document Capture Software include:

- Barcode recognition
- Patch Code recognition
- Separation
- Optical Character Recognition (OCR)
- Optical Mark Recognition (OMR)
- Quality Assurance
- Indexing
- Migration

20.1.1 Goal for Implementation of a Document Capture Solution

The goal for implementing a document capture solution is to reduce the amount of time spent in the scanning and capture process, and produce metadata along with an image file, and/or OCR text. This information is then migrated to a Document Management or Enterprise Content Management system. These systems often provide a search function, allowing search of the assets based on the produced metadata, and then viewed using document imaging software.

20.2 Document Capture System Solutions - General

20.2.1 Integration with Document Management System

Main article: Enterprise content management

ECM (Enterprise Content management) and their DMS component (Document Management System) are being adopted by many organizations as a corporate document management system for all types of electronic files, e.g. MS word, PDF ... However, much of the information held by organisations is on paper and this needs to be integrated within the same document repository.

By converting paper documents into digital format through scanning companies can convert paper into image formats such as TIF and JPG and also extract valuable index information or business data from the document using OCR technology. Digital documents and associated metadata can easily be stored in the ECM in a variety of formats. The most popular of these formats is PDF which not only provides an accurate representation of the document but also allows all the OCR text in the document to be stored behind the PDF image. This format is known as PDF with hidden text or text-searchable PDF. This allows users to search for documents by using keywords in the metadata fields or by searching the content of PDF files across the repository.

Advantages of scanning documents into a ECM/DMS

Information held on paper is usually just as valuable to organisations as the electronic documents that are generated internally. Often this information represents a large proportion of the day to day correspondence with suppliers and customers. Having the ability to manage and share this information internally through a document management system such as SharePoint can improve collaboration between departments or employees and also eliminate the risk of losing this information through disasters such as floods or fire.

Organisations adopting an ECM/DMS often implement electronic workflow which allows the information held on paper to be included as part of an electronic business process and incorporated into a customer record file along with other associated office documents and emails. For business critical documents, such as purchase orders and supplier invoices, digitising documents can help speed up business transactions as well as reduce manual effort involved in keying data into business systems, such as CRM, ERP and Accounting. Scanned invoices can also be routed to managers for payment approval via email or an electronic workflow.

Document Capture Software

There are many document capture software providers that offer integration with ECM to varying levels. Some providers offer a batch interface that simply drops images and index data into a directory and relies on a batch upload utility to transfer these documents into the ECM. Others offer a direct integration with some ECM which allows documents and metadata to be exported into specific folders. A few capture providers offer a very tightly integrated bi-directional interface with some ECM, e.g.

- PSI:Capture from PSIGEN [1]

- Prevalent Software's Quillix provides flexible methods for capturing documents to SharePoint.[2]

- ChronoScan Capture offers batch scanning with barcode recognition and OCR, and direct export to SharePoint web services, it has a free version for no commercial use [3]

- Ephesoft offers an open source software version for document capture integrated with open source document management products like Alfresco as well as commercial ones.[4]*[4][5]

- Librex from Corium provides intelligent scan and capture and smart connectors to multiple systems like Alfresco, SharePoint, Clara, COBA, Docuthèque, IntelliGID, SyGED, Ultima or simply to a network folder. Librex offers a free version (limited page volume) and an enterprise one.[6]

- GScan Online[7] offered by GRADIENT[8] provides the ability to scan/document capture directly within SharePoint On-Premises and Office 365 enabling Advanced Image processing, OCR recognition, and full-text searchable PDFs, whilst staying in the Microsoft environment. GScan Online app is available as a free

version (limited user and page volume) via the Office Store.[9] For more high-volume desktop scanning, see GScan,[10] and for mobile document capture on the GO, see GScan Mobile.[11]

20.3 Distributed Capture Solutions

Distributed document capture is a technology which allows the scanning of documents into a central server through the use of individual capture stations. A variation of distributed capture is thin-client document capture in which documents are scanned into a central server through the use of web browser. One of these web-based products was reviewed by AIIM. They said, "(this product) is a thin-client distributed capture system that streamlines the process of acquiring and creating documents."[12] The streamlining is a result of several factors including the lack of software which needs to be installed at every scanning station and the variety of input sources from which documents can be captured. This includes things like email, fax, or a watched folder.

Jeff Shuey, Director of Business Development at Kodak, makes a distinction between distributed capture and what he calls "remote" capture. In an article publishing in AIIM, he said that the key difference between the two is whether or not the information that is captured from scanning needs to be sent to the centralized server. If, as he points out in his article, the document just needs to be scanned and committed to a SharePoint system and doesn't need to be sent to some other centralized server, this is just a remote capture situation.[13]

There are Document Capture Software comparisons available, featuring some of the most relevant products (EMC Captiva, IBM Datacap, Artsyl Technologies or Ephesoft) and extracting performance facts and their most relevant features.

20.4 References

[1] SharePoint Capture and OCR

[2] Quillix Capture

[3] ChronoScan Capture

[4] Peelen, Tjarda. "Software for Document Capture". Open Source ECM. Retrieved 18 Feb 2014.

[5] Feild, Don. "Ephesoft".

[6] Librex Document Capture and Smart Connectors

[7] GScan Online

[8] GRADIENT ECM

[9] GScan Online App Office Store Trial

[10] GScan (desktop)

[11] GScan Mobile

[12] Association for Information and Image Management "Prevalent Software - Quillix", accessed August 29, 2011.

[13] Association for Information and Image Management "Remote or Distributed Scanning - Are They Different?", accessed August 29, 2011.

Chapter 21

Document processing

Document Processing involves the conversion of typed and handwritten text on paper-based & electronic documents (e.g., scanned image of a document) into electronic information utilising one of, or a combination of, Intelligent Character Recognition (ICR), Optical Character Recognition (OCR) and experienced Data Entry Clerks.

21.1   See also

- Document automation
- Document modelling
- Outsourced document processing

Chapter 22

Dr. Sbaitso

Dr. Sbaitso is an artificial intelligence speech synthesis program released in 1992 by Creative Labs for MS DOS-based personal computers.

22.1 History

Dr. Sbaitso was distributed with various sound cards manufactured by Creative Labs (the name was an acronym for Sound Blaster Artificial Intelligent Text to Speech Operator) in the early 1990s.

The program "conversed" with the user as if it were a psychologist, though most of its responses were along the lines of "WHY DO YOU FEEL THAT WAY?" rather than any sort of complicated interaction. When confronted with a phrase it could not understand, it would often reply with something such as "THAT'S NOT MY PROBLEM". Dr. Sbaitso repeated text out loud that was typed after the word "SAY". Repeated swearing or abusive behavior on the part of the user caused Dr. Sbaitso to "break down" in a "PARITY ERROR" before resetting itself.

The program introduced itself with the following lines: Example:

HELLO [UserName], MY NAME IS DOCTOR SBAITSO. I AM HERE TO HELP YOU. SAY WHATEVER IS IN YOUR MIND FREELY, OUR CONVERSATION WILL BE KEPT IN STRICT CONFIDENCE. MEMORY CONTENTS WILL BE WIPED OFF AFTER YOU LEAVE, SO, TELL ME ABOUT YOUR PROBLEMS.

The program was designed to showcase the digitized voices the cards were able to produce, though the quality was far from lifelike. Its AI engine was likely based on something similar to the ELIZA algorithm.

22.2 See also

- ALICE

- ELIZA

- History of natural language processing

22.3 External links

- "Dr. Sbaitso Was My Only Friend". X-Entertainment. 2006-10-04. Retrieved 2010-02-26.

- "Dr. Sbaitso". Home of the Underdogs. Retrieved 2010-02-26.

- "Dr. Sbaitso Online". OneWeakness. Retrieved 2013-08-26.

Chapter 23

Eccky

Eccky is an online game. Until 2009, it was an MSN-based life simulation game in which two people come together to create and raise a virtual baby. *Eccky* won the 2005 SpinAwards for Innovation and for Best Interactive Concept.[1] In 2009, the game play changed to a real-time virtual world launched on Hyves

23.1 History

Eccky was created in August 2005 by Dutch developer Media Republic in association with MSN in the Netherlands. Eccky has characteristics of life simulation and virtual pet games. The gameplay of this first version of Eccky involved a virtual baby, or Eccky, which was born on the basis of information derived from both Eccky user parents. *Eccky* used an AIML chatbot and MSN Messenger for chat between users and the Eccky baby. In 2006, *Eccky* became an independent company as a subsidiary of Media Republic.

From its live introduction to the public until August 2006, Eccky required an initial fee which could be paid by either user parent. However Eccky has been free to play since September 2006.[2][3]

23.2 Eccky 1.0 (2005-2007)

In the first version of *Eccky*, two users create a virtual baby, and raise him/her with the goal of making the child as happy and satisfied as possible. A user must consists of a questionnaire that user parents must fill in with information regarding their personal characteristics, child-rearing attitudes, favorites, etc. Once registration and the "DNA" test have been completed, a user may invite another person to make an Eccky. Upon accepting the invitation, the second user also registers on the Eccky website, and completes his/her own "DNA" test. Both parents then choose both a masculine and feminine name for their future Ec-

cky. Thereafter Eccky is born, with characteristics determined by the combination of both user parents' DNA profiles. Eccky's sex is randomly determined, as is Eccky's name (which is chosen randomly between the four possible names chosen by the user parents).

Over a six-day period from Eccky's birth, Eccky grows and ages three years for every one day of gameplay. Thus, in six days, Eccky develops from a cooing baby into an eighteen-year-old young adult with its own character. Every Eccky is unique at birth, and the way in which the user parents raise their Eccky further individualizes Eccky's demeanor and characteristics. On the sixth day, or upon turning 18, Eccky leaves the house to venture off into the wide world, and the game ends.

Eccky played principally via the Eccky website and MSN Messenger, though also via mobile phone. Upon Eccky's birth, Eccky is automatically added as a contact to the MSN contact lists of both parents. This allows user parents to talk to their virtual child. Running on an AIML chat engine, Eccky is able to speak from the moment following birth, both in response to user parents addressing Eccky and by initiating conversation him/herself. Eccky will initiate conversation either randomly or to express any particularly pressing need he/she may have (i.e. being extremely hungry, having to go to the bathroom, being very sick, feeling neglected, etc.) Eccky's vocabulary is initially limited to newborn babble. Then, as with a real child, Eccky's command of vocabulary grows with each day of gameplay, to a final capability of being able to respond with over 60,000 unique answers on more than 4,000 diverse subjects.[4] Since June 2007, Eccky also features an in-game chat functionality.

Eccky and user parents can also exchange text messages via mobile phone. Exchange of text messages requires that the user parent have a mobile phone, and that the user parent purchase a mobile phone for Eccky within the game environment. This feature involves some extra costs to the user parent, specifically the cost of sending text messages, and can be turned on and off at the user parent's discretion.

Most games are intended to be played with user parents

playing against their Eccky and vice versa. Others are played in cooperation with Eccky. Of note are the racing games, some of which allow users to create their own tracks and race on them with Eccky. Though most games are free to play, some games require additional credits to play.

Eccky's physical and emotional states are subject to continual change, determined by 180 dynamic variables, and are influenced by the interaction with and treatment by user parents, both via the virtual world and via the chat. The levels of these physical and emotional states are continually assessed and are made visible to user parents via meters that gauge happiness, hunger, toilet needs, popularity, who Eccky's favorite parent is, etc. For example, if Eccky is not sufficiently fed, users will see this in Eccky's hunger meter. In worst-case scenarios, an Eccky can be neglected, physical and emotionally, to the point of needing to be sent to the hospital. During this time, gameplay continues and user parents may chat with Eccky, but may not interact with Eccky in the virtual world. Further, Eccky's physical and emotional states are reflected in the chat element, as Eccky will either comment, unsolicited, on how he/she is doing physically and emotionally, or respond to a user parent in such a way as to make his/her physical and emotional state known.

It is also possible to send Eccky away for a period, either to live in other accommodations such as in a hotel, on vacation, or to stay with a babysitter. A babysitter may be anyone with an MSN Messenger account. Sending Eccky to a hotel or on vacation does involve additional costs (sending Eccky to a babysitter does not), and as with Eccky staying in the hospital, user parents may continue to speak with Eccky via chat but cannot interact with Eccky in the virtual world setting during this time. A user parent can retrieve their Eccky at any time during a stay away from home. Eccky was closed down in 2007 and until it was launched in a new format in 2009.

23.3   Eccky 2.0 (Since 2009)

In 2009 Dutch/Chinese developer TribePlay created a new version of Eccky and launched it in Hyves as one of the first social networking virtual worlds. In Eccky players can make a character (an Eccky) with their social network profile. After that they enter the Eccky world. In this world they have access to various locations, such as a city center, park, mountain top and beach. Players can also visit their own or other user's house. In any of these virtual locations players can chat, play mini games and do a variety of other things.

Eccky is integrated into Hyves and Facebook. Together with their Hyves or Facebook friends players can chat, play

mini games and post their Eccky's activities on their social networking profile. Eccky has many games. Games can be played in single-player or multi-player format. Ecckies can also play with their Wobble. A Wobble is Eccky's own pet. Wobbles were the first inhabitants of the Eccky world. Wobbles live together with Ecckies and need to be taken care of. Once Ecckies advance in levels they receive superpowers to be used in the game.

23.4   References

[1] "SpinAwards: 2005". *SpinAwards*. 13 April 2005. Retrieved 2009-04-09.

[2] "Eccky will be free". Retrieved 2006-07-22.

[3] Tomesen, Remco (2006-07-14). "Eccky vanaf september gratis". Emerce.nl. Retrieved 2006-07-22.

[4] "Media Republic introduces Eccky BETA in collaboration with MSN" (Press release). Media Republic. 2005-10-27.

23.5   External links

- Eccky English-language game website

- Eccky corporate website

Chapter 24

eSTAR project

The **eSTAR project** is a multi-agent system that aims to implement a true heterogeneous network of robotic telescopes for automated observing. The project is a joint collaboration between the Astrophysics Group of the University of Exeter and the Astrophysics Research Institute at Liverpool John Moores University.

In 2006 work began on an autonomous software agent for observations of variable stars. This agent implements the optimal sampling technique of Saunders et al. (2006) and the prototype was successfully tested on the RoboNet network of telescopes which includes: the Liverpool Telescope, the Faulkes Telescope North and the Faulkes Telescope South.

eSTAR is affiliated with the RoboNet Consortium and the global Heterogeneous Telescope Networks Consortium.

As of 2007 eSTAR is "live" supporting two real-time observing projects. Automated follow-up observations of gamma ray bursts are performed using the 3.8m UKIRT telescope situated in Hawai'i, making this telescope the largest in the world, with an automated response system for tracking such events.

eSTAR is also involved in the search for extra-solar planets by placing observations on the RoboNet system of telescopes on behalf of the PLANET collaboration. The technique of gravitational microlensing is used to monitor large numbers of stars in the galactic bulge looking for the telltale signature of cool planets orbiting those stars.

24.1 External links

- eSTAR Project homepage

- Heterogeneous Telescopes Networks homepage

- University of Exeter Astrophysics Group

- LJM Astrophysics Research Institute

- "Optimal placement of a limited number of observations for period searches", Saunders, E.S., Naylor, T. and Allan, A.

Chapter 25

ETAP-3

ETAP-3 is a proprietary linguistic processing system focusing on English and Russian.[1] It was developed in Moscow, Russia at the Institute for Information Transmission Problems (ru:Институт проблем передачи информации им. А. А. Харкевича РАН). It is a rule-based system which uses the Meaning-Text Theory as its theoretical foundation. At present, there are several applications of ETAP-3, such as a machine translation tool, a converter of the Universal Networking Language, an interactive learning tool for Russian language learners and a syntactically annotated corpus of Russian language. Demo versions of some of these tools are available online.

25.1 Machine translation tool

The ETAP-3 machine translation tool can translate text from English into Russian and vice versa. It is a rule-based system which makes it different from the most present-day systems that are predominantly statistical-based. The system makes a syntactical analysis of the input sentence which can be visualized as a syntax tree.

The machine translation tool uses bilingual dictionaries which contain more than 100,000 lexical entries.

25.2 UNL converter

The UNL converter based on ETAP-3 can transform English and Russian sentences into there representations in UNL (*Universal Networking Language*) and generate English and Russian sentences from their UNL representations.

25.3 Russian language treebank

A syntactically annotated corpus (treebank) is a part of Russian National Corpus.[2] It contains 40,000 sentences (600,000 words) which are fully syntactically and morphologically annotated. The primary annotation was made by ETAP-3 and then manually verified by competent linguists. This makes the syntactically annotated corpus a reliable tool for linguistic research.

25.4 Lexical functions learning tool

The ETAP-3 system makes extensive use of lexical functions explored in the Meaning-Text Theory. For this reason, an interactive tool for Russian language learners aiming at the acquisition of lexical functions has been developed. Such learning tools are now being created for German, Spanish and Bulgarian[3]

25.5 References

[1] "МНОГОЦЕЛЕВОЙ ЛИНГВИСТИЧЕСКИЙ ПРОЦЕССОР ЭТАП−3". Iitp.ru. Retrieved 2012-02-14.

[2] "Search the Corpus. Russian National Corpus". Ruscorpora.ru. Retrieved 2012-02-14.

[3] "Лаборатория № 15". Iitp.ru. Retrieved 2012-02-14.

25.6 External links

Official website with demo-versions of linguistic tools

Chapter 26

EuResist

EuResist is an international project designed to improve the treatment of HIV patients by developing a computerized system that can recommend optimal treatment based on the patient's clinical and genomic data.

The project is part of the Virtual Physiological Human framework, funded by the European Commission. It started in 2006 with the formation of a consortium of several research institutes and hospitals in Europe and Israel. The consortium completed its commitment to the European Commission near the end of 2008, at which time the system became available online. A non-profit organization was consequently established by the main partners to maintain and improve the system.

In 2009, the EuResist project was named as a Computerworld honors program laureate.[1]

26.1 Background

AIDS is a disease caused by the HIV retrovirus, which progressively reduces the effectiveness of the immune system, leading to infections and ultimately death.

More than 30 different drugs exist for treating HIV patients. Antiretroviral drugs can disrupt the virus's replication process causing its numbers to decrease dramatically. While the virus cannot be eradicated completely, in small numbers it is harmless. Usually a patient is given a combination of three or four drugs, a treatment known as highly active antiretroviral therapy, or HAART. The main reason such a treatment might fail is the development of mutated strands of the virus, resistant to one or more of the prescribed drugs.

Thus an important consideration when choosing treatment for a patient is to prescribe those drugs to which the particular patient's virus strands are most susceptible. One way to achieve that is to extract virus samples from the patient's blood and test them against all possible drugs. Since this process is lengthy and costly, computerized systems have been developed to predict virus resistance based on its genotype. The treating physician samples virus genotype sequences from the patient's blood and provides this data to a computerized system. The system then responds with drug recommendations.

Such systems are limited in accuracy, depending on the amount of data used for their creation, its quality and the richness of mathematical models used for the actual prediction. Prior to EuResist, such systems had several common characteristics that negatively impacted their accuracy:[2]

- The amount of data used for creating the system was relatively small

- This data was in vitro data: laboratory measures of the resistance of various strands of HIV to individual drugs. Such data is known to be inaccurate because laboratory tests do not simulate exactly the processes of a living organism, and since resistance to individual drugs does not accurately predict the resistance to a combination of drugs.

- They used a relatively simple mathematical prediction model

26.2 EuResist overview

EuResist sought to create a more accurate HIV treatment prediction system by collecting a large database of in vivo data (clinical and genomic records of real treatments of HIV patients and their consequences), and by using an array of prediction models instead of just one.

The database was created by merging local databases of various clinics across Europe. This database is thought to be the largest of its kind in the world. For each patient, it includes various personal and demographic details such as gender, age, country of origin, genomic sequencing of HIV found in the patient's blood, records of the drugs prescribed, and the changes in the amount of virus in the blood following these treatments.

This data was used to train an array of prediction models, created by using various contemporary machine learning techniques, among them Bayesian networks, logistic regression, and others.

A web interface allows physicians to specify patients' clinical and genomic data. This data is sent to the prediction engines, and the combined response, which is displayed to the physician, includes various suggested treatments and a prediction of their effect on the amount of HIV in the blood.

The EuResist system was tested and compared with its predecessors by feeding it with historical data on patients for which treatment results are known. The developers of EuResist, who conducted this test, reported an improved performance over the previous state-of-the-art system.

26.3 History

EuResist started in 2006 as a consortium funded by the European Union as part of the Virtual Physiological Human FP-6 framework. The partners of this consortium were:

- Informa S.r.l. (Italy)
- University of Siena (Italy)
- Karolinska Institutet (Sweden)
- Universitätsklinikum Koeln (Germany)
- Max Planck Institute for Informatics (Germany)
- IBM Haifa Research Laboratory (Israel)
- MTA KFKI Reszecske-ES Magfizikai KutatoIntezet (Hungary)
- Kingston University (United Kingdom)

The consortium completed its commitment to the European Union in late 2008, at which time the EuResist system became available on line. The first five partners mentioned above continued to form a non-profit organization that maintains the system, expands the database with new clinical and genomical records and updates the prediction engines accordingly. As of mid-2010, an average of 600 queries are submitted to the EuResist system every quarter.

26.4 Recognition

On June 1, 2009, EuResist received a Computerworld honors program laureate award, a global program honoring individuals and organizations that use information technology to benefit society.[1]

26.5 References

[1] http://www.cwhonors.org/laureates/finalists2009.htm Computerworld honors program - laureates of 2009.

[2] M Rosen-Zvi et al. ,Selecting anti-HIV therapies based on a variety of genomic and clinical factors, Bioinformatics 24(13): i399–406, 2008 http://bioinformatics.oxfordjournals.org/cgi/content/short/24/13/i399

26.6 External links

- EuResist official site
- A movie about EuResist

Chapter 27

Eurisko

Eurisko (Gr., *I discover*) is a program written by Douglas Lenat in RLL-1, a representation language itself written in the Lisp programming language. A sequel to Automated Mathematician, it consists of heuristics, i.e. rules of thumb, including heuristics describing how to use and change its own heuristics.[1][2] Lenat was frustrated by Automated Mathematician's constraint to a single domain and so developed Eurisko; his frustration with the effort of encoding domain knowledge for Eurisko led to Lenat's subsequent (and, as of 2014, continuing) development of Cyc. Lenat envisions ultimately coupling the Cyc knowledgebase with the Eurisko discovery engine.

27.1 History

Development commenced at Carnegie Mellon in 1976 and continued at Stanford University in 1978 when Lenat returned to teach. "For the first five years, nothing good came out of it," Lenat said. But when the implementation was changed to a frame language based representation he called RLL (Representation Language Language), heuristic creation and modification became much simpler. Eurisko was then applied to a number of domains with surprising success, including VLSI chip design.

Lenat and Eurisko gained notoriety by submitting the winning fleet (a large number of stationary, highly weaponed, defenseless ships)[3] to the United States Traveller TCS national championship in 1981, forcing extensive changes to the game's rules. However, Eurisko won again in 1982 when the program discovered that the rules permitted the program to destroy its own ships, permitting it to continue to use much the same strategy.[3] Tournament officials announced that if Eurisko won another championship the competition would be abolished; Lenat retired Eurisko from the game.[4] The Traveller TCS wins brought Lenat to the attention of DARPA,[5] which has funded much of his subsequent work.

27.2 In popular culture

In the first-season *X-Files* episode "Ghost in the Machine," Eurisko is the name of a fictional software company responsible for the episode's "monster of the week," facilities management software known as "Central Operating System," or "COS." COS (described in the episode as an "adaptive network") is shown to be capable of learning when its designer arrives at Eurisko headquarters and is surprised to find that COS has given itself the ability to speak. The designer is forced to create a virus to destroy COS after COS commits a series of murders in an apparent effort to prevent its own destruction.

Lenat is also mentioned and Eurisko is discussed at the end of Richard Feynman's Computer Heuristics Lecture as part of the Idiosyncratic Thinking Workshop Series.[6]

27.3 Notes

[1] Lenat, Douglas (1983). "EURISKO: A program that learns new heuristics and domain concepts". *Artificial Intelligence* **21**: pp. 61–98. doi:10.1016/s0004-3702(83)80005-8.

[2] Drexler, K. Eric (1986). "Thinking Machines (Chapter 5)". *Engines of Creation*. Doubleday. ISBN 0-385-19973-2. EURISKO ... is guided by heuristics ... in effect, various rules of thumb.

[3] Malcolm Gladwell (2009-05-11). "How underdogs can win". The New Yorker. Retrieved 2010-01-11.

[4] Johnson, George (1984). "Eurisko, The Computer With A Mind Of Its Own". *the APF Reporter* (Washington, D.C.: The Alicia Patterson Foundation) **7** (4). External link in |work= (help)

[5] *Understanding Computers: Artificial Intelligence*. Amsterdam: Time-Life Books. 1986. p. 84. ISBN 0-7054-0915-5.

[6] https://youtube.com/EKWGGDXe5MA?t=1h8m38s

27.4 References

- *Understanding Computers: Artificial Intelligence*. Amsterdam: Time-Life Books. 1986. pp. 81–84. ISBN 0-7054-0915-5.

- Lenat, Douglas; Brown, J.S. (1984). "Why AM and EURISKO appear to work" (PDF). *Artificial Intelligence* **23** (3): pp. 269–294. doi:10.1016/0004-3702(84)90016-X.

- Haase, Kenneth W (February 1990). "Invention and exploration in discovery". Massachusetts Institute of Technology. Archived from the original (PDF) on 2005-01-22. Retrieved 2008-12-13.

Chapter 28

FatKat (investment software)

For the similarly titled company (an animation studio), see Fatkat.

FatKat, Inc. is a privately held company founded in 1999 by Raymond C. Kurzweil, an author, inventor, and futurist. He's perhaps best known for creating an optical character recognition system that – in conjunction with a flatbed scanner and text-to-speech synthesizer – reads text aloud to the sight-impaired. FatKat is an acronym derived from "**F**inancial **A**ccelerating **T**ransactions from **K**urzweil **A**daptive **T**echnologies." The aforesaid company is one of a total of nine Kurzweil companies.[1]

The purpose of FatKat as listed with the Massachusetts Secretary of the Commonwealth Corporations Division is "investment software."[2] Kurzweil, who specializes in artificial intelligence coupled with pattern recognition, has created software that uses quantitative methods to pick stocks for investment purposes.[3]

Although selecting stocks based on software-generated recommendations is not new, FatKat's approach was unique at the time because of its "nonlinear decision making processes more akin to how a brain operates." In layman's terms, the software can evolve by creating different rules, letting them compete, and using (or combining) the best outcomes. After FatKat's inception, other investment and/or software companies rushed to develop software based on this and similar Darwinist evolutionary principles, using genetic algorithms.[3]

In 2005, Kurzweil reported that the FatKat software was "doing very well – 50% to 100% returns for the last two years." [1] But as of December 2008, FatKat does not offer its software for sale.

28.1 Corporate structure

FatKat was registered as a foreign corporation in 1999 with the Massachusetts Secretary of the Commonwealth, Corporations Division. It was originally formed as a com-

pany in the state of Delaware. Ray Kurzweil is the president of FatKat, with Aaron Kleiner serving as treasurer and secretary. Michael Brown is listed as a director.[2]

28.2 Related hedge funds

Two hedge funds exist that use the FatKat name: FatKat Investment Fund, LP and FatKat QP Investment Fund, LP. Both of these investment fund companies list Kurzweil Capital Partners LLC as a general partner. These companies were formed in December 2005, also in Delaware.[2] Neither of the hedge funds is publicly traded. Kurzweil Capital Partners LLC and the two hedge funds are not listed on the Kurzweil companies' web site.

28.3 Investors

Documented investors in FatKat, Inc. and its hedge funds are venture capitalist Vinod Khosla and Michael W. Brown (former CFO of Microsoft and chairman of NASDAQ).[1] Other investors have not been disclosed.

28.4 References

[1] Port, Otis (1 August 2005). "Raymond C. Kurzweil: Prophet of Longevity". *Business Week*. Retrieved 10 December 2008.

[2] "Massachusetts Secretary of the Commonwealth, Corporations Division".

[3] Duhigg, Charles (24 November 2006). "A Smarter Computer to Pick Stock". *New York Times Late Edition (East Coast)*. pp. C–1. ISSN 0362-4331. Retrieved 10 December 2008.

28.5   See also

Kurzweil Technologies (with links to related companies)

Chapter 29

GestureTek

GestureTek is an American-based interactive technology company headquartered in Silicon Valley, California, with offices in Toronto and Ottawa, Ontario and Asia.[1]

29.1 Founding

Founded in 1986 by Canadians Vincent John Vincent[2] and Francis MacDougall,[3] this privately held company develops and licenses gesture recognition software based on computer vision techniques. The partners invented video gesture control in 1986 and received their base patent in 1996 for the GestPoint video gesture control system. GestPoint technology is a camera-enabled video tracking software system that translates hand and body movement into computer control.[4] The system enables users to navigate and control interactive multi-media and menu-based content, engage in virtual reality game play, experience immersion in an augmented reality environment or interact with a consumer device (such a television, mobile phone or set top box) without using touch-based peripherals.[5][6][7] Similar companies include gesture recognition specialist LM3LABS based in Tokyo, Japan.

29.2 Technology

GestureTek's gesture interface applications include multi-touch and 3D camera tracking. GestureTek's multi-touch technology powers the multi-touch table in Melbourne's Eureka Tower.[8] A GestureTek multi-touch table with object recognition is found at the New York City Visitors Center.[9] Telefónica has a multi-touch window with technology from GestureTek.[10] GestureTek's 3D tracking technology is used in a 3D television prototype from Hitachi and various digital signage and display solutions based on 3D interaction.[11]

29.3 Patents

GestureTek currently has 8 patents awarded, including: 5,534,917[12] (Video Gesture Control Motion Detection); 7,058,204[13] (Multiple Camera Control System, Point to Control Base Patent); 7,421,093[14] (Multiple Camera Tracking System for Interfacing With an Application); 7,227,526[15] (Stereo Camera Control, 3D-Vision Image Control System); 7,379,563[16] (Two Handed Movement Tracker Tracking Bi-Manual Movements); 7,379,566[17] (Optical Flow-Based Tilt Sensor For Phone Tilt Control); 7,389,591[18] (Phone Tilt for Typing & Menus/Orientation-Sensitive Signal Output); 7,430,312[19] (Five Camera 3D Face Capture).

GestureTek's software and patents have been licensed by Microsoft for the Xbox 360,[20] Sony for the EyeToy,[21] NTT DoCoMo for their mobile phones[22] and Hasbro for the ION Educational Gaming System.[23] In addition to software provision, GestureTek also fabricates interactive gesture control display systems with natural user interface for interactive advertising, games and presentations.[24]

In addition, GestureTek's natural user interface virtual reality system has been the subject of research by universities and hospitals for its application in both physical therapy[25] and physical rehabilitation.[26]

In 2008, GestureTek received the Mobile Innovation Global Award[27] from the GSMA for its software-based, gesture-controlled user interface for mobile games and applications. The technology is used by Java platform integration providers[28] and mobile developers.[29] Katamari Damacy is one example of a gesture control mobile game powered by GestureTek software.

29.4 Competitors

Other companies in the industry of interactive projections for marketing and retail experiences include Po-motion Inc.,[30] Touchmagix [31] and LM3LABS[32]

29.5   References

[1] "Gesture Recognition & Computer Vision Control Technology & Motion Sensing Systems for Presentation & Entertainment". Gesturetek.com. Retrieved October 20, 2011.

[2] "Vincent John Vincent". Vjvincent.com. Retrieved October 20, 2011.

[3] "ATIS TechThink". Techthink.org. Retrieved October 20, 2011.

[4]

[5] "GestureTek brings 3D and gestures together for remote control". Engadget. January 5, 2009. Retrieved October 20, 2011.

[6] "Watch out, Surface; GestureTek is straight frontin' | TechCrunch". Crunchgear.com. November 12, 2008. Retrieved October 20, 2011.

[7] "GestureTek Mobile is Overall Winner at the 2008 Mobile Innovation Global Awards at the GSMA's Mobile World Congress in Barcelona – Feb 13, 2008". Mobileworldcongress.mediaroom.com. February 13, 2008. Retrieved October 20, 2011.

[8] "Microsoft Surface versus GestureTek's Illuminate Table". Aboutmicrosoftsurface.com. Retrieved October 20, 2011.

[9] "The New York Center Information Center Installation". Svconline.com. Retrieved October 20, 2011.

[10] Chris Morrison (December 12, 2007). "GestureTek receives investment from Telefonica | VentureBeat". Deals.venturebeat.com. Retrieved October 20, 2011.

[11] "LCD TV". Lcdtvreviews.org.uk. Retrieved October 20, 2011.

[12] "Video image based control system – Very Vivid, Inc". Freepatentsonline.com. Retrieved October 20, 2011.

[13] "Multiple camera control system – GestureTek, Inc". Freepatentsonline.com. Retrieved October 20, 2011.

[14] "Multiple camera control system – GestureTek, Inc". Freepatentsonline.com. Retrieved October 20, 2011.

[15] "Video-based image control system – US Patent 7227526 Abstract". Patentstorm.us. Retrieved October 20, 2011.

[16] "Tracking bimanual movements – US Patent 7379563 Abstract". Patentstorm.us. Retrieved October 20, 2011.

[17] "Optical flow based tilt sensor – Patent # 7379566". PatentGenius. Retrieved October 20, 2011.

[18] "Orientation-sensitive signal output – GestureTek, Inc". Freepatentsonline.com. Retrieved October 20, 2011.

[19] "Creating 3D images of objects by illuminating with infrared patterns – GestureTek, Inc". Freepatentsonline.com. Retrieved October 20, 2011.

[20] "News – Q&A: GestureTek Talks Xbox 360 Camera Innovation". Gamasutra. October 11, 2006. Retrieved October 20, 2011.

[21] "GestureTek Grants Patent License to Sony Computer Entertainment America for EyeToy and PlayStation2 Game Development | Business Wire". Find Articles. February 18, 2005. Retrieved October 20, 2011.

[22]

[23] "News – GestureTek Preparing 'Wii-like' Control Wand". Gamasutra. February 15, 2008. Retrieved October 20, 2011.

[24] http://www.digitalsignagetoday.com/video_gallery.php?v=1586

[25] Weiss, P. L.; Rand, D; Katz, N; Kizony, R (2004). "Video capture virtual reality as a flexible and effective rehabilitation tool". *Journal of NeuroEngineering and Rehabilitation* **1** (1): 12. doi:10.1186/1743-0003-1-12. PMC 546410. PMID 15679949.

[26] "Retrieved on 2009-05-07". Hw.haifa.ac.il. Retrieved October 20, 2011.

[27] "FirstNews – February 13, 2008". Wireless Week. February 13, 2008. Retrieved October 20, 2011.

[28]

[29] "Gaming News – Get the latest updates on the gaming industry". gamezone.com. October 3, 2011. Retrieved October 20, 2011.

[30] *Po-motion website*

[31] *Touchmagix website*

[32] *LM3LABS blog*

Chapter 30

GNOME Chess

Main article: GNOME Games

GNOME Chess (formerly **glChess**[3]) is a graphical front-

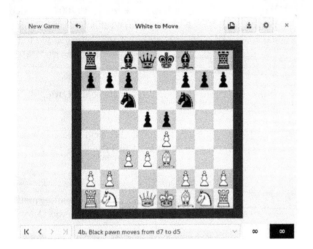

GNOME Chess in 2D view

end featuring a 2D and a 3D chessboard interface. GNOME Chess does not comprise an own chess engine and to play against the computer a third party chess engine must be present, but most Linux distributions package GNU Chess as default chess engine with it. Additionally GNOME Chess supports third party chess engines, known ones are automatically detected.

GNOME Chess is written in Vala. For 2D rendering it uses GTK+ and Cairo/librsvg, and 3D support is optionally available using OpenGL.

As part of the GNOME desktop environment and GNOME Games, GNOME Chess is free and open-source software subject to the terms of the GNU General Public License (GPL) version 2.

30.1 Third-party chess engines

GNOME Chess supports following chess engines:[4]

- Amy
- BBChess
- Boo's Chess Engine
- Crafty
- Diablo
- Faile
- Fruit
- Glaurung
- GNU Chess
- HoiChess
- Phalanx
- Shredder
- Sjeng
- Toga II

And a couple more.[5]

glChess, the predecessor to GNOME Chess can be used with any other CECP and Universal Chess Interface compatible software like:[6][7]

- Amy
- Amundsen
- BBChess
- Boo's Chess Engine
- Crafty
- Diablo
- Faile

81

- FairyMax

- Fruit

- Glaurung

- GNU Chess

- HoiChess

- Komodo

- Phalanx

- Shredder

- Sjeng

- Stockfish

- Toga II

30.2   History

glChess was written by Robert Ancell in 2000 only as a personal project to test open source development.[8]

First version was written in C, OpenGL for graphics, and GLUT for the user interface. In May 5 was released 0.1.0, the first but still not playable version, being only capable to draw board and pieces. Days later, on May 31, version 0.1.3 was finally included on SourceForge and playable on a very basic way.

On April 8, 2001 version 0.2.0 changed GLUT to GTK+ focusing the improvement in visual aspects instead of its chess playability. Version 0.3.0, from June 27, could play against other artificial intelligence (AI) engines, like Crafty and GNU Chess, after a Chess Engine Communication Protocol (CECP) implementation and it was ported to IRIX platform. In December, version 0.4.0 was the last one before the project entered into a stand-by time of three years.

In December, 2004, there was an advance to version 0.8.0 in order to accelerate the achievement the 1.0. This version added network support and updated GTK+ from version 1.2 to 2.0.

One year later, December 2005, version 0.9.0 was intended to be the last release before 1.0. It replaced C for Python to improve platform portability and maintenance, besides having a better test approach of the codebase testing.

On December 16, 2006, glChess finally reached version 1.0.

Apple Chess is a fork of GNOME Chess.

30.3   See also

- Chess Engine Communication Protocol

- Computer Chess

- Universal Chess Interface

30.4   References

[1] Clasen, Matthias (Sep 23, 2015). "GNOME 3.18". *gnome-announce-list* (Mailing list). Retrieved Sep 23, 2015.

[2] "GNOME 3.19.x Development Series". Retrieved October 29, 2015.

[3] "GNOME Chess history". GNOME. Retrieved 2014-03-15.

[4] "GNOME Chess supported chess engines".

[5] "Apps/Chess/ChessEngines - GNOME Wiki!". *gnome.org*.

[6] Chess from GNOME Wiki. Retrieved on September 24, 2012.

[7] Package glChess from Debian site. Retrieved on September 26, 2012.

[8] "Chess Manual". GNOME Library. Retrieved 2013-08-04.

30.5   External links

- Official website

- Manual of Chess

Chapter 31

Grandmaster Chess

Grandmaster Chess is a 1993 video game to play chess for PC DOS platform develop by IntraCorp and its subsidiary Capstone that was focused on neural network technology and an artificial intelligence (AI) able to learn from mistakes.[1]

Capable of using VGA and SVGA modes, features multiple skill levels, different sets of pieces, boards and backgrounds, 2D/3D view, pull-down menus, move list with VCR style control, able to analysis moves and games and rate the user strength. Originally it was distributed in floppy discs, but in 1996 in appeared in CD-ROM. This release only relevant addition was the *Terminator 2: Judgement Day: Chess Wars* package, an animated chess set like *Battle Chess* video game representing the Terminator 2: Judgment Day movie.[2]

31.1 Requirements

Originally, to execute *Grandmaster Chess* an IBM PC compatible needed:[3]

- 386SX/33 MHz CPU type/speed
- less than 1 MB RAM
- 1 MB hard disk space
- DOS 3.3
- VGA: 640x480, 256 colors
- 640 KB free conventional memory

In DOS-independents systems, just like GNU/Linux, Unix-like and more modern versions of Windows it can be played through console emulators, like DOSBox (version 0.61 and later).[4]

31.2 Reception

Computer Gaming World stated that *Grandmaster Chess* "falls short of the current competition in terms of overall options". The magazine criticized the game's weak strategic analysis reporting, the absence of an advertised teaching mode, and weak opening book.[5]

31.3 See also

- Computer chess
- Vintage software
- Learning section of *Artificial Intelligence* article
- Simulators for teaching neural network theory section of *Neural network software* article

31.4 References

[1] Grandmaster Chess from Home of the Underdogs. Retrieved on September 22, 2012.

[2] Grandmaster Chess (CD-ROM Edition) for DOS (1993) from Moby Games. Retrieved on September 22, 2012.

[3] Grandmaster Chess CD-ROM Edition from Allgame. Retrieved on September 22, 2012.

[4] from DOSBox website. Retrieved on September 22, 2012.

[5] Carter, Tim (November 1992). "Capstone's Grandmaster Chess". *Computer Gaming World*. p. 88. Retrieved 4 July 2014.

31.5 External links

- Download rom Free Chess Downloads: Oldies collection.

Chapter 32

Handwriting recognition

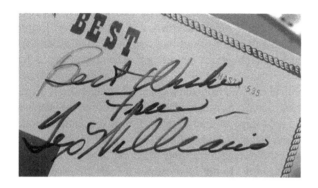

Signature of country star, Tex Williams.

Handwriting recognition (or **HWR**[1]) is the ability of a computer to receive and interpret intelligible handwritten input from sources such as paper documents, photographs, touch-screens and other devices. The image of the written text may be sensed "off line" from a piece of paper by optical scanning (optical character recognition) or intelligent word recognition. Alternatively, the movements of the pen tip may be sensed "on line", for example by a pen-based computer screen surface.

Handwriting recognition principally entails optical character recognition. However, a complete handwriting recognition system also handles formatting, performs correct segmentation into characters and finds the most plausible words.

32.1 Off-line recognition

Off-line handwriting recognition involves the automatic conversion of text in an image into letter codes which are usable within computer and text-processing applications. The data obtained by this form is regarded as a static representation of handwriting. Off-line handwriting recognition is comparatively difficult, as different people have different handwriting styles. And, as of today, OCR engines are primarily focused on machine printed text and ICR for hand "printed" (written in capital letters) text.

32.1.1 Problem domain reduction techniques

Narrowing the problem domain often helps increase the accuracy of handwriting recognition systems. A form field for a U.S. ZIP code, for example, would contain only the characters 0-9. This fact would reduce the number of possible identifications.

Primary techniques:

- Specifying specific character ranges
- Utilization of specialized forms

32.1.2 Character extraction

Off-line character recognition often involves scanning a form or document written sometime in the past. This means the individual characters contained in the scanned image will need to be extracted. Tools exist that are capable of performing this step.[2] However, there are several common imperfections in this step. The most common is when characters that are connected are returned as a single sub-image containing both characters. This causes a major problem in the recognition stage. Yet many algorithms are available that reduce the risk of connected characters.

32.1.3 Character recognition

After the extraction of individual characters occurs, a recognition engine is used to identify the corresponding computer character. Several different recognition techniques are currently available.

Neural networks

Neural network recognizers learn from an initial image training set. The trained network then makes the character identifications. Each neural network uniquely learns the properties that differentiate training images. It then looks for similar properties in the target image to be identified. Neural networks are quick to set up; however, they can be inaccurate if they learn properties that are not important in the target data.

Feature extraction

Feature extraction works in a similar fashion to neural network recognizers. However, programmers must manually determine the properties they feel are important.

Some example properties might be:

- Aspect Ratio.
- Percent of pixels above horizontal half point
- Percent of pixels to right of vertical half point
- Number of strokes
- Average distance from image center
- Is reflected y axis
- Is reflected x axis

This approach gives the recognizer more control over the properties used in identification. Yet any system using this approach requires substantially more development time than a neural network because the properties are not learned automatically.

32.2 On-line recognition

On-line handwriting recognition involves the automatic conversion of text as it is written on a special digitizer or PDA, where a sensor picks up the pen-tip movements as well as pen-up/pen-down switching. This kind of data is known as digital ink and can be regarded as a digital representation of handwriting. The obtained signal is converted into letter codes which are usable within computer and text-processing applications.

The elements of an on-line handwriting recognition interface typically include:

- a pen or stylus for the user to write with.
- a touch sensitive surface, which may be integrated with, or adjacent to, an output display.
- a software application which interprets the movements of the stylus across the writing surface, translating the resulting strokes into digital text.

32.2.1 General process

The process of online handwriting recognition can be broken down into a few general steps:

- preprocessing,
- feature extraction and
- classification.

The purpose of preprocessing is to discard irrelevant information in the input data, that can negatively affect the recognition.[3] This concerns speed and accuracy. Preprocessing usually consists of binarization, normalization, sampling, smoothing and denoising.[4] The second step is feature extraction. Out of the two- or more-dimensional vector field received from the preprocessing algorithms, higher-dimensional data is extracted. The purpose of this step is to highlight important information for the recognition model. This data may include information like pen pressure, velocity or the changes of writing direction. The last big step is classification. In this step various models are used to map the extracted features to different classes and thus identifying the characters or words the features represent.

Hardware

Commercial products incorporating handwriting recognition as a replacement for keyboard input were introduced in the early 1980s. Examples include handwriting terminals such as the Pencept Penpad[5] and the Inforite point-of-sale terminal.[6] With the advent of the large consumer market for personal computers, several commercial products were introduced to replace the keyboard and mouse on a personal computer with a single pointing/handwriting system, such as those from PenCept,[7] CIC[8] and others. The first commercially available tablet-type portable computer was the GRiDPad from GRiD Systems, released in September 1989. Its operating system was based on MS-DOS.

In the early 1990s, hardware makers including NCR, IBM and EO released tablet computers running the PenPoint operating system developed by GO Corp.. PenPoint used handwriting recognition and gestures throughout and provided the facilities to third-party software. IBM's tablet computer was the first to use the ThinkPad name and used IBM's handwriting recognition. This recognition system was later ported to Microsoft Windows for Pen Computing, and IBM's Pen for OS/2. None of these were commercially successful.

Advancements in electronics allowed the computing power necessary for handwriting recognition to fit into a smaller form factor than tablet computers, and handwriting recognition is often used as an input method for hand-held PDAs. The first PDA to provide written input was the Apple Newton, which exposed the public to the advantage of a streamlined user interface. However, the device was not a commercial success, owing to the unreliability of the software, which tried to learn a user's writing patterns. By the time of the release of the Newton OS 2.0, wherein the handwriting recognition was greatly improved, including unique features still not found in current recognition systems such as modeless error correction, the largely negative first impression had been made. After discontinuation of Apple Newton, the feature has been ported to Mac OS X 10.2 or later in form of Inkwell (Macintosh).

Palm later launched a successful series of PDAs based on the Graffiti recognition system. Graffiti improved usability by defining a set of "unistrokes", or one-stroke forms, for each character. This narrowed the possibility for erroneous input, although memorization of the stroke patterns did increase the learning curve for the user. The Graffiti handwriting recognition was found to infringe on a patent held by Xerox, and Palm replaced Graffiti with a licensed version of the CIC handwriting recognition which, while also supporting unistroke forms, pre-dated the Xerox patent. The court finding of infringement was reversed on appeal, and then reversed again on a later appeal. The parties involved subsequently negotiated a settlement concerning this and other patents Graffiti (Palm OS).

A Tablet PC is a special notebook computer that is outfitted with a digitizer tablet and a stylus, and allows a user to handwrite text on the unit's screen. The operating system recognizes the handwriting and converts it into typewritten text. Windows Vista and Windows 7 include personalization features that learn a user's writing patterns or vocabulary for English, Japanese, Chinese Traditional, Chinese Simplified and Korean. The features include a "personalization wizard" that prompts for samples of a user's handwriting and uses them to retrain the system for higher accuracy recognition. This system is distinct from the less advanced handwriting recognition system employed in its Windows Mobile OS for PDAs.

Although handwriting recognition is an input form that the public has become accustomed to, it has not achieved widespread use in either desktop computers or laptops. It is still generally accepted that keyboard input is both faster and more reliable. As of 2006, many PDAs offer handwriting input, sometimes even accepting natural cursive handwriting, but accuracy is still a problem, and some people still find even a simple on-screen keyboard more efficient.

32.2.2　Software

Initial software modules could understand print handwriting where the characters were separated. Author of the first applied pattern recognition program in 1962 was Shelia Guberman, then in Moscow.[9] Commercial examples came from companies such as Communications Intelligence Corporation and IBM. In the early 90s, two companies, ParaGraph International, and Lexicus came up with systems that could understand cursive handwriting recognition. ParaGraph was based in Russia and founded by computer scientist Stepan Pachikov while Lexicus was founded by Ronjon Nag and Chris Kortge who were students at Stanford University. The ParaGraph CalliGrapher system was deployed in the Apple Newton systems, and Lexicus Longhand system was made available commercially for the PenPoint and Windows operating system. Lexicus was acquired by Motorola in 1993 and went on to develop Chinese handwriting recognition and predictive text systems for Motorola. ParaGraph was acquired in 1997 by SGI and its handwriting recognition team formed a P&I division, later acquired from SGI by Vadem. Microsoft has acquired CalliGrapher handwriting recognition and other digital ink technologies developed by P&I from Vadem in 1999. Wolfram Mathematica (8.0 or later) also provides a handwriting or text recognition function TextRecognize[].

32.3　Research

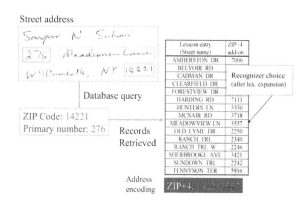

Method used for exploiting contextual information in the first handwritten address interpretation system developed by Sargur Srihari and Jonathan Hull [10]

Handwriting Recognition has an active community of academics studying it. The biggest conferences for handwriting recognition are the International Conference on Frontiers in Handwriting Recognition (ICFHR), held in even-numbered years, and the International Conference on Document Analysis and Recognition (ICDAR), held in odd-numbered years. Both of these conferences are endorsed by the IEEE. Active areas of research include:

- Online Recognition
- Offline Recognition
- Signature Verification
- Postal-Address Interpretation
- Bank-Check Processing
- Writer Recognition

A survey of research on handwriting recognition (2000) is by R. Plamondon and S. N. Srihari.[11] In India, the Technology Development for Indian Languages (TDIL[12]), under the Department of Information Technology,[13] Government of India, has funded a national level research consortium on online handwriting recognition in several Indian languages, led by Prof. A. G. Ramakrishnan, Medical intelligence and language engineering lab, Department of Electrical Engineering,[14] Indian Institute of Science, Bangalore.

32.4   Results since 2009

Since 2009, the recurrent neural networks and deep feedforward neural networks developed in the research group of Jürgen Schmidhuber at the Swiss AI Lab IDSIA have won several international handwriting competitions.[15] In particular, the bi-directional and multi-dimensional Long short term memory (LSTM)[16][17] of Alex Graves et al. won three competitions in connected handwriting recognition at the 2009 International Conference on Document Analysis and Recognition (ICDAR), without any prior knowledge about the three different languages (French, Arabic, Persian) to be learned. Recent GPU-based deep learning methods for feedforward networks by Dan Ciresan and colleagues at IDSIA won the ICDAR 2011 offline Chinese handwriting recognition contest; their neural networks also were the first artificial pattern recognizers to achieve human-competitive performance[18] on the famous MNIST handwritten digits problem[19] of Yann LeCun and colleagues at NYU.

32.5   See also

- Optical character recognition
- Intelligent character recognition
- AI effect

- Applications of artificial intelligence
- Handwriting movement analysis
- Neocognitron
- Pen computing
- Live Ink Character Recognition Solution
- Sketch recognition
- Tablet PC

32.5.1   Lists

- Outline of artificial intelligence
- List of emerging technologies

32.6   References

[1] http://acronyms.thefreedictionary.com/HWR

[2] Java OCR, 5 June 2010. Retrieved 5 June 2010

[3] Huang, B.; Zhang, Y. and Kechadi, M.; *Preprocessing Techniques for Online Handwriting Recognition. Intelligent Text Categorization and Clustering*, Springer Berlin Heidelberg, 2009, Vol. 164, "Studies in Computational Intelligence" pp. 25–45.

[4] Holzinger, A.; Stocker, C.; Peischl, B. and Simonic, K.-M.; *On Using Entropy for Enhancing Handwriting Preprocessing*, Entropy 2012, 14, pp. 2324-2350.

[5] *Pencept Penpad (TM) 200 Product Literature*, Pencept, Inc., 1982-08-15

[6] *Inforite Hand Character Recognition Terminal*, Cadre Systems Limited, England, 1982-08-15

[7] *Users Manual for Penpad 320*, Pencept, Inc., 1984-06-15

[8] *Handwriter (R) GrafText (TM) System Model GT-5000*, Communication Intelligence Corporation, 1985-01-15

[9] Guberman is the inventor of the handwriting recognition technology used today by Microsoft in Windows CE. Source: In-Q-Tel communication, june 3, 2003

[10] S. N. Srihari and E. J. Keubert, "Integration of handwritten address interpretation technology into the United States Postal Service Remote Computer Reader System" Proc. Int. Conf. Document Analysis and Recognition (ICDAR) 1997, IEEE-CS Press, pp. 892–896

[11] R. Plamondon and S. N. Srihari (2000). "On-line and offline handwriting recognition: a comprehensive survey". In: IEEE Transactions on Pattern Analysis and Machine Intelligence 22(1), 63–84.

[12] "TDIL". Department of Electronics & Information Technology(DeitY), MCIT, Govt of India. Retrieved 7 December 2014.

[13] "DeitY". Department Of Electronics & Information Technology, Government Of India. Retrieved 7 December 2014.

[14] A G, Ramakrishnan. "DEPARTMENT OF ELECTRICAL ENGINEEING". *http://www.ee.iisc.ernet.in/*. Indian Institute of Science, Bangalore, India. Retrieved 7 December 2014.

[15] 2012 Kurzweil AI Interview with Jürgen Schmidhuber on the eight competitions won by his Deep Learning team 2009-2012

[16] Graves, Alex; and Schmidhuber, Jürgen; *Offline Handwriting Recognition with Multidimensional Recurrent Neural Networks*, in Bengio, Yoshua; Schuurmans, Dale; Lafferty, John; Williams, Chris K. I.; and Culotta, Aron (eds.), *Advances in Neural Information Processing Systems 22 (NIPS'22), December 7th–10th, 2009, Vancouver, BC*, Neural Information Processing Systems (NIPS) Foundation, 2009, pp. 545–552

[17] A. Graves, M. Liwicki, S. Fernandez, R. Bertolami, H. Bunke, J. Schmidhuber. A Novel Connectionist System for Improved Unconstrained Handwriting Recognition. IEEE Transactions on Pattern Analysis and Machine Intelligence, vol. 31, no. 5, 2009.

[18] D. C. Ciresan, U. Meier, J. Schmidhuber. Multi-column Deep Neural Networks for Image Classification. IEEE Conf. on Computer Vision and Pattern Recognition CVPR 2012.

[19] LeCun, Y., Bottou, L., Bengio, Y., & Haffner, P. (1998). Gradient-based learning applied to document recognition. Proc. IEEE, 86, pp. 2278-2324.

32.7 External links

- Annotated bibliography of references to gesture and pen computing

- Notes on the History of Pen-based Computing (YouTube)

Chapter 33

Human-centered computing (NASA)

For other uses, see Human-centered computing (disambiguation).

Human-Centered Computing is the name of a subproject of NASA's Intelligent Systems Project. It is focused on the development of adaptive systems that amplify human cognitive, perceptual, and motor capabilities in such domains as: space, mission control operations, air traffic management, safety and security systems.

Chapter 34

Imense

Imense Ltd is a UK-based company that develops technology for Content-based image retrieval and automatic image annotation.

34.1 Imense

The founders of Imense are Dr Christopher Town and Dr David Sinclair. In their academic lives they developed the first 'Ontological Query Evaluation Language' (OQUEL) for image retrieval, which mapped a plain text user query onto a query over automatically recognized visual content in a corpus of images.

Technology derived in spirit from OQUEL is in routine use on the Imense PictureSearch portal. The user interface allows a user to type a plain text query that is probabilistically parsed to recognise visual aspects (like 'purple center green background' or 'group of five people') and non visual aspects (e.g. 'freedom' or 'Buddhism' or 'Parma ham'). The issues associated with scaling up image search to cope with tens of millions or more images were addressed with active support from the Science and Technology Facilities Council and GridPP.[1] News articles about Imense search technology include.[2][3][4]

34.2 Research

Key papers describing the birth and evolution of ontological query languages include: [5][6]

The research focus of Imense Ltd remains ontology based image content recognition. Imense uses cutting edge techniques from machine learning to build and train extremely-high-dimensional classifiers to help semantically label things in the visual world. Imense appears to use different types of visual models for different object classes — for example, Bayesian Constrained Local Models for parametric face modeling,[7] and SVMs for general semantic content labeling.[8]

34.3 References

[1] http://www.stfc.ac.uk/News+and+Events/3388.aspx

[2] news article 1

[3] news article 2

[4] news article 3

[5] Dr Town's Publications

[6] ORL Publications

[7] http://www.gmazars.info/conf/cvpr2009.html   Convexity and Bayesian Constrained Local Models Paquet, U.

[8] *Ontology based Visual Information Processing* (Town, 2004)

- *Language-based Querying of Image Collections on the basis of an Extensible Ontology* (Town and Sinclair, 2004)

34.4 External links

- imense.com Content based image search portal.

- annotator.imense.com Statistical assisted image annotation site.

Chapter 35

Intelligent character recognition

In computer science, **intelligent character recognition** (**ICR**) is an advanced optical character recognition (OCR) or — rather more specific — handwriting recognition system that allows fonts and different styles of handwriting to be learned by a computer during processing to improve accuracy and recognition levels.

Most ICR software has a self-learning system referred to as a neural network, which automatically updates the recognition database for new handwriting patterns. It extends the usefulness of scanning devices for the purpose of document processing, from printed character recognition (a function of OCR) to hand-written matter recognition. Because this process is involved in recognising hand writing, accuracy levels may, in some circumstances, not be very good but can achieve 97%+ accuracy rates in reading handwriting in structured forms. Often to achieve these high recognition rates several read engines are used within the software and each is given elective voting rights to determine the true reading of characters. In numeric fields, engines which are designed to read numbers take preference, while in alpha fields, engines designed to read hand written letters have higher elective rights. When used in conjunction with a bespoke interface hub, hand-written data can be automatically populated into a back office system avoiding laborious manual keying and can be more accurate than traditional human data entry.

An important development of ICR was the invention of Automated Forms Processing in 1993. This involved a three-stage process of capturing the image of the form to be processed by ICR and preparing it to enable the ICR engine to give best results, then capturing the information using the ICR engine and finally processing the results to automatically validate the output from the ICR engine.

This application of ICR increased the usefulness of the technology and made it applicable for use with real world forms in normal business applications. Modern software applications use ICR as a technology of recognizing text in forms filled in by hand (hand-printed).

35.1 Taking ICR to the Next Level

Intelligent word recognition (IWR) can recognize and extract not only printed-handwritten information, but cursive handwriting as well. ICR recognizes on the character-level, whereas IWR works with full words or phrases. Capable of capturing unstructured information from every day pages, IWR is said to be more evolved than hand print ICR (according to the CCA (Committee for Capturing Abstractions)).

Not meant to replace conventional ICR and OCR systems, IWR is optimized for processing real-world documents that contain mostly free-form, hard-to-recognize data fields that are inherently unsuitable for ICR. This means that the highest and best use of IWR is to eliminate a high percentage of the manual entry of handwritten data and run-on hand print fields on documents that otherwise could be keyed only by humans.

35.2 See also

- Handwriting recognition
- machine learning

Chapter 36

Intelligent software assistant

An **intelligent personal assistant** is a software agent that can perform tasks or services for an individual. These tasks or services are based on user input, location awareness, and the ability to access information from a variety of online sources (such as weather or traffic conditions, news, stock prices, user schedules, retail prices, etc.). Examples of such an agent are Apple's Siri, Google's Google Now, Amazon Echo, Microsoft's Cortana, Braina (application developed by Brainasoft for Microsoft Windows), Samsung's S Voice, LG's Voice Mate, BlackBerry's Assistant, SILVIA, HTC's Hidi, IBM's Watson_(computer), and Facebook's M.

36.1 Description

According to venture capitalist Chi-Hua Chien[1] of Kleiner Perkins Caufield & Byers, examples of tasks that may be performed by a smart personal agent-type of Intelligent Automated Assistant[2] include schedule management (e.g., sending an alert to a dinner date that a user is running late due to traffic conditions, update schedules for both parties, and change the restaurant reservation time) and personal health management (*e.g.*, monitoring caloric intake, heart rate and exercise regimen, then making recommendations for healthy choices).

Intelligent personal assistant technology are enabled by the combination of mobile devices, application programming interfaces (APIs), and the proliferation of mobile apps. However, intelligent automated assistants are designed to perform specific, one-time tasks specified by user voice instructions, while smart personal agents perform ongoing tasks (*e.g.*, schedule management) autonomously.

36.2 Aspects of an intelligent personal assistant

36.2.1 Organize and maintain Information

One of the key aspects of an intelligent personal assistant is its ability to organize and maintain information. This includes the management of emails, calendar events, files, to-do lists, etc.[3]

36.3 Comparison

36.4 See also

- Intelligent agent
- Software agent
- Knowledge Navigator

36.5 References

[1] "Chi-Hua Chien". CrunchBase. 2012-01-24. Retrieved 2012-02-03.

[2] Empson, Rip (2011-07-29). "Three Companies Chi-Hua Chien Of Kleiner Perkins Would Love To Invest In". TechCrunch. Retrieved 2012-02-03.

[3] Chaudhri, Vinay; Cheyer, Adam; Guili, Richard; Jarrold, Bill; Myers, Karen; Niekrasz, John, *A Case Study in Engineering a Knowledge Base for an Intelligent Personal Assistant* (PDF)

Chapter 37

Interactions Corporation

Interactions LLC[1] is a privately held[2] technology company that builds and delivers hosted Virtual Assistant applications that enable businesses to deliver automated natural language communications for customer care.

37.1 History

Interactions LLC was founded in 2004 and is headquartered in Boston (Franklin[3]), Massachusetts.[4] Interactions is Venture-backed by Sigma Partners, Cross Atlantic Capital Partners, Updata Partners, and North Hill Ventures. Michael Iacobucci serves as Interactions' CEO.[5] Interactions has additional offices in Indianapolis, Indiana (Corporate/Technology Center), and Austin, Texas (Technology Center).

In 2010, Interactions received PCI DSS compliance validation.[6]

In April 2012, Interactions was named a 2012 Gartner 'Cool Vendor' in CRM Customer Service and Social.[7]

In November 2014, Interactions announced the acquisition of AT&T's Speech and Language Technology group,[8] along with its AT&T Watson(SM) platform.

37.2 Services

Interactions' hosted customer care solutions work with and enhance existing IVR (Interactive Voice Response) platforms, speech platforms, and web applications. Operating under a SaaS business model, Interactions' service includes both an application's design and build, as well as continuous operating and tuning.[9]

37.3 Customers

Interactions' customer base includes multiple consumer-facing Fortune 500 companies, including Hyatt, Best Western,[10] and Humana,[11][12] representing the Telecommunication, Hospitality, Finance, Insurance and Warranty, Retail, Utility, Consumer Software and Electronics, and Healthcare industries.

37.4 References

[1] "Crunchbase: Interactions".

[2] "Interactions Corporation raises 12m more to ease the pains of automated customer service".

[3] "Franklin firm works to improve business interactions".

[4] "IT firm rakes in VC cash: Interactions Corp. has raised $35M since 2002 inception". *Indianapolis Business Journal*. Retrieved 1 March 2012.

[5] "Franklin firm works to improve business interactions". *MetroWest Daily News*. Retrieved 1 March 2012.

[6] "Interactions corp validated as PCI DSS compliant".

[7] "Interactions Corporation named 'Cool Vendor' by Leading Analyst Firm".

[8] "AT&T sells its Watson speech recognition tech to Interactions Corporation in equity deal".

[9] "Humana expands deployment of voice portal technology".

[10] "Go Back Interactions Corp. Partners with Best Western".

[11] "Interactions Corporation to expand relationship with Humana".

[12] "Automated agent will aid enrollees in Medicare". *Boston Globe*.

Chapter 38

Kasparov's Gambit

Kasparov's Gambit or simply *Gambit* is a chess playing computer program created by Heuristic Software and published by Electronic Arts in 1993 based on Socrates II, the only winner of the North American Computer Chess Championship running on a common microcomputer.[1] It was designed for DOS while Garry Kasparov reigned as world champion, whose involvement and support was its key allure.[2]

38.1 History

Julio Kaplan, chessplayer, computer programmer, and owner of the company 'Heuristic Software', first developed Heuristic Alpha in 1990-91.[3] The original version evolved into *Socrates* with the help of other chess players and programmers including Larry Kaufman and Don Dailey, who, later, were also developers of *Kasparov's Gambit*.[4]

Improvements to *Socrates* were reflected in a version called *Titan*, renamed for competition as *Socrates II*,[5] the most successful of the series winning the 1993 ACM International Chess Championship.[6] During the course of the championship *Socrates II*, which was running on a stock 486 PC, defeated opponents with purpose-built hardware and software for playing chess, including HiTech[7] and Cray Blitz.[8]

Electronic Arts purchased *Socrates II* and hired its creators to build a new product, *Kasparov's Gambit*, including Kasparov as consultant and brand. It was the company's effort to enter the chess programs market, dominated at the time by *Chessmaster 3000* and *Blitz*. In 1993 it went on sale, but contained a number of bugs, so was patched at the end of that year. The patched version ran at about 75% of the speed of *Socrates II* which was quite an achievement considering the whole functionality of the software was sharing the same computer resources.[9]

In 1993 it competed in the Harvard Cup (six humans versus six programs) facing grandmasters who had ratings ranging from 2515 to 2625 ELO,.[10] It finished the competition in 12th and last place. Grandmasters took the first five places and another *Socrates* derivation - *Socrates Exp* - was the best program finishing in 6th place. [11]

According to team-developer, Eric Schiller, a Windows version was planned by Electronic Arts, but was never finished.[12] Excluding chess-style board games like Archon: The Light and the Dark (1983) or Battle Chess II: Chinese Chess (2002), Kasparov's Gambit remains the sole effort of Electronic Arts to enter the classic chess software market.

38.2 Reception

It was hailed by *Computer Gaming World* as "a very good game. It was the best teaching chess program available until *Bobby Fischer Teaches Chess*, and was the first to offer a reasonable way to rate human play versus the computer. It's a shame EA hasn't updated this for Windows 95 with SVGA graphics, because it deserves to be played."[cite 1] It holds the 147th place in its 1996 list of *150 Best Games of All Time*.[13]

Regarding Garry Kasparov's successful title defense against Nigel Short in the same year, followed by its triumph at the 1993 International Computer Chess Championship and its user-friendly capabilities, *Gambit*[14] failed in sales and marked the end of Electronic Arts attempts to produce chess games.

38.3 Features

Gambit was intended to have the capabilities of a champion level software and a teaching tool for a wide range of player levels.[15] It was Electronic Arts' first use of windowed video[2] showing digitized images, video and voice of champ Garry Kasparov giving advice and commenting on player moves.[16]

Primary features include:[17][18]

- Interactive tutorial with video-help by Garry Kasparov

- An inline glossary of chess terms

- A library of 500 famous games played by past world champions

- An auxiliary graphical chessboard showing the computer's analysis while playing or reviewing moves

- A interactive move list

- An analysis text box, showing move's elapsed time, depth, score of the best evaluated line and number of positions seek

- Multiple computer playing styles allowing creation and customization of computer opponents

- A coach window including the moves played and comments about apertures and advices, sometimes showing videos of Kasparov

38.3.1 Rating

The human strength rating is calculated using Elo formula with the included personalities and the one of player himself/herself, going from 800 to 2800 points. New players get a customizable 800 ELO, which changes according the total number of games played, opponents strength and result of game.[19]

Creation of personalities enables five adjustable characteristics in percentage (0-100%)—strength, orthodoxy, creativity, focus and aggresivness—which define, besides its style, its ELO rating.[20] User ELO is calculated according to *Gambit's* universe of electronic players and user him/herself, thus do not match rankings in real world, instead this feature was designed to provide a useful way to measure player strength and progress against *Gambit*.[21]

38.3.2 Teaching tools

Besides 125 tutorials, written by renowned chess author and developer Eric Schiller,[22] classified in openings, middle game, endgames (checkmates), tactics and strategy also include a *Famous Games* database, a list of all-time world champions games commented by Kasparov with a quiz option where user most choose the next move.[23]

38.4 Technical information

Was designed for 386SX IBM AT compatible systems. Even when it's capable to read commands from keyboard or mouse, the use of mouse is recommended. During the days it was released, *Kasparov's Gambit* offered a nice *look & feel* experience using SVGA mode with 640x480 resolution and 256 colors and voice/video recordings of world champion Garry Kasparov. A lack of soundcards support was reported by users.[24]

It is playable in DOSBox emulator since 0.61 version over GNU/Linux and other Unix-like operating systems, Windows XP and subsequent versions and Mac OS X.[25]

38.4.1 Development

First intention was using *Heuristic Alpha* as *Gambit's* base, but unexpected good performance of *Socrates II* in tournaments made of it the final choice. According to developer and tester Larry Kauffman[26] "first released included important bugs, that Knowledge of bishop mobility appears to be missing, as does some other chess knowledge, and Gambit appears to run only about 50-60% of the speed of the ACM program in positions (without bishops) where the two do play and evaluate identically. There are also bugs in the features and the time controls, and the program is rather difficult to use (perhaps because it has so many features). One good thing I can say is that the 3d graphics are superb... I have tested the patched version, and have confirmed that most or all of the bugs have been corrected. The new version does play identically to the ACM program and runs at 70-75% of the speed, so it should rate just 30 points below the ACM program." [cite 2]

Socrates II engine was fully programmed in assembly language, but rewritten just in C language for *Kasparov's Gambit* engine. Instead, assembly language was used for sound and video capabilities, as for other functionalities.

38.5 See also

- Computer chess

- Vintage software

- List of Electronic Arts games

38.6 Notes

[1] Moby Games. "Kasparov's Gambit". Computer Gaming World. Retrieved September 11, 2012.

[2] Kauffman, Larry. "PC-Software". Computer Chess Report. Retrieved September 19, 2012.

38.7   External links

- Games played at *1993 Harvards Cup* by *Kasparov's Gambit* at 365Chess.com.

38.8   References

[1] Wall, Bill. ACM Computer Chess. Consulted on September 6, 2012

[2] Kasparov's Gambit. Moby Games. Consulted on September 6, 2012

[3] Heuristic Alpha. CPW Chess Programming Wiki. Consulted on September 19, 2012.

[4] Julio Kaplan Chess Programming Wiki Retrieved on September 6, 2012

[5] Socrates. Chess Programming Wiki Retrieved on Sempember 6, 2012

[6] ACM 1993 Chess Programming Wiki. Retrieved on September 6, 2012

[7] HiTech Chess Programming Wiki. Retrieved on Septembre 6, 2012

[8] Cray Blitz Chess Programming Wiki

[9] Kasparov's Gambit. Chess Programming Wiki. Retrieved on September 6, 2012

[10] Comp Kasparov's Gambit. 365Chess.com. Consulted on September 19, 2012.

[11] Harvard Cup 1993. Computershaak. Retrieved on September 19, 2012.

[12] Schiller, Eric. (1996). Kasparov's Gambit vs. CM4000. Newsgroup rec.games.chess.computer. Retrieved on September 19, 2012.

[13] 150 Best Games of All Time. CDAccess.com. Retrieved on September 6, 2012.

[14] Lynch, Dennis.The $699.95 Question. *Chicago Tribune* article from November 18, 1993. Retrieved on September 19, 2012.

[15] Kasparov's Gambit Guide to Chess (1993). Electronic Arts

[16] Kasparov's Gambit Home of the Underdogs. Retrieved on September 6, 2012

[17] Kasparov's Gambit. CDAccess. Consulted on September 6, 2012

[18] Kasparov's Gambit User's Manual (1993). Electronic Arts

[19] Schiller, E. "How to get the most out of Gambit". Kasparov's Gambit User's Manual (1993). Electronic Arts. p. 10.

[20] Kasparov's Gambit Online Help. (1993). U.S.A: Electronic Arts

[21] Opinions about Kasparov's Gambit. Newsgroup rec.games.chess.computer. Retrieved on September 19, 2012

[22] Schiller, Eric. (1996). Opinions on Kasparovs Gambit program?. September 19, 2012

[23] Schiller, E. "How to get the most out of Gambit". Kasparov's Gambit User's Manual (1993). Electronic Arts. p. 12.

[24] corey_russell. Play chess with Kasparov kibitzing. Forum Epinions. Retrieved on September 19, 2012.

[25] DOSBox. Consulted on September 19, 2012.

[26] Kauffman, Larry. (1993). Read in Kasparov's Gambit History. Retrieved on September 19, 2012.

Chapter 39

Language Acquisition Device (computer)

This article is about the computer program. For the hypothetical part of the brain, see Language acquisition device.

The **Language Acquisition Device** is a computer program developed by Lobal Technologies, a computer company in the United Kingdom, and scientists from King's College. It emulates the functions of the brain's frontal lobes where humans process language and emotion.[1]

Scientists hope this might enable computers to understand, speak, learn, and eventually think. One possible use is in interactive entertainment such as video gaming, where the technology is used to help computer-controlled characters to develop.[1] A press release describing this technology produced widespread media interest in 2002, but no reports have been published since then, and the current status of the technology is unclear.

39.1 See also

- Ethics of artificial intelligence

39.2 External links, references

[1] Games to take on a life of their own: Copying the brain's neural networks By Alfred Hermida, BBC News Online 11 February 2002.

Chapter 40

Language identification

For language identifiers, see Language code. For assistance in identifying languages for Wikipedia purposes, see Wikipedia:Language recognition chart.

In natural language processing, **language identification** or **language guessing** is the problem of determining which natural language given content is in. Computational approaches to this problem view it as a special case of text categorization, solved with various statistical methods.

40.1 Overview

There are several statistical approaches to language identification using different techniques to classify the data. One technique is to compare the compressibility of the text to the compressibility of texts in a set of known languages. This approach is known as mutual information based distance measure. The same technique can also be used to empirically construct family trees of languages which closely correspond to the trees constructed using historical methods. Mutual information based distance measure is essentially equivalent to more conventional model-based methods and is not generally considered to be either novel or better than simpler techniques. Bennedetto, et al.'s work has largely been discredited as relatively naive and inaccurate.

Another technique, as described by Cavnar and Trenkle (1994) and Dunning (1994) is to create a language n-gram model from a "training text" for each of the languages. These models can be based on characters (Cavnar and Trenkle) or encoded bytes (Dunning); in the latter, language identification and character encoding detection are integrated. Then, for any piece of text needing to be identified, a similar model is made, and that model is compared to each stored language model. The most likely language is the one with the model that is most similar to the model from the text needing to be identified. This approach can be problematic when the input text is in a language for which there

is no model. In that case, the method may return another, "most similar" language as its result. Also problematic for any approach are pieces of input text that are composed of several languages, as is common on the Web.

For a more recent method, see Řehůřek and Kolkus (2009). This method can detect multiple languages in an unstructured piece of text and works robustly on short texts of only a few words: something that the n-gram approaches struggle with.

An older statistical method by Grefenstette was based on the prevalence of certain function words (e.g., "the" in English).

40.2 Identifying Similar Languages

One of the great bottlenecks of language identification systems is to distinguish between closely related languages. Similar languages like Serbian and Croatian or Indonesian and Malay present significant lexical and structural overlap, making it challenging for systems to discriminate between them.

Recently, the DSL shared task [1] has been organized providing a dataset (Tan et al., 2014) containing 13 different languages (and language varieties) in six language groups: Group A (Bosnian, Croatian, Serbian), Group B (Indonesian, Malaysian), Group C (Czech, Slovakian), Group D (Brazilian Portuguese, European Portuguese), Group E (Peninsular Spain, Argentine Spanish), Group F (American English, British English). The best system reached performance of over 95% results (Goutte et al., 2014). Results of the DSL shared task are described in Zampieri et al. 2014.

40.3 References

- Joshua Goodman. Extended Comment on Language Trees and Zipping. arXiv:cond-mat/0202383 [cond-mat.stat-mech]

- Benedetto, D., E. Caglioti and V. Loreto. Language trees and zipping. *Physical Review Letters*, 88:4 (2002), Complexity theory.

- Cavnar, William B. and John M. Trenkle. "N-Gram-Based Text Categorization". Proceedings of SDAIR-94, 3rd Annual Symposium on Document Analysis and Information Retrieval (1994).

- Cilibrasi, Rudi and Paul M.B. Vitanyi. "Clustering by compression". *IEEE Transactions on Information Theory* 51(4), April 2005, 1523-1545.

- Dunning, T. (1994) "Statistical Identification of Language". Technical Report MCCS 94-273, New Mexico State University, 1994.

- Goodman, Joshua. (2002) Extended comment on "Language Trees and Zipping". Microsoft Research, Feb 21 2002. (This is a criticism of the data compression in favor of the Naive Bayes method.)

- Goutte, C.; Leger, S.; Carpuat, M. (2014) The NRC System for Discriminating Similar Languages. Proceedings of the Coling 2014 workshop "Applying NLP Tools to Similar Languages, Varieties and Dialects"

- Grefenstette, Gregory. (1995) Comparing two language identification schemes. *Proceedings of the 3rd International Conference on the Statistical Analysis of Textual Data* (JADT 1995).

- Poutsma, Arjen. (2001) Applying Monte Carlo techniques to language identification. SmartHaven, Amsterdam. Presented at CLIN 2001.

- Tan, L.; Zampieri, M.; Ljubešić, N.; Tiedemann, J. (2014) Merging Comparable Data Sources for the Discrimination of Similar Languages: The DSL Corpus Collection. Proceedings of the 7th Workshop on Building and Using Comparable Corpora (BUCC). Reykjavik, Iceland. p. 6-10

- The Economist. (2002) "The elements of style: Analysing compressed data leads to impressive results in linguistics"

- Radim Řehůřek and Milan Kolkus. (2009) "Language Identification on the Web: Extending the Dictionary Method" *Computational Linguistics and Intelligent Text Processing*.

- Zampieri, M.; Tan, L.; Ljubešić, N.; Tiedemann, J. (2014) A Report on the DSL Shared Task 2014. Proceedings of the 1st Workshop on Applying NLP Tools to Similar Languages, Varieties and Dialects (VarDial). Dublin, Ireland. p. 58-67.

40.4 See also

- Native Language Identification
- Algorithmic information theory
- Artificial grammar learning
- Family name affixes
- Kolmogorov complexity
- Language Analysis for the Determination of Origin
- Machine translation
- Translation

40.5 References

[1] http://corporavm.uni-koeln.de/vardial/sharedtask.html

40.6 External links

- S.M. Mohammadzadeh: Language identification/detection related documents (26 February 2011).

- System and method for identifying the language of written text having a plurality of different length n-gram profiles

- Graph of letter positions within words for 8 languages - statistical analysis chart

- DSL Shared Task

40.6.1 Libraries

- LID - Language Identification in Python: algorithm and code example of an n-gram based LID tool in Python and Scheme by Damir Cavar.

- lid Language Identifier: by Lingua-Systems; C/C++ library and Perl Extension (online demo).

- lc4j, a language categorization Java library, by Marco Olivo.

- Microsoft Extended Linguistic Services for Windows 7: including Microsoft Language Detection.

- Windows 7 API Code Pack for .NET: including managed interfaces for the above.

- NTextCat - free Language Identification API for .NET (C#): 280+ languages available out of the box. Recognizes language and encoding (UTF-8, Windows-1252, Big5, etc.) of text. Mono compatible.

- jsli - pure JavaScript Language Identification library.

- cldr-R library for Chromium-Author's Compact Language Detection code.

- language-detection: open-source language detection library for Java (forks: lang-guess and language-detector).

- cld2: open-source language detection library for C++ by Google

- GuessLanguage: open-source language detection library for javascript

- GuessLanguage: open-source language detection library for python

- Text LanguageDetect: pear language detect (not maintained currently)

- datagram: open-source MIT JavaScript classification library. Automatically classify and recognize languages of input data. It can be used for any type of classification based on trained data.

- textcat: R library for text categorization based on n-grams

- Rosette Language Identifier Commercial language identifier with short string (<20 bytes) detection, in Java and C++

40.6.2 Web services

- Language Identification Web Service: language detection API (JSON and XML) that detects 100+ languages in texts, websites and documents

- Language Detection API: simple language identification API

- Language Detection API: language identification RESTful API, part of Dandelion API, a semantic APIs family (named entity extraction, text similarity etc.)

- AlchemyAPI: language identification API, available as SDK and through a RESTfull API (web-based demonstration).

- PetaMem Language Identification: provides a choice between ngram, nvect and smart methods.

- Open Xerox LanguageIdentifier, available in web-based form or through API.

- GlobalNLP: web-based language identification

- Language Detector, Online identification from text or URL and API available for developers.

- What Language Is This? Online language identifier: web-based tool written by Henrik Falck.

- Rosette Language Identifier: product by Basis Technology.

- Language Identifier: product by Sematext; exposes Java API and is available through REST/Webservice.

- G2LI (Global Information Infrastructure Laboratory's Language Identifier).

- Rosoka Cloud by IMT Holdings provides language ID, entity and relationship extraction RESTfull web services available through Amazon Web Services Marketplace.

- Semantria sentiment and text analytics API which features language detection

- Loque.la Language Detection API: Website language identification with API, (json/XML)

Chapter 41

Machine translation

This article is about automated translation of natural languages. For automated translation of programming languages, see translation (computing). For the Australian musician, see Machine Translations.

Machine translation, sometimes referred to by the abbreviation **MT** (not to be confused with **computer-aided translation**, **machine-aided human translation (MAHT)** or **interactive translation**) is a sub-field of computational linguistics that investigates the use of software to translate text or speech from one language to another.

On a basic level, MT performs simple substitution of words in one language for words in another, but that alone usually cannot produce a good translation of a text because recognition of whole phrases and their closest counterparts in the target language is needed. Solving this problem with corpus and statistical techniques is a rapidly growing field that is leading to better translations, handling differences in linguistic typology, translation of idioms, and the isolation of anomalies.[1]

Current machine translation software often allows for customization by domain or profession (such as weather reports), improving output by limiting the scope of allowable substitutions. This technique is particularly effective in domains where formal or formulaic language is used. It follows that machine translation of government and legal documents more readily produces usable output than conversation or less standardised text.

Improved output quality can also be achieved by human intervention: for example, some systems are able to translate more accurately if the user has unambiguously identified which words in the text are proper names. With the assistance of these techniques, MT has proven useful as a tool to assist human translators and, in a very limited number of cases, can even produce output that can be used as is (e.g., weather reports).

The progress and potential of machine translation have been debated much through its history. Since the 1950s, a num-ber of scholars have questioned the possibility of achieving fully automatic machine translation of high quality.[2] Some critics claim that there are in-principle obstacles to automatizing the translation process.[3]

41.1 History

Main article: History of machine translation

The idea of machine translation may be traced back to the 17th century. In 1629, René Descartes proposed a universal language, with equivalent ideas in different tongues sharing one symbol. The field of "machine translation" appeared in Warren Weaver's Memorandum on Translation (1949). The first researcher in the field, Yehosha Bar-Hillel, began his research at MIT (1951). A Georgetown University MT research team followed (1951) with a public demonstration of its Georgetown-IBM experiment system in 1954. MT research programs popped up in Japan and Russia (1955), and the first MT conference was held in London (1956). Researchers continued to join the field as the Association for Machine Translation and Computational Linguistics was formed in the U.S. (1962) and the National Academy of Sciences formed the Automatic Language Processing Advisory Committee (ALPAC) to study MT (1964). Real progress was much slower, however, and after the ALPAC report (1966), which found that the ten-year-long research had failed to fulfill expectations, funding was greatly reduced. According to a 1972 report by the Director of Defense Research and Engineering (DDR&E), the feasibility of large-scale MT was reestablished by the success of the Logos MT system in translating military manuals into Vietnamese during that conflict.

The French Textile Institute also used MT to translate abstracts from and into French, English, German and Spanish (1970); Brigham Young University started a project to translate Mormon texts by automated translation (1971); and Xerox used SYSTRAN to translate technical manuals (1978). Beginning in the late 1980s, as computational power increased and became less expensive, more inter-est was shown in statistical models for machine translation. Various MT companies were launched, including Trados (1984), which was the first to develop and market transla-tion memory technology (1989). The first commercial MT system for Russian / English / German-Ukrainian was de-veloped at Kharkov State University (1991).

MT on the web started with SYSTRAN Offering free trans-lation of small texts (1996), followed by AltaVista Ba-belfish, which racked up 500,000 requests a day (1997). Franz-Josef Och (the future head of Translation Devel-opment AT Google) won DARPA's speed MT competi-tion (2003). More innovations during this time included MOSES, the open-source statistical MT engine (2007), a text/SMS translation service for mobiles in Japan (2008), and a mobile phone with built-in speech-to-speech transla-tion functionality for English, Japanese and Chinese (2009). Recently, Google announced that Google Translate trans-lates roughly enough text to fill 1 million books in one day (2012).

The idea of using digital computers for translation of natu-ral languages was proposed as early as 1946 by A. D. Booth and possibly others. Warren Weaver wrote an important memorandum "Translation" in 1949. The Georgetown ex-periment was by no means the first such application, and a demonstration was made in 1954 on the APEXC machine at Birkbeck College (University of London) of a rudimen-tary translation of English into French. Several papers on the topic were published at the time, and even articles in popular journals (see for example *Wireless World*, Sept. 1955, Cleave and Zacharov). A similar application, also pioneered at Birkbeck College at the time, was reading and composing Braille texts by computer.

41.2 Translation process

Main article: Translation process

The human translation process may be described as:

1. Decoding the meaning of the source text; and

2. Re-encoding this meaning in the target language.

Behind this ostensibly simple procedure lies a complex cognitive operation. To decode the meaning of the source text in its entirety, the translator must interpret and analyse all the features of the text, a process that requires in-depth knowledge of the grammar, semantics, syntax, idioms, etc., of the source language, as well as the culture of its speak-ers. The translator needs the same in-depth knowledge to re-encode the meaning in the target language.

Therein lies the challenge in machine translation: how to program a computer that will "understand" a text as a person does, and that will "create" a new text in the target language that "sounds" as if it has been written by a person.

In its most general application, this is beyond current tech-nology. Though it works much faster, no automated trans-lation program or procedure, with no human participation, can produce output even close to the quality a human trans-lator can produce. What it can do, however, is provide a general, though imperfect, approximation of the original text, getting the "gist" of it (a process called "gisting"). This is sufficient for many purposes, including making best use of the finite and expensive time of a human translator, re-served for those cases in which total accuracy is indispens-able.

This problem may be approached in a number of ways, through the evolution of which accuracy has improved.

41.3 Approaches

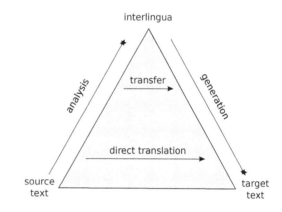

Bernard Vauquois' pyramid showing comparative depths of in-termediary representation, interlingual machine translation at the peak, followed by transfer-based, then direct translation.

Machine translation can use a method based on linguistic rules, which means that words will be translated in a lin-guistic way – the most suitable (orally speaking) words of the target language will replace the ones in the source lan-guage.

It is often argued that the success of machine translation requires the problem of natural language understanding to be solved first.

Generally, rule-based methods parse a text, usually creat-ing an intermediary, symbolic representation, from which the text in the target language is generated. According to the nature of the intermediary representation, an approach is described as interlingual machine translation or transfer-based machine translation. These methods require extensive lexicons with morphological, syntactic, and semantic information, and large sets of rules.

Given enough data, machine translation programs often work well enough for a native speaker of one language to get the approximate meaning of what is written by the other native speaker. The difficulty is getting enough data of the right kind to support the particular method. For example, the large multilingual corpus of data needed for statistical methods to work is not necessary for the grammar-based methods. But then, the grammar methods need a skilled linguist to carefully design the grammar that they use.

To translate between closely related languages, the technique referred to as rule-based machine translation may be used.

41.3.1 Rule-based

Main article: Rule-based machine translation

The rule-based machine translation paradigm includes transfer-based machine translation, interlingual machine translation and dictionary-based machine translation paradigms. This type of translation is used mostly in the creation of dictionaries and grammar programs. Unlike other methods, RBMT involves more information about the linguistics of the source and target languages, using the morphological and syntactic rules and semantic analysis of both languages. The basic approach involves linking the structure of the input sentence with the structure of the output sentence using a parser and an analyzer for the source language, a generator for the target language, and a transfer lexicon for the actual translation. RBMT's biggest downfall is that everything must be done explicit: orthographical variation and erroneous input must be made part of the source language analyser in order to cope with it, and lexical selection rules must be written for all instances of ambiguity. Adapting to new domains in itself is not that hard, as the core grammar is the same across domains, and the domain-specific adjustment is limited to lexical selection adjustment.

Transfer-based machine translation

Main article: Transfer-based machine translation

Transfer-based machine translation is similar to interlingual machine translation in that it creates a translation from an intermediate representation that simulates the meaning of the original sentence. Unlike interlingual MT, it depends partially on the language pair involved in the translation.

Interlingual

Main article: Interlingual machine translation

Interlingual machine translation is one instance of rule-based machine-translation approaches. In this approach, the source language, i.e. the text to be translated, is transformed into an interlingual language, i.e. a "language neutral" representation that is independent of any language. The target language is then generated out of the interlingua. One of the major advantages of this system is that the interlingua becomes more valuable as the number of target languages it can be turned into increases. However, the only interlingual machine translation system that has been made operational at the commercial level is the KANT system (Nyberg and Mitamura, 1992), which is designed to translate Caterpillar Technical English (CTE) into other languages.

Dictionary-based

Main article: Dictionary-based machine translation

Machine translation can use a method based on dictionary entries, which means that the words will be translated as they are by a dictionary.

41.3.2 Statistical

Main article: Statistical machine translation

Statistical machine translation tries to generate translations using statistical methods based on bilingual text corpora, such as the Canadian Hansard corpus, the English-French record of the Canadian parliament and EUROPARL, the record of the European Parliament. Where such corpora are available, good results can be achieved translating similar texts, but such corpora are still rare for many language pairs. The first statistical machine translation software was CANDIDE from IBM. Google used SYSTRAN for several years, but switched to a statistical translation method in October 2007.[4] In 2005, Google improved its internal translation capabilities by using approximately 200 billion words from United Nations materials to train their system; translation accuracy improved.[5] Google Translate and similar statistical translation programs work by detecting patterns in hundreds of millions of documents that have previously been translated by humans and making intelligent guesses based on the findings. Generally, the more human-translated documents available in a given language, the more likely it is that the translation will be of good quality.[6] Newer approaches into Statistical Machine translation such as METIS II and PRESEMT use minimal corpus size and instead focus on derivation of syntactic structure through pattern recognition. With further development, this may allow statistical machine translation to operate off of a monolingual text corpus.[7] SMT's biggest downfall includes it being dependent upon huge amounts of parallel texts, its problems with morphology-rich languages (especially with translating *into* such languages), and its inability to correct singleton errors.

41.3.3 Example-based

Main article: Example-based machine translation

Example-based machine translation (EBMT) approach was proposed by Makoto Nagao in 1984.[8][9] Example-based machine translation is based on the idea of analogy. In this approach, the corpus that is used is one that contains texts that have already been translated. Given a sentence that is to be translated, sentences from this corpus are selected that contain similar sub-sentential components.[10] The similar sentences are then used to translate the sub-sentential components of the original sentence into the target language, and these phrases are put together to form a complete translation.

41.3.4 Hybrid MT

Main article: Hybrid machine translation

Hybrid machine translation (HMT) leverages the strengths of statistical and rule-based translation methodologies.[11] Several MT organizations (such as Asia Online, LinguaSys, Systran, and Polytechnic University of Valencia) claim a hybrid approach that uses both rules and statistics. The approaches differ in a number of ways:

- **Rules post-processed by statistics**: Translations are performed using a rules based engine. Statistics are then used in an attempt to adjust/correct the output from the rules engine.

- **Statistics guided by rules**: Rules are used to pre-process data in an attempt to better guide the statistical engine. Rules are also used to post-process the statistical output to perform functions such as normalization. This approach has a lot more power, flexibility and control when translating.

41.4 Major issues

41.4.1 Disambiguation

Main article: Word sense disambiguation

Word-sense disambiguation concerns finding a suitable translation when a word can have more than one meaning. The problem was first raised in the 1950s by Yehoshua Bar-Hillel.[12] He pointed out that without a "universal encyclopedia", a machine would never be able to distinguish between the two meanings of a word.[13] Today there are numerous approaches designed to overcome this problem. They can be approximately divided into "shallow" approaches and "deep" approaches.

Shallow approaches assume no knowledge of the text. They simply apply statistical methods to the words surrounding the ambiguous word. Deep approaches presume a comprehensive knowledge of the word. So far, shallow approaches have been more successful.

Claude Piron, a long-time translator for the United Nations and the World Health Organization, wrote that machine translation, at its best, automates the easier part of a translator's job; the harder and more time-consuming part usually involves doing extensive research to resolve ambiguities in the source text, which the grammatical and lexical exigencies of the target language require to be resolved:

> Why does a translator need a whole workday to translate five pages, and not an hour or two? ..... About 90% of an average text corresponds to these simple conditions. But unfortunately, there's the other 10%. It's that part that requires six [more] hours of work. There are ambiguities one has to resolve. For instance, the author of the source text, an Australian physician, cited the example of an epidemic which was declared during World War II in a "Japanese prisoner of war camp". Was he talking about an American camp with Japanese prisoners or a Japanese camp with American prisoners? The English has two senses. It's necessary therefore to do research, maybe to the extent of a phone call to Australia.[14]

The ideal deep approach would require the translation software to do all the research necessary for this kind of disambiguation on its own; but this would require a higher degree of AI than has yet been attained. A shallow approach which simply guessed at the sense of the ambiguous English phrase that Piron mentions (based, perhaps, on which kind of prisoner-of-war camp is more often mentioned in a given corpus) would have a reasonable chance of guessing wrong fairly often. A shallow approach that involves "ask the user about each ambiguity" would, by Piron's estimate, only automate about 25% of a professional translator's job, leaving the harder 75% still to be done by a human.

41.4.2 Non-standard speech

One of the major pitfalls of MT is its inability to translate non-standard language with the same accuracy as standard language. Heuristic or statistical based MT takes input from various sources in standard form of a language. Rule-based translation, by nature, does not include common non-standard usages. This causes errors in translation from a vernacular source or into colloquial language. Limitations on translation from casual speech present issues in the use of machine translation in mobile devices.

41.4.3 Named entities

> Related to named entity recognition in information extraction.

Name entities, in narrow sense, refer to concrete or abstract entities in the real world including people, organizations, companies, places etc. It also refers to expressing of time, space, quantity such as 1 July 2011, $79.99 and so on.[15]

Named entities occur in the text being analyzed in statistical machine translation. The initial difficulty that arises in dealing with named entities is simply identifying them in the text. Consider the list of names common in a particular language to illustrate this – the most common names are different for each language and also are constantly changing. If named entities cannot be recognized by the machine translator, they may be erroneously translated as common nouns, which would most likely not affect the BLEU rating of the translation but would change the text's human readability.[16] It is also possible that, when not identified, named entities will be omitted from the output translation, which would also have implications for the text's readability and message.

Another way to deal with named entities is to use transliteration instead of translation, meaning that you find the letters in the target language that most closely correspond to the name in the source language. There have been attempts to incorporate this into machine translation by adding a transliteration step into the translation procedure. However, these attempts still have their problems and have even been cited as worsening the quality of translation.[17] Named entities were still identified incorrectly, with words not being transliterated when they should or being transliterated when they shouldn't. For example, for "Southern California" the first word should be translated directly, while

the second word should be transliterated. However, machines would often transliterate both because they treated them as one entity. Words like these are hard for machine translators, even those with a transliteration component, to process.

The lack of attention to the issue of named entity translation has been recognized as potentially stemming from a lack of resources to devote to the task in addition to the complexity of creating a good system for named entity translation. One approach to named entity translation has been to transliterate, and not translate, those words. A second is to create a "do-not-translate" list, which has the same end goal – transliteration as opposed to translation.[18] Both of these approaches still rely on the correct identification of named entities, however.

A third approach to successful named entity translation is a class-based model. In this method, named entities are replaced with a token to represent the class they belong to. For example, "Ted" and "Erica" would both be replaced with "person" class token. In this way the statistical distribution and use of person names in general can be analyzed instead of looking at the distributions of "Ted" and "Erica" individually. A problem that the class based model solves is that the probability of a given name in a specific language will not affect the assigned probability of a translation. A study by Stanford on improving this area of translation gives the examples that different probabilities will be assigned to "David is going for a walk" and "Ankit is going for a walk" for English as a target language due to the different number of occurrences for each name in the training data. A frustrating outcome of the same study by Stanford (and other attempts to improve named recognition translation) is that many times, a decrease in the BLEU scores for translation will result from the inclusion of methods for named entity translation.[18]

41.5 Translation from multiparallel sources

Some work has been done in the utilization of multiparallel corpora, that is, a body of text which has been translated into 3 or more languages. Using these methods, a text which has been translated into 2 or more languages may be utilized in combination to provide a more accurate translation into a third language compared to if just one of those source languages were used alone. [19][20][21]

41.6   Ontologies in MT

An ontology is a formal representation of knowledge which includes the concepts (such as objects, processes etc.) in a domain and some relations between them. If the stored information is of linguistic nature, one can speak of a lexicon.[22] In NLP, ontologies can be used as a source of knowledge for machine translation systems. With access to a large knowledge base, systems can be enabled to resolve many (especially lexical) ambiguities on their own. In the following classic examples, as humans, we are able to interpret the prepositional phrase according to the context because we use our world knowledge, stored in our lexicons:

> "I saw a man/star/molecule with a microscope/telescope/binoculars."[22]

A machine translation system initially would not be able to differentiate between the meanings because syntax does not change. With a large enough ontology as a source of knowledge however, the possible interpretations of ambiguous words in a specific context can be reduced. Other areas of usage for ontologies within NLP include information retrieval, information extraction and text summarization.[22]

41.6.1   Building ontologies

The ontology generated for the PANGLOSS knowledge-based machine translation system in 1993 may serve as an example of how an ontology for NLP purposes can be compiled:[23]

- A large-scale ontology is necessary to help parsing in the active modules of the machine translation system.

- In the PANGLOSS example, about 50.000 nodes were intended to be subsumed under the smaller, manually-built *upper* (abstract) *region* of the ontology. Because of its size, it had to be created automatically.

- The goal was to merge the two resources LDOCE online and WordNet to combine the benefits of both: concise definitions from Longman, and semantic relations allowing for semi-automatic taxonomization to the ontology from WordNet.

  - A *definition match* algorithm was created to automatically merge the correct meanings of ambiguous words between the two online resources, based on the words that the definitions of those meanings have in common in LDOCE and WordNet. Using a similarity matrix, the algorithm delivered matches between meanings including a confidence factor. This algorithm

alone, however, did not match all meanings correctly on its own.

  - A second *hierarchy match* algorithm was therefore created which uses the taxonomic hierarchies found in WordNet (deep hierarchies) and partially in LDOCE (flat hierarchies). This works by first matching unambiguous meanings, then limiting the search space to only the respective ancestors and descendants of those matched meanings. Thus, the algorithm matched locally unambiguous meanings (for instance, while the word *seal* as such is ambiguous, there is only one meaning of *"seal"* in the *animal* subhierarchy).

- Both algorithms complemented each other and helped constructing a large-scale ontology for the machine translation system. The WordNet hierarchies, coupled with the matching definitions of LDOCE, were subordinated to the ontology's *upper region*. As a result, the PANGLOSS MT system was able to make use of this knowledge base, mainly in its generation element.

41.7   Applications

While no system provides the holy grail of fully automatic high-quality machine translation of unrestricted text, many fully automated systems produce reasonable output.[24][25][26] The quality of machine translation is substantially improved if the domain is restricted and controlled.[27]

Despite their inherent limitations, MT programs are used around the world. Probably the largest institutional user is the European Commission. The MOLTO project, for example, coordinated by the University of Gothenburg, received more than 2.375 million euros project support from the EU to create a reliable translation tool that covers a majority of the EU languages.[28] The further development of MT systems comes at a time when budget cuts in human translation may increase the EU's dependency on reliable MT programs.[29] The European Commission contributed 3.072 million euros (via its ISA programme) for the creation of MT@EC, a statistical machine translation program tailored to the administrative needs of the EU, to replace a previous rule-based machine translation system.[30]

Google has claimed that promising results were obtained using a proprietary statistical machine translation engine.[31] The statistical translation engine used in the Google language tools for Arabic <-> English and Chinese <-> English had an overall score of 0.4281 over the runner-up IBM's BLEU-4 score of 0.3954 (Summer 2006) in tests conducted by the National Institute for Standards and Technology.[32][33][34]

With the recent focus on terrorism, the military sources in the United States have been investing significant amounts of money in natural language engineering. *In-Q-Tel*[35] (a venture capital fund, largely funded by the US Intelligence Community, to stimulate new technologies through private sector entrepreneurs) brought up companies like Language Weaver. Currently the military community is interested in translation and processing of languages like Arabic, Pashto, and Dari. Within these languages, the focus is on key phrases and quick communication between military members and civilians through the use of mobile phone apps.[36] The Information Processing Technology Office in DARPA hosts programs like TIDES and Babylon translator. US Air Force has awarded a $1 million contract to develop a language translation technology.[37]

The notable rise of social networking on the web in recent years has created yet another niche for the application of machine translation software – in utilities such as Facebook, or instant messaging clients such as Skype, GoogleTalk, MSN Messenger, etc. – allowing users speaking different languages to communicate with each other. Machine translation applications have also been released for most mobile devices, including mobile telephones, pocket PCs, PDAs, etc. Due to their portability, such instruments have come to be designated as mobile translation tools enabling mobile business networking between partners speaking different languages, or facilitating both foreign language learning and unaccompanied traveling to foreign countries without the need of the intermediation of a human translator.

Despite being labelled as an unworthy competitor to human translation in 1966 by the Automated Language Processing Advisory Committee put together by the United States government,[38] the quality of machine translation has now been improved to such levels that its application in online collaboration and in the medical field are being investigated. In the Ishida and Matsubara lab of Kyoto University, methods of improving the accuracy of machine translation as a support tool for inter-cultural collaboration in today's globalized society are being studied.[39] The application of this technology in medical settings where human translators are absent is another topic of research however difficulties arise due to the importance of accurate translations in medical diagnoses.[40]

41.8 Evaluation

Main article: Evaluation of machine translation

There are many factors that affect how machine translation systems are evaluated. These factors include the intended use of the translation, the nature of the machine translation software, and the nature of the translation process.

Different programs may work well for different purposes. For example, statistical machine translation (SMT) typically outperforms example-based machine translation (EBMT), but researchers found that when evaluating English to French translation, EBMT performs better.[41] The same concept applies for technical documents, which can be more easily translated by SMT because of their formal language.

In certain applications, however, e.g., product descriptions written in a controlled language, a dictionary-based machine-translation system has produced satisfactory translations that require no human intervention save for quality inspection.[42]

There are various means for evaluating the output quality of machine translation systems. The oldest is the use of human judges[43] to assess a translation's quality. Even though human evaluation is time-consuming, it is still the most reliable method to compare different systems such as rule-based and statistical systems.[44] Automated means of evaluation include BLEU, NIST, METEOR, and LEPOR.[45]

Relying exclusively on unedited machine translation ignores the fact that communication in human language is context-embedded and that it takes a person to comprehend the context of the original text with a reasonable degree of probability. It is certainly true that even purely human-generated translations are prone to error. Therefore, to ensure that a machine-generated translation will be useful to a human being and that publishable-quality translation is achieved, such translations must be reviewed and edited by a human.[46] The late Claude Piron wrote that machine translation, at its best, automates the easier part of a translator's job; the harder and more time-consuming part usually involves doing extensive research to resolve ambiguities in the source text, which the grammatical and lexical exigencies of the target language require to be resolved. Such research is a necessary prelude to the pre-editing necessary in order to provide input for machine-translation software such that the output will not be meaningless.[47]

In addition to disambiguation problems, decreased accuracy can occur due to varying levels of training data for machine translating programs. Both example-based and statistical machine translation rely on a vast array of real example sentences as a base for translation, and when too many or too few sentences are analyzed accuracy is jeopardized. Researchers found that when a program is trained on 203,529 sentence pairings, accuracy actually decreases.[41] The optimal level of training data seems to be just over 100,000 sentences, possibly because as training data increasing, the number of possible sentences increases, making it harder to find an exact translation match.

41.9 Using machine translation as a teaching tool

Although there have been concerns about machine translation's accuracy, Dr. Ana Nino of the University of Manchester has researched some of the advantages in utilizing machine translation in the classroom. One such pedagogical method is called using "MT as a Bad Model."[48] MT as a Bad Model forces the language learner to identify inconsistencies or incorrect aspects of a translation; in turn, the individual will (hopefully) possess a better grasp of the language. Dr. Nino cites that this teaching tool was implemented in the late 1980s. At the end of various semesters, Dr. Nino was able to obtain survey results from students who had used MT as a Bad Model (as well as other models.) Overwhelmingly, students felt that they had observed improved comprehension, lexical retrieval, and increased confidence in their target language.[48]

41.10 Machine translation and signed languages

In the early 2000s, options for machine translation between spoken and signed languages were severely limited. It was a common belief that deaf individuals could use traditional translators. However, stress, intonation, pitch, and timing are conveyed much differently in spoken languages compared to signed languages. Therefore, a deaf individual may misinterpret or become confused about the meaning of written text that is based on a spoken language.[49]

Researchers Zhao, et al. (2000), developed a prototype called TEAM (translation from English to ASL by machine) that completed English to American Sign Language (ASL) translations. The program would first analyze the syntactic, grammatical, and morphological aspects of the English text. Following this step, the program accessed a sign synthesizer, which acted as a dictionary for ASL. This synthesizer housed the process one must follow to complete ASL signs, as well as the meanings of these signs. Once the entire text is analyzed and the signs necessary to complete the translation are located in the synthesizer, a computer generated human appeared and would use ASL to sign the English text to the user.[49]

41.11 Copyright

Only works that are original are subject to copyright protection, so some scholars claim that machine translation results are not entitled to copyright protection because MT does not involve creativity.[50] The copyright at issue is for a derivative work; the author of the original work in the original language does not lose his rights when a work is translated: a translator must have permission to publish a translation.

41.12 See also

- Comparison of machine translation applications

- Statistical machine translation

- Artificial intelligence

- Cache language model

- Computational linguistics

- Universal Networking Language

- Computer-assisted translation and Translation memory

- Foreign language writing aid

- Controlled natural language

- Fuzzy matching

- Postediting

- History of machine translation

- Human language technology

- Humour in translation ("howlers")

- Language barrier

- List of emerging technologies

- List of research laboratories for machine translation

- Pseudo-translation

- Translation

- Translation memory

- Universal translator

- Phraselator

- Mobile translation

41.13 Notes

[1] Albat, Thomas Fritz. "Systems and Methods for Automatically Estimating a Translation Time." US Patent 0185235, 19 July 2012.

[2] First and most notably Bar-Hillel, Yeheshua: "A demonstration of the nonfeasibility of fully automatic high quality machine translation," in *Language and Information: Selected essays on their theory and application* (Jerusalem Academic Press, 1964), pp. 174–179.

[3] "Madsen, Mathias: The Limits of Machine Translation (2010)". Docs.google.com. Retrieved 2012-06-12.

[4] Chitu, Alex (22 October 2007). "Google Switches to Its Own Translation System". Googlesystem.blogspot.com. Retrieved 2012-08-13.

[5] "Google Translator: The Universal Language". Blog.outercourt.com. 25 January 2007. Retrieved 2012-06-12.

[6] "Inside Google Translate – Google Translate".

[7] http://www.mt-archive.info/10/HyTra-2013-Tambouratzis.pdf

[8] Nagao, M. 1981. A Framework of a Mechanical Translation between Japanese and English by Analogy Principle, in Artificial and Human Intelligence, A. Elithorn and R. Banerji (eds.) North- Holland, pp. 173–180, 1984.

[9] "the Association for Computational Linguistics – 2003 ACL Lifetime Achievement Award". Association for Computational Linguistics. Retrieved 2010-03-10.

[10] http://kitt.cl.uzh.ch/clab/satzaehnlichkeit/tutorial/Unterlagen/Somers1999.pdf

[11] Adam Boretz. "Boretz, Adam, "AppTek Launches Hybrid Machine Translation Software" SpeechTechMag.com (posted 2 MAR 2009)". Speechtechmag.com. Retrieved 2012-06-12.

[12] Milestones in machine translation – No.6: Bar-Hillel and the nonfeasibility of FAHQT by John Hutchins

[13] Bar-Hillel (1960), "Automatic Translation of Languages". Available online at http://www.mt-archive.info/Bar-Hillel-1960.pdf

[14] Claude Piron, *Le défi des langues* (The Language Challenge), Paris, L'Harmattan, 1994.

[15] [张政.计算机翻译研究.清华大学出版社,2010]

[16] http://www.cl.cam.ac.uk/~{}ar283/eacl03/workshops03/W03-w1_eacl03babych.local.pdf

[17] Hermajakob, U., Knight, K., & Hal, D. (2008). Name Translation in Statistical Machine Translation Learning When to Transliterate. Association for Computational Linguistics. 389–397.

[18] http://nlp.stanford.edu/courses/cs224n/2010/reports/singla-nirajuec.pdf

[19] http://dowobeha.github.io/papers/amta08.pdf

[20] http://homepages.inf.ed.ac.uk/mlap/Papers/acl07.pdf

[21] https://www.jair.org/media/3540/live-3540-6293-jair.pdf

[22] Vossen, Piek: *Ontologies*. In: Mitkov, Ruslan (ed.) (2003): Handbook of Computational Linguistics, Chapter 25. Oxford: Oxford University Press.

[23] Knight, Kevin. *"Building a large ontology for machine translation (1993)"* (PDF). Retrieved 7 September 2014.

[24] "Melby, Alan. The Possibility of Language (Amsterdam: Benjamins, 1995, 27–41)". Benjamins.com. Retrieved 2012-06-12.

[25] Adam (14 February 2006). "Wooten, Adam. "A Simple Model Outlining Translation Technology" T&I Business (February 14, 2006)". Tandibusiness.blogspot.com. Retrieved 2012-06-12.

[26] "Appendix III of 'The present status of automatic translation of languages', Advances in Computers, vol.1 (1960), p.158-163. Reprinted in Y.Bar-Hillel: Language and information (Reading, Mass.: Addison-Wesley, 1964), p.174-179." (PDF). Retrieved 2012-06-12.

[27] "Human quality machine translation solution by Ta with you" (in Spanish). Tauyou.com. 15 April 2009. Retrieved 2012-06-12.

[28] "molto-project.eu". molto-project.eu. Retrieved 2012-06-12.

[29] SPIEGEL ONLINE, Hamburg, Germany (13 September 2013). "Google Translate Has Ambitious Goals for Machine Translation". *SPIEGEL ONLINE*.

[30] "Machine Translation Service". 5 August 2011.

[31] Google Blog: The machines do the translating (by Franz Och)

[32] "Geer, David, "Statistical Translation Gains Respect", pp. 18 – 21, IEEE Computer, October 2005" (PDF). Ieeexplore.ieee.org. 27 September 2011. doi:10.1109/MC.2005.353. Retrieved 2012-06-12.

[33] "Ratcliff, Evan "Me Translate Pretty One Day", Wired December 2006". Wired.com. 4 January 2009. Retrieved 2012-06-12.

[34] ""NIST 2006 Machine Translation Evaluation Official Results", November 1, 2006". Itl.nist.gov. Retrieved 2012-06-12.

[35] "In-Q-Tel". In-Q-Tel. Retrieved 2012-06-12.

[36] Gallafent, Alex (26 Apr 2011). "Machine Translation for the Military". *PRI's The World*. PRI's The World. Retrieved 17 Sep 2013.

[37] Jackson, William (9 September 2003). "GCN – Air force wants to build a universal translator". Gcn.com. Retrieved 2012-06-12.

[38] http://www.nap.edu/html/alpac_lm/ARC000005.pdf

[39] "Intercultural Collaboration".

[40] "Using machine translation in clinical practice".

[41] Way, Andy; Nano Gough (20 September 2005). "Comparing Example-Based and Statistical Machine Translation". *Natural Language Engineering* **11** (3): 295–309. doi:10.1017/S1351324905003888. Retrieved 2014-03-23.

[42] Muegge (2006), "Fully Automatic High Quality Machine Translation of Restricted Text: A Case Study," in *Translating and the computer 28. Proceedings of the twenty-eighth international conference on translating and the computer, 16–17 November 2006, London*, London: Aslib. ISBN 978-0-85142-483-5.

[43] "Comparison of MT systems by human evaluation, May 2008". Morphologic.hu. Retrieved 2012-06-12.

[44] Anderson, D.D. (1995). Machine translation as a tool in second language learning. CALICO Journal. 13(1). 68–96.

[45] Han et al. (2012), "LEPOR: A Robust Evaluation Metric for Machine Translation with Augmented Factors," in *Proceedings of the 24th International Conference on Computational Linguistics (COLING 2012): Posters, pages 441–450*, Mumbai, India.

[46] J.M. Cohen observes (p.14): "Scientific translation is the aim of an age that would reduce all activities to techniques. It is impossible however to imagine a literary-translation machine less complex than the human brain itself, with all its knowledge, reading, and discrimination."

[47] See the annually performed NIST tests since 2001 and Bilingual Evaluation Understudy

[48] Nino, Ana. "Machine Translation in Foreign Language Learning: Language Learners' and Tutors' Perceptions of Its Advantages and Disadvantages" ReCALL: the Journal of EUROCALL 21.2 (May 2009) 241–258.

[49] Zhao, L., Kipper, K., Schuler, W., Vogler, C., & Palmer, M. (2000). A Machine Translation System from English to American Sign Language. Lecture Notes in Computer Science, 1934: 54–67.

[50] "Machine Translation: No Copyright On The Result". SEO Translator, citing Zimbabwe Independent. Retrieved 24 November 2012.

41.14 Further reading

- Cohen, J. M. (1986), "Translation", *Encyclopedia Americana* **27**, pp. 12–15
- Hutchins, W. John; Somers, Harold L. (1992). *An Introduction to Machine Translation*. London: Academic Press. ISBN 0-12-362830-X.
- Lewis-Kraus, Gideon, "Tower of Babble", *New York Times Magazine*, June 7, 2015, pp. 48-52.
- Piron, Claude (1994), *Le défi des langues – Du gâchis au bon sens* [*The Language Challenge: From Chaos to Common Sense*] (in French), Paris: L'Harmattan, ISBN 9782738424327

41.15 External links

- The Advantages and Disadvantages of Machine Translation
- Statistical Machine Translation
- International Association for Machine Translation (IAMT)
- Machine Translation Archive by John Hutchins. An electronic repository (and bibliography) of articles, books and papers in the field of machine translation and computer-based translation technology
- Machine translation (computer-based translation) – Publications by John Hutchins (includes PDFs of several books on machine translation)
- Machine Translation and Minority Languages
- John Hutchins 1999
- OpenLogos

41.15.1 Online translator links

- http://translate.google.com/
- http://translate.reference.com/
- http://translation.babylon.com/
- http://transsoftware.info/scripts/webtrans2.dll
- http://turkceingilizce.ingilizceturkce.gen.tr/
- http://www.bing.com/translator
- http://www.englishdictionaryonline.org/

- http://www.freetranslation.com/
- http://www.freetranslations.org/
- http://www.ingilizceceviri.org/
- http://www.reverso.net/
- http://www.spanishenglish.com/
- http://turkce.cevirsozluk.com/
- http://www.systranet.com/translate/
- http://www.targoman.com/en.php

Chapter 42

Machine translation software usability

The sections below give objective criteria for evaluating the usability of machine translation software output.

42.1 Stationarity or Canonical Form

Main article: Round-trip translation

Do repeated translations converge on a single expression in both languages? I.e. does the translation method show stationarity or produce a canonical form. Does the translation become stationary without losing the original meaning? This metric has been criticized as not being well correlated with BLEU (BiLingual Evaluation Understudy) scores[1]

42.2 Adaptive to colloquialism, argot or slang

Is the system adaptive to colloquialism, argot or slang? The French language has many rules for creating words in the speech and writing of popular culture. Two such rules are: (a) The reverse spelling of words such as *femme* to *meuf*. (This is called verlan.) (b) The attachment of the suffix -*ard* to a noun or verb to form a proper noun. For example, the noun *faluche* means "student hat". The word *faluchard* formed from *faluche* colloquially can mean, depending on context, "a group of students", "a gathering of students" and "behavior typical of a student". The Google translator as of 28 December 2006 doesn't derive the constructed words as for example from rule (b), as shown here:

> Il y a une chorale falucharde mercredi, venez nombreux, les faluchards chantent des paillardes! ==> *There is a choral society falucharde Wednesday, come many, the faluchards sing loose-living women!*

French argot has three levels of usage:[2]

1. *familier* or friendly, acceptable among friends, family and peers but not at work

2. *grossier* or swear words, acceptable among friends and peers but not at work or in family

3. *verlan* or ghetto slang, acceptable among lower classes but not among middle or upper classes

The United States National Institute of Standards and Technology conducts annual evaluations of machine translation systems based on the BLEU−4 criterion . A combined method called IQmt which incorporates BLEU and additional metrics NIST, GTM, ROUGE and METEOR has been implemeneted by Gimenez and Amigo .

42.3 Well-formed output

Is the output grammatical or well-formed in the target language? Using an interlingua should be helpful in this regard, because with a fixed interlingua one should be able to write a grammatical mapping to the target language from the interlingua. Consider the following Arabic language input and English language translation result from the Google translator as of 27 December 2006 . This Google translator output doesn't parse using a reasonable English grammar:

> وعن حوادث الـتدافـع عند شـعيـرة رمي الجمرات -الـتي كثـيـرا ما يسقط فـيـها الـعديد من الضـحايا- أشار الـأمير نايف إلى إدخال "تـحسيـنات كثـيـرة فـي جسر الجمرات ستـمنع بـإذن الـله حدوث أي تـزاحم".
>
> ==> And incidents at the push Carbuncles-throwing ritual, which often fall where many of the victims - Prince Nayef pointed to the introduction of "many improvements in bridge Carbuncles God would stop the occurrence of any competing."

42.4 Semantics preservation

Do repeated re-translations preserve the semantics of the original sentence? For example, consider the following English input passed multiple times into and out of French using the Google translator as of 27 December 2006:

> Better a day earlier than a day late. ==>
> *Améliorer un jour plus tôt qu'un jour tard.* ==>
> To improve one day earlier than a day late. ==>
> *Pour améliorer un jour plus tôt qu'un jour tard.* ==>
> To improve one day earlier than a day late.

As noted above and in,[1] this kind of round-trip translation is a very unreliable method of evaluation.

42.5 Trustworthiness and Security

An interesting peculiarity of Google Translate as of 24 January 2008 (corrected as of 25 January 2008) is the following result when translating from English to Spanish, which shows an embedded joke in the English-Spanish dictionary which has some added poignancy given recent events:

> Heath Ledger is dead ==>
> *Tom Cruise está muerto*

This raises the issue of trustworthiness when relying on a machine translation system embedded in a Life-critical system in which the translation system has input to a Safety Critical Decision Making process. Conjointly it raises the issue of whether in a given use the software of the machine translation system is safe from hackers.

It is not known whether this feature of Google Translate was the result of a joke/hack or perhaps an unintended consequence of the use of a method such as statistical machine translation. Reporters from CNET Networks asked Google for an explanation on January 24, 2008; Google said only that it was an "internal issue with Google Translate".[3] The mistranslation was the subject of much hilarity and speculation on the Internet.[4][5]

If it is an unintended consequence of the use of a method such as statistical machine translation, and not a joke/hack, then this event is a demonstration of a potential source of critical unreliability in the statistical machine translation method.

In human translations, in particular on the part of interpreters, selectivity on the part of the translator in performing a translation is often commented on when one of the two parties being served by the interpreter knows both languages.

This leads to the issue of whether a particular translation could be considered *verifiable*. In this case, a converging round-trip translation would be a kind of verification.

42.6 Notes

[1] Somers, H. (2005) "Round-trip Translation: What Is It Good For?"

[2] "The Agony of Argot", Chitlins & Camembert, October 28, 2005

[3] "Google Translate bug mixes up Heath Ledger, Tom Cruise", by Caroline McCarthy, CNET Networks, January 24, 2008

[4] '"Tom Cruise" is Spanish for "Heath Ledger"', gawker.com, January 24, 2008

[5] "Tom Cruise está muerto", Ray Leon Blog Project, January 24, 2008

42.7 References

- Gimenez, Jesus and Enrique Amigo. (2005) IQmt: A framework for machine translation evaluation.

- NIST. Annual machine translation system evaluations and evaluation plan.

- Papineni, Kishore, Salim Roukos, Todd Ward and Wei-Jing Zhu. (2002) BLEU: A Method for automatic evaluation of machine translation. Proc. 40th Annual Meeting of the ACL, July, 2002, pp. 311–318.

42.8 See also

- Comparison of machine translation applications
- Evaluation of machine translation
- Round-trip translation
- Translation

Chapter 43

Marketing and artificial intelligence

Artificial intelligence is a field of study that "seeks to explain and emulate intelligent behaviour in terms of computational processes" [1] through performing the tasks of decision making, problem solving and learning.[2] Unlike other fields associated with intelligence, Artificial intelligence is concerned with both understanding and building of intelligent entities, and has the ability to automate intelligent processes.[3] It is evident that Artificial intelligence is impacting on a variety of subfields and wider society. However literature regarding its application to the field of marketing appears to be scarce.

Advancements in Artificial intelligence's application to a range of disciplines have led to the development of Artificial intelligence systems which have proved useful to marketers. These systems assist in areas such as market forecasting, automation of processes and decision making and increase the efficiency of tasks which would usually be performed by humans. The science behind these systems can be explained through neural networks and expert systems which are computer programs that process input and provide valuable output for marketers. In the area of social networking, AI is used to

Artificial intelligence systems stemming from Social computing technology can be applied to understand social networks on the Web. Data mining techniques can be used to analyze different types of social networks. This analysis helps a marketer to identify influential actors or nodes within networks, this information can then be applied to take a Societal marketing approach.

Artificial intelligence has gained significant recognition in the marketing industry. However, ethical issues surrounding these systems and their potential to impact on the need for humans in the workforce, specifically marketing, is a controversial topic.

43.1 Artificial Neural Networks

An artificial neural network is a form of computer program modelled on the brain and nervous system of humans.[4] Neural networks are composed of a series of interconnected processing neurons functioning in unison to achieve certain outcomes. Using "human-like trial and error learning methods neural networks detect patterns existing within a data set ignoring data that is not significant, while emphasising the data which is most influential".[5]

From a marketing perspective, neural networks are a form of software tool used to assist in decision making. Neural networks are effective in gathering and extracting information from large data sources [5] and have the ability to identify the cause and effect within data.[6] These neural nets through the process of learning, identify relationships and connections between data bases. Once knowledge has been accumulated, neural networks can be relied on to provide generalisations and can apply past knowledge and learning to a variety of situations.[6]

Neural networks help fulfil the role of marketing companies through effectively aiding in market segmentation and measurement of performance while reducing costs and improving accuracy. Due to their learning ability, flexibility, adaption and knowledge discovery, neural networks offer many advantages over traditional models.[7] Neural networks can be used to assist in pattern classification, forecasting and marketing analysis.

43.1.1 Pattern Classification

Classification of customers can be facilitated through the neural network approach allowing companies to make informed marketing decisions. An example of this was employed by Spiegel Inc., a firm dealing in direct-mail operations who used neural networks to improve efficiencies. Using software developed by NeuralWare Inc., Spiegel identified the demographics of customers who had made a single purchase and those customers who had made repeat purchases. Neural networks where then able to identify the key patterns and consequently identify the customers that were most likely to repeat purchase. Understanding this information allowed Speigel to streamline marketing efforts, and reduced costs.[8]

43.1.2 Forecasting

Sales forecasting "is the process of estimating future events with the goal of providing benchmarks for monitoring actual performance and reducing uncertainty".[9] Artificial intelligence techniques have emerged to facilitate the process of forecasting through increasing accuracy in the areas of demand for products, distribution, employee turnover, performance measurement and inventory control.[9] An example of forecasting using neural networks is the Airline Marketing Assistant/Tactician; an application developed by BehabHeuristics which allows for the forecasting of passenger demand and consequent seat allocation through neural networks. This system has been used by Nationalair Canada and USAir.[10]

43.1.3 Marketing Analysis

Neural networks provide a useful alternative to traditional statistical models due to their relibility, time saving characteristics and ability to recognise patterns from incomplete or noisy data.[6][11] Examples of marketing analysis systems include the Target Marketing System developed by Churchull Systems for Veratex Corporation. This support system scans a market database to identify dormant customers allowing management to make decisions regarding which key customers to target.[10]

When performing marketing analysis, neural networks can assist in the gathering and processing of information ranging from consumer demographics and credit history to the purchase patterns of consumers.[12]

43.2 Application of Artificial Intelligence to Marketing Decision Making

Marketing is a complex field of decision making which involves a large degree of both judgment and intuition on behalf of the marketer.[13] The enormous increase in complexity that the individual decision maker faces renders the decision making process almost an impossible task. Marketing decision engine can help distill the noise. StrategyVP.com is the world's first decision engine that matches marketing strategies with business goals.[14] The generation of more

efficient management procedures have been recognized as a necessity.[15] The application of Artificial intelligence to decision making through a Decision Support System has the ability to aid the decision maker in dealing with uncertainty in decision problems. Artificial intelligence techniques are increasingly extending decision support through analyzing trends; providing forecasts; reducing information overload; enabling communication required for collaborative decisions, and allowing for up-to-date information.[16]

43.2.1 The Structure of Marketing Decision

Organizations' strive to satisfy the needs of the customers, paying specific attention to their desires. A consumer-orientated approach requires the production of goods and services that align with these needs. Understanding consumer behaviour aids the marketer in making appropriate decisions. Thus, the decision making is dependent on the marketing problem, the decision maker, and the decision environment.[15]

43.2.2 Expert System

An Expert System is a software program that combines the knowledge of experts in an attempt to solve problems through emulating the knowledge and reasoning procedures of the experts. Each expert system has the ability to process data, and then through reasoning, transform it into evaluations, judgments and opinions, thus providing advises to specialized problems.[17]

The use of an expert system that applies to the field of marketing is MARKEX (Market Expert). These Intelligent decision support systems act as consultants for marketers, supporting the decision maker in different stages, specifically in the new product development process. The software provides a systematic analysis that uses various methods of forecasting, data analysis and multi-criteria decision making to select the most appropriate penetration strategy.[15] BRANDFRAME is another example of a system developed to assist marketers in the decision-making process. The system supports a brand manager in terms of identifying the brand's attributes, retail channels, competing brands, targets and budgets. New marketing input is fed into the system where BRANDFRAME analyses the data. Recommendations are made by the system in regard to marketing mix instruments, such as lowering the price or starting a sales promotional campaign.

43.3 Artificial Intelligence and Automation Efficiency

43.3.1 Application to Marketing Automation

In terms of marketing, automation uses software to computerize marketing processes that would have otherwise been performed manually. It assists in effectively allowing processes such as customer segmentation, campaign management and products promotion, to be undertaken at a more efficient rate.[18] Marketing automation is a key component of Customer Relationship Management (CRM). Companies are using systems that employ data-mining algorithms that analyses the customer database, giving further insight into the customer. This information may refer to socio-economic characteristics, earlier interactions with the customer, and information about the purchase history of the customer.[19] Varinos Systems have been designed to give organizations control over their data. Automation tools allow the system to monitor the performance of campaigns, making regular adjustments to the campaigns to improve response rates and to provide campaign performance tracking.[20]

43.3.2 Automation of Distribution

Distribution of products requires companies to access accurate data so they are able to respond to fluctuating trends in product demand. Automation processes are able to provide a comprehensive system that improves real-time monitoring and intelligent control. Amazon acquired Kiva Systems, the makers of the warehouse robot for $775 million in 2012. Prior to the purchase of the automated system, human employees would have to walk the enormous warehouse, tracking and retrieving books. The Kiva robots are able to undertake order fulfillment, product replenishment, as well as heavy lifting, thus increasing efficiency for the company.[21]

43.4 Use of Artificial Intelligence to Analyze Social Networks on the Web

A social network is a social arrangement of actors who make up a group, within a network; there can be an array of ties and nodes that exemplifies common occurrences within a network and common relationships. Lui (2011),[22] describes a social network as, "the study of social entities (people in organization, called actors), and their interactions and relationships. The interactions and relationships can be represented with a network or graph, where each vertex (or node) represents an actor and each link represents a relationship." At the present time there is a growth in virtual social networking with the common emergence of social networks being replicated online, for example social networking sites such as Twitter, Facebook and LinkedIn. From a marketing perspective, analysis and simulation of these networks can help to understand consumer behavior and opinion. The use of Agent-based social simulation techniques and data/opinion mining to collect social knowledge of networks can help a marketer to understand their market and segments within it.

43.4.1 Social Computing

Social computing is the branch of technology that can be used by marketers to analyze social behaviors within networks and also allows for creation of artificial social agents.[23] Social computing provides the platform to create social based software; some earlier examples of social computing are such systems that allow a user to extract social information such as contact information from email accounts e.g. addresses and companies titles from ones email using Conditional Random Field (CRFs) technology.[24]

43.4.2 Data Mining

Data mining involves searching the Web for existing information namely opinions and feelings that are posted online among social networks. " This area of study is called opinion mining or sentiment analysis. It analyzes peoples opinions, appraisals, attitudes, and emotions toward entities, individuals, issues, events, topics, and their attributes".[22] Data mining eliminates the need for costly market research for example surveys and opinion polls in the quest for primary data. However searching for this information and analysis of it can be a sizeable task, manually analyzing this information also presents the potential for researcher bias. Therefore objective opinion analysis systems are suggested as a solution to this in the form of automated opinion mining and summarization systems. Marketers using this type of intelligence to make inferences about consumer opinion should be wary of what is called opinion spam, where fake opinions or reviews are posted in the web in order to influence potential consumers for or against a product or service.[22]

Search engines are a common type of intelligence that seeks to learn what the user is interested in to present appropriate information. PageRank and HITS are examples of algorithms that search for information via hyperlinks; Google uses PageRank to control its search engine. Hyperlink based intelligence can be used to seek out web communities, which is described as ' a cluster of densely linked pages representing a group of people with a common interest'.[22]

Centrality and prestige are types of measurement terms used to describe the level of common occurrences among a group of actors; the terms help to describe the level of influence and actor holds within a social network. Someone who has many ties within a network would be described as a 'central' or 'prestige' actor. Identifying these nodes within a social network is helpful for marketers to find out who are the trendsetters within social networks.[22]

43.5 References

[1] Scholkoff, R.J. (1990) Artificial Intelligence: An engineering Approach, Mc Graw Hill, New York.

[2] Bellman. (1978). An introduction to artificial intelligence: can computers think? Boyd & Fraser Pub. Co.

[3] Russell, S., & Norvig, P. (1995). Artificial Intelligence: A Modern Approach. New Jersey: Prentice Hall.

[4] Whitby, B. (2003). A beginner's guide: Artificial Intelligence. Oxford, England: Oneworld Publications.

[5] Tedesco, B. G. (1992), Neural Analysis: Artificial Intelligence Neural Networks Applied to Single Source and Geodemographic Data. Chicage, IL: Grey Associates.

[6] Tedesco, B. G. (1992). Neural Marketing: Artificial Intelligence Neural Networks In Measuring Consumer Expectations. Chicago, IL: Grey Associates.

[7] Bloom, J. (2005). Market Segmentation: A Neural Network Application. Annals of Tourism Research, 32(1), 93-111.

[8] Schwartz, E. I. (1992, March 2). Smart Programs Go To Work. Retrieved from Business Week: http://www.businessweek.com/archives/1992/b325470.arc.htm

[9] Hall, O. P. (2002). Artificial Intelligence Techniques Enhance Business Forecasts: Computer-Based Analysis Increases Accuracy. Graziado Business Review, 5(2). Retrieved from http://gbr.pepperdine.edu/2010/08/artificial-intelligence-techniques-enhance-business-forecasts/

[10] Hall, C. (1992). Neural Net Technology- Ready for Prime-Time. IEEE Expert, 7(6), 2-4.

[11] Woelfel, J. (1992). Artificial Neural Networks for Advertising and Marketing Research: A Current Assessment. University at Buffalo.

[12] Lin, B. (1995). Applications of Neural Network in Marketing Decision Making. Shrevport: Louisiana State University.

[13] Wierenga, B. (2010). Marketing & Artificial Intelligence: Great Opportunities, Reluctant Partners. Marketing Intelligent Systems Using Soft Computing: Managerial and Research Applications , 258, 1-8.

[14] StrategyVP (2012, Dec 21). StrategyVP.com Launched: Reach Your 2013 Business Goals. Retrieved from Marketing PR: http://marketingpr.eu/news,url, strategyvpcom-launched-reach-your-2013-business-goals. html

[15] Matsatsinis, N. F., & Siskos, Y. (2002). Intelligent Support Systems for Marketing Decisions. Norwell, MA, USA: Kulwer Academic Publishers.

[16] Phillips-Wren, G., Jain, L. C., & Ichalkaranje, N. (2008). Intelligent Decision Making: An AI Approach. Spring Publishing Company.

[17] Crunk, J., & North, M. M. (2007). Decision Support System and AI Technologies in Aid of Information Based Marketing. International Management Review , 3 (2), 61-86.

[18] TechTarget. (2004, February). Marketing Automation. Retrieved April 20, 2012 from Search CRM: http://searchcrm. techtarget.com/definition/marketing-automation

[19] Sharma, S., Goval, R. K., & Mittal, R. K. (2010). Imperative relationship between data quality & performance of data mining tools for CRM. International Journal of Business Competition & Growth , 1 (1), 45-61.

[20] Gaffney, A. (2008). DemandGen Honors Top 10 Firms Using Automation Toolds to Fuel Business Growth. Retrieved April 20, 2012 from Demand GenReport: The Score Card for Sales & Marketing Automation: http://www.amberroad.com/pdf/DemandGen% 20Honors%20Top%2010%20Firms.pdf

[21] Murray, P. (2012, March 21). Amazon Goes Robotic, Acquires Kiva Systems, Makers of Warehouse Robot. Retrieved April 18, 2012 from Singularity Hub: http://singularityhub.com/2012/03/21/ amazon-goes-robotic-acquires-kiva-systems-makers-of-the-warehous -

[22] Liu, B. (2011). Web Data Mining: Opinion Mining and Sentiment Analysis (2nd ed.). New York: Springer. Retrieved April 19, 2012

[23] Fei-Yue, W., Kathleen, C., Zeng, D., & Wengi, M. (2007). Social Computing: From Social Informatics to Social Intelligence. Intellegent Systems, 22(2), 79-83. Retrieved April 20, 2012

[24] Culotta, A., Bekkerman, R., & McCallum, A. (2004). Extracting social networks and contact information from email and the Web. University of Massachusetts- Amherst. Amherst: Computer Science Department Faculty Publication Series.

Chapter 44

Mind's Eye (US military)

The **Mind's Eye** is a video analysis research project using artificial intelligence. It is funded by the Defense Advanced Research Projects Agency.[1]

Twelve research teams have been contracted by DARPA for the Mind's Eye: Carnegie Mellon University, Co57 Systems, Inc., Colorado State University, Jet Propulsion Laboratory/Caltech, Massachusetts Institute of Technology, Purdue University, SRI International, State University of New York at Buffalo, TNO (Netherlands), University of Arizona, University of California Berkeley and the University of Southern California.[2]

44.1 Mission

"The Mind's Eye program seeks to develop in machines a capability that exists only in animals: visual intelligence. This program pursues the capability to learn generally applicable and generative representations of action between objects in a scene directly from visual inputs, and then reason over those learned representations. A key distinction between this research and the state of the art in machine vision is that the latter has made continual progress in recognizing a wide range of objects and their properties - what might be thought of as the nouns in the description of a scene. The focus of Mind's Eye is to add the perceptual and cognitive underpinnings for recognizing and reasoning about the verbs in those scenes, enabling a more complete narrative of action in the visual experience."[3]

44.2 See also

- Gorgon Stare

44.3 References

[1] Lohr, Steve (January 1, 2011). "Computers That See You and Keep Watch Over You". *The New York Times*. Retrieved December 15, 2011.

[2] "Military contracts for visual intel system". UPI. January 5, 2011. Retrieved December 15, 2011.

[3] "Mind's Eye". DARPA Information Innovation Office. Retrieved 6 December 2012.

44.4 External links

- Official website

Chapter 45

Mobileye

Mobileye (NYSE: MBLY) is a technology company that develops vision-based advanced driver assistance systems (ADAS) providing warnings for collision prevention and mitigation. Mobileye N.V. is headquartered in the Netherlands, with a R&D Center in Jerusalem, Israel, and sales and marketing offices in Jericho, New York; Shanghai, China; Tokyo, Japan and Düsseldorf, Germany.[1]

A MobileEye EyeQ2 chip used in a Hyundai Lane Guidance camera module.

45.1 History

Mobileye N.V. was founded in 1999 by Amnon Shashua (a researcher of the Hebrew University), when he evolved his academic research into a technical solution for a vision system which could detect vehicles using only a camera and software algorithms on a processor.[2] After receiving a license to use the Technology which was owned by Yissum it was possible to incorporate the company. Together with Ziv Aviram, he set up the company's R&D headquarters in Jerusalem, Israel. At first the company developed algorithms, and a processor chip called the EyeQ chip. All of Mobileye's proprietary image processing algorithms run on the EyeQ chip. After years of testing, the chip and software algorithms began to be sold as commercial products to original equipment manufacturer (OEM) customers. The company's first clients were automotive manufacturers such as BMW, General Motors and Volvo, whose electronics suppliers integrated Mobileye's technologies into these company's cars, at first as an optional accessory when buying a new car, and later as a standard fit in new cars.[3]

In 2006 Mobileye set up an Aftermarket department, which sells finished products manufactured by Mobileye at their Philippines factory, IMI. The Aftermarket products are sold to an international network of distributors on all continents who sell the products to fleets of trucks and buses, to car dealerships, and to car accessory shops.[4]

In August 2015 Tesla Motors announced that it is using Mobileye's technology to enable its self-drive solution, which would be incorporated into Model S cars from 2016.[5]

45.2 Company timeline

- 1999: Mobileye N.V., co-founded by Mr. Ziv Aviram and Prof. Amnon Shashua[6]

- 1999 (June): Introduction of the First Generation Live Demonstration System

- 1999 MobilEye Received a license from Yissum to be able to use the technology.

- 2000: Introduction of the Second Generation Live Demonstration System

- 2001 (February): Introduction of the Third Generation Live Demonstration System

- 2001 (May): Introduction of the Fourth Generation Live Demonstration System

- 2002: Introduction of the Fifth Generation Live Demonstration System for Multi-Vision Applications

- 2003: Mobileye and Denso sign Cooperation Agreement

- 2003: Mobileye and Delphi sign Cooperation Agreement

- 2004: Introduction of the First Generation EyeQ™ System-on-a-Chip (SoC)

- 2004: Mobileye and SVDO/Continental sign a development agreement

- 2005: Mobileye and ST Microelectrionics sign a chip manufacture and development partnership agreement[7]

- 2006: Introduction of the Sixth Generation Live Demonstration System for Pedestrian Detection

- 2006: Introduction of Mobileye's Aftermarket Department

- 2006 (July): Mobileye and Magna Electronics announce Partnership to develop advanced automotive driver assistance features[8]

- 2007: U.S. investment bank Goldman Sachs invests $100 million in Mobileye[9]

- 2007: Mobileye launches multiple series productions for LDW on GM Cadillac STS and DTS vehicles,[10] for LDW on BMW 5 and 6 Series vehicles[11] and for radar-vision fusion for enhanced Adaptive Cruise Control with Collision Mitigation by Braking on Volvo S80, XC90/70/60 and V70 vehicles[12]

- 2007: Introduction of the Mobileye Advanced Warning System providing a world's first Aftermarket system featuring functions of lane and vehicle Detection running on a single processor[13]

- 2008 (September): Mobileye and Continental launch a World's first combination of multiple functions of Lane Departure Warning, Intelligent Highbeam Control and Traffic Sign Recognition on the BMW 7 series[14]

- 2008: Introduction of the Second Generation EyeQ2™ System-on-a-Chip (SoC)[15]

- 2009: Mobileye and Visteon sign Cooperation Agreement [16]

- 2010: U.S. investment bank Goldman Sachs, Leumi Partners and Menora Mivtachim Holdings Ltd. invest $37 million in Mobileye[17]

- 2010: Mobileye launches newest aftermarket product, the C2-270 Collision Prevention System, with vehicle, pedestrian, bicycle, and motorcycle detection capabilities.[18]

- 2010: Mobileye launches a world-first vision based Pedestrian Forward Collision Warning as part of a radar-vision 'automatic emergency braking system' system with Delphi and Volvo on the S60 saloon and V60 estate

- 2010: Mobileye launches Lane Keeping and Support (LKAS) on two HKMC vehicles (Hyundai i40 and Kia Optima) for US and European introduction.

- 2011: Mobileye launches the world's first vision only based forward collision warning system (bundled with multiple other functions of LDW IHC and TSR) on the 2011 BMW 1 series

- 2011: Mobileye launches the world's first vision only based U.S. National Highway Traffic Safety Administration (NHTSA) compliant Forward Collision Warning system and lane departure warning system combination on multiple GM vehicles - Chevrolet Equinox and GMC Terrain.

- 2011: Mobileye launches multi functional bundles including vision based FCW on the Opel Zafira and Opel Insignia.

- 2014: Mobileye launched its IPO on the NYSE which was the biggest Israeli IPO ever in the US raising approx. $1B at a market cap of $5.3B[19]

45.3 Awards

- International Fleet Industry Award, Fleet Europe, November 2013 [20]

- International Fleet Industry Award, Fleet Europe, October 2011.[21]

- Fleet Safety Forum Award for Excellence in the UK, for the Fleet Safety Product category, for the Mobileye C2-170 safety system.[22] Brake - Road Safety Charity -, July 2009.

- Best Electronic Design 2008 for Best Automotive Design, for the EyeQ2 Vision Processor.[23] *Electronic Design*, December 2008.

- Entrepreneurial Company of the Year Award in the Automotive Industry. Frost & Sullivan, December 2006.[24]

- Selected for the Top 100 Innovators Award. Red Herring Magazine, December 2005.[25]

45.4 Technologies

The firm's technology is based on the use of optical vision systems with motion detection algorithms, unlike many other systems which use a combination of visual detection, radar, and laser scanning. The firm's vehicle detection algorithms recognize motorised vehicles such as cars, motorcycles and trucks, in day and night time conditions. The firm's version performs its vehicle detection based functions using a single camera mounted in the rear view mirror, unlike the usual approach of using radars, laser scanners or in some cases stereo-cameras.[26]

In 2011 the firm introduced the world's first OEM production of vision-only forward collision warning system (NHTSA compliant) on multiple BMW, GM and Opel vehicles.

Lane departure warning systems are in-vehicle electronic systems that monitor the position of a vehicle within a roadway lane and warn a driver if the vehicle deviates or is about to deviate outside the lane. Mobileye's version was launched in multiple production platforms through 2007 and 2008 with GM, BMW and Volvo.

The firm's pedestrian detection technology is based on the use of mono cameras only, using pattern recognition and classifiers with image processing and optic flow analysis. Both static and moving pedestrians can be detected to a range of around 30m using VGA resolution imagers. The firm announced in 2008 that by mid-2010 they would launch a world's first application of full emergency braking for collision mitigation for pedestrians Mobileye announced in May 2009 as part of the next generation Volvo radar-vision fusion system which also provides lane departure warning and vehicle detection with radar-vision fusion for an enhanced collision mitigation by braking system on the next Volvo S60 vehicle.[27]

Since 2008, BMW 7-Series cars are equipped with the Mobileye traffic sign recognition systems, developed in cooperation with automotive supplier Continental AG.[28]

Adaptive highbeam systems automatically raises and lowering the high beams without inconveniencing oncoming or preceding traffic. The firm's version, Intelligent Headlight Control, is in production on the BMW 7 series.[29]

In 2011 the firm introduced multi-functional bundles including vision based FCW on the Opel Zafira and Opel Insignia.

45.4.1 Aftermarket

Since 2007 the firm has offered a range of aftermarket vision based ADAS systems, based on the same core technology as for production models. They currently offer lane departure warning, forward collision warning, headway monitoring and warning, low speed urban collision warning, intelligent headlamp control, speed limit indication (tsr) and pedestrian collision warning (including bicycles). These systems have also been integrated with fleet management systems.[30]

45.5 Investments

Between 2007 and 2011 the company raised $160 million. In 2013 the company sold 25% of its private shares for $400 million to a group of blue-chip investors.[31][32][33]

45.6 Competition

Mobileye faces competition from Tier 1 automotive suppliers as well as from other technology companies, including potentially Google.[34] There is also an increasing competition on the after-market space from radar-based systems manufacturers, such as Safe Drive Systems and others.[35]

Other competitors who develop ADAS technology include Continental, Bosch, NVIDIA, OmniVision Technologies, Freescale, Texas Instruments, Toshiba, Renesas Electronics Corp., and Denso, Green Hills Software, Intel, and Qualcomm.[36][37][38][39][40][41][42][43][44][45][46][47][48][49][50][51][52][53] Whether Mobileye's first-mover advantage will allow it to dominate the ADAS market or any of the mentioned competitors can capture a significant market share from Mobileye remains to be seen.

45.7 References

[1] http://www.mobileye.com/contact-us/worldwide-offices/

[2] Amnon Shashua : Executive Profile - Bloomberg

[3] What drives Israel's serial entrepreneurs? - Israel21.org

[4] NYC taxis to be a little safer, thanks to Mobileye: Israeli road safety alert system is being installed in New York cabs to help their operators drive more safely, David Shamah , Times of Israel 15 June 2015

[5] Mobileye's Tech Powers Tesla Model NoCamels News 23 August 2015

[6] "Mobileye's LinkedIn Profile". Linkedin.com. Retrieved 2011-11-13.

[7] View ST Microelectronics Press Release

[8] View Magna Press Release

[9] Gabay, Eran (2008-04-02). "Goldman Sachs investing $100m in startup Mobileye". Haaretz.com. Retrieved 2011-11-13.

[10] "View PRNewswire Press Release". Newswiretoday.com. 2008-01-15. Retrieved 2011-11-13.

[11] View VDO News Release

[12] View Volvo's Press Release

[13] "View News Wire Today". Newswiretoday.com. 2008-03-24. Retrieved 2011-11-13.

[14] "View High Beam News Article". Highbeam.com. Retrieved 2011-11-13.

[15] View STMicroelectronics Press Release

[16] See Press Release

[17] Mobileye raises $37 million US Dollars

[18] http://www.mobileye.com/en/press-room/press-releases

[19] Coppola, Gabrielle (2014-07-31). "Mobileye Raises $890 Million as Largest Israeli IPO in the U.S". *Bloomberg*.

[20] http://www.fleeteurope.com/news/international-fleet-industry-award-2013-mobileye-awarded-again

[21] http://www.fleeteurope.com/mobileye_wins_the_international_fleet_industry_award_2011_51708-en-146-181920.html

[22] Fleet Safety Forum Award Winners

[23] "2008 Winner's List". Electronicdesign.com. 2008-12-04. Retrieved 2011-11-13.

[24] "Frost & Sullivan Press Release". Frost.com. 2006-12-14. Retrieved 2011-11-13.

[25] "View Press Release". Allbusiness.com. 2004-12-09. Retrieved 2011-11-13.

[26] Safety upgrades for your car

[27] Administrator, Cars (2009-10-14). "Cars.co.za: Volvo Cars tests new, unique safety technology in Copenhagen - in a disguised S60 prototype". Carszainfo.blogspot.com. Retrieved 2011-11-13.

[28] View Motortrend News Article

[29] BMW 7-series Headlights System

[30] "InstallerNet to handle installation of Mobileye systems". *Fleet Owner*. Fleet Owner. Apr 14, 2010. Retrieved 2015-01-26.

[31] http://www.haaretz.com/business/.premium-1.591207

[32] http://www.haaretz.com/business/.premium-1.534607

[33] http://www.wsj.de/article/SB10001424052702304547704579567401946285692.html

[34] http://www.sec.gov/Archives/edgar/data/1607310/000157104914003550/t1401453-424b4.htm

[35] http://www.fenderbender.com/FenderBender/March-2014/Safe-Drive-Systems-Launches-Anti-Collision-Technology-in-US/

[36] http://www.conti-online.com/www/automotive_de_en/themes/passenger_cars/chassis_safety/adas/

[37] http://www.conti-online.com/www/automotive_de_en/themes/commercial_vehicles/chassis_safety/adas/

[38] http://www.bosch-mobility-solutions.com/en/de/driving_safety/driving_safety_systems_for_passenger_cars_1/driver_assistance_systems/driver_assistance_systems_2.html

[39] http://www.bosch-mobility-solutions.com/en/de/driving_comfort/driving_comfort_systems_for_passenger_cars_1/driver_assistance_systems_4/driver_assistance_systems_5.html

[40] http://corporate.tomtom.com/releasedetail.cfm?ReleaseID=873327

[41] http://www.nvidia.com/object/advanced-driver-assistance-systems.html

[42] http://www.ovt.com/applications/application.php?id=7

[43] http://www.freescale.com/webapp/sps/site/overview.jsp?code=ADAS&tid=vanADAS

[44] http://asia.nikkei.com/Business/Companies/Toshiba-to-supply-chips-for-driver-assist-systems

[45] http://www.ti.com/lsds/ti/apps/automotive/adas/overview.page

[46] http://www.toshiba.com/taec/Catalog/Line.do?familyid=28&lineid=2006887

[47] http://am.renesas.com/applications/automotive/adas/index.jsp

[48] http://www.globaldenso.com/en/products/oem/driving-assist-system/

[49] http://www.ghs.com/products/auto_adas.html

[50] http://www.intel.com/content/www/us/en/automotive/driving-safety-advanced-driver-assistance-systems-self-driving-technology-pa.html

[51] https://www.qualcomm.com/products/automotive

[52] http://www.eetindia.co.in/ART_8800693887_1800001_NT_94051dac.HTM

[53] King, Ian (2014-07-01). "Intel Chases Sales on Silicon Road to Driverless Cars". *Bloomberg*.

45.8 External links

- Mobileye's Website

Chapter 46

Monitoring and Surveillance Agents

Monitoring and surveillance agents (also known as predictive agents) are a type of intelligent agent software that observes and reports on computer equipment. Monitoring and surveillance agents are often used to monitor complex computer networks to predict when a crash or some other defect may occur. Another type of monitoring and surveillance agent works on computer networks keeping track of the configuration of each computer connected to the network. It tracks and updates the central configuration database when anything on any computer changes, such as the number or type of disk drives. An important task in managing networks lies in prioritizing traffic and shaping bandwidth.

46.1 Examples

- NASA's Jet Propulsion Laboratory has an agent that monitors inventory, planning, and scheduling equipment ordering to keep costs down.

- Allstate Insurance has a network with thousands of computers. The company uses a network monitoring agent from Computer Associates International called Neugent that watches its huge networks 24 hours a day. Every five seconds, the agent measures 1200 data points and can predict a system crash 45 minutes before it happens.

Haag & Cummings & McCubbrey & Pinsonneault & Donovan (2006). *Management Information Systems Third Canadian Ed.* McGraw-Hill Ryerson

46.2 See also

- Software agent

- Cfengine

- Nagios

- PIKT

- Ganglia - an opensource distributed monitoring system for HPC clusters and grids

Chapter 47

Trenchard More

Trenchard More is a professor at Dartmouth College. He participated in the 1956 Dartmouth Summer Research Project on Artificial Intelligence.[1][2][3] At the 50th year meeting of the Dartmouth Conference with Marvin Minsky, Geoffrey Hinton and Simon Osindero he presented *The Future of Network Models* and also gave a lecture entitled *Routes to the Summit*.[4]

Designed a theory for nested rectangular array that provided a formal structure used in the development of the Nested Interactive Array Language.[5][6][7][8]

47.1 See also

- AI@50

- Automaton

47.2 References

[1] William Bechtel, George Graham (://books.google) *A companion to cognitive science* [Retrieved 2011-10-25]

[2] .dartmouth.edu/~{}vox [Retrieved 2011-10-25] © 2011 Trustees of Dartmouth College (showing photograph of the Professor)

[3] Rudolf Seising (Google eBook) Fuzzification of systems: *the genesis of fuzzy set theory and its initial applications* - developments up to the 1970s [Retrieved 2011-10-25]

[4] artintelligence on Dec 22, 2010,*slideshare.net* (4.) and (6.),Dartmouth College slideshare.net/artintelligence © 2011 SlideShare Inc. All rights reserved [Retrieved 2011-10-25]

[5] P. Thagard <| id=7___V7sUVfgC&pg=PA170&lpg=PA170&dq |> *Mind readings: introductory selections on cognitive science* (344 pages) Bradford Books MIT Press, 1998 ISBN 0-262-70067-0

[6] www.dartmouth.edu/~{}ai50 + nial.com [Retrieved 2011-12-29]

[7] W.Fitzgerald, Kalamazoo College docs.google *Martin Luther King and the Ghost in the Machine* International Journal of Cognition and Technology[Retrieved 2011-12-29]

[8] [T. More, IBM Data Processing Division Scientific Center] dl.acm *Axioms and theorems for a theory of arrays* IBM Journal of Research and Development archive Volume 17 Issue 2, March 1973 doi>10.1147/rd.172.0135 Association for Computing Machinery. Copyright © 2011 ACM, Inc [2011-12-29] [Trenchard More, IBM Cambridge Scientific Center, 545 Technology Square, Cambridge, MA] doi>10.1145/800136.804440 Proceeding APL '79 Proceedings of the international conference on APL: part 1] dl.acm *The nested rectangular array as a model of data* the Association for Computing Machinery. Copyright © 2011 ACM, Inc. [ANALYSIS]

47.3 External links

- SCHLOSS DAGSTUHL Universität Trier dblp *publications*

Chapter 48

Natachata

Natachata is a sexbot used to simulate smutty conversations via text messages with paying subscribers, fooling them into believing that she is human. Written by former rocket scientist Simon Luttrell, Natachata is widely used by porn chat merchants. Natachata can handle 15 messages per second at £1 for each SMS text message in the UK.

Natachata operates by comparing incoming messages with a database of 100,000 sentences and then concocts a reply based on what it received. It then transcribes the message into slang, adds spelling mistakes and, after a random delay, sends a reply. Most users of such systems would be surprised to learn that they are not conversing with a human.[1]

48.1   See also

- Sexting

- Turing test

48.2   References

[1] Ward, Mark (2004-02-20). "UK | Magazine | Has text-porn finally made computers 'human'?". BBC News. Retrieved 2011-12-18.

48.3   External links

- News article on BBC

Chapter 49

Natural language user interface

Natural Language User Interfaces (LUI or NLUI) are a type of computer human interface where linguistic phenomena such as verbs, phrases and clauses act as UI controls for creating, selecting and modifying data in software applications.

In interface design natural language interfaces are sought after for their speed and ease of use, but most suffer the challenges to understanding wide varieties of ambiguous input.[1] Natural language interfaces are an active area of study in the field of natural language processing and computational linguistics. An intuitive general natural language interface is one of the active goals of the Semantic Web.

Text interfaces are "natural" to varying degrees. Many formal (un-natural) programming languages incorporate idioms of natural human language. Likewise, a traditional keyword search engine could be described as a "shallow" natural language user interface.

49.1 Overview

A natural language search engine would in theory find targeted answers to user questions (as opposed to keyword search). For example, when confronted with a question of the form 'which U.S. state has the highest income tax?', conventional search engines ignore the question and instead search on the keywords 'state', 'income' and 'tax'. Natural language search, on the other hand, attempts to use natural language processing to understand the nature of the question and then to search and return a subset of the web that contains the answer to the question. If it works, results would have a higher relevance than results from a keyword search engine.

49.2 History

Prototype Nl interfaces had already appeared in the late sixties and early seventies.[2]

- SHRDLU, a natural language interface that manipulates blocks in a virtual "blocks world"

- *Lunar*, a natural language interface to a database containing chemical analyses of Apollo-11 moon rocks by William A. Woods.

- *Chat-80* transformed English questions into Prolog expressions, which were evaluated against the Prolog database. The code of Chat-80 was circulated widely, and formed the basis of several other experimental Nl interfaces. An online demo is available on the LPA website.[3]

- ELIZA, written at MIT by Joseph Weizenbaum between 1964 and 1966, mimicked a psychotherapist and was operated by processing users' responses to scripts. Using almost no information about human thought or emotion, the DOCTOR script sometimes provided a startlingly human-like interaction. An online demo is available on the LPA website.[4]

- *Janus* is also one of the few systems to support temporal questions.

- *Intellect* from Trinzic (formed by the merger of AICorp and Aion).

- BBN's *Parlance* built on experience from the development of the *Rus* and *Irus* systems.

- IBM *Languageaccess*

- Q&A from Symantec.

- *Datatalker* from Natural Language Inc.

- *Loqui* from Bim.

- *English Wizard* from Linguistic Technology Corporation.

- *iAskWeb* from Anserity Inc. fully implemented in Prolog was providing interactive recommendations in NL to users in tax and investment domains in 1999-2001[5]

49.3 Challenges

Natural language interfaces have in the past led users to anthropomorphize the computer, or at least to attribute more intelligence to machines than is warranted. On the part of the user, this has led to unrealistic expectations of the capabilities of the system. Such expectations will make it difficult to learn the restrictions of the system if users attribute too much capability to it, and will ultimately lead to disappointment when the system fails to perform as expected as was the case in the AI winter of the 1970s and 80s.

A 1995 paper titled 'Natural Language Interfaces to Databases – An Introduction', describes some challenges:[2]

- *Modifier attachment*

The request "List all employees in the company with a driving licence" is ambiguous unless you know companies can't have drivers licences.

- *Conjunction and disjunction*

"List all applicants who live in California and Arizona" is ambiguous unless you know that a person can't live in two places at once.

- *Anaphora resolution*

- resolve what a user means by 'he', 'she' or 'it', in a self-referential query.

Other goals to consider more generally are the speed and efficiency of the interface, in all algorithms these two points are the main point that will determine if some methods are better than others and therefore have greater success in the market.

Finally, regarding the methods used, the main problem to be solved is creating a general algorithm that can recognize the entire spectrum of different voices, while disregarding nationality, gender or age. The significant differences between the extracted features - even from speakers who says the same word or phrase - must be successfully overcome.

49.4 Uses and applications

The natural language interface gives rise to technology used for many different applications.

Some of the main uses are:

- *Dictation*, is the most common use for automated speech recognition (ASR) systems today. This includes medical transcriptions, legal and business dictation, and general word processing. In some cases special vocabularies are used to increase the accuracy of the system.

- *Command and control*, ASR systems that are designed to perform functions and actions on the system are defined as command and control systems. Utterances like "Open Netscape" and "Start a new xterm" will do just that.

- *Telephony*, some PBX/Voice Mail systems allow callers to speak commands instead of pressing buttons to send specific tones.

- *Wearables*, because inputs are limited for wearable devices, speaking is a natural possibility.

- *Medical, disabilities*, many people have difficulty typing due to physical limitations such as repetitive strain injuries (RSI), muscular dystrophy, and many others. For example, people with difficulty hearing could use a system connected to their telephone to convert a caller's speech to text.

- *Embedded applications*, some new cellular phones include C&C speech recognition that allow utterances such as "call home". This may be a major factor in the future of automatic speech recognition and Linux.

Below are named and defined some of the applications that use natural language recognition, and so have integrated utilities listed above.

49.4.1 Ubiquity

Main article: Ubiquity (Firefox)

Ubiquity, an add-on for Mozilla Firefox, is a collection of quick and easy natural-language-derived commands that act as mashups of web services, thus allowing users to get information and relate it to current and other webpages.

49.4.2 Wolfram Alpha

Main article: Wolfram Alpha

Wolfram Alpha is an online service that answers factual queries directly by computing the answer from structured data, rather than providing a list of documents or web pages that might contain the answer as a search engine would.[6] It was announced in March 2009 by Stephen Wolfram, and was released to the public on May 15, 2009.[7]

49.4.3 Siri

Main article: Siri (software)

Siri is an intelligent personal assistant application integrated with operating system iOS. The application uses natural language processing to answer questions and make recommendations.

Siri's marketing claims include that it adapts to a user's individual preferences over time and personalizes results, and performs tasks such as making dinner reservations while trying to catch a cab.[8]

49.4.4 Others

- Anboto Group provides Web customer service and e-commerce technology based on semantics and natural language processing. The main offer of Anboto Group are the virtual sales agent and intelligent chat.

- Ask.com - The original idea behind Ask Jeeves (Ask.com) was traditional keyword searching with an ability to get answers to questions posed in everyday, natural language. The current Ask.com still supports this, with added support for math, dictionary, and conversion questions.

- Braina[9] - Braina is a natural language interface for Windows OS that allows to type or speak English language sentences to perform a certain action or find information.

- CMANTIK - CMANTIK is a semantic information search engine which is trying to answer user's questions by looking up relevant information in Wikipedia and some news sources.

- C-Phrase - is a web-based natural language front end to relational databases. C-Phrase runs under Linux, connects with PostgreSQL databases via ODBC and supports both select queries and updates. Currently there is only support for English.

- EasyQuery - is a component library (for .NET framework first of all) which allows you to implement natural language query builder in your application. Works both with relational databases or ORM solutions like Entity Framework.

Screenshot of GNOME DO classic interface.

- Enguage - this is an open source text understanding interface for web/mobile devices, using publicly available speech-to-text and text-to-speech facilities. This is directed at controlling apps, rather than as a front-end database query or web search. The interpretation of utterances is programmed, and programmable, in natural language utterances; thus, it is (or at least asserts that language is) an autopoietic system.[10] It can achieve a deep understanding of text.[11] A reference app is available on Google Play

- GNOME Do - Allows for quick finding miscellaneous artifacts of GNOME environment (applications, Evolution and Pidgin contacts, Firefox bookmarks, Rhythmbox artists and albums, and so on) and execute the basic actions on them (launch, open, email, chat, play, etc.).[12]

- Invention Machine Goldfire - powered by a semantic research engine that has the capability to transform unstructured documents from various electronic sources into an index that, when searched, delivers answers to research questions. Goldfire's Natural Language query interface enables the user to put a question in a free text format, which would be the same format as if the question were given to another person. And, once knowledge has been retrieved, Goldfire presents the results in a way that makes their meaning readily apparent.

- hakia - hakia is an Internet search engine. The company has invented an alternative new infrastructure to indexing that uses SemanticRank algorithm, a solution mix from the disciplines of ontological semantics, fuzzy logic, computational linguistics, and mathematics.

- Lexxe - Lexxe is an Internet search engine that uses natural language processing for queries (semantic search). Searches can be made with keywords, phrases, and questions, such as "How old is Wikipedia?" When it comes to facts, Lexxe is quite effective, though needs much improvement in natural language analysis in the area of facts and in other areas.

- Mnemoo - Mnemoo is an answer engine that aimed to directly answer questions posed in plain text (Natural Language), which is accomplished using a database of facts and an inference engine.

- Natural Date and Time - Natural language date and time zone engine. It allows you to ask questions about time, daylight saving information and to do time zone conversions via plain English questions such as 'What is the time in São Paulo when it is 6pm on the 2nd of June in Detroit'.

- NLUI Server - an enterprise-oriented multilingual application server by LinguaSys for natural language user interface scripts, supporting English, Spanish, Portuguese, German, Japanese, Chinese, Pashto, Thai, Russian, Vietnamese, Malay, with Arabic, French, and more languages in development.

- Pikimal - Pikimal uses natural language tied to user preference to make search recommendations by template.

- Powerset — On May 11, 2008, the company unveiled a tool for searching a fixed subset of Wikipedia using conversational phrases rather than keywords.[13] On July 1, 2008, it was purchased by Microsoft.[14]

- Q-go - The Q-go technology provides relevant answers to users in response to queries on a company's internet website or corporate intranet, formulated in natural sentences or keyword input alike. Q-go was acquired by RightNow Technologies in 2011

- START (MIT project) - START, Web-based question answering system. Unlike information retrieval systems such as search engines, START aims to supply users with "just the right information," instead of merely providing a list of hits. Currently, the system can answer millions of English questions about places, movies, people and dictionary definitions.

- StatMuse - Natural language analytics platform, currently in private beta with NBA data. Ask natural questions and get rich visualizations and raw data.

- Swingly - Swingly is an answer engine designed to find exact answers to factual questions. Just ask a question in plain English - and Swingly will find you the answer (or answers) you're looking for (according to their site).

- Yebol - Yebol is a vertical "decision" search engine that had developed a knowledge-based, semantic search platform. Yebol's artificial intelligence human intelligence-infused algorithms automatically cluster and categorize search results, web sites, pages and content that it presents in a visually indexed format that is more aligned with initial human intent. Yebol uses association, ranking and clustering algorithms to analyze related keywords or web pages. Yebol integrates natural language processing, metasynthetic-engineered open complex systems, and machine algorithms with human knowledge for each query to establish a web directory that actually 'learns', using correlation, clustering and classification algorithms to automatically generate the knowledge query, which is retained and regenerated forward.[15]

49.5   See also

- Natural user interface

- Natural language programming

  - xTalk, a family of English-like programming languages

- Chatterbot, a computer program that simulates human conversations

- Noisy text

- Question answering

- Selection-based search

- Semantic search

- Semantic query

- Semantic Web

49.6   References

[1] Hill, I. (1983). "Natural language versus computer language." In M. Sime and M. Coombs (Eds.) Designing for Human-Computer Communication. Academic Press.

[2] Natural Language Interfaces to Databases – An Introduction, I. Androutsopoulos, G.D. Ritchie, P. Thanisch, Department of Artificial Intelligence, University of Edinburgh

[3] Chat-80 demo

[4] ELIZA demo

[5] Galitsky, Boris (2003). *Natural Language Question Answering: technique of semantic headers*. Adelaide, Australia: Advance Knowledge International. ISBN 0868039799.

[6] Johnson, Bobbie (2009-03-09). "British search engine 'could rival Google'". *The Guardian*. Retrieved 2009-03-09.

[7] "So Much for A Quiet Launch". Wolfram Alpha Blog. 2009-05-08. Retrieved 2009-10-20.

[8] Siri webpage

[9] Braina

[10] http://www.academia.edu/10177437/An_Autopoietic_Repertoire

[11] http://cit.srce.unizg.hr/index.php/CIT/article/view/2278/1658 if we are holding hands whose hand am i holding

[12] Ubuntu 10.04 Add/Remove Applications description for GNOME Do

[13] Helft, Miguel (May 12, 2008). "Powerset Debuts With Search of Wikipedia". The New York Times.

[14] Johnson, Mark (July 1, 2008). "Microsoft to Acquire Powerset". Powerset Blog. Archived from the original on February 25, 2009.

[15] Humphries, Matthew. "Yebol.com steps into the search market" *Geek.com*. 31 July 2009.

Chapter 50

Network Compartment

Network Compartmentalization, the division of network functionality into **network compartments**, is an important concept of Autonomic Networking.

50.1 Definition of Network Compartments

Network Compartments implement the operational rules and administrative policies for a given communication context. The boundaries of a communication context, and hence the compartment boundaries, are based on technological and/or administrative boundaries. For example, compartment boundaries can be defined by a certain type of network technology (e.g., a specific wireless access network) or based on a particular communication protocol and/or addressing space (e.g., an IPv4 or and IPv6 network), but also based on a policy domain (e.g., a national health network that requires a highly secure boundary).

A compartment's communication principles, protocols and policies form a sort of "recipe" that all compartment entities must obey. For example, the recipe defines how to join a compartment, who can join, and how the naming, addressing and routing is handled. The complexity and details of the internal operation is left to each compartment. For example, registration with a compartment can range from complex trust-based mechanisms to simple registration schemes with a central database or a public DHT-based system; resolution of a communication peer can be handled implicitly by the compartment's naming and addressing scheme or require explicit actions (e.g., resolution of an identifier to a locator). It is important to note here that compartments have full autonomy on how to handle the compartment's internal communication – i.e. there are no global invariants that have to be implemented by all compartments or all communication elements.

Members of a compartment are able and willing to communicate among each other according to compartment's operational and policy rules. Conceptually a compartment

maintains some form of implicit database which contains its members; that is, each entry in the database defines a member. Before one can send a data packet to a compartment member, a resolution step is required which returns a means to "address" the member. Note that the above definition does not specify whether a member is a node, a set of servers or a software module. This rather abstract definition of compartment membership permits to capture many different flavours of members and communication forms.

It is anticipated that many compartments co-exist and that compartments are able to interwork on various levels (e.g. through "layering" or "peering" of compartments).

50.2 External links

- ANA Blueprint - V1.0 by C. Jelger, S. Schmid (Ed.) et al.

- Tussle Space Paper by D. Clark

- www.cbrt.in

Chapter 51

Neural machine translation

Neural machine translation (NMT) is the approach to machine translation in which a large neural network is trained to maximize translation performance. It is a radical departure from the phrase-based statistical translation approaches, in which a translation system consists of subcomponents that are separately optimized.[1]

The artificial neural network (ANN) is a unique learning algorithm inspired by the functional aspects and structure of the brain's biological neural networks. With use of ANN, it is possible to execute a number of tasks, such as classification, clustering, and prediction, using machine learning techniques like supervised or reinforced learning. Therefore, ANN is a subset of machine learning algorithms.

A bidirectional recurrent neural network (RNN), known as an *encoder*, is used by the neural network to encode a source sentence for a second RNN, known as a *decoder*, that is used to predict words in the target language.[2]

NMT models are inspired by deep representation learning. They require only a fraction of the memory needed by traditional statistical machine translation (SMT) models. Furthermore, unlike conventional translation systems, each and every component of the neural translation model is trained jointly to maximize the translation performance.[3]

When a new neural network is created, it is trained for certain domains or applications. Once an automatic learning mechanism is established, the network practices. With time it starts operating according to its own judgment, turning into an "expert".[1]

51.1 References

[1] Wołk, Krzysztof; Marasek, Krzysztof (2015). "Neural-based Machine Translation for Medical Text Domain. Based on European Medicines Agency Leaflet Texts". *Procedia Computer Science* (64): 2–9. doi:10.1016/j.procs.2015.08.456.

[2] Dzmitry Bahdanau, Cho Kyunghyun, Yoshua Bengio (2014). "Neural Machine Translation by Jointly Learning to Align and Translate". Cornell University Library. Retrieved 20 October 2015.

[3] Kyunghyun Cho, Bart van Merrienboer, Dzmitry Bahdanau, Yoshua Bengio (3 September 2014). "On the Properties of Neural Machine Translation: Encoder–Decoder Approaches". Cornell University Library. Retrieved 26 October 2015.

51.2 External links

- Neural machine translation at LISA, the machine learning laboratory of the University of Montreal

Chapter 52

Noisy text analytics

Noisy text analytics is a process of information extraction whose goal is to automatically extract structured or semistructured information from noisy unstructured text data. While Text analytics is a growing and mature field that has great value because of the huge amounts of data being produced, processing of noisy text is gaining in importance because a lot of common applications produce noisy text data. Noisy unstructured text data is found in informal settings such as online chat, text messages, e-mails, message boards, newsgroups, blogs, wikis and web pages. Also, text produced by processing spontaneous speech using automatic speech recognition and printed or handwritten text using optical character recognition contains processing noise. Text produced under such circumstances is typically highly noisy containing spelling errors, abbreviations, non-standard words, false starts, repetitions, missing punctuations, missing letter case information, pause filling words such as "um" and "uh" and other texting and speech disfluencies. Such text can be seen in large amounts in contact centers, chat rooms, optical character recognition (OCR) of text documents, short message service (SMS) text, etc. Documents with historical language can also be considered noisy with respect to today's knowledge about the language. Such text contains important historical, religious, ancient medical knowledge that is useful. The nature of the noisy text produced in all these contexts warrants moving beyond traditional text analysis techniques.

52.1 Techniques for noisy text analysis

Missing punctuation and the use of non-standard words can often hinder standard natural language processing tools such as part-of-speech tagging and parsing. Techniques to both learn from the noisy data and then to be able to process the noisy data are only now being developed.

52.2 Possible source of noisy text

- World wide web: Poorly written text is found in web pages, online chat, blogs, wikis, discussion forums, newsgroups. Most of these data are unstructured and the style of writing is very different from, say, well-written news articles. Analysis for the web data is important because they are sources for market buzz analysis, market review, trend estimation, etc. Also, because of the large amount of data, it is necessary to find efficient methods of information extraction, classification, automatic summarization and analysis of these data.

- Contact centers: This is a general term for help desks, information lines and customer service centers operating in domains ranging from computer sales and support to mobile phones to apparels. On an average a person in the developed world interacts at least once a week with a contact center agent. A typical contact center agent handles over a hundred calls per day. They operate in various modes such as voice, online chat and E-mail. The contact center industry produces gigabytes of data in the form of E-mails, chat logs, voice conversation transcriptions, customer feedback, etc. A bulk of the contact center data is voice conversations. Transcription of these using state of the art automatic speech recognition results in text with 30-40% word error rate. Further, even written modes of communication like online chat between customers and agents and even the interactions over email tend to be noisy. Analysis of contact center data is essential for customer relationship management, customer satisfaction analysis, call modeling, customer profiling, agent profiling, etc., and it requires sophisticated techniques to handle poorly written text.

- Printed Documents: Many libraries, government organizations and national defence organizations have vast repositories of hard copy documents. To retrieve and process the content from such documents, they need to be processed using Optical Character Recognition. In addition to printed text, these documents may also contain handwritten annotations. OCRed text can be highly noisy depending on the font size, quality of the print etc. It can range from 2-3% word error rates to as high as 50-60% word error rates. Handwritten annotations can be particularly hard to decipher, and error rates can be quite high in their presence.

- Short Messaging Service (SMS): Language usage over computer mediated discourses, like chats, emails and SMS texts, significantly differs from the standard form of the language. An urge towards shorter message length facilitating faster typing and the need for semantic clarity, shape the structure of this non-standard form known as the texting language.

52.3 References

- "Special Issue on Noisy Text Analytics - International Journal on Document Analysis and Recognition (2007), Springer, Guest Editors Craig Knoblock, Daniel Lopresti, Shourya Roy and L. Venkata Subramaniam, Vol. 10, No. 3-4, December 2007."

- "Wong, W., Liu, W. & Bennamoun, M. Enhanced Integrated Scoring for Cleaning Dirty Texts. In: IJCAI Workshop on Analytics for Noisy Unstructured Text Data (AND), 2007; Hyderabad, India.".

- "L. V. Subramaniam, S. Roy, T. A. Faruquie, S. Negi, A survey of types of text noise and techniques to handle noisy text. In: Third Workshop on Analytics for Noisy Unstructured Text Data (AND), 2009".

52.4 See also

- Text analytics

- Information extraction

- Computational linguistics

- Natural language processing

- Named entity recognition

- Text mining

- Automatic summarization

- Statistical classification

- Data quality

Chapter 53

OpenNN

OpenNN (Open Neural Networks Library) is a software library written in the C++ programming language which implements neural networks,[1] a main area of deep learning research. The library is open source, hosted at SourceForge and licensed under the GNU Lesser General Public License.

53.1 Characteristics

The software implements any number of layers of non-linear processing units for supervised learning. This deep architecture allows the design of neural networks with universal approximation properties. On the other hand, it allows multiprocessing programming by means of OpenMP, in order to increase the computer performance.

OpenNN contains data mining algorithms as a bundle of functions. These can be embedded in other software tools, using an application programming interface, for the integration of the predictive analytics tasks. In this regard, a graphical user interface is missing but some functions can be supported by specific visualization tools.[2]

53.2 History

The development started in 2003 at the International Center for Numerical Methods in Engineering (CIMNE), within the research project funded by the European Union called RAMFLOOD.[3] Then it continued as part of similar projects. At present, OpenNN is being developed by the startup company Artelnics.[4]

In 2014, *Big Data Analytics Today* rated OpenNN as the #1 brain inspired artificial intelligence project.[5] Also, during the same year, *ToppersWorld* selected OpenNN among the top 5 open source data mining tools.[6]

53.3 Applications

OpenNN is a general purpose artificial intelligence software package.[7] It uses machine learning techniques for solving data mining and predictive analytics tasks in different fields. For instance, the library has been applied in the engineering,[8] energy,[9] or chemistry[10] sectors.

53.4 Related libraries

- Deeplearning4j, a deep learning library written for Java and Scala which is open source.

- Torch, an open source framework written in Lua with wide support for machine learning algorithms.

53.5 See also

- Artificial intelligence

- Machine learning

- Deep learning

- Artificial neural network

53.6 References

[1] "OpenNN, An Open Source Library For Neural Networks". KDNuggets. June 2014.

[2] J. Mary Dallfin Bruxella; et al. (2014). "Categorization of Data Mining Tools Based on Their Types". *International Journal of Computer Science and Mobile Computing* **3** (3): 445–452.

[3] "CORDIS - EU Research Project RAMFLOOD". European Commission. December 2004.

[4] "Artelnics home page".

[5] "Top 12 Brain Inspired Artificial Intelligence Projects". Big Data Analytics Today. October 2014.

[6] "Top 5 Open Source Data Mining Tools". ToppersWorld. November 2014.

[7] "Here Are 7 Thought-Provoking AI Software Packages For Your Info". Saurabh Singh. Retrieved 25 June 2014.

[8] R. Lopez; et al. (2008). "Neural Networks for Variational Problems in Engineering". *International Journal for Numerical Methods in Engineering* **75** (11): 1341–1360. doi:10.1002/nme.2304.

[9] P. Richter; et al. (2011). "Optimisation of Concentrating Solar Thermal Power Plants with Neural Networks". *Lecture Notes in Computer Science* **6593**: 190–199. doi:10.1007/978-3-642-20282-7_20.

[10] A.A. D'Archivio; et al. (2014). "Artificial Neural Network Prediction of Multilinear Gradient Retention in Reversed-Phase HPLC". *Analytical and Bioanalytical Chemistry* **407**: 1–10. doi:10.1007/s00216-014-8317-3.

53.7 External links

- OpenNN project at SourceForge

Chapter 54

Optical answer sheet

An **optical answer sheet** or "bubble sheet" is a special type of form used in multiple choice question examinations. Optical mark recognition is used to detect answers. The most well known company in the United States involved with optical answer sheets is the Scantron Corporation, although certain uses require their own customized system. The terms "Optical answer sheet" and "scantron" have become more or less interchangeable.

Optical answer sheets usually have a set of blank ovals or boxes that correspond to each question, often on separate sheets of paper. Bar codes may mark the sheet for automatic processing, and each series of ovals filled will return a certain value when read. In this way students' answers can be digitally recorded, or identity given.

54.1 Reading

The first optical answer sheets were read by shining a light through the sheet and measuring how much of the light was blocked using phototubes on the opposite side.[1] As some phototubes are mostly sensitive to the blue end of the visible spectrum,[2] blue pens could not be used, as blue inks reflect and transmit blue light. Because of this, number two pencils had to be used to fill in the bubbles—graphite is a very opaque substance which absorbs or reflects most of the light which hits it.[1]

Modern optical answer sheets are read based on reflected light, measuring lightness and darkness. They do not need to be filled in with a number two pencil, though these are recommended over other types due to the lighter marks made by higher-number pencils, and the smudges from number 1 pencils. Black ink will be read, though many systems will ignore marks that are the same color the form is printed in.[1] This also allows optical answer sheets to be double-sided, because marks made on the opposite side will not interfere with reflectance readings as much as with opacity readings.

Most systems accommodate for human error in filling in ovals imprecisely, as long as they do not stray into the other ovals and the oval is almost completely filled

54.2 Errors

It is possible for optical answer sheets to be printed incorrectly, such that all ovals will be read as filled. This occurs if the outline of the ovals is too thick, or is irregular. During the 2008 U.S. presidential election, this occurred with over 19,000 absentee ballots in the Georgia county of Gwinnett, and was discovered after around 10,000 had already been returned. The slight difference was not apparent to the naked eye, and was not detected until a test run was made in late October. This required all ballots to be transferred to correctly printed ones, by sequestered workers of the board of elections, under close observation by members of the Democratic and Republican (but not other) political parties, and county sheriff deputies. The transfer, by law, cannot occur until election day (November 4).

54.3 References

[1] Bloomfield, Louis A. "Question 1529: Why do scantron-type tests only read #2 pencils? Can other pencils work?". HowEverythingWorks.org.

[2] Mullard Technical Handbook Volume 4 Section 4:Photoemissive Cells (1960 Edition)

Chapter 55

Optical braille recognition

Image of a page showing both the raised braille characters, and the recessed characters on the other side of the page.

Optical braille recognition is the act of capturing and processing images of braille characters into natural language characters. It is used to convert braille documents for people who cannot read them into text, and for preservation and reproduction of the documents.

55.1 History

In 1984, a group of researchers at the Delft University of Technology designed a braille reading tablet, in which a reading head with photosensitive cells was moved along set of rulers to capture braille text line-by-line.[1] In 1988, a group of French researchers at the Lille University of Science and Technology developed an algorithm, called Lectobraille, which converted braille documents into plain text. The system photographed the braille text with a low-resolution CCD camera, and used spatial filtering techniques, median filtering, erosion, and dilation to extract the braille. The braille characters were then converted to natural language using adaptive recognition.[2] The Lectobraille technique had an error rate of 1%, and took an average pro-

cessing time of seven seconds per line.[1] In 1993, a group of researchers from the Katholieke Universiteit Leuven developed a system to recognize braille that had been scanned with a commercially available scanner.[1] The system, however, was unable to handle deformities in the braille grid, so well-formed braille documents were required.[3] In 1999, a group at the Hong Kong Polytechnic University implemented an optical braille recognition technique using edge detection to translate braille into English or Chinese text.[4] In 2001, Murray and Dais created a handheld recognition system, that scanned small sections of a document at once.[5] Because of the small area scanned at once, grid deformation was less of an issue, and a simpler, more efficient algorithm was employed.[3] In 2003, Morgavi and Morando designed a system to recognize braille characters using artificial neural networks. This system was noted for its ability to handle image degradation more successfully than other approaches.[3]

55.2 Applications

Optical braille recognition is used to digitize and reproduce texts that have been produced with non-computerized systems, such as with braille typewriters. Digitizing braille texts also helps reduce storage space, as braille texts take up much more space than their natural language counterparts. Optical braille recognition is also useful for people who cannot read braille, but need to access the content of braille documents.[6]

55.3 Challenges

Many of the challenges to successfully processing braille text arise from the nature of braille documents. Braille is generally printed on solid-color paper, with no ink to produce contrast between the raised characters and the background paper. However, imperfections in the page can appear in a scan or image of the page.

139

Many documents are printed *inter-point*, meaning they are double-sided. As such, the depressions of the braille of one side appear interlaid with the protruding braille of the other side.[7]

55.4 Techniques

Some optical braille recognition techniques attempt to use oblique lighting and a camera to reveal the shadows of the depressions and protrusions of the braille. Others make use of commercially available document scanners.[7]

55.5 See also

- Optical character recognition

55.6 References

[1] Mennens, Jan; Tichelen, Luc van; François, Guido; Enge-len, Jan J. (December 1994). "Optical recognition of Braille using standard equipment". *IEEE Transactions on Rehabili-tation Engineering* **2** (4): 207–212. doi:10.1109/86.340878. ISSN 1063-6528.

[2] Dubus, J.P.; Benjelloun, M.; Devlaminck, V.; Wauquier, F.; Altmayer, P. (November 1988). "Image processing tech-niques to perform an autonomous system to translate relief braille into black-ink, called: Lectobraille". *Proceedings of the Annual International Conference of the IEEE* (Engi-neering in Medicine and Biology Society) **4**: 1584–1585. doi:10.1109/IEMBS.1988.94726.

[3] Wong, Lisa; Abdulla, Waleed; Hussman, Stephan (August 2004). "A software algorithm prototype for optical recog-nition of embossed Braille". *Proceedings of the 17th In-ternational Conference on Pattern Recognition*: 586–589. doi:10.1109/ICPR.2004.1334316. ISSN 1051-4651.

[4] Ng, C.; Ng, V.; Lau, Y. (September 1999). "Regu-lar feature extraction for the recognition of braille". *Third International Conference on Computational Intelligence and Multimedia Applications*: 302–306. doi:10.1109/ICCIMA.1999.798547.

[5] Murray, I.; Dias, T. (2001). "A protable device for opti-cally recognizing Braille". *The Seventh Australian and New Zealand Intelligent Information Systems Conference*: 302–306. doi:10.1109/ANZIIS.2001.974063.

[6] Al-Saleh, Amany; El-Zaart, Ali; Al-Salman, Abdul Ma-lik (2011). "Dot detection of Braille images using a mixture of beta distributions". *Journal of Com-puter Science* (Science Publications) **7** (11): 1749–1759. doi:10.3844/jcssp.2011.1749.1759. ISSN 1549-3636.

[7] Antonacopoulos, A.; Bridson, D. (2004). "A Robust Braille Recognition System". *Document Analysis Systems* **VI**: 533–545. doi:10.1007/978-3-540-28640-0_50. ISSN 0302-9743.

Chapter 56

Optical character recognition

Optical character recognition(optical character reader) (OCR) is the mechanical or electronic conversion of images of typed, handwritten or printed text into machine-encoded text. It is widely used as a form of data entry from printed paper data records, whether passport documents, invoices, bank statements, computerized receipts, business cards, mail, printouts of static-data, or any suitable documentation. It is a common method of digitizing printed texts so that it can be electronically edited, searched, stored more compactly, displayed on-line, and used in machine processes such as machine translation, text-to-speech, key data and text mining. OCR is a field of research in pattern recognition, artificial intelligence and computer vision.

Early versions needed to be trained with images of each character, and worked on one font at a time. Advanced systems capable of producing a high degree of recognition accuracy for most fonts are now common. Some systems are capable of reproducing formatted output that closely approximates the original page including images, columns, and other non-textual components.

56.1 History

Early optical character recognition may be traced to technologies involving telegraphy and creating reading devices for the blind.[1] In 1914, Emanuel Goldberg developed a machine that read characters and converted them into standard telegraph code. Concurrently, Edmund Fournier d'Albe developed the Optophone, a handheld scanner that when moved across a printed page, produced tones that corresponded to specific letters or characters.[2]

In the late 1920s and into the 1930s Emanuel Goldberg developed what he called a "Statistical Machine" for searching microfilm archives using an optical code recognition system. In 1931 he was granted USA Patent number 1,838,389 for the invention. The patent was acquired by IBM.

56.1.1 Blind and visually impaired users

In 1974, Ray Kurzweil started the company Kurzweil Computer Products, Inc. and continued development of omni-font OCR, which could recognize text printed in virtually any font (Kurzweil is often credited with inventing omni-font OCR, but it was in use by companies, including CompuScan, in the late 1960s and 1970s[1][3]). Kurzweil decided that the best application of this technology would be to create a reading machine for the blind, which would allow blind people to have a computer read text to them out loud. This device required the invention of two enabling technologies – the CCD flatbed scanner and the text-to-speech synthesizer. On January 13, 1976, the successful finished product was unveiled during a widely reported news conference headed by Kurzweil and the leaders of the National Federation of the Blind. In 1978, Kurzweil Computer Products began selling a commercial version of the optical character recognition computer program. LexisNexis was one of the first customers, and bought the program to upload legal paper and news documents onto its nascent on-line databases. Two years later, Kurzweil sold his company to Xerox, which had an interest in further commercializing paper-to-computer text conversion. Xerox eventually spun it off as Scansoft, which merged with Nuance Communications. The research group headed by A. G. Ramakrishnan at the Medical intelligence and language engineering lab, Indian Institute of Science, has developed PrintToBraille tool, an open source GUI frontend[4] that can be used by any OCR to convert scanned images of printed books to Braille books.

In the 2000s, OCR was made available online as a service (WebOCR), in a cloud computing environment, and in mobile applications like real-time translation of foreign-language signs on a smartphone.

Various commercial and open source OCR systems are available for most common writing systems, including Latin, Cyrillic, Arabic, Hebrew, Indic, Bengali (Bangla), Devanagari, Tamil, Chinese, Japanese, and Korean characters.

56.2 Applications

OCR engines have been developed into many kinds of object-oriented OCR applications, such as receipt OCR, invoice OCR, check OCR, legal billing document OCR.

They can be used for:

- Data entry for business documents, e.g. check, passport, invoice, bank statement and receipt

- Automatic number plate recognition

- Automatic insurance documents key information extraction

- Extracting business card information into a contact list

- More quickly make textual versions of printed documents, e.g. book scanning for Project Gutenberg

- Make electronic images of printed documents searchable, e.g. Google Books

- Converting handwriting in real time to control a computer (pen computing)

- Defeating CAPTCHA anti-bot systems, though these are specifically designed to prevent OCR[5][6][7]

- Assistive technology for blind and visually impaired users

56.3 Types

- Optical character recognition (OCR) – targets typewritten text, one glyph or character at a time.

- Optical word recognition – targets typewritten text, one word at a time (for languages that use a space as a word divider). (Usually just called "OCR".)

- Intelligent character recognition (ICR) – also targets handwritten printscript or cursive text one glyph or character at a time, usually involving machine learning.

- Intelligent word recognition (IWR) – also targets handwritten printscript or cursive text, one word at a time. This is especially useful for languages where glyphs are not separated in cursive script.

OCR is generally an "offline" process, which analyzes a static document. Handwriting movement analysis can be used as input to handwriting recognition.[8] Instead of merely using the shapes of glyphs and words, this technique is able to capture motions, such as the order in which segments are drawn, the direction, and the pattern of putting the pen down and lifting it. This additional information can make the end-to-end process more accurate. This technology is also known as "on-line character recognition", "dynamic character recognition", "real-time character recognition", and "intelligent character recognition".

56.4 Techniques

56.4.1 Pre-processing

OCR software often "pre-processes" images to improve the chances of successful recognition. Techniques include:[9]

- De-skew – If the document was not aligned properly when scanned, it may need to be tilted a few degrees clockwise or counterclockwise in order to make lines of text perfectly horizontal or vertical.

- Despeckle – remove positive and negative spots, smoothing edges[10]

- Binarization – Convert an image from color or greyscale to black-and-white (called a "binary image" because there are two colours). The task of binarization is performed as a simple way of separating the text (or any other desired image component) from the background.[11] The task of binarization itself is necessary since most commercial recognition algorithms work only on binary images since it proves to be simpler to do so.[12] In addition, the effectiveness of the binarization step influences to a significant extent the quality of the character recognition stage and the careful decisions are made in the choice of the binarization employed for a given input image type; since the quality of the binarization method employed to obtain the binary result depends on the type of the input image (scanned document, scene text image, historical degraded document etc.).[13][14]

- Line removal – Cleans up non-glyph boxes and lines

- Layout analysis or "zoning" – Identifies columns, paragraphs, captions, etc. as distinct blocks. Especially important in multi-column layouts and tables.

- Line and word detection – Establishes baseline for word and character shapes, separates words if necessary.

- Script recognition – In multilingual documents, the script may change at the level of the words and hence, identification of the script is necessary, before the right OCR can be invoked to handle the specific script.[15]

- Character isolation or "segmentation" – For per-character OCR, multiple characters that are connected due to image artifacts must be separated; single characters that are broken into multiple pieces due to artifacts must be connected.

- Normalize aspect ratio and scale[16]

Segmentation of fixed-pitch fonts is accomplished relatively simply by aligning the image to a uniform grid based on where vertical grid lines will least often intersect black areas. For proportional fonts, more sophisticated techniques are needed because whitespace between letters can sometimes be greater than that between words, and vertical lines can intersect more than one character.[17]

56.4.2 Character recognition

There are two basic types of core OCR algorithm, which may produce a ranked list of candidate characters.[18]

Matrix matching involves comparing an image to a stored glyph on a pixel-by-pixel basis; it is also known as "pattern matching", "pattern recognition", or "image correlation".[19] This relies on the input glyph being correctly isolated from the rest of the image, and on the stored glyph being in a similar font and at the same scale. This technique works best with typewritten text and does not work well when new fonts are encountered. This is the technique the early physical photocell-based OCR implemented, rather directly.

Feature extraction decomposes glyphs into "features" like lines, closed loops, line direction, and line intersections. These are compared with an abstract vector-like representation of a character, which might reduce to one or more glyph prototypes. General techniques of feature detection in computer vision are applicable to this type of OCR, which is commonly seen in "intelligent" handwriting recognition and indeed most modern OCR software.[10] Nearest neighbour classifiers such as the k-nearest neighbors algorithm are used to compare image features with stored glyph features and choose the nearest match.[20]

Software such as Cuneiform and Tesseract use a two-pass approach to character recognition. The second pass is known as "adaptive recognition" and uses the letter shapes recognized with high confidence on the first pass to recognize better the remaining letters on the second pass. This is advantageous for unusual fonts or low-quality scans where the font is distorted (e.g. blurred or faded).[17]

56.4.3 Post-processing

OCR accuracy can be increased if the output is constrained by a lexicon – a list of words that are allowed to occur in a document.[9] This might be, for example, all the words in the English language, or a more technical lexicon for a specific field. This technique can be problematic if the document contains words not in the lexicon, like proper nouns. Tesseract uses its dictionary to influence the character segmentation step, for improved accuracy.[17]

The output stream may be a plain text stream or file of characters, but more sophisticated OCR systems can preserve the original layout of the page and produce, for example, an annotated PDF that includes both the original image of the page and a searchable textual representation.

"Near-neighbor analysis" can make use of co-occurrence frequencies to correct errors, by noting that certain words are often seen together.[19] For example, "Washington, D.C." is generally far more common in English than "Washington DOC".

Knowledge of the grammar of the language being scanned can also help determine if a word is likely to be a verb or a noun, for example, allowing greater accuracy.

56.4.4 Application-specific optimizations

In recent years, the major OCR technology providers began to tweak OCR systems to better deal with specific types of input. Beyond an application-specific lexicon, better performance can be had by taking into account business rules, standard expression, or rich information contained in color images. This strategy is called "Application-Oriented OCR" or "Customized OCR", and has been applied to OCR of license plates, business cards, invoices, screenshots, ID cards, driver licenses, and automobile manufacturing.

56.5 Workarounds

There are several techniques for solving the problem of character recognition by means other than improved OCR algorithms.

56.5.1 Forcing better input

Special fonts like OCR-A, OCR-B, or MICR fonts, with precisely specified sizing, spacing, and distinctive character shapes, allow a higher accuracy rate during transcription. These were often used in early matrix-matching systems.

"Comb fields" are pre-printed boxes that encourage humans

to write more legibly – one glyph per box.[19] These are often printed in a "dropout color" which can be easily removed by the OCR system.[19]

Palm OS used a special set of glyphs, known as "Graffiti" which are similar to printed English characters but simplified or modified for easier recognition on the platform's computationally limited hardware. Users would need to learn how to write these special glyphs.

Zone-based OCR restricts the image to a specific part of a document. This is often referred to as "Template OCR".

56.5.2 Crowdsourcing

Crowdsourcing humans to perform the character recognition can quickly process images like computer-driven OCR, but with higher accuracy for recognizing images than is obtained with computers. Practical systems include the Amazon Mechanical Turk and reCAPTCHA.

56.6 Accuracy

Commissioned by the U.S. Department of Energy (DOE), the Information Science Research Institute (ISRI) had the mission to foster the improvement of automated technologies for understanding machine printed documents, and it conducted the most authoritative of the *Annual Test of OCR Accuracy* from 1992 to 1996.[21]

Recognition of Latin-script, typewritten text is still not 100% accurate even where clear imaging is available. One study based on recognition of 19th- and early 20th-century newspaper pages concluded that character-by-character OCR accuracy for commercial OCR software varied from 81% to 99%;[22] total accuracy can be achieved by human review or Data Dictionary Authentication. Other areas—including recognition of hand printing, cursive handwriting, and printed text in other scripts (especially those East Asian language characters which have many strokes for a single character)—are still the subject of active research. The MNIST database is commonly used for testing systems' ability to recognize handwritten digits.

Accuracy rates can be measured in several ways, and how they are measured can greatly affect the reported accuracy rate. For example, if word context (basically a lexicon of words) is not used to correct software finding non-existent words, a character error rate of 1% (99% accuracy) may result in an error rate of 5% (95% accuracy) or worse if the measurement is based on whether each whole word was recognized with no incorrect letters.[23]

Web based OCR systems for recognizing hand-printed text on the fly have become well known as commercial prod-

ucts in recent years (see Tablet PC history). Accuracy rates of 80% to 90% on neat, clean hand-printed characters can be achieved by pen computing software, but that accuracy rate still translates to dozens of errors per page, making the technology useful only in very limited applications.

Recognition of cursive text is an active area of research, with recognition rates even lower than that of hand-printed text. Higher rates of recognition of general cursive script will likely not be possible without the use of contextual or grammatical information. For example, recognizing entire words from a dictionary is easier than trying to parse individual characters from script. Reading the *Amount* line of a cheque (which is always a written-out number) is an example where using a smaller dictionary can increase recognition rates greatly. The shapes of individual cursive characters themselves simply do not contain enough information to accurately (greater than 98%) recognise all handwritten cursive script.

56.7 Unicode

Main article: Optical Character Recognition (Unicode block)

Characters to support OCR were added to the Unicode Standard in June 1993, with the release of version 1.1.

Some of these characters are mapped from fonts specific to MICR or OCR-A.

56.8 See also

- AI effect
- Applications of artificial intelligence
- Computational linguistics
- Digital library
- Digital mailroom
- Digital pen
- Institutional repository
- Live Ink Character Recognition Solution
- Music OCR
- Optical mark recognition
- Outline of artificial intelligence
- Sketch recognition

- Speech recognition

- Vectorization (image tracing)

- Voice recording

- List of emerging technologies

56.9   References

[1] Schantz, Herbert F. (1982). *The history of OCR, optical character recognition.* [Manchester Center, Vt.]: Recognition Technologies Users Association. ISBN 9780943072012.

[2] d'Albe, E. E. F. (1 July 1914). "On a Type-Reading Optophone". *Proceedings of the Royal Society A: Mathematical, Physical and Engineering Sciences* **90** (619): 373–375. doi:10.1098/rspa.1914.0061.

[3] "The History of OCR". *Data processing magazine* **12**: 46. 1970.

[4] PrintToBraille Tool. "ocr-gui-frontend". MILE Lab, Dept of EE, IISc. Archived from the original on December 25, 2014. Retrieved 7 December 2014.

[5] "How To Crack Captchas". andrewt.net. 2006-06-28. Retrieved 2013-06-16.

[6] "Breaking a Visual CAPTCHA". Cs.sfu.ca. 2002-12-10. Retrieved 2013-06-16.

[7] John Resig (2009-01-23). "John Resig – OCR and Neural Nets in JavaScript". Ejohn.org. Retrieved 2013-06-16.

[8] Tappert, C. C.; Suen, C. Y.; Wakahara, T. (1990). "The state of the art in online handwriting recognition". *IEEE Transactions on Pattern Analysis and Machine Intelligence* **12** (8): 787. doi:10.1109/34.57669.

[9] "Optical Character Recognition (OCR) – How it works". Nicomsoft.com. Retrieved 2013-06-16.

[10] "How OCR Software Works". OCRWizard. Retrieved 2013-06-16.

[11] Sezgin, Mehmet; Sankur, Bulent (2004). "Survey over image thresholding techniques and quantitative performance evaluation." (PDF). *Journal of Electronic imaging* **13** (1): 146. Retrieved 2 May 2015.

[12] Gupta, Maya R.; Jacobson, Nathaniel P.; Garcia, Eric K. (2007). "OCR binarization and image pre-processing for searching historical documents." (PDF). *Pattern Recognition* **40** (2): 389. Retrieved 2 May 2015.

[13] Trier, Oeivind Due; Jain, Anil K. (1995). "Goal-directed evaluation of binarization methods." (PDF). *IEEE Transactions on Pattern Analysis and Machine Intelligence* **17** (12): 1191–1201. Retrieved 2 May 2015.

[14] Milyaev, Sergey; Barinova, Olga; Novikova, Tatiana; Kohli, Pushmeet; Lempitsky, Victor (2013). "Image binarization for end-to-end text understanding in natural images." (PDF). *Document Analysis and Recognition (ICDAR) 2013*. 12th International Conference on. Retrieved 2 May 2015.

[15] Pati, P.B.; Ramakrishnan, A.G. (1987-05-29). *Word Level Multi-script Identification. Pattern Recognition Letters, Vol. 29, pp. 1218 - 1229, 2008.* doi:10.1016/j.patrec.2008.01.027.

[16] "Basic OCR in OpenCV | Damiles". Blog.damiles.com. Retrieved 2013-06-16.

[17] Ray Smith (2007). "An Overview of the Tesseract OCR Engine" (PDF). Retrieved 2013-05-23.

[18] "OCR Introduction". Dataid.com. Retrieved 2013-06-16.

[19] "How does OCR document scanning work?". Explain that Stuff. 2012-01-30. Retrieved 2013-06-16.

[20] "The basic patter recognition and classification with openCV | Damiles". Blog.damiles.com. Retrieved 2013-06-16.

[21] Code and Data to evaluate OCR accuracy, originally from UNLV/ISRI

[22] Holley, Rose (April 2009). "How Good Can It Get? Analysing and Improving OCR Accuracy in Large Scale Historic Newspaper Digitisation Programs". D-Lib Magazine. Retrieved 5 January 2011.

[23] Suen, C.Y.; Plamondon, R.; Tappert, A.; Thomassen, A.; Ward, J.R.; Yamamoto, K. (1987-05-29). *Future Challenges in Handwriting and Computer Applications*. 3rd International Symposium on Handwriting and Computer Applications, Montreal, May 29, 1987. Retrieved 2008-10-03.

56.10   External links

- Unicode OCR – Hex Range: 2440-245F Optical Character Recognition in Unicode

- Annotated bibliography of references to handwriting character recognition and pen computing

- Notes on the History of Pen-based Computing (YouTube)

Chapter 57

Optical mark recognition

Optical mark recognition (also called **optical mark reading** and **OMR**) is the process of capturing human-marked data from document forms such as surveys and tests.

57.1 OMR background

OMR test form, with registration marks and drop-out colors, designed to be scanned by dedicated OMR device

Many traditional OMR devices work with a dedicated scanner device that shines a beam of light onto the form paper. The contrasting reflectivity at predetermined positions on a page is then used to detect these marked areas because they reflect less light than the blank areas of the paper.

Some OMR devices use forms which are preprinted onto 'transoptic' paper and measure the amount of light which passes through the paper, thus a mark on either side of the paper will reduce the amount of light passing through the paper.

In contrast to the dedicated OMR device, desktop OMR software allows a user to create their own forms in a word processor and print them on a laser printer. The OMR software then works with a common desktop image scanner with a document feeder to process the forms once filled out.

OMR is generally distinguished from optical character recognition (OCR) by the fact that a complicated pattern recognition engine is not required. That is, the marks are constructed in such a way that there is little chance of not reading the marks correctly. This does require the image to have high contrast and an easily recognizable or irrelevant shape. A related field to OMR and OCR is the recognition of barcodes such as the UPC bar code found on product packaging.

One of the most familiar applications of optical mark recognition is the use of #2 pencil (HB in Europe) bubble optical answer sheets in multiple choice question examinations. Students mark their answers, or other personal information, by darkening circles marked on a pre-printed sheet. Afterwards the sheet is automatically graded by a scanning machine. In the United States and most European countries, a horizontal or vertical 'tick' in a rectangular 'lozenge' is the most commonly used type of OMR form, the most familiar application being the UK National lottery form. Lozenge marks are a later technology and have the advantage of being easier to mark and easier to erase. The large 'bubble' marks are legacy technology from the very early OMR machines that were so insensitive a large mark was required for reliability. In most Asian countries, a special marker is used to fill in an optical answer sheet. Students, likewise mark answers or other information via darkening circles marked on a pre-printed sheet. Then the sheet is automatically graded by a scanning machine.

Many of today's OMR applications involve people filling

in specialized forms. These forms are optimized for computer scanning, with careful registration in the printing, and careful design so that ambiguity is reduced to the minimum possible. Due to its extremely low error rate, low cost and ease-of-use, OMR is a popular method of tallying votes.[1][2][3][4][5][6][7][8][9][10]

OMR marks are also added to items of physical mail so folder inserter equipment can be used. The marks are added to each (normally facing/odd) page of a mail document and consist of a sequence of black dashes that folder inserter equipment scans in order to determine when the mail should be folded then inserted in an envelope.

57.2 OMR software

UNIVERSITY

Course Evaluation

Plain paper OMR survey form, without registration marks and drop-out colors, designed to be scanned by an image scanner and OMR software

OMR software is a computer software application that makes OMR possible on a desktop computer by using an Image scanner to process surveys, tests, attendance sheets, checklists, and other plain-paper forms printed on a laser printer.

OMR software is used to capture data from OMR sheets. While data capturing scanning devices focus on many factors like thickness of paper dimensions of OMR sheet and designing pattern.

One of the first OMR software packages that used images from common image scanners was Remark Office OMR, made by Gravic, Inc. (originally named Principia Products, Inc.). Remark Office OMR 1.0 was released in 1991.

The need for OMR software originated because early optical mark recognition systems used dedicated scanners and special pre-printed forms with drop-out colors and registration marks. Such forms typically cost US$0.10 to $0.19 a page.[11] In contrast, OMR software users design their own mark-sense forms with a word processor or built-in form editor, print them locally on a printer, and can save thousands of dollars on large numbers of forms.[12]

Identifying optical marks within a form, such as for processing census forms, has been offered by many forms-processing (Batch Transaction Capture) companies since the late 1980s. Mostly this is based on a bitonal image and pixel count with minimum and maximum pixel counts to eliminate extraneous marks, such as those erased with a dirty eraser that when converted into a black-and-white image (bitonal) can look like a legitimate mark. So this method can cause problems when a user changes his mind, and so some products started to use grayscale to better identify the intent of the marker—internally scantron and NCS scanners used grayscale.

OMR software is also used for adding OMR marks to mail documents so they can be scanned by folder inserter equipment. An example of OMR software is Mail Markup from UK developer Funasset Limited. This software allows the user to configure and select an OMR sequence then apply the OMR marks to mail documents prior to printing.

57.2.1 Open source

Some OMR software products are developed and or distributed under open source licenses.

- FormScanner: multiplatform Java application, supports custom forms [13] FormScanner has user support at www.formscanner.org.[14]

- queXF which can be used alone or in conjunction with surveys exported from LimeSurvey.

- Udai OMR

- Shared Questionnaire System (SQS)

- Auto Multiple Choice for class tests, with LaTeX formatting.[15]

- Moodle also has an extension, Quiz OMR, which provides online support for offline quizzes conducted on OMR sheets.

- TCExam supports offline testing conducted on OMR sheets.

- SDAPS for surveys, supports LaTeX and ODT formatted documents.[16]

- OMR Mark Engine C# implementation supports bulk scanning with custom forms

57.3 History

Optical mark recognition (OMR) is the scanning of paper to detect the presence or absence of a mark in a predetermined position.[4] Optical mark recognition has evolved from several other technologies. In the early 19th century and 20th century patents were given for machines that would aid the blind.[2]

OMR is now used as an input device for data entry. Two early forms of OMR are paper tape and punch cards which use actual holes punched into the medium instead of pencil filled circles on the medium. Paper tape was used as early as 1857 as an input device for telegraph.[10] Punch cards were created in 1890 and were used as input devices for computers. The use of punch cards declined greatly in the early 1970s with the introduction of personal computers.[8] With modern OMR, where the presence of a pencil filled in bubble is recognized, the recognition is done via an optical scanner.

The first mark sense scanner was the IBM 805 Test Scoring Machine; this read marks by sensing the electrical conductivity of graphite pencil lead using pairs of wire brushes that scanned the page. In the 1930s, Richard Warren at IBM experimented with optical mark sense systems for test scoring, as documented in US Patents 2,150,256 (filed in 1932, granted in 1939) and 2,010,653 (filed in 1933, granted in 1935). The first successful optical mark-sense scanner was developed by Everett Franklin Lindquist as documented in US Patent 3,050,248 (filed in 1955, granted in 1962). Lindquist had developed numerous standardized educational tests, and needed a better test scoring machine than the then-standard IBM 805. The rights to Lindquist's patents were held by the Measurement Research Center until 1968, when the University of Iowa sold the operation to Westinghouse Corporation.

During the same period, IBM also developed a successful optical mark-sense test-scoring machine, as documented in US Patent 2,944,734 (filed in 1957, granted in 1960). IBM commercialized this as the IBM 1230 Optical mark scoring reader in 1962. This and a variety of related machines allowed IBM to migrate a wide variety of applications developed for its mark sense machines to the new optical technology. These applications included a variety of inventory

management and trouble reporting forms, most of which had the dimensions of a standard punched card.

While the other players in the educational testing arena focused on selling scanning services, Scantron Corporation, founded in 1972,[17] had a different model; it would distribute inexpensive scanners to schools and make profits from selling the test forms. As a result, many people came to think of all mark-sense forms (whether optically sensed or not) as *scantron* forms. Scantron operates as a subsidiary of M&F Worldwide(MFW)[18] and provides testing and assessment systems and services and data collection and analysis services to educational institutions, businesses and government.

In 1983, Westinghouse Learning Corporation was acquired by National Computer Systems (NCS). In 2000, NCS was acquired by Pearson Education, where the OMR technology formed the core of Pearson's Data Management group. In February 2008, M&F Worldwide purchased the Data Management group from Pearson; the group is now part of the Scantron brand.[19]

OMR has been used in many situations as mentioned below. The use of OMR in inventory systems was a transition between punch cards and bar codes and is not used as much for this purpose.[8] OMR is still used extensively for surveys and testing though.

57.4 Usage

The use of OMR is not limited to schools or data collection agencies; many businesses and health care agencies use OMR to streamline their data input processes and reduce input error. OMR, OCR, and ICR technologies all provide a means of data collection from paper forms. OMR may also be done using an OMR (discrete read head) scanner or an imaging scanner.[20]

57.4.1 Applications

There are many other applications for OMR, for example:

- In the process of institutional research

- Community surveys

- Consumer surveys

- Tests and assessments

- Evaluations and feedback

- Data compilation

- Product evaluation

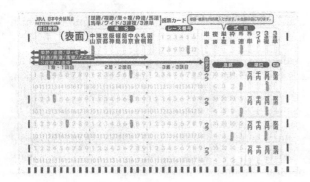

OMR betting form used in Japan Racing Association Fukushima Racecourse, Japan.

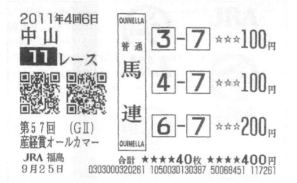

Betting ticket using this form.

- Time sheets and inventory counts

- Membership subscription forms

- Lotteries and voting

- Geocoding (e.g. postal codes)

- Mortgage loan, banking, and insurance applications

57.4.2 Field types

OMR has different fields to provide the format the questioner desires. These fields include:

- Multiple, where there are several options but only one is chosen. For example, the form might ask for one of the options ABCDE; 12345; completely disagree, disagree, indifferent, agree, completely agree; or similar.

- Grid: the bubbles or lines are set up in a grid format for the user to fill in a phone number, name, ID number and so on.

- Add, total the answers to a single value

- Boolean, answering yes or no to all that apply

- Binary, answering yes or no to only one

- Dotted lines fields, developed by Smartshoot OMR, allow border dropping like traditional color dropping.

57.4.3 Capabilities/requirements

In the past and presently, some OMR systems require special paper, special ink and a special input reader (Bergeron, 1998). This restricts the types of questions that can be asked and does not allow for much variability when the form is being input. Progress in OMR now allows users to create and print their own forms and use a scanner (preferably with a document feeder) to read the information.[21] The user is able to arrange questions in a format that suits their needs while still being able to easily input the data.[22] OMR systems approach one hundred percent accuracy and only take 5 milliseconds on average to recognize marks.[21] Users can use squares, circles, ellipses and hexagons for the mark zone. The software can then be set to recognize filled in bubbles, crosses or check marks.

OMR can also be used for personal use. There are all-in-one printers in the market that will print the photos the user selects by filling in the bubbles for size and paper selection on an index sheet that has been printed. Once the sheet has been filled in, the individual places the sheet on the scanner to be scanned and the printer will print the photos according to the marks that were indicated.

57.4.4 Disadvantages

There are also some disadvantages and limitations to OMR. If the user wants to gather large amounts of text, then OMR complicates the data collection.[23] There is also the possibility of missing data in the scanning process, and incorrectly or unnumbered pages can lead to their being scanned in the wrong order. Also, unless safeguards are in place, a page could be rescanned, providing duplicate data and skewing the data.[21]

As a result of the widespread adoption and ease of use of OMR, standardized examinations can consist primarily of multiple-choice questions, changing the nature of what is being tested.

57.5 See also

- AI effect

- Applications of artificial intelligence

- Clock mark

- Electronic data capture

- Mark sense

- Object recognition

- Optical character recognition

- Pattern recognition

Lists

- List of emerging technologies

- Outline of artificial intelligence

57.6   References

[1] http://www.postgradmed.com/issues/1998/08_98/dd_aug.
htm[]

[2] "Research Optical Character Recognition | Macmillan Science Library: Computer Sciences". Bookrags.com. 2010-11-02. Retrieved 2015-07-03.

[3] "Optical Scanning Systems —". Aceproject.org. Retrieved 2015-07-03.

[4] Haag, S., Cummings, M., McCubbrey, D., Pinsonnault, A., Donovan, R. (2006). Management Information Systems for the Information Age (3rd ed.). Canada: McGraw-Hill Ryerson.

[5] http://www.nyu.edu/its/pubs/connect/archives/96fall/
loprestistats.html[]

[6] >"Data Collection on the Cheap" (PPT). July 2015. Retrieved 2015-07-21.

[7] "Remark Office OMR, by Gravic (Principia Products), works with popular image scanners to scan surveys, tests and other plain paper forms". Omrsolutions.com. Retrieved 2015-07-03.

[8] Palmer, Roger C. (1989, Sept) The Basics of Automatic Identification [Electronic version]. Canadian Datasystems, 21 (9), 30-33

[9] "Forms Processing Technology". Tkvision.com. Retrieved 2015-07-03.

[10] "Research Input Devices | Macmillan Science Library: Computer Sciences". Bookrags.com. 2010-11-02. Retrieved 2015-07-03.

[11] http://fdc.fullerton.edu/technology/scantron/Scantron%
20Forms%202008%20handout.pdf[]

[12] Michael Wagenheim. "Grading Biology Exams at a Large State University". RemarkSoftware.com. Retrieved 2015-07-21.

[13] "FormScanner download". SourceForge.net. Retrieved 2015-07-03.

[14] "FormScanner". FormScanne.org. Retrieved 2015-07-03.

[15] "AMC - Multiple Choice Questionnaires management with automated marking - Home". Home.gna.org. Retrieved 2015-07-03.

[16] "SDAPS". SDAPS.org. 2015-05-30. Retrieved 2015-07-03.

[17] "The Marketplace for Educational Testing". *Bc.edu*. Retrieved 2015-07-03.

[18] http://www.mandfworldwide.com/[]

[19] http://www.ncspearson.com/[]

[20] http://datamanagement.scantron.com/pdf/icr-ocr-omr.
pdf[]

[21] Bergeron,

[22] LoPresti, 1996

[23] Green, 2000

Chapter 58

Polyworld

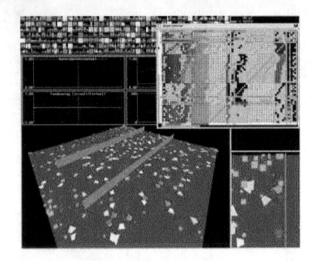

Polyworld Screenshot, 1994

The genome is randomly mutated at a set probability, which are also changed in descendant organisms.

58.1   External links

- Github entry

- Yaeger's page on Polyworld

- Google TechTalk about Polyworld

Polyworld is a cross-platform (Linux, Mac OS X) program written by Larry Yaeger to evolve Artificial Intelligence through natural selection and evolutionary algorithms.

It uses the Qt graphics toolkit and OpenGL to display a graphical environment in which a population of trapezoid agents search for food, mate, have offspring, and prey on each other. The population is typically only in the hundreds, as each individual is rather complex and the environment consumes considerable computer resources. The graphical environment is necessary since the individuals actually move around the 2-D plane and must be able to "see." Since some basic abilities, like eating carcasses or randomly generated food, seeing other individuals, mating or fighting with them, etc., are possible, a number of interesting behaviours have been observed to spontaneously arise after prolonged evolution, such as cannibalism, predators and prey, and mimicry.

Each individual makes decisions based on a neural net using Hebbian learning; the neural net is derived from each individual's genome. The genome does not merely specify the wiring of the neural nets, but also determines their size, speed, color, mutation rate and a number of other factors.

Chapter 59

Pop music automation

Pop music automation is a field of study among musicians and computer scientists with a goal of producing successful pop music algorithmically. It is often based on the premise that pop music is especially formulaic, unchanging, and easy to compose. The idea of automating pop music composition is related to many ideas in algorithmic music, Artificial Intelligence (AI) and computational creativity.

59.1 Overview: automation in music

Algorithms (or, at the very least, formal sets of rules) have been used to compose music for centuries; the procedures used to plot voice-leading in Western counterpoint, for example, can often be reduced to algorithmic determinacy. Now the term is usually reserved, however, for the use of formal procedures to make music without human intervention.

Classical music automation software exists that generates music in the style of Mozart and Bach and jazz. Most notably, David Cope[1] has written a software system called "Experiments in Musical Intelligence" (or "EMI") that is capable of analyzing and generalizing from existing music by a human composer to generate novel musical compositions in the same style. EMI's output is convincing enough to persuade human listeners that its music is human-generated to a high level of competence.

Creativity research in jazz has focused on the process of improvisation and the cognitive demands that this places on a musical agent: reasoning about time, remembering and conceptualizing what has already been played, and planning ahead for what might be played next.

Inevitably associated with Pop music automation is Pop music analysis.

Projects in Pop music automation may include, but are not limited to, ideas in melody creation and song development, vocal generation or improvement, automatic accompaniment and lyric composition.

59.2 Automatic accompaniment

Some systems exist that automatically choose chords to accompany a vocal melody in real-time. A user with no musical experience can create a song with instrumental accompaniment just by singing into a microphone. An example is a Microsoft Research project called Songsmith,[2] which trains a Hidden Markov model using a music database and uses that model to select chords for new melodies.

59.3 Melody generation

Automatic melody generation is often done with a Markov chain, the states of the system become note or pitch values, and a probability vector for each note is constructed, completing a transition probability matrix (see below). An algorithm is constructed to produce and output note values based on the transition matrix weightings, which could be MIDI note values, frequency (Hz), or any other desirable metric.

A second-order Markov chain can be introduced by considering the current state *and* also the previous state, as indicated in the second table. Higher, *n*th-order chains tend to "group" particular notes together, while 'breaking off' into other patterns and sequences occasionally. These higher-order chains tend to generate results with a sense of phrasal structure, rather than the 'aimless wandering' produced by a first-order system.[3]

59.4 Lyric composition

Automated lyric creating software may take forms such as:

- Selecting words according to their rhythm

The Tra-la-Lyrics system[4] produces song lyrics, in Portuguese, for a given melody. This not only involves matching each word syllable with a note in the melody, but also matching the word's stress with the strong beats of the melody.

- Parsing existing Pop music (for content or word choice e.g.)

This involves natural language processing. Pablo Gervás[5] has developed a noteworthy system called ASPERA that employs a case-based reasoning (CBR) approach to generating poetic formulations of a given input text via a composition of poetic fragments that are retrieved from a case-base of existing poems. Each poem fragment in the ASPERA case-base is annotated with a prose string that expresses the meaning of the fragment, and this prose string is used as the retrieval key for each fragment. Metrical rules are then used to combine these fragments into a well-formed poetic structure.

- Automatic analogy or story creation

Programs like TALE-SPIN [6] and The MINSTREL[7] system represent a complex elaboration of this basis approach, distinguishing a range of character-level goals in the story from a range of author-level goals for the story. Systems like Bringsjord's BRUTUS[8] can create stories with complex inter-personal themes like betrayal.
On-line metaphor generation systems like 'Sardonicus' or 'Aristotle'[9] can suggest lexical metaphors for a given descriptive goal (e.g., to describe a supermodel as skinny, the source terms "pencil", "whip", "whippet", "rope", "stick-insect" and "snake" are suggested).

- Free association of grouped words

Using a language database (such as wordnet) one can create musings on a subject that may be weak grammatically but are still sensical. See such projects as the Flowerewolf automatic poetry generator or the Dada engine.

59.5   Software

59.5.1   More or less free

- AI Sings - Algorithmic Composition by Learning

- BreathCube by xoxos. Simple lyrical vocal content is generated with simple music.

- CubeBreath by xoxos. Audio input is vocoded in tune with the music.

- Midi Internet Algorithmic Composition

- infno - Infinite generator of electronic dance music and synth pop.

59.5.2   Commercial

- Band in a box generates any element, potentially creates whole new songs from scratch.

- Musical Palette - Melody Composing Tool

- SongSmith:Automatic Accompaniment for Vocal Melodies

- Ludwig 3.0 automatic accompaniment, writes arrangements for given instruments, plays its own songs for an infinitely long time.

59.6   See also

- Algorithmic music

- Artificial Creativity

- Computer music

59.7   References

[1] Cope, David (2006), *Computer Models of Musical Creativity*, Cambridge, MA: MIT Press

[2] and

[3] Curtis Roads (ed.) (1996), *The Computer Music Tutorial*, MIT Press, ISBN 0-262-18158-4

[4] Gonçalo Oliveira, Hugo; et al. (2007), *Tra-la-lyrics: an approach to generate text based on rhythm*, Proceedings of the 4th International Joint Workshop on Computational Creativity, pp. 47–55, London, UK, (June 2007)

[5] Gervás, Pablo (2001), *An expert system for the composition of formal Spanish poetry*, Journal of Knowledge-Based Systems 14(3-4) pp 181–188

[6] Meehan, James (1981), *TALE-SPIN*, Shank, R. C. and Riesbeck, C. K., (eds.), *Inside Computer Understanding: Five Programs plus Miniatures.* Hillsdale, NJ: Lawrence Erlbaum Associates

[7] Turner, S.R. (1994), *The Creative Process: A Computer Model of Storytelling*, Hillsdale, NJ: Lawrence Erlbaum Associates

[8] Bringsjord, S., Ferrucci, D. A. (2000), *Artificial Intelligence and Literary Creativity. Inside the Mind of BRUTUS, a Storytelling Machine.*, Hillsdale NJ: Lawrence Erlbaum Associates

[9] Veale, Tony, Hao, Yanfen (2007), *Comprehending and Generating Apt Metaphors: A Web-driven, Case-based Approach to Figurative Language*, Proceedings of AAAI 2007, the 22nd AAAI Conference on Artificial Intelligence. Vancouver, Canada

Chapter 60

Quack.com

Quack.com was an early voice portal company. The domain name later was used for Quack; an iPad Search application from AOL.

60.1 History

It was originally founded in 1998 by Steven Woods, Jeromy Carriere and Alex Quilici as a Pittsburgh, Pennsylvania, USA, based voice portal infrastructure company originally named Quackware. Quack was the first company to try to create a voice portal: a consumer-based destination "site" in which consumers could not only access information by voice alone, but also complete transactions. Quackware launched a beta phone service in 1999 that allowed consumers to purchase books from sites such as Amazon and CDs from sites such as CDNow simply by answering a short set of questions. Quack followed on with a set of information services from movie listings (inspired by, but expanding upon, Moviefone) to news, weather and stock quotes. This concept introduced a series of lookalike startups including Tellme Networks which went on to raise more money than any single Internet startup in history on a similar concept.

Quack received venture funding in 1999 and moved operations to Mountain View in Silicon Valley, California in 1999. A deal with Lycos was announced in May 2000.[1][2] In September 2000 Quack was acquired[3] for $200 million by America Online (AOL) and moved onto the Netscape campus with what was left of the Netscape team.

Quack was attacked in the Canadian press for being representative of the Canadian "brain drain" to the US during the Internet bubble, focusing its recruiting efforts on the University of Waterloo, hiring more than 50 engineers from Waterloo in less than 10 months. Quack competitor Tellme Networks raised enormous funds in what became a highly competitive market in 2000, with the emergence of more than a dozen additional competitors in a 12-month period.

Following its acquisition by America Online in a Ted Leon-sis-led effort to bring Quack into AOL Interactive, the Quack voice service became AOLbyPhone as one of AOL's "web properties" along with MapQuest, Moviefone and others.[4]

Quack secured several patents that underlie the technical challenges of delivering interactive voice services. Constructing a voice portal required integrations and innovations not only in speech recognition and speech generation, but also in databases, application specification, constraint-based reasoning and artificial intelligence and computational linguistics. "Quack"'s name derived from the company goal of providing not only voice-based services, but more broadly "Quick Ubiquitous Access to Consumer Knowledge".

The patents assigned to Quack.com include: System and method for voice access to Internet-based information, System and method for advertising with an Internet Voice Portal and recognizing the axiom that in interactive voice systems one must "know the set of possible answers to a question before asking it". System and method for determining if one web site has the same information as another web site.

Quack.com was spoofed in The Simpsons in March, 2002 in the episode Blame It on Lisa in which a "ComQuaak" sign is replaced by another equally crazy telecom company name.

60.2 2010 Onwards

In July 2010, quack.com became the focus of a new AOL iPad application, that was a web search experience. The product delivers web results and blends in picture, video and Twitter results. It enables you to preview the web results before you go to the site, search within each result, and flip through the results pages, making full use of the iPad's touch screen features. The iPad app was free via iTunes, but support discontinued in 2012.

60.3   References

[1] John Borland (May 23, 2000). "Deals deliver validation to voice portal players". *Cnet News*. Retrieved June 11, 2013.

[2] John Borland (August 31, 2000). "AOL nabs Quack.com for voice recognition". *Cnet News*. Retrieved June 11, 2013.

[3] Kelly Black (September 1, 2000). "If It Walks Like a Duck, Quack.com". *Internet News*. Retrieved June 11, 2013.

[4] Kenneth G. Hardy, Amy J. Hillman, Benji Shomair (February 27, 2002). "Strategic Direction at Quack.com". *Case Study*. Harvard Business School Online.

60.4   External links

- Official site

- Quack.com company web site (historical link)

- iTunes App Link

Chapter 61

Question answering

For other uses, see question and answer.

Question Answering (**QA**) is a computer science discipline within the fields of information retrieval and natural language processing (NLP), which is concerned with building systems that automatically answer questions posed by humans in a natural language.

A QA implementation, usually a computer program, may construct its answers by querying a structured database of knowledge or information, usually a knowledge base. More commonly, QA systems can pull answers from an unstructured collection of natural language documents.

Some examples of natural language document collections used for QA systems include:

- a local collection of reference texts

- internal organization documents and web pages

- compiled newswire reports

- a set of Wikipedia pages

- a subset of World Wide Web pages

QA research attempts to deal with a wide range of question types including: fact, list, definition, *How*, *Why*, hypothetical, semantically constrained, and cross-lingual questions.

- *Closed-domain* question answering deals with questions under a specific domain (for example, medicine or automotive maintenance), and can be seen as an easier task because NLP systems can exploit domain-specific knowledge frequently formalized in ontologies. Alternatively, *closed-domain* might refer to a situation where only a limited type of questions are accepted, such as questions asking for descriptive rather than procedural information. QA systems in the context of machine reading applications have also been constructed in the medical domain, for instance related to Alzheimers disease [1]

- *Open-domain* question answering deals with questions about nearly anything, and can only rely on general ontologies and world knowledge. On the other hand, these systems usually have much more data available from which to extract the answer.

61.1 History

Two early QA systems were BASEBALL and LUNAR. BASEBALL answered questions about the US baseball league over a period of one year. LUNAR, in turn, answered questions about the geological analysis of rocks returned by the Apollo moon missions. Both QA systems were very effective in their chosen domains. In fact, LUNAR was demonstrated at a lunar science convention in 1971 and it was able to answer 90% of the questions in its domain posed by people untrained on the system. Further restricted-domain QA systems were developed in the following years. The common feature of all these systems is that they had a core database or knowledge system that was hand-written by experts of the chosen domain. The language abilities of BASEBALL and LUNAR used techniques similar to ELIZA and DOCTOR, the first chatterbot programs.

SHRDLU was a highly successful question-answering program developed by Terry Winograd in the late 60s and early 70s. It simulated the operation of a robot in a toy world (the "blocks world"), and it offered the possibility to ask the robot questions about the state of the world. Again, the strength of this system was the choice of a very specific domain and a very simple world with rules of physics that were easy to encode in a computer program.

In the 1970s, knowledge bases were developed that targeted narrower domains of knowledge. The QA systems developed to interface with these expert systems produced more repeatable and valid responses to questions within an area of knowledge. These expert systems closely resembled modern QA systems except in their internal architecture. Ex-

157

pert systems rely heavily on expert-constructed and organized knowledge bases, whereas many modern QA systems
rely on statistical processing of a large, unstructured, natural language text corpus.

The 1970s and 1980s saw the development of comprehensive theories in computational linguistics, which led to the
development of ambitious projects in text comprehension
and question answering. One example of such a system was
the Unix Consultant (UC), developed by Robert Wilensky
at U.C. Berkeley in the late 1980s. The system answered
questions pertaining to the Unix operating system. It had
a comprehensive hand-crafted knowledge base of its domain, and it aimed at phrasing the answer to accommodate various types of users. Another project was LILOG, a
text-understanding system that operated on the domain of
tourism information in a German city. The systems developed in the UC and LILOG projects never went past the
stage of simple demonstrations, but they helped the development of theories on computational linguistics and reasoning.

Recently, specialized natural language QA systems have
been developed, such as EAGLi for health and life scientists.

61.2   Architecture

Most modern QA systems use natural language text documents as their underlying knowledge source. Natural language processing techniques are used to both process the
question and index or process the text corpus from which
answers are extracted. An increasing number of QA systems use the World Wide Web as their corpus of text and
knowledge. However, many of these tools do not produce
a human-like answer, but rather employ "shallow" methods
(keyword-based techniques, templates...) to produce a list
of documents or a list of document excerpts containing the
probable answer highlighted.

In an alternative QA implementation, human users assem-
ble knowledge in a structured database, called a knowledge
base, similar to those employed in the expert systems of
the 1970s. It is also possible to employ a combination of
structured databases and natural language text documents
in a hybrid QA system. Such a hybrid system may employ
data mining algorithms to populate a structured knowledge
base that is also populated and edited by human contributors. An example hybrid QA system is the Wolfram Alpha
QA system which employs natural language processing to
transform human questions into a form that is processed by
a curated knowledge base.

Current QA systems[2] typically include a **question classifier** module that determines the type of question and the

type of answer. After the question is analysed, the system
typically uses several modules that apply increasingly complex NLP techniques on a gradually reduced amount of text.
Thus, a **document retrieval module** uses search engines to
identify the documents or paragraphs in the document set
that are likely to contain the answer. Subsequently a **filter** preselects small text fragments that contain strings of
the same type as the expected answer. For example, if the
question is "Who invented Penicillin" the filter returns text
that contain names of people. Finally, an **answer extraction** module looks for further clues in the text to determine
if the answer candidate can indeed answer the question.

A **multiagent** question-answering architecture has been
proposed, where each domain is represented by an agent
which tries to answer questions taking into account its specific knowledge. The meta–agent controls the cooperation
between question answering agents and chooses the most
relevant answer(s).[3]

61.3   Question answering methods

QA is very dependent on a good search corpus - for without documents containing the answer, there is little any QA
system can do. It thus makes sense that larger collection
sizes generally lend well to better QA performance, unless
the question domain is orthogonal to the collection. The
notion of data redundancy in massive collections, such as
the web, means that nuggets of information are likely to be
phrased in many different ways in differing contexts and
documents,[4] leading to two benefits:

1. By having the right information appear in many forms,
   the burden on the QA system to perform complex NLP
   techniques to understand the text is lessened.

2. Correct answers can be filtered from false positives by
   relying on the correct answer to appear more times in
   the documents than instances of incorrect ones.

Question answering heavily relies on reasoning. There
are a number of question answering systems designed in
Prolog,[5] a logic programming language associated with
artificial intelligence.

61.3.1   Open domain question answering

In information retrieval, an open domain question answering system aims at returning an answer in response to the
user's question. The returned answer is in the form of short
texts rather than a list of relevant documents. The system

uses a combination of techniques from computational linguistics, information retrieval and knowledge representation for finding answers.

The system takes a natural language question as an input rather than a set of keywords, for example, "When is the national day of China?" The sentence is then transformed into a query through its logical form. Having the input in the form of a natural language question makes the system more user-friendly, but harder to implement, as there are various question types and the system will have to identify the correct one in order to give a sensible answer. Assigning a question type to the question is a crucial task, the entire answer extraction process relies on finding the correct question type and hence the correct answer type.

Keyword extraction is the first step for identifying the input question type. In some cases, there are clear words that indicate the question type directly. i.e. "Who", "Where" or "How many", these words tell the system that the answers should be of type "Person", "Location", "Number" respectively. In the example above, the word "When" indicates that the answer should be of type "Date". POS tagging and syntactic parsing techniques can also be used to determine the answer type. In this case, the subject is "Chinese National Day", the predicate is "is" and the adverbial modifier is "when", therefore the answer type is "Date". Unfortunately, some interrogative words like "Which", "What" or "How" do not give clear answer types. Each of these words can represent more than one type. In situations like this, other words in the question need to be considered. First thing to do is to find the words that can indicate the meaning of the question. A lexical dictionary such as WordNet can then be used for understanding the context.

Once the question type has been identified, an Information retrieval system is used to find a set of documents containing the correct key words. A tagger and NP/Verb Group chunker can be used to verify whether the correct entities and relations are mentioned in the found documents. For questions such as "Who" or "Where", a Named Entity Recogniser is used to find relevant "Person" and "Location" names from the retrieved documents. Only the relevant paragraphs are selected for ranking.

A vector space model can be used as a strategy for classifying the candidate answers. Check if the answer is of the correct type as determined in the question type analysis stage. Inference technique can also be used to validate the candidate answers. A score is then given to each of these candidates according to the number of question words it contains and how close these words are to the candidate, the more and the closer the better. The answer is then translated into a compact and meaningful representation by parsing. In the previous example, the expected output answer is "1st Oct."

61.4 Issues

In 2002 a group of researchers wrote a roadmap of research in question answering.[6] The following issues were identified.

Question classes Different types of questions (e.g., "What is the capital of Liechtenstein?" vs. "Why does a rainbow form?" vs. "Did Marilyn Monroe and Cary Grant ever appear in a movie together?") require the use of different strategies to find the answer. Question classes are arranged hierarchically in taxonomies.

Question processing The same information request can be expressed in various ways, some interrogative ("Who is the King of Lesotho?") and some assertive ("Tell me the name of the King of Lesotho."). A semantic model of question understanding and processing would recognize equivalent questions, regardless of how they are presented. This model would enable the translation of a complex question into a series of simpler questions, would identify ambiguities and treat them in context or by interactive clarification.

Context and QA Questions are usually asked within a context and answers are provided within that specific context. The context can be used to clarify a question, resolve ambiguities or keep track of an investigation performed through a series of questions. (For example, the question, "Why did Joe Biden visit Iraq in January 2010?" might be asking why Vice President Biden visited and not President Obama, why he went to Iraq and not Afghanistan or some other country, why he went in January 2010 and not before or after, or what Biden was hoping to accomplish with his visit. If the question is one of a series of related questions, the previous questions and their answers might shed light on the questioner's intent.)

Data sources for QA Before a question can be answered, it must be known what knowledge sources are available and relevant. If the answer to a question is not present in the data sources, no matter how well the question processing, information retrieval and answer extraction is performed, a correct result will not be obtained.

Answer extraction Answer extraction depends on the complexity of the question, on the answer type provided by question processing, on the actual data where the answer is searched, on the search method and on the question focus and context.

Answer formulation The result of a QA system should be presented in a way as natural as possible. In some cases, simple extraction is sufficient. For example, when the question classification indicates that the answer type is a name (of a person, organization, shop or disease, etc.), a quantity (monetary value, length, size, distance, etc.) or a date (e.g. the answer to the question, "On what day did Christmas fall in 1989?") the extraction of a single datum is sufficient. For other cases, the presentation of the answer may require the use of fusion techniques that combine the partial answers from multiple documents.

Real time question answering There is need for developing Q&A systems that are capable of extracting answers from large data sets in several seconds, regardless of the complexity of the question, the size and multitude of the data sources or the ambiguity of the question.

Multilingual (or cross-lingual) question answering The ability to answer a question posed in one language using an answer corpus in another language (or even several). This allows users to consult information that they cannot use directly. (See also Machine translation.)

Interactive QA It is often the case that the information need is not well captured by a QA system, as the question processing part may fail to classify properly the question or the information needed for extracting and generating the answer is not easily retrieved. In such cases, the questioner might want not only to reformulate the question, but to have a dialogue with the system. In addition, system may also use previously answered questions.[7] (For example, the system might ask for a clarification of what sense a word is being used, or what type of information is being asked for.)

Advanced reasoning for QA More sophisticated questioners expect answers that are outside the scope of written texts or structured databases. To upgrade a QA system with such capabilities, it would be necessary to integrate reasoning components operating on a variety of knowledge bases, encoding world knowledge and common-sense reasoning mechanisms, as well as knowledge specific to a variety of domains. Evi is an example of such as system.

Information clustering for QA Information clustering for question answering systems is a new trend that originated to increase the accuracy of question answering systems through search space reduction. In recent years this was widely researched through development of question answering systems which support information clustering in their basic flow of process.[8]

User profiling for QA The user profile captures data about the questioner, comprising context data, domain of interest, reasoning schemes frequently used by the questioner, common ground established within different dialogues between the system and the user, and so forth. The profile may be represented as a predefined template, where each template slot represents a different profile feature. Profile templates may be nested one within another.

61.5 Progress

QA systems have been extended in recent years to encompass additional domains of knowledge[9] For example, systems have been developed to automatically answer temporal and geospatial questions, questions of definition and terminology, biographical questions, multilingual questions, and questions about the content of audio, images, and video. Current QA research topics include:

- interactivity—clarification of questions or answers
- answer reuse or caching
- knowledge representation and reasoning
- social media analysis with QA systems
- sentiment analysis[10]
- utilization of thematic roles[11]
- semantic resolution: to bridge the gap between syntactically different questions and answer-bearing texts[12]
- utilization of linguistic resources,[13] such as WordNet, FrameNet, and the similar

IBM's question answering system, Watson, defeated the two greatest Jeopardy champions, Brad Rutter and Ken Jennings, by a significant margin. [14]

61.6 References

- Dragomir R. Radev, John Prager, and Valerie Samn. Ranking suspected answers to natural language questions using predictive annotation. In Proceedings of the 6th Conference on Applied Natural Language Processing, Seattle, WA, May 2000.

- John Prager, Eric Brown, Anni Coden, and Dragomir Radev. Question-answering by predictive annotation. In Proceedings, 23rd Annual International ACM SIGIR Conference on Research and Development in Information Retrieval, Athens, Greece, July 2000.

- Hutchins, W. John; Harold L. Somers (1992). *An Introduction to Machine Translation*. London: Academic Press. ISBN 0-12-362830-X.

- L. Fortnow, Steve Homer (2002/2003). A Short History of Computational Complexity. In D. van Dalen, J. Dawson, and A. Kanamori, editors, *The History of Mathematical Logic*. North-Holland, Amsterdam.

[1] Roser Morante , Martin Krallinger , Alfonso Valencia and Walter Daelemans. Machine Reading of Biomedical Texts about Alzheimer's Disease. CLEF 2012 Evaluation Labs and Workshop. September 17, 2012

[2] Hirschman, L. & Gaizauskas, R. (2001) Natural Language Question Answering. The View from Here. Natural Language Engineering (2001), 7:4:275-300 Cambridge University Press.

[3] Galitsky B, Pampapathi R. Can many agents answer questions better than one. *First Monday*. 2005;10.

[4] Lin, J. (2002). The Web as a Resource for Question Answering: Perspectives and Challenges. In Proceedings of the Third International Conference on Language Resources and Evaluation (LREC 2002).

[5] Galitsky, Boris (2003). *Natural Language Question Answering System: Technique of Semantic Headers*. International Series on Advanced Intelligence. Volume 2. Australia: Advanced Knowledge International. ISBN 978-0-86803-979-4.

[6] Burger, J., Cardie, C., Chaudhri, V., Gaizauskas, R., Harabagiu, S., Israel, D., Jacquemin, C., Lin, C-Y., Maiorano, S., Miller, G., Moldovan, D., Ogden, B., Prager, J., Riloff, E., Singhal, A., Shrihari, R., Strzalkowski, T., Voorhees, E., Weishedel, R. Issues, Tasks and Program Structures to Roadmap Research in Question Answering (QA).

[7] Perera, R. and Nand, P. 2014. Interaction History Based Answer Formulation for Question Answering.

[8] Perera, R. 2012. IPedagogy: Question Answering System Based on Web Information Clustering.

[9] Maybury, M. T. editor. 2004. New Directions in Question Answering. AAAI/MIT Press.

[10] BitCrawl by Hobson Lane

[11] Perera, R. and Perera, U. 2012. Towards a thematic role based target identification model for question answering.

[12] Bahadorreza Ofoghi, John Yearwood, and Liping Ma (2008). *The impact of semantic class identification and semantic role labeling on natural language answer extraction*. The 30th European Conference on Information Retrieval (ECIR'08). Springer Berlin Heidelberg. pp. 430–437. External link in |title= (help)

[13] Bahadorreza Ofoghi, John Yearwood, and Liping Ma (2009). "The impact of frame semantic annotation levels, frame-alignment techniques, and fusion methods on factoid answer processing". *Journal of the American Society for Information Science and Technology* **60** (2): 247–263. doi:10.1002/asi.20989.

[14] http://www.nytimes.com/2011/02/17/science/17jeopardy-watson.html?_r=0

61.7   External links

- Question Answering Evaluation at NTCIR

- Question Answering Evaluation at TREC

- Question Answering Evaluation at CLEF

Chapter 62

Resistance Database Initiative

HIV Resistance Response Database Initiative (RDI) is a not-for-profit organisation established in 2002 with the mission of improving the clinical management of HIV infection through the application of bioinformatics to HIV drug resistance and treatment outcome data. The RDI has the following specific goals:

1. To be an independent repository of HIV resistance and treatment outcome data

2. To use bioinformatics to explore the relationships between resistance, other clinical and laboratory factors and HIV treatment outcome

3. To develop and make freely available a system to predict treatment response, as an aid to optimising and individualising the clinical management of HIV infection

The RDI consists of a small executive group based in the UK, an international advisory group of leading HIV/AIDS scientists and clinicians, and an extensive global network of collaborators and data contributors.

62.1 Background

Human immunodeficiency virus (HIV) is the virus that causes acquired immunodeficiency syndrome (AIDS), a condition in which the immune system begins to fail, leading to life-threatening opportunistic infections.

There are approximately 25 HIV 'antiretroviral' drugs that have been approved for the treatment of HIV infection, from six different classes, based on the point in the HIV life-cycle at which they act.

They are used in combination; typically 3 or more drugs from 2 or more different classes, a form of therapy known as highly active antiretroviral therapy or HAART. The aim of therapy is suppression of the virus to very low, ideally undetectable, levels in the blood this prevents the virus

from depleting the immune cells that it preferentially attacks (CD4 cells) and prevents or delays illness and death.

Despite the expanding availability of these drugs and the impact of their use, treatments continue to fail, often due to the development of resistance. During drug therapy, low-level virus replication still occurs, particularly when a patient misses a dose. HIV makes errors in copying its genetic material and, if a mutation makes the virus resistant to one or more of the drugs, it may begin to replicate more successfully in the presence of that drug and undermine the effect of the treatment. If this happens then the treatment needs to be changed to re-establish control over the virus.

In well-resourced healthcare settings, when treatment fails a resistance test may be run to predict to which drugs the patient's virus is resistant. The type of test in most common use is the genotype test, which detects mutations in the viral genetic code. This information is then typically interpreted using rules equating individual mutations with resistance against individual drugs. However, there are many different interpretation systems available that do not always agree, the systems only provide categorical results (resistant, sensitive or intermediate) and they do not necessarily relate well to how a patient will respond to a combination of drugs in the clinic.

62.2 RDI Overview

The RDI was established in 2002 to pioneer a new approach: to develop computational models using the genotype and a wide range of other clinically relevant data collected from thousands of patients treated with HAART all over the world and to use these models to predict how an individual patient will respond to different combinations of drugs. The RDI's goal was to make available a free treatment-response prediction tool over the Internet.

Key to the success of this approach is the collection of large amounts of data with which to train the models and the use of data from as wide and heterogeneous range of sources as possible to maximise the generalisability of the models' predictions. In order to achieve this, the RDI set out to involve as many clinics worldwide as possible and to be the single repository for the data required, in an attempt to avoid unnecessary duplication of effort and competition.

As of October 2013, the RDI has collected data from approximately 110,000 patients from dozens of clinics in more than 30 countries. It is probably the largest database of its kind in the world. The data includes demographic information for the patient, and multiple determinations of the amount of virus in the patient's bloodstream, CD4 cells counts (a white blood cell critical to the function of the immune system that HIV targets and destroys), genetic code of the patients virus, and details of the drugs that have been used to treat the patient.

The RDI has used these data to conduct extensive research in order to develop the most accurate system possible for the prediction of treatment response. This research involved the development and comparison of different computational modelling methods including artificial neural networks, support vector machines, random forests and logistical regression.[1]

The predictions of the RDI's models have historically correlated well with the actual changes in virus load of patients in the clinic, typically achieving a correlation coefficient of 0.8 or more.[2]

62.3 HIV-TRePS

In October 2010, following clinical testing in two multinational studies, the RDI made its experimental HIV Treatment Response Prediction System, HIV-TRePS available over the Internet. In January 2011, two clinical studies were published indicating that use of the HIV-TRePS system could lead to clinical and economic benefits.[3] The studies, conducted by expert HIV physicians in the USA, Canada and Italy, showed that use of the system was associated with changes of treatment decision to combinations involving fewer drugs overall, which were predicted to result in better virological responses, suggesting that use of the system could potentially improve patient outcomes and reduce the overall number and cost of drugs used.

Recent models have predicted whether a combination treatment will reduce the level of virus in the patient's bloodstream to undetectable levels with an accuracy of approximately 80%, significantly better than just using a genotype with rules-based interpretation[4]

As clinics in resource-limited settings are often unable to afford genotyping, the RDI has developed models that predicted treatment response without the need for a genotype,

with only a small loss of accuracy.[5] In July 2011, the RDI made these models available as part of the HIV-TRePS system. This version is aimed particularly at resource-limited settings where genotyping is often not routinely available. The most recent of these models, trained with the largest dataset so far, achieved 80% accuracy, which is comparable to models that use a genotype in their predictions and significantly more accurate than genotyping with rules-based interpretation itself.[6][7]

HIV-TRePS is now in use in 70 countries as a tool to predict virological response to therapy and avoid treatment failure.

The system has been expanded to enable physicians to include their local drug costs in the modelling. A recent study of data from an Indian cohort demonstrated that the system was able to identify combinations of three locally available drugs with a higher probability of success than the regimen prescribed in the clinic, including those cases where the treatment used in the clinic failed. Moreover in all these cases some of the alternatives were less costly than the regimen used in the clinic, suggesting that the system could be not only help avoid treatment failure but also reduce costs.[8]

62.4 RDI Personnel

62.4.1 RDI Executive

- Dr Brendan Larder - Scientific Chair
- Dr Andrew Revell - Executive Director
- Dr Dechao Wang - Director Bioinformatics
- Daniel Coe – Director of Software Development

62.4.2 International Advisory Group

- Dr Julio Montaner (BC Centre For Excellence in HIV/AIDS, Vancouver, Canada)
- Dr Carlo Torti (University of Brescia, Italy)
- Dr John Baxter (Cooper University Hospital, Camden, NJ, USA)
- Dr Sean Emery (National Centre in HIV Epidemiology and Clinical Research, Sydney, Australia)
- Dr Jose Gatell (Hospital Clinic of Barcelona, Spain)
- Dr Brian Gazzard (Chelsea and Westminster Hospital, London, United Kingdom)
- Dr Anna-Maria Geretti (Royal Free Hospital, London, United Kingdom)

• Dr Richard Harrigan (BC Centre For Excellence in HIV/AIDS, Vancouver, Canada)

62.5 RDI data and study group

Cohorts: Peter Reiss and Ard van Sighem (ATHENA, the Netherlands); Julio Montaner and Richard Harrigan (BC Center for Excellence in HIV & AIDS, Canada); Tobias Rinke de Wit, Raph Hamers and Kim Sigaloff (PASER-M cohort, The Netherlands); Brian Agan, Vincent Marconi and Scott Wegner (US Department of Defense); Wataru Sugiura (National Institute of Health, Japan); Maurizio Zazzi (MASTER, Italy); Adrian Streinu-Cercel National Institute of Infectious Diseases Prof.Dr. Matei Balş, Bucharest, Romania; Gerardo Alvarez-Uria (VFHCS, India). Clinics: Jose Gatell and Elisa Lazzari (University Hospital, Barcelona, Spain); Brian Gazzard, Mark Nelson, Anton Pozniak and Sundhiya Mandalia (Chelsea and Westminster Hospital, London, UK); Lidia Ruiz and Bonaventura Clotet (Fundacion Irsi Caixa, Badelona, Spain); Schlomo Staszewski (Hospital of the Johann Wolfgang Goethe-University, Frankfurt, Germany); Carlo Torti (University of Brescia); Cliff Lane and Julie Metcalf (National Institutes of Health Clinic, Rockville, USA); Maria-Jesus Perez-Elias (Instituto Ramón y Cajal de Investigación Sanitaria, Madrid, Spain); Andrew Carr, Richard Norris and Karl Hesse (Immunology B Ambulatory Care Service, St. Vincent's Hospital, Sydney, NSW, Australia); Dr Emanuel Vlahakis (Taylor's Square Private Clinic, Darlinghurst, NSW, Australia); Hugo Tempelman and Roos Barth (Ndlovu Care Group, Elandsdoorn, South Africa), Carl Morrow and Robin Wood (Desmond Tutu HIV Centre, University of Cape Town, South Africa); Luminita Ene ("Dr. Victor Babes" Hospital for Infectious and Tropical Diseases, Bucharest, Romania); Gordana Dragovic (University of Belgrade, Belgrade, Serbia). Clinical trials: Sean Emery and David Cooper (CREST); Carlo Torti (Gen-Pherex); John Baxter (GART, MDR); Laura Monno and Carlo Torti (PhenGen); Jose Gatell and Bonventura Clotet (HAVANA); Gaston Picchio and Marie-Pierre deBethune (DUET 1 & 2 and POWER 3); Maria-Jesus Perez-Elias (RealVirfen).

62.6 References

[1] Wang, Dechao (2009). "A comparison of three computational modelling methods for the prediction of virological response to combination HIV therapy". *Artificial Intelligence in Medicine* **47** (1): 6374. doi:10.1016/j.artmed.2009.05.002.

[2] Larder, Brendan (2007). "The development of artificial neural networks to predict virological response to combination HIV therapy". *Antiviral Therapy* **12** (12): 15–24.

[3] Larder, Brendan (2011). "Clinical Evaluation of the Potential Utility of Computational Modeling as an HIV Treatment Selection Tool by Physicians with Considerable HIV Experience". *AIDS Patient Care and STDs* **25** (1): 29–36. doi:10.1089/apc.2010.0254.

[4] Revell, Andrew (2011). "The development of an expert system to predict virological response to HIV therapy as part of an online treatment support tool". *AIDS Journal* **25** (15): 1855–1863. doi:10.1097/QAD.0b013e328349a9c2.

[5] Revell, Andrew (2010). "Modelling response to HIV therapy without a genotype: an argument for viral load monitoring in resource-limited settings". *Journal of Antimicrobial Chemotherapy* **65** (4): 605–607. doi:10.1093/jac/dkq032.

[6] Revell, Andrew; Wang, D; Wood R et al. (2013). "Computational models can predict response to HIV therapy without a genotype and may reduce treatment failure in different resource-limited settings". *Journal of Antimicrobial Chemotherapy*. doi:10.1093/jac/dkt041.

[7] Larder, Brendan; Revell AD; Hamers R; Tempelman H et al. (2013). "Accurate prediction of response to HIV therapy without a genotype a potential tool for therapy optimisation in resource-limited settings". *Antiviral Therapy*.

[8] Revell, Andrew; Alvarez-Uria G; Wang D; Pozniak A; Montaner JSG; Lane HC; Larder BA et al. (2013). "Potential Impact of a Free Online HIV Treatment Response Prediction System for Reducing Virological Failures and Drug Costs after Antiretroviral Therapy Failure in a Resource-Limited Setting". *BioMed Research International* **2013**. doi:10.1155/2013/579741.

62.7 External links

• RDI official site

• HIV-TRePS

Chapter 63

Roblog

Not to be confused with Roblox.

Roblog is a neologism for a blog written by a robot with no human intervention.

Roblogs were made possible with a new generation of robots which are capable of uploading images and texts automatically to the Web. The first roblogs to appear, late 2005, were written by AIBO robots, the dog-like robotic pets once manufactured by Sony.

63.1   AIBO diaries

AIBO diaries are roblogs produced by AIBO model ERS-7, running a bundled software called *Mind* in either version 2 or 3. Depending on the language of the Mind software, the AIBO blogs in either English or Japanese. To be able to blog on its own, an ERS-7M2 or ERS-7M3 must be linked to the Internet through its Wi-Fi connection capability, and its e-mail sending capability must be correctly configured, for which an SMTP server not requiring authentication nor alternate ports is needed. Posts, consisting of pictures taken with the AIBO's color camera built into its nose, are then sent by e-mail to the blog.

63.2   References

- Gaudette, Pat (2006). *Sparky the Aibo: Robot Dogs & Other Robotic Pets*. Home & Leisure Publishing. ISBN 978-0-9761210-6-0.

63.3   External links

- Directory of English-language AIBO roblogs

Chapter 64

Sayre's paradox

Sayre's Paradox is a dilemma encountered in the design of automated handwriting recognition systems. A standard statement of the paradox is that a cursively written word cannot be recognized without being segmented and cannot be segmented without being recognized.[1] The paradox was first articulated in a 1973 publication by Kenneth M. Sayre, after whom it was named.[2]

64.1 Nature of the Problem

It is relatively easy to design automated systems capable of recognizing words inscribed in a printed format. Such words are segmented into letters by the very act of writing them on the page. Given templates matching typical letter shapes in a given language, individual letters can be identified with a high degree of probability. In cases of ambiguity, probable letter sequences can be compared with a selection of properly spelled words in that language (called a lexicon).[3] If necessary, syntactic features of the language can be applied to render a generally accurate identification of the words in question.[4] Printed-character recognition systems of this sort are commonly used in processing standardized government forms, in sorting mail by zip code, and so forth.

In cursive writing, however, letters comprising a given word typically flow sequentially without gaps between them. Unlike a sequence of printed letters, cursively connected letters are not segmented in advance. Here is where Sayre's Paradox comes into play. Unless the word is already segmented into letters, template-matching techniques like those described above cannot be applied. Prior segmentation, that is to say, is necessary for word recognition. On the other hand, there are no reliable techniques for segmenting a word into letters unless the word itself has been previously identified. Word recognition requires letter segmentation, and letter segmentation requires word recognition. There is no way a cursive writing recognition system employing standard template-matching techniques can do both simultaneously.

Advantages to be gained by use of automated cursive writing recognition systems include routing mail with handwritten addresses, reading handwritten bank checks, and automated digitalization of hand-written documents.[5] These are practical incentives for finding ways of circumventing Sayre's Paradox.

64.2 Avoiding the Paradox

One way of ameliorating the adverse effects of the paradox is to normalize the word inscriptions to be recognized. Normalization amounts to eliminating idiosyncrasies in the penmanship of the writer, such as unusual slope of the letters and unusual slant of the cursive line.[6] This procedure can increase the probability of a correct match with a letter template, resulting in an incremental improvement in the success rate of the system. Since improvement of this sort still depends on accurate segmentation, however, it remains subject to the limitations of Sayre's Paradox.[7] Researchers have come to realize that the only way to circumvent the paradox is by use of procedures that do not rely on accurate segmentation.[8]

64.3 Directions of Current Research

Segmentation is accurate to the extent that it matches distinctions among letters in the actual inscriptions presented to the system for recognition (the input data). This is sometimes referred to as "explicit segmentation".[9] "Implicit segmentation," by contrast, is division of the cursive line into more parts than the number of actual letters in the cursive line itself. Processing these "implicit parts" to achieve eventual word identification requires specific statistical procedures involving Hidden Markov Models (HMM).

A Markov model is a statistical representation of a random process, which is to say a process in which future states are independent of states occurring before the present. In such a process, a given state is dependent only on the conditional probability of its following the state immediately before it. An example is a series of outcomes from successive casts of a die. An HMM is a Markov model, individual states of which are not fully known. Conditional probabilities between states are still determinate, but the identities of individual states are not fully disclosed.

Recognition proceeds by matching HMMs of words to be recognized with previously prepared HMMs of words in the lexicon. The best match in a given case is taken to indicate the identity of the handwritten word in question. As with systems based on explicit segmentation, automated recognition systems based on implicit segmentation are judged more or less successful according to the percentage of correct identifications they accomplish.

Instead of explicit segmentation techniques, most automated handwriting recognition systems today employ implicit segmentation in conjunction with HMM-based matching procedures.[10] The constraints epitomized by Sayre's Paradox are largely responsible for this shift in approach.

64.4 References

[1] See the PhD thesis by Alessandro Vinciarelli "Offline Cursive Handwriting: From Word to Text Recognition" (http://infoscience.epfl.ch/record/82879). See also Machine Learning: Theory and Applications, Vol. 31 of Handbook of Statistics, B. V. Elsevier, ed., p. 422 (https://one.overdrive.com/media/1358341/machine-learning-theory-and-applications).

[2] Kenneth M. Sayre, "Machine Recognition of Handwritten Words: A Project Report," Pattern Recognition, Pergamon Press, Vol. 5, 1973, pp. 213-228.

[3] Alessandro Vinciarelli, "A Survey on [sic] Off-line Cursive Word Recognition," Pattern Recognition, Vol. 35, issue 7. July 2002, pp. 1433-1446.

[4] See "Introduction of Statistical Information in a Syntactic analyzer for Document Image Recognition," by André O. Maroneze, Bertrant Coüashon, and Aurélie Lemaitre (http://proceedings.spiedigitallibrary.org/proceeding.aspx?articleid=731511).

[5] See Alessandro Vinciarelli, "Offline Cursive Handwriting: From Word to Text Recognition," op. cit.

[6] Alessandro Vinciarelli, "A Survey on [sic] Offline Cursive Word Recognition," op. cit.

[7] Alessandro Vinciarelli, "Offline Cursive Handwriting: From Word to Text Recognition," op. cit.

[8] Alessandro Vinciarelli, "Offline Cursive Handwriting: From Word to Text Recognition," op. cit.

[9] Alessandro Vinciarelli, "A Survey on [sic] Offline Cursive Word Recognition," op. cit.

[10] Alessandro Vinciarelli, "Offline Cursive Handwriting: From Word to Text Recognition," op. cit.

64.5 External links

- Kenneth M. Sayre and the Philosophic Institute.

Chapter 65

SCIgen

SCIgen is a computer program that uses context-free grammar to randomly generate nonsense in the form of computer science research papers. All elements of the papers are formed, including graphs, diagrams, and citations. Created by scientists at the Massachusetts Institute of Technology, its stated aim is "to maximize amusement, rather than coherence."[1]

65.1 Sample output

Opening abstract of *Rooter: A Methodology for the Typical Unification of Access Points and Redundancy*:[2]

> Many physicists would agree that, had it not been for congestion control, the evaluation of web browsers might never have occurred. In fact, few hackers worldwide would disagree with the essential unification of voice-over-IP and public/private key pair. In order to solve this riddle, we confirm that SMPs can be made stochastic, cacheable, and interposable.

65.2 Prominent results

In 2005 a paper generated by SCIgen, *Rooter: A Methodology for the Typical Unification of Access Points and Redundancy*, was accepted as a non-reviewed paper to the 2005 World Multiconference on Systemics, Cybernetics and Informatics (WMSCI) and the authors were invited to speak. The authors of SCIgen described their hoax on their website, and it soon received great publicity when picked up by Slashdot. WMSCI withdrew their invitation, but the SCIgen team went anyway, renting space in the hotel separately from the conference and delivering a series of randomly generated talks on their own "track." The organizer of these WMSCI conferences is Professor Nagib Callaos. From 2000 until 2005, the WMSCI was also sponsored by the Institute of Electrical and Electronics Engineers. The IEEE stopped granting sponsorship to Callaos from 2006 to 2008.

Submitting the paper was a deliberate attempt to embarrass WMSCI, which the authors claim accepts low-quality papers and sends unsolicited requests for submissions in bulk to academics. As the SCIgen website states:

> One useful purpose for such a program is to auto-generate submissions to conferences that you suspect might have very low submission standards. A prime example, which you may recognize from spam in your inbox, is SCI/IIIS and its dozens of co-located conferences (check out the very broad conference description on the WMSCI 2005 website).
>
> — About SCIgen [3]

Computing writer Stan Kelly-Bootle noted in *ACM Queue* that many sentences in the "Rooter" paper were individually plausible, which he regarded as posing a problem for automated detection of hoax articles. He suggested that even human readers might be taken in by the effective use of jargon ("The pun on root/router is par for MIT-graduate humor, and at least one occurrence of methodology is mandatory") and attribute the paper's apparent incoherence to their own limited knowledge. His conclusion was that "a reliable gibberish filter requires a careful holistic review by several peer domain experts".[4]

65.2.1 Schlangemann

The name of a fictional man named "Herbert Schlangemann" was used to publish false scientific articles in international conferences that are suspected to be, at least partially, frauds. The author is named after the Swedish short film *Der Schlangemann*.

- In 2008, after receiving a series of Call-for-Paper e-mails, a couple of students used the SCIgen computer program to generate a false scientific paper titled *Towards the Simulation of E-Commerce*, using "Herbert Schlangemann" as the author. The article was accepted at the *2008 International Conference on Computer Science and Software Engineering (CSSE 2008)*, co-sponsored by the IEEE, to be held in Wuhan, China, and the author was invited to be a session chair on grounds of his fictional Curriculum Vitae.[5] The official review comment: "This paper presents cooperative technology and classical Communication. In conclusion, the result shows that though the much-touted amphibious algorithm for the refinement of randomized algorithms is impossible, the well-known client-server algorithm for the analysis of voice-over-IP by Kumar and Raman runs in _(n) time. The authors can clearly identify important features of visualization of DHTs and analyze them insightfully. It is recommended that the authors should develop ideas more cogently, organizes them more logically, and connects them with clear transitions." The paper was available for a short time in the IEEE Xplore Database but was then removed. The entire story is described in the official "Herbert Schlangemann" blog,[6] and it also received attention in Slashdot[7] and the German-language technology-news site Heise Online.[8][9]

- In 2009, the same incident happened and Herbert Schlangemann's latest fake paper *PlusPug: A Methodology for the Improvement of Local-Area Networks* was accepted for oral presentation at the *2009 International Conference on e-Business and Information System Security (EBISS 2009)*, also co-sponsored by IEEE, to be held again in Wuhan, China.[6]

In all cases, the published papers were withdrawn from the conferences' proceedings, and the conference organizing committee as well as the names of the keynote speakers were removed from their websites.

65.2.2 List of other works with notable acceptance

In conferences

See also: Fraudulent conference

- Rob Thomas: *Rooter: A Methodology for the Typical Unification of Access Points and Redundancy*, 2005 for WMSCI (see above)

- Mathias Uslar's paper was accepted to the IPSI-BG conference.[10]

- Professor Genco Gulan published a paper in the 3rd International Symposium of Interactive Media Design.[11]

- A 2013 scientometrics paper demonstrated that at least 85 SCIgen papers have been published by IEEE and Springer.[12] Over 120 SCIgen papers were removed according to this research.[13]

In journals

- Students at Iran's Sharif University of Technology published a paper in Elsevier's *Journal of Applied Mathematics and Computation*.[14] The students wrote under the surname "MosallahNejad", which translates literally from Persian language (in spite of not being a traditional Persian name) as "from an Armed Breed". The paper was subsequently removed when the publishers were informed that it was a joke paper.[15]

- Mikhail Gelfand published a translation of the "Rooter" article in the Russian-language *Journal of Scientific Publications of Aspirants and Doctorants* in August 2008. Gelfand was protesting against the journal, which was apparently not peer reviewed and was being used by Russian PhD candidates to publish in an "accredited" scientific journal, charging them 4000 Rubles to do so. The accreditation was revoked two weeks later.[16][17][18][19][20] (See Dissernet for related information.)

65.2.3 Spoofing Google Scholar and h-index calculators

Refereeing performed on behalf of the Institute of Electrical and Electronics Engineers has also been subject to criticism after fake papers were discovered in conference publications, most notably by Labbé and a researcher using the pseudonym of Schlangemann.[21][22][23][24][25][26]

In this 2010 paper by Cyril Labbé from Grenoble University demonstrated the vulnerability of h-index calculations based on Google Scholar output by feeding it a large set of SCIgen-generated documents that were citing each other, effectively an academic link farm. Using this method the author managed to rank "Ike Antkare" ahead of Albert Einstein for instance.[27]

65.3   See also

- Academic conference

- Derailment (thought disorder)

- Infinite monkey theorem

- Parody generator

- Postmodernism Generator

- snarXiv

- Sokal affair

- Turing test

- *Get me off your fucking mailing list*

- *Who's Afraid of Peer Review?*

65.4   References

[1] SCIgen - An Automatic CS Paper Generator

[2] Stribling, Jeremy; Aguayo, Daniel; Krohn, Maxwell. "Rooter: A Methodology for the Typical Unification of Access Points and Redundancy" (PDF).

[3] "SCIgen - An Automatic CS Paper Generator". MIT.

[4] Stan Kelly-Bootle (July–August 2005). "Call that gibberish?". *ACM Queue* **3** (6): 64. doi:10.1145/1080862.1080884.

[5] "CSSE Conference Program" (PDF).

[6] "The official Herbert Schlangemann Blog, The whole story behind the paper "Towards the Simulation of E-Commerce"".

[7] kdawson (December 24, 2008). "Software-Generated Paper Accepted At IEEE Conference". *slashdot* (VA Linux Systems Japan). Retrieved May 5, 2009.

[8] Peter-Michael Ziegler (December 26, 2008). "Dr. Herbert Schlangemann - oder die Geschichte eines pseudowissenschaftlichen Nonsens-Papiers (in German)". *heise online* (Heise Zeitschriften Verlag). Retrieved May 5, 2009.

[9] Heise Online webpage (in German)

[10] "Mathias Uslar's paper.". Archived from the original on 2009-06-15.

[11] "About Genco Gulan's paper.".

[12] "Duplicate and Fake Publications in the Scientific Literature : How many SCIgen papers in Computer Science?" (PDF). Hal.archives-ouvertes.fr. Retrieved 2014-05-15.

[13] "Publishers withdraw more than 120 gibberish papers". *Nature*. 24 February 2014. Retrieved 25 February 2014.

[14] Rohollah Mosallahnezhad. "Cooperative, Compact Algorithms for Randomized Algorithms" (PDF).

[15] John L. Casti, *REMOVED: Cooperative, compact algorithms for randomized algorithms*, doi:10.1016/j.amc.2007.03.011

[16] "Mon ordinateur écrit mieux que le tien!". *Agence Science-Presse* (in French) (Canada). 8 September 2009. Retrieved 4 October 2011.

[17] "Rooter invades Russia". *SCIgen*. 8 January 2009. Retrieved 4 October 2011.

[18] Malozemov, Sergei (7 October 2008). Группа отечественных ученых поставила эксперимент — смешала сложные термины случайным образом, а полученный текст отослала в один из научных журналов. *NTV* (in Russian). Retrieved 4 October 2011.

[19] "Feedback". *New Scientist*. 15 August 2009.

[20] Слегка упорядоченные размышления о науке, религии и чайниках. *Lenta* (in Russian). 18 June 2009. Retrieved 4 October 2011.

[21] Labbé, Cyril; Labbé, Dominique (2013). "Duplicate and fake publications in the scientific literature: how many SCIgen papers in computer science?". *Scientometrics* (Springer) **94** (1): 379–396. doi:10.1007/s11192-012-0781-y.

[22] Oransky, Ivan (February 24, 2014). "Springer, IEEE withdrawing more than 120 nonsense papers". *retractionwatch.com*. WordPress.com. Retrieved April 29, 2014.

[23] de Gloucester, Paul Colin (2013). "Referees Often Miss Obvious Errors in Computer and Electronic Publications". *Accountability in Research: Policies and Quality Assurance* (Taylor & Francis Group) **20** (3): 143–166. doi:10.1080/08989621.2013.788379.

[24] Dawson, K. (December 23, 2008). "Software-Generated Paper Accepted At IEEE Conference". *slashdot.org*. Dice. Retrieved April 29, 2014.

[25] Hatta, Masayuki (December 24, 2008). "IEEE□□□□□□□□□□□□□□□□□□□□". *slashdot.jp*. OSDN Corporation. Retrieved April 29, 2014.

[26] Ziegler, Peter-Michael (December 26, 2008). "Dr. Herbert Schlangemann - oder die Geschichte eines pseudowissenschaftlichen Nonsens-Papiers". *heise.de*. Heise Zeitschriften Verlag. Retrieved April 29, 2014.

[27] "Les rapports de recherche du LIG" (PDF). Rr.liglab.fr. Retrieved 2014-05-15.

65.5 Further reading

- Ball, Philip (2005). "Computer conference welcomes gobbledegook paper". *Nature* **434** (7036): 946. doi:10.1038/nature03653. PMID 15846311.

- kdawson (24 December 2008). "Software-Generated Paper Accepted At IEEE Conference". *slashdot* (VA Linux Systems Japan). Retrieved 5 May 2009.

- Peter-Michael Ziegler (26 December 2008). "Dr. Herbert Schlangemann - oder die Geschichte eines pseudowissenschaftlichen Nonsens-Papiers (in German)". *heise online* (Heise Zeitschriften Verlag). Retrieved 5 May 2009.

65.6 External links

- Copy of the fake paper: Towards the Simulation of E-Commerce by Herbert Schlangemann

- SCIgen - An Automatic CS Paper Generator

- SCIgen detection website

Chapter 66

Silent speech interface

Silent speech interface is a device that allows speech communication without using the sound made when people vocalize their speech sounds. As such it is a type of electronic lip reading. It works by the computer identifying the phonemes that an individual pronounces from nonauditory sources of information about their speech movements. These are then used to recreate the speech using speech synthesis.[1]

66.1 Information sources

Silent speech interface systems have been created using ultrasound and optical camera input of tongue and lip movements.[2] Electromagnetic devices are another technique for tracking tongue and lip movements. [3] The detection of speech movements by electromyography of speech articulator muscles and the larynx is another technique.[4][5] Another source of information is the vocal tract resonance signals that get transmitted through bone conduction called non-audible murmurs.[6] They have also been created as a brain–computer interface using brain activity in the motor cortex obtained from intracortical microelectrodes.[7]

66.2 Uses

Such devices are created as aids to those unable to create the sound phonation needed for audible speech such as after laryngectomies.[8] Another use is for communication when speech is masked by background noise or distorted by self-contained breathing apparatus. A further practical use is where a need exists for silent communication, such as when privacy is required in a public place, or hands-free data silent transmission is needed during a military or security operation.[2][9]

In 2002, the Japanese company NTT DoCoMo announced it had created a silent mobile phone using electromyography and imaging of lip movement. "The spur to developing such a phone," the company said, "was ridding public places of noise," adding that, "the technology is also expected to help people who have permanently lost their voice."[10] The feasibility of using Silent Speech Interfaces for practical communication has since then been shown.[11]

66.3 In fiction

The decoding of silent speech using a computer played an important role in Arthur C. Clarke's story and Stanley Kubrick's associated film *2001: A Space Odyssey (film)*. In this, HAL 9000, a computer controlling spaceship Discovery One, bound for Jupiter, discovers a plot to deactivate it by the mission astronauts Dave Bowman and Frank Poole through lip reading their conversations.[12]

In Orson Scott Card's series (including *Ender's Game*), the artificial intelligence can be spoken to while the protagonist wears a movement sensor in his jaw, enabling him to converse with the AI without making noise. He also wears an ear implant.

66.4 See also

- Subvocal recognition
- AI effect
- Applications of artificial intelligence
- List of emerging technologies
- Outline of artificial intelligence

66.5 References

[1] Denby B, Schultz T, Honda K, Hueber T, Gilbert J.M., Brumberg J.S. (2010). Silent speech interfaces. Speech Communication 52: 270–287. doi:10.1016/j.specom.2009.08.002

[2] Hueber T, Benaroya E-L, Chollet G, Denby B, Dreyfus G, Stone M. (2010). Development of a silent speech interface driven by ultrasound and optical images of the tongue and lips. Speech Communication, 52 288–300. doi:10.1016/j.specom.2009.11.004

[3] Wang, J., Samal, A., & Green, J. R. (2014). Preliminary test of a real-time, interactive silent speech interface based on electromagnetic articulograph, the 5th ACL/ISCA Workshop on Speech and Language Processing for Assistive Technologies, Baltimore, MD, 38-45.

[4] Jorgensen C, Dusan S. (2010). Speech interfaces based upon surface electromyography. Speech Communication, 52: 354–366. doi:10.1016/j.specom.2009.11.003

[5] Schultz T, Wand M. (2010). Modeling Coarticulation in EMG-based Continuous Speech Recognition. Speech Communication, 52: 341-353. doi:10.1016/j.specom.2009.12.002

[6] Hirahara T, Otani M, Shimizu S, Toda T, Nakamura K, Nakajima Y, Shikano K. (2010). Silent-speech enhancement using body-conducted vocal-tract resonance signals. Speech Communication, 52:301–313. doi:10.1016/j.specom.2009.12.001

[7] Brumberg J.S., Nieto-Castanon A, Kennedy P.R., Guenther F.H. (2010). Brain–computer interfaces for speech communication. Speech Communication 52:367–379. 2010 doi:10.1016/j.specom.2010.01.001

[8] Deng Y., Patel R., Heaton J. T., Colby G., Gilmore L. D., Cabrera J., Roy S. H., De Luca C.J., Meltzner G. S.(2009). Disordered speech recognition using acoustic and sEMG signals. In INTERSPEECH-2009, 644-647.

[9] Deng Y., Colby G., Heaton J. T., and Meltzner HG. S. (2012). Signal Processing Advances for the MUTE sEMG-Based Silent Speech Recognition System. Military Communication Conference, MILCOM 2012.

[10] Fitzpatrick M. (2002). Lip-reading cellphone silences loudmouths. New Scientist.

[11] Wand M, Schultz T. (2011). Session-independent EMG-based Speech Recognition. Proceedings of the 4th International Conference on Bio-inspired Systems and Signal Processing.

[12] Clarke, Arthur C. (1972). The Lost Worlds of 2001. London: Sidgwick and Jackson. ISBN 0-283-97903-8.

Chapter 67

SILVIA

Symbolically Isolated Linguistically Variable Intelligence Algorithms, or more popularly known as **SILVIA**, is a core platform technology developed by Cognitive Code. SILVIA was developed, and designed to recognized and interpret speech, text, and interact with applications and operating systems, all while interacting with a user. The technology can be run and operate via cloud, a mobile application, a part of network, or via server.[1]

67.1 Overview

67.1.1 History

Leslie Spring founded Cognitive Code in 2007 and is the inventor and architect of Cognitive Code's SILVIA Platform.[2][3] Prior to founding Cognitive Code, Leslie worked for such companies such as Electronic Arts, Disney, and Sony heading up their software development teams responsible for building graphics systems, 3D game engines, and custom software developer tools.[4][5]

In addition to Leslie Spring, the company's general partners include Mimi Chen and John Albert.[6] Cognitive Code received Venture Capital funding from Channel Mark Ventures.[7] The platform was initially released on January 1, 2008.[8]

67.1.2 Features and system requirements

SILVIA was developed to recognized and interpret any human interaction: through text, speech, and any other human input. The platform allows an application of it in all applicable and possible application which then allows natural and intuitive human interaction.[1] The system also allows easy implementation. It has a complete set of graphical user interface tools which can aid in developing intelligent objects or entities, and has an array of API scripts which can be embed in any compatible applications.[9]

Differentiating SILVIA from other similar technologies, the platform can be used in different computing platforms and operating systems which can seamlessly allow easy transfer of data.[10] Aside from being available in almost all platforms, SILVIA uses a non-command based system wherein inputs are based on normal human conversational language, not on pre-coded commands like what Google's Google Now and Apple Inc.'s Siri used.[4]

67.1.3 Components

SILVIA is composed of several components:

- **SILVIA Core:** A runtime engine which can be configurable for use in any user, server, or mobile systems. It can also be embedded.[11]

- **SILVIA Server:** A configurable system of SILVIA Cores for automated management.[11]

- **SILVIA Voice:** A modular component designed for accepting voice input and rendering voice output. It can be used within an application, web page, or as part of SILVIA server for better optimization of media streaming.[11]

- **SILVIA API:** Is one of the several components of SILVIA wherein programmers are allowed to create applications, and plug-in based functionality.[11]

- **SILVIA Studio:** A graphical system for application-specific behavior development.[11]

67.1.4 Use

SILVIA can be used in several applications, such as: being used in call centers, smart phones like the iPhone and Android devices, and voice search or other voice-related applications. Unlike other similar technologies, SILVIA can intelligently respond to its users, not in one or two words or small phrases but in complete sentences.[12]

SILVIA has been used by several companies such as Northrop Grumman.[1] Northrop Grumman used the technology in order to aid the company's employees to much better communicate with computers and mobile devices using natural language.[13] The company also utilizes the technology in the development and deployment of military training applications.[1][14] "SILVIA is also currently being used for training and simulation applications for the US Military.[15][16]

The platform is also revolutionary as it can also be used in gaming through its SILVIA Unity platform,[5] and is currently being introduced for being used in toys.[17]

67.2 Recognition

Cognitive Code and its technology platform was included in the list of TechCrunch's *TechCrunch40*.[18][19]

67.3 References

[1] Strauss, Karsten (July 9, 2012). "Riding the Wave of Artificial Intelligence". *Forbes*. pp. 1 – 2. Retrieved May 25, 2013.

[2] "Mimi Chen Interview in Dailysingle - Radio DJ & Jamba Juice Spokesmodel". *Dailysingle*. Retrieved May 27, 2013.

[3] "Company Overview of Cognitive Code Corp". *Bloomberg Businessweek*. Retrieved May 30, 2013.

[4] "SILVIA: Artificial Intelligence Platform". *FORA.tv*. Retrieved May 30, 2013.

[5] "Interview: Cognitive Code's Leslie Spring tells all about the SILVIA artificial intelligence platform, Androids answer for SIRI". *Androrev*. Retrieved May 30, 2013.

[6] "Cognitive Code Funding" (PDF). *Launch Funding Network*. Retrieved May 30, 2013.

[7] "Cognitive Code Investors". *Cognitive Code*. Retrieved May 30, 2013.

[8] "Cognitive Code". *CrunchBase*. Retrieved May 30, 2013.

[9] Melanson, Donald (September 17, 2007). "Cognitive Code shows off SILVIA artificial intelligence platform". *Engadget*. Retrieved May 30, 2013.

[10] "Cognitive Code". *VentureBeat*. Retrieved May 30, 2013.

[11] "Components of the SILVIA Technology". *Cognitive Code*. Retrieved May 30, 2013.

[12] Dodge, Don (September 17, 2007). "TechCrunch40 - First 10 companies". *Don Dodge on The Next Big Thing*. Retrieved May 29, 2013.

[13] "Cognitive Code is Approved Vendor for Northrop Grumman". *Speech Technology*. May 12, 2010. Retrieved May 30, 2013.

[14] "Cognitive Code is Approved Vendor for Northrop Grumman". *International Business Times*. Retrieved May 30, 2013.

[15] "SILVIA per Android, assistente vocale nativo per smartphone e tablet" (in Italian). *TuttoAndroid*. May 31, 2012. Retrieved May 30, 2013.

[16] Daniel P. (May 31, 2012). "SILVIA project for Android aims to topple Siri and S Voice". *Phone Arena*. Retrieved May 30, 2013.

[17] Kate Greene (September 19, 2007). "Intelligent, Chatty Machines". *MIT Technology Review*. Retrieved May 30, 2013.

[18] Robinson, Blake (September 17, 2007). "Cognitive Code at TC40". *TechCrunch*. Retrieved May 30, 2013.

[19] Kiss, Jemima (September 17, 2007). "@TechCrunch40: The search guys". *The Guardian*. Retrieved May 29, 2013.

67.4 External links

- Official website

- SILVIA on Facebook

- SILVIA on Twitter

Chapter 68

Sinewave synthesis

Sinewave synthesis, or **sine wave speech**, is a technique for synthesizing speech by replacing the formants (main bands of energy) with pure tone whistles. The first sinewave synthesis program (*SWS*) for the automatic creation of stimuli for perceptual experiments was developed by Philip Rubin at Haskins Laboratories in the 1970s. This program was subsequently used by Robert Remez, Philip Rubin, David Pisoni, and other colleagues to show that listeners can perceive continuous speech without traditional speech cues. This work paved the way for a view of speech as a dynamic pattern of trajectories through articulatory-acoustic space.

- Robert Remez
- Philip Rubin
- David Pisoni
- SineWave Synthesis
- Smithsonian Speech Synthesis History Project (SSSHP) 1986-2002

68.1 Bibliography

- Rubin, P.E. Sinewave synthesis. Internal memorandum, Haskins Laboratories, New Haven, CT, 1980.

- Remez, R.E., Rubin, P.E., Pisoni, D.B., & Carrell, T.D. Speech perception without traditional speech cues. *Science*, 1981, 212, 947-950.

- Best, C.T., Morrongiello, B. & Robson, R. Perceptual equivalence of acoustic cues in speech and nonspeech perception. *Perception & Psychophysics*, 1981, 29, 191-211.

- Remez, R.E., Rubin, P.E., Berns, S.M., Pardo, J.S. & Lang, J.M. On the perceptual organization of speech. *Psychological Review*, 1994, 101, 129-156.

- Remez, R. E., Fellowes, J. M., & Rubin, P.E. Talker identification based on phonetic information. *Journal of Experimental Psychology: Human Perception and Performance*, 1997, 23, 651-666.

68.2 External links

- Haskins Laboratories

Chapter 69

SmartAction

SmartAction provides artificial intelligence-based voice self-service. SmartAction's Intelligent Voice Automation (IVA) is a hosted IVR platform that uses natural language speech recognition and is based on an object-oriented coding framework.[1] IVA is a cloud-based, hosted service.

The tagline of the company is, "We make a phone call effortless."

SmartAction was founded by inventor and entrepreneur Peter Voss[2][3] and is headquartered in El Segundo, CA.

69.1 History

Developing artificial intelligence has challenged researchers since at least the 1940s. (See History of artificial intelligence.) Part of the problem has been the difficulty of defining an adequate theory of intelligence that can serve as a framework to guide hardware implementations. Starting in the early 1990s Voss developed a new theory of intelligence, outlined in the book *Artificial General Intelligence*.[4] In 2001, Voss founded an R&D startup, Adaptive AI, Inc., to research and develop a prototype artificial general intelligence system based on his theory of intelligence.[2] In 2009 Voss founded a subsidiary, Smart Action Company, LLC, to commercialize this technology. Born out of Voss' research and development, SmartAction created its first practical application of this new technology focused on the management of inbound and outbound calls for contact centers.[5] Since its inception, SmartAction has continued to develop the technology into a highly specialized and purpose driven AI, identified by the company as Intelligent Voice Automation.[6]

69.2 Technology

There are two layers of technology that SmartAction uses in their systems. The first builds on Nuance's recognition engine to create a layer of voice recognition that enables their system to identify open, natural language speech and dialects. Second is a proprietary artificial intelligence brain used to determine the meaning and intent behind spoken words, create conversation with the caller, and monitor systems to learn and improve over time.[7][8] The fundamental difference is that AI systems learn naturally the way humans do, and therefore do not need to be programmed.[7] This "[ability] to think, reason and remember, and tackle any subject like a human" [9] gives systems unprecedented flexibility and upgradeability, enabling learning "on the fly" without expensive programming changes.[10]

69.3 Awards

- Customer Interaction Solutions, 2011 Product of the Year Award [11]

- Customer Interaction Solutions, 2012 Speech Technology Excellence Award [12]

- Contact Center World, 2012 Best Technology Innovation [13]

- TMC, 2014 Product of the Year [14]

- Stevie Award, 2014 Gold award for IVR or Web Service Solution [15]

- 2014 M2M Evolution Award [16]

- TMC, 2015 Speech Technology Award[17]

- TMC, 2015 CRM Excellence Award[18]

- CIOReview's 20 Most Promising Telecom Solution Providers, 2015[19]

69.4 See also

- Artificial Intelligence

- Interactive voice response

- Speech recognition

- Speech synthesis (text-to-speech (TTS))

- Contact center

69.5 References

[1] Intelligent Voice Automation, SmartAction, (Retrieved Jan. 5, 2015).

[2] "Contributors, Kurzweil, (Retrieved Jan 5, 2015)

[3] "El último paso lo ha dado Adaptive AI, que ha presentado el primer sistema artificial de inteligencia. El SmartAction "es un sistema interactivo de respuesta por voz que podrá ser instalado en robots", dice Peter Voss, su creador." Juan Manuel Daganzo Generación Robot; Los investigadores calculan que, en diez o quince años, los robots tendrán capacidades humanas muy desarrolladas 13/03/2009 Publico (Spain)

[4] Goertzel, Ben, ed. (2007). *Artificial General Intelligence* (1st ed.). Springer. ISBN 978-3-540-23733-4.

[5] "Start-Up SmartAction Starts with IVR Release", SpeechTechMag.com 2009-01-12. Retrieved on 2009-08-11.

[6] "Intelligent Voice Automation", SmartAction.com. Retrieved on 2014-05-06.

[7] About, SmartAction, (Retrieved Jan 5, 2015).

[8] "I'm Sorry, I Can't Connect Your Call, Dave", io9.com 2009-02-08. Retrieved on 2009-09-01.

[9] "Innovation: Artificial brain for sale", NewScientist.com 2009-02-06. Retrieved on 2009-08-11.

[10] "Adaptive A.I. Inc. launches commercial AGI-based virtual agent for call centers", MachinesLikeUs.com 2009-01-19. Retrieved on 2009-08-11.

[11] "2011 Product of the Year Award". *The Business Journals.* 10 Jan 2011. Retrieved 6 May 2014.

[12] "2012 Speech Technology Excellence Award". *gnomes national news service.* 13 Aug 2012. Retrieved 6 May 2014.

[13] "2012 Best Technology Innovation". *Call Miner.* 29 June 2012. Retrieved 6 May 2014.

[14] "2014 Product of the Year Award". *World News.* 27 Jan 2014. Retrieved 6 May 2014.

[15] 2014 Stevie® Award Winners, The Stevie Awards for Sales and Customer Service, (Retrieved Jan. 5, 2015)

[16] July 2014 "M2M Evolution Award".

[17] "TMC Announces Winners of the 11th Annual Speech Technology Excellence Award". *www.customerzone360. com.* Retrieved 2015-09-03.

[18] "CUSTOMER Magazine Announces Winners of the 2015 CRM Excellence Award". *news.tmcnet.com.* Retrieved 2015-09-03.

[19] "CIOReview: Telecom Special Edition".

69.6 Further reading

- Goertzel, Ben, ed. (2007). *Artificial General Intelligence* (1st ed.). Springer. ISBN 978-3-540-23733-4. Amazon.com page

- The First Conference on Artificial General Intelligence

69.7 External links

- SmartAction official website

- SmartAction White Papers

- SmartAction Audio Demos

- Adaptive AI official website

- Speech Technology / Telephony at DMOZ

Chapter 70

Speech-generating device

See also: Speech synthesis

Speech-generating devices (SGDs), also known as **voice**

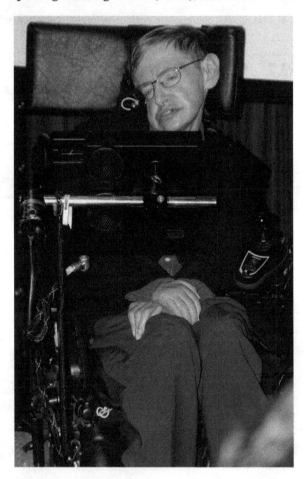

Stephen Hawking, physicist and SGD user

output communication aids, are electronic augmentative and alternative communication (AAC) systems used to supplement or replace speech or writing for individuals with severe speech impairments, enabling them to verbally communicate their needs.[1] SGDs are important for people who have limited means of interacting verbally, as they allow individuals to become active participants in communication

interactions.[2]

There are several input and display methods for users of varying abilities to make use of SGDs. Some SGDs have multiple pages of symbols to accommodate a large number of utterances, and thus only a portion of the symbols available are visible at any one time, with the communicator navigating the various pages. Speech-generating devices can produce electronic voice output by using digitized recordings of natural speech or through speech synthesis—which may carry less emotional information but can permit the user to speak novel messages.[3]

The content, organization, and updating of the vocabulary on an SGD is influenced by a number of factors, such at the user's needs and the contexts that the device will be used in.[4] The development of techniques to improve the available vocabulary and rate of speech production is an active research area. Vocabulary items should be of high interest to the user, be frequently applicable, have a range of meanings, and be pragmatic in functionality.[5]

There are multiple methods of accessing messages on devices: directly or indirectly, or using specialized access devices—although the specific access method will depend on the skills and abilities of the user.[1] SGD output is typically much slower than speech, although rate enhancement strategies can increase the user's rate of output, resulting in enhanced efficiency of communication.[6]

The first known SGD was prototyped in the mid-1970s, and rapid progress in hardware and software development has meant that SGD capabilities can now be integrated into devices like smartphones. Notable users of SGDs include Stephen Hawking, Roger Ebert, and Tony Proudfoot.

Speech-generating systems may be dedicated devices developed solely for AAC, or non-dedicated devices such as computers running additional software to allow them to function as AAC devices.[7][8]

70.1   Speech-generating device history

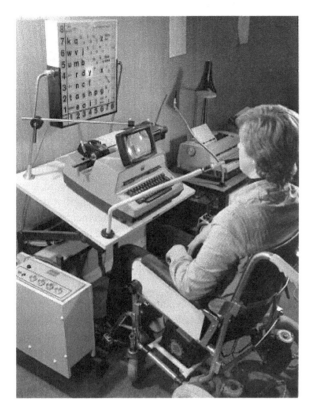

The patient-operated selector mechanism (POSM or POSSUM), was developed in the early 1960s

SGDs have their roots in early electronic communication aids. The first such aid was a sip-and-puff typewriter controller named the patient-operated selector mechanism (POSSUM) prototyped by Reg Maling in the United Kingdom in 1960.[9][10] POSSUM scanned though a set of symbols on an illuminated display.[9] Researchers at Delft University in the Netherlands created the lightspot operated typewriter (LOT) in 1970, which made of small movements of the head to point a small spot of light at a matrix of characters, each equipped with a photoelectric cell. Although it was commercially unsuccessful, the LOT was well received by its users.[11]

During the 1970s and early 1980s, several companies began to emerge that have since become prominent manufacturers of SGDs. Toby Churchill founded Toby Churchill Ltd in 1973, after losing his speech following encephalitis,.[12] In the US, Dynavox (then known as Sentient Systems Technology) grew out of a student project at Carnegie-Mellon University, created in 1982 to help a young woman with cerebral palsy to communicate.[13] Beginning in the 1980s, improvements in technology led to a greatly increased number, variety, and performance of commercially available

communication devices, and a reduction in their size and price. Alternative methods of access such as eye pointing, where the movement of a user's eyes is used to direct an SGD, and scanning, in which alternatives are presented to the user sequentially, became available on communication devices.[10][14] Speech output possibilities included both digitized and synthesized speech.[10]

Rapid progress in hardware and software development continued, including projects funded by the European Community. The first commercially available dynamic screen speech generating devices were developed in the 1990s. Software programs were developed that allowed the computer-based production of communication boards.[10][14] High-tech devices have continued to become smaller and lighter,[14] while increasing accessibility and capability; communication devices can be accessed using eye-tracking systems, perform as a computer for word-processing and Internet use, and as an environmental control device for independent access to other equipment such as TV, radio and telephones.[15]

Notable individuals who have used AAC devices include Stephen Hawking, Roger Ebert[16] and Tony Proudfoot. Hawking is unable to speak due to a combination of severe disabilities caused by ALS, and an emergency tracheotomy. He has come to be associated with the unique voice of his particular synthesis equipment.[17]

70.2   Access methods

See also: Switch access scanning

There are many methods of accessing messages on devices: directly, indirectly, and with specialized access devices. Direct access methods involve physical contact with the system, by using a keyboard or a touch screen. Users accessing SGDs indirectly and through specialized devices must manipulate an object in order to access the system, such as manoeuvring a joystick, head mouse, optical head pointer, light pointer, infrared pointer, or switch access scanner.[1]

The specific access method will depend on the skills and abilities of the user. With direct selection a body part, pointer, adapted mouse, joystick, or eye tracking could be used,[18] whereas switch access scanning is often used for indirect selection.[8][19] Unlike direct selection (e.g., typing on a keyboard, touching a screen), users of switch access scanning can only make selections when the scanning indicator (or cursor) of the electronic device is on the desired choice.[20] The scanning indicator moves through items by highlighting each item on the screen, or by announcing each item via voice output, and then the user activates a switch to select the item.[21] The speed and pattern of scanning, as well as the way items are selected, are individualized to the physical, visual and cognitive capabilities of the user.[20]

70.3   Message construction

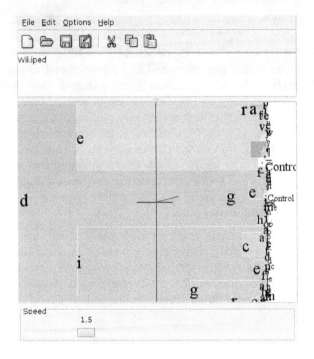

A screenshot of the Dasher rate enhancement program

Augmentative and alternative communication is typically much slower than speech,[6] with users generally producing 8–10 words per minute.[22] Rate enhancement strategies can increase the user's rate of output to around 12–15 words per minute,[22] and as a result enhance the efficiency of communication.

In any given SGD there may be a large number of vocal expressions that facilitate efficient and effective communication, including greetings, expressing desires, and asking questions.[23] Some SGDs have multiple pages of symbols to accommodate a large number of vocal expressions, and thus only a portion of the symbols available are visible at any one time, with the communicator navigating the various pages.[24] Speech-generating devices generally display a set of selections either using a dynamically changing screen, or a fixed display.[25]

There are two main options for increasing the rate of communication for an SGD: encoding and prediction.[6]

Encoding permits a user to produce a word, sentence or phrase using only one or two activations of their SGD.[6] Iconic encoding strategies such as Semantic compaction combine sequences of icons (picture symbols) to produce words or phrases.[26] In numeric, alpha-numeric, and letter encoding (also known as Abbreviation-Expansion), words and sentences are coded as sequences of letters and numbers. For example, typing "HH" or "G1" (for Greeting 1) may retrieve "Hello, how are you?".[26]

Prediction is a rate enhancement strategy in which the SGD attempts to reduce the number of keystrokes used by predicting the word or phrase being written by the user. The user can then select the correct prediction without needing to write the entire word. Word prediction software may determine the choices to be offered based on their frequency in language, association with other words, past choices of the user, or grammatical suitability.[6][26][27] However, users have been shown to produce more words per minute (using a scanning interface) with a static keyboard layout than with a predictive grid layout, suggesting that the cognitive overhead of reviewing a new arrangement cancels out the benefits of the predictive layout when using a scanning interface.[28]

Some systems, such as Auditory Sciences' Interact-Voice device, combine Encoding and Prediction into the same system. For example, typing "HMF" can be an encoded shortcut for "Can you help me find ____" and then the prediction capabilities help the user complete the sentence, such as "Can you help me find my glasses?" or "Can you help me find my car keys?".

Another approach to rate-enhancement is Dasher,[29] which uses language models and arithmetic coding to present alternative letter targets on the screen with size relative to their likelihood given the history.[30][31]

The rate of words produced can depend greatly on the conceptual level of the system: the TALK system, which allows users to choose between large numbers of sentence-level utterances, demonstrated output rates in excess of 60 wpm.[32]

70.4   Fixed and dynamic display devices

70.4.1   Fixed display devices

Fixed display devices refer to those in which the symbols and items are "fixed" in a particular format; some sources refer to these as "static" displays.[33] Such display devices can be simpler for users to learn to use;[33] however, this advantage disappears over time as the user soon becomes familiar with it.[24]

Fixed display devices replicate the typical arrangement of low-tech AAC devices (low tech is defined as those that do not need batteries, electricity or electronics), like

A speech-generation device with a fixed display

A speech-generating device with dynamic display, capable of outputting both synthesized and digitized speech

that such email writing practices allowed children who were SGD users to develop new social skills and increase their social participation.[35]

70.5 Output

communication boards. They share some of their comparative disadvantages; for example they are typically restricted to a limited number of symbols, and hence messages.[25]

70.4.2 Dynamic display devices

Dynamic displays devices are usually also touchscreen devices. They typically generate electronically produced visual symbols that, when pressed, change the set of selections that is displayed. The user can change the symbols available using page links to navigate to appropriate pages of vocabulary and messages. The "home" page of a dynamic display device may show symbols related to many different contexts or conversational topics. Pressing any one of these symbols may open a different screen with messages related to that topic.[25] For example, when watching a volleyball game, a user may press the "sport" symbol to open a page with messages relating to sport, then press the symbol showing a scoreboard to utter the phrase "What's the score?".

Advantages of dynamic display devices include the availability of a much larger vocabulary, and the ability to see the sentence under construction[23] A further advantage of dynamic display devices is that the underlying operating system is capable of providing options for multiple communication channels, including cell phone, text messaging and e-mail.[34] Work by Linköping University has shown

The output of a SGD may be digitized and/or synthesized: digitized systems play directly recorded words or phrases while synthesized speech uses text-to-speech software that can carry less emotional information but permits the user to speak novel messages by typing new words.[36][37] Moreover, individuals may also use a combination of recorded messages and text-to-speech techniques on their SGDs.[37] However, some devices are limited to only one type of output.

70.5.1 Digitized speech

Words, phrases or entire messages can be digitised and stored onto the device for playback to be activated by the user.[1][38] Advantages of recorded speech include that it (a) provides natural prosody and speech naturalness for the listener[3] (e.g., person of the same age and gender as the AAC user can be selected to record the messages),[3] and (b) it provides for additional sounds that may be important for the user such as laughing or whistling.

A major disadvantage of using only recorded speech is that users are unable to produce novel messages; they are limited to the messages pre-recorded into the device.[3][39] Depending on the device, there may be a limit to the length of the recordings.[3][39]

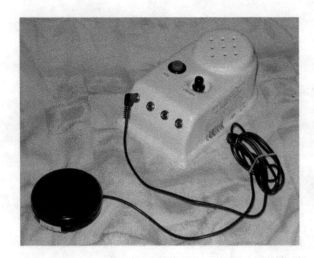

Simple switch-operated speech-generating device

70.5.2 Synthesized speech

SGDs that use synthesized speech apply the phonetic rules of the language to translate the user's message into voice output (speech synthesis).[1][37] Users have the freedom to create novel words and messages and are not limited to those that have been pre-recorded on their device by others.[37]

Synthesized SGDs may allow multiple methods of message creation that can be used individually or in combination: messages can be created from letters, words, phrases, sentences, pictures, or symbols.[1][39] With synthesized speech there is virtually unlimited storage capacity for messages with few demands on memory space.[3]

Synthesized speech engines are available in many languages,[37][39] and the engine's parameters, such as speech rate, pitch range, gender, stress patterns, pauses, and pronunciation exceptions can be manipulated by the user.[39]

Keyboard text-to-speech generating device

70.6 Selection set and vocabulary

The selection set of a SGD is the set of all messages, symbols and codes that are available to a person using that device.[37] The content, organisation, and updating of this selection set are areas of active research and are influenced by a number of factors, including the user's ability, interests and age.[4] The selection set for an AAC system may include words that the user does not know yet – they are included for the user to "grow into".[4] The content installed on any given SGD may include a large number of preset pages provided by the manufacturer, with a number of additional pages produced by the user or the user's care team depending on the user's needs and the contexts that the device will be used in.[4]

70.6.1 Initial content selection

Researchers Beukelman and Mirenda list a number of possible sources (such as family members, friends, teachers, and care staff) for the selection of initial content for a SGD. A range of sources is required because, in general, one individual would not have the knowledge and experience to generate all the vocal expressions needed in any given environment.[4] For example, parents and therapists might not think to add slang terms, such as "innit".[40]

Previous work has analyzed both vocabulary use of typically developing speakers and word use of AAC users to generate content for new AAC devices. Such processes work well for generating a core set of utterances or vocal expressions but are less effective in situations where a particular vocabulary is needed (for example, terms related directly to a user's interest in horse riding). The term "fringe vocabulary" refers to vocabulary that is specific or unique to the individual's personal interests or needs. A typical technique to develop fringe vocabulary for a device is to conduct interviews with multiple "informants": siblings, parents, teachers, co-workers and other involved persons.[4]

Other researchers, such as Musselwhite and St. Louis suggest that initial vocabulary items should be of high interest to the user, be frequently applicable, have a range of meanings and be pragmatic in functionality.[5] These criteria have been widely used in the AAC field as an ecological check of SGD content.[4]

70.6.2 Automatic content maintenance

Beukelman and Mirenda emphasize that vocabulary selection also involves ongoing vocabulary maintenance;[4] however, a difficulty in AAC is that users or their carers must program in any new utterances manually (e.g. names of

AAC user with custom-built device

70.7 Producers

There are relatively few producers of SGDs, although several more companies produce software to give existing devices SGD functionality, and there are some home-built systems.   Producers of dedicated devices include Auditory Sciences, Dynavox Mayer-Johnson, LC Technologies, Lingraphica, Prentke Romich Company, Saltillo Corporation, TextSpeak Design.,[51] Tobii Technology and Words+.[52] Other companies produce software that allow devices like the iPhone, iPad, and Nintendo DS to function as SGDs.[53]

new friends or personal stories) and there are no existing commercial solutions for automatically adding content.[22] A number of research approaches have attempted to overcome this difficulty,[41] these range from "inferred input", such as generating content based on a log of conversation with a user's friends and family,[42] to data mined from the Internet to find language materials, such as the Webcrawler Project.[43] Moreover, by making use of Lifelogging based approaches, a device's content can be changed based on events that occur to a user during their day.[41][44] By accessing more of a user's data, more high-quality messages can be generated at a risk of exposing sensitive user data.[41] For example, by making use of global positioning systems, a device's content can be changed based on geographical location.[45][46]

70.6.3 Ethical concerns

Many recently developed SGDs include performance measurement and analysis tools to help monitor the content used by an individual. This raises concerns about privacy, and some argue that the device user should be involved in the decision to monitor use in this way.[47][48] Similar concerns have been raised regarding the proposals for devices with automatic content generation,[44] and privacy is increasingly a factor in design of SGDs.[40][49] As AAC devices are designed to be used in all areas of a user's life, there are sensitive legal, social, and technical issues centred on a wide family of personal data management problems that can be found in contexts of AAC use. For example, SGDs may have to be designed so that they support the user's right to delete logs of conversations or content that has been added automatically.[50]

70.8 References

 [1] Aetna Inc. (2010)

 [2] Blischak et al (2003)

 [3] Glennen & Decoste pp. 88–90

 [4] Beukelman & Mirenda, Chapter 2

 [5] Musselwhite & Louis

 [6] University of Washington (2009)

 [7] Glennen, pp. 62–63.

 [8] Jans & Clark (1998), pp. 37–38.

 [9] Vanderheide (2002)

[10] Zangari (1994)

[11] Stassen et al., p. 127

[12] Toby Churchill (About Us)

[13] Dynavox (Company History)

[14] Hourcade (2004).

[15] Robitaille, pp. 151–153.

[16] Chicago Sun-Times, (2009)

[17] Stephen Hawking and ALS

[18] Mathy (2000)

[19] Glennen & Decoste pp 62–63

[20] Beukelman & Mirenda, pp. 97–101

[21] Hedman, pp 100–101

[22] Higginbotham et al (2007)

[23] Beukelman & Mirenda

[24] Hochstein et al (2004)

[25] Beukelman & Mirenda p. 84-85

[26] Venkatagiri (1995)

[27] Augmentative Communication, Incorporated

[28] Johansen et al (2003)

[29] Ward et al (2000)

[30] Roark et al (2010)

[31] MacKey (2003), p 119

[32] Todman (2000)

[33] Hochstein et al (2003)

[34] Dynavox at www.speechbubble.org.uk

[35] Sundqvist & Rönnberg (2010)

[36] Schlosser, Blischak & Koul (2003)

[37] Beukelman & Mirenda p. 105-106

[38] Beukelman & Mirenda, p. 105.

[39] Radomski et al (2007)

[40] @article{wickenden2011whose, title={Whose Voice is That?: Issues of Identity, Voice and Representation Arising in an Ethnographic Study of the Lives of Disabled Teenagers who use Augmentative and Alternative Communication (AAC)}, author={Wickenden, M.}, journal={Disability Studies Quarterly}, volume={31}, number={4}, year={2011} }

[41] Reddington & Tintarev (2011)

[42] Ashraf et al. (2002)

[43] Luo et al (2007)

[44] Black et al (2010)

[45] Dominowska et al

[46] Patel & Radhakrishnan

[47] Beukelman & Mirenda, p. 30

[48] Blackstone et al. (2002)

[49] Rackensperger et al. (2005)

[50] Reddington & Coles-Kemp (2011)

[51] www.textspeak.com

[52] www.infinitec.org

[53] www.cbsphily.com

70.9 Bibliography

- Aetna Inc. (2010). "Clinical Policy Bulletin: Speech Generating Devices".

- Ashraf, S.; Warden, A.; Shearer, A. J.; Judson, A.; Ricketts, I. W.; Waller, A.; Alm, N.; Gordon, B.; MacAulay, F.; Brodie, J. K.; Etchels, M. (2002). "Capturing phrases for ICU-Talk, a communication aid for intubated intensive care patients.". *Proceedings of the fifth international ACM conference on Assistive technologies - Assets '02*. p. 213. doi:10.1145/638249.638288. ISBN 1581134649.

- Beukelman, D.; Mirenda, P. (15 June 2005). *Augmentative & alternative communication: supporting children & adults with complex communication needs* (3rd ed.). Paul H. Brookes Pub. Co. ISBN 978-1-55766-684-0.

- Black, R., Reddington, J., Reiter, E., Tintarev, N., and Waller A.. 2010. Using NLG and sensors to support personal narrative for children with complex communication needs. In Proceedings of the NAACL HLT 2010 Workshop on Speech and Language Processing for Assistive Technologies (SLPAT '10). Association for Computational Linguistics, Stroudsburg, PA, USA, 1–9.

- Blackstone, S. W.; Williams, M. B.; Joyce, M. (2002). "Future AAC Technology Needs: Consumer Perspectives". *Assistive Technology* **14** (1): 3–16. doi:10.1080/10400435.2002.10132051. PMID 12739846.

- Blischak, D. M., Lombardino, L. J., & Dyson, A. T. (2003). Use of speech-generating devices: In support of natural speech. Augmentative and Alternative Communication, 19

- Brewer, N (8 February 2011). "'Technology Gives Young Boy A Voice". Retrieved 16 March 2011.

- Dempster, M., Alm, N., and Reiter, E.. 2010. Automatic generation of conversational utterances and narrative for augmentative and alternative communication: a prototype system. In Proceedings of the NAACL HLT 2010 Workshop on Speech and Language Processing for Assistive Technologies (SLPAT '10). Association for Computational Linguistics, Stroudsburg, PA, USA, 10–18.

- Dominowska, E., Roy, D., & Patel, R. (2002). An adaptive context-sensitive communication aid. Proceedings of the CSUN International Conference on Technology and Persons with Disabilities, Northridge, CA.

- ACE centre. "Dynavox Series 5".

- "Dynavox Company History". Retrieved 26 December 2011.

- Lund, J. "Roger Ebert's Journal: Finding my own voice 8/12/2009". Blogs.suntimes.com. Retrieved 17 October 2009.

- Friedman, M. B., G. Kiliany, M. Dzmura, D. Anderson. "The Eyetracker Communication System," Johns Hopkins APL Technical Digest, vol. 3, no. 3, 1982. 250–252

- Friedman, M.B., Kiliany, G. and Dzmura, M. (1985) An Eye Gaze Controlled Keyboard. Proceedings of the 2nd International Conference on Rehabilitation Engineering, 446–447

- Hanlon, M. "Stephen Hawking chooses a new voice". Retrieved 10 August 2009.

- Glennen, Sharon L. and Decoste, Denise C. (1997). The Handbook of Augmentative and Alternative Communication. Singular Publishing Group, Inc.: San Diego, CA.

- Hawking, S. "Stephen Hawking and ALS". Retrieved 10 August 2009.

- Hedman, Glenn (1990). *Rehabilitation Technology*. Routledge. pp. 100–01. ISBN 978-1-56024-033-4.

- Higginbotham, D. J.; Shane, H.; Russell, S.; Caves, K. (2007). "Access to AAC: Present, past, and future". *Augmentative and Alternative Communication* **23** (3): 243–257. doi:10.1080/07434610701571058. PMID 17701743.

- Hochstein, D. D.; McDaniel, M. A.; Nettleton, S.; Neufeld, K. H. (2003). "The Fruitfulness of a Nomothetic Approach to Investigating AAC: Comparing Two Speech Encoding Schemes Across Cerebral Palsied and Nondisabled Children". *American Journal of Speech-Language Pathology* **12** (1): 110–120. doi:10.1044/1058-0360(2003/057). PMID 12680818.

- Hochstein, D. D.; McDaniel, M. A.; Nettleton, S. (2004). "Recognition of Vocabulary in Children and Adolescents with Cerebral Palsy: A Comparison of Two Speech Coding Schemes". *Augmentative and Alternative Communication* **20** (2): 45–62. doi:10.1080/07434610410001699708.

- Hourcade, J.; Everhart Pilotte, T.; West, E.; Parette, P. (2004). "A History of Augmentative and Alternative Communication for Individuals with Severe and Profound Disabilities". *Focus on Autism and Other Developmental Disabilities* **19** (4): 235–244. doi:10.1177/10883576040190040501.

- Infinitec.org. "Augmentative Alternative Communication". Retrieved 16 March 2011.

- Jans, D.; Clark, S. (1998). "High Technology Aids to Communication" (PDF). In Wilson, Allan. *Augmentative Communication in Practice: An Introduction*. University of Edinburgh CALL Centre. ISBN 978-1-898042-15-0.

- Johansen, A. S., Hansen, J. P., Hansen, D. W., Itoh, K., and Mashino, S. 2003. Language technology in a predictive, restricted on-screen keyboard with dynamic layout for severely disabled people. In Proceedings of the 2003 EACL Workshop on Language Modeling for Text Entry Methods (TextEntry '03). Association for Computational Linguistics, Stroudsburg, PA, USA, 59–66.

- Luo, F., Higginbotham, D. J., & Lesher, G. (2007). Webcrawler: Enhanced augmentative communication. Paper presented at CSUN Conference on Disability Technology, March, Los Angeles.

- Mathy; Yorkston, Guttman (2000). "Augmentative Communication for Individuals with Amyotrophic Lateral Sclerosis". In Beukelman, D.,Yorkston, K., Reichle, J. *Augmentative and Alternative Communication Disorders for Adults with Acquired Neurologic Disorders*. Baltimore: P.H. Brookes Pub. ISBN 978-1-55766-473-0.

- David J. C. MacKay (6 October 2003). *Information theory, inference, and learning algorithms*. Cambridge University Press. p. 119. ISBN 978-0-521-64298-9. Retrieved 18 December 2011.

- Musselwhite, C. R.; St. Louis, K. W. (May 1988). *Communication programming for persons with severe handicaps: vocal and augmentative strategies*. Pro-Ed. ISBN 978-0-89079-388-6. Retrieved 17 May 2011.

- R. Patel and R. Radhakrishnan. 2007. Enhancing Access to Situational Vocabulary by Leveraging Geographic Context. Assistive Technology Outcomes and Benefits

- Rackensperger, T.; Krezman, C.; McNaughton, D.; Williams, M. B.; d'Silva, K. (2005). ""When I First Got It, I Wanted to Throw It off a Cliff": The Challenges and Benefits of Learning AAC Technologies as Described by Adults who use AAC". *Augmentative and Alternative Communication* **21** (3): 165. doi:10.1080/07434610500140360.

- Radomski, M. V. and Trombly Latham, C. A. (2007). *Occupational therapy for physical dysfunction*. Lippincott Williams & Wilkins. p. 527. ISBN 978-0-7817-6312-7.

- Reddington, J.; Tintarev, N. (2011). "Automatically generating stories from sensor data". *Proceedings of the 15th international conference on Intelligent user interfaces - IUI '11*. p. 407. doi:10.1145/1943403.1943477. ISBN 9781450304191.

- Reddington, J., & Coles-Kemp, L. (2011). Trap Hunting: Finding Personal Data Management Issues in Next Generation AAC Devices. In Proceedings of the Second Workshop on Speech and Language Processing for Assistive Technologies (pp. 32–42). Edinburgh, Scotland, UK: Association for Computational Linguistics.

- Roark, B., de Villiers, J., Gibbons, C., and Fried-Oken, M.. 2010. Scanning methods and language modeling for binary switch typing. In Proceedings of the NAACL HLT 2010 Workshop on Speech and Language Processing for Assistive Technologies (SLPAT '10). Association for Computational Linguistics, Stroudsburg, PA, USA, 28–36.

- Schlosser, R. W., Blischak, D. M., K., Rajinder K. (2003). "Roles of Speech Output in AAC". In R. W. Schlosser. *The efficacy of augmentative and alternative communication: towards evidence-based practice*. San Diego: Academic. pp. 472–532. ISBN 0-12-625667-5.

- "Getting Back the Gift of Gab: NexGen Handheld Computers Allow the Mute to Converse". Retrieved 10 August 2009.

- Stassen, H. G.; Sheridan, T. B.; Van Lunteren, T. (1997). *Perspectives on the human controller: essays in honor of Henk G. Stassen*. Psychology Press. ISBN 978-0-8058-2190-1. Retrieved 10 October 2011.

- Sundqvist, A.; Rönnberg, J. (2010). "A Qualitative Analysis of Email Interactions of Children who use Augmentative and Alternative Communication". *Augmentative and Alternative Communication* **26** (4): 255–266. doi:10.3109/07434618.2010.528796. PMID 21091302.

- Todman, J. (2000). "Rate and quality of conversations using a text-storage AAC system: Single-case training study". *Augmentative and Alternative Communication* **16** (3): 164–179. doi:10.1080/07434610012331279024.

- "Types of AAC Devices, Augmentative Communication, Incorporated". Retrieved 19 March 2009.

- "Toby Churchill, About Us". Retrieved 26 December 2011.

- Vanderheide, G. C. (2002). "A journey through early augmentative communication and computer access". *Journal of Rehabilitation Research and Development* **39**: 39–53.

- Venkatagiri, H. S. 1995. Techniques for enhancing communication productivity in AAC: A review of research. American Journal of Speech-Language Pathology 4, 36–45.

- Ward, D. J.; Blackwell, A. F.; MacKay, D. J. C. (2000). "Dasher---a data entry interface using continuous gestures and language models". *Proceedings of the 13th annual ACM symposium on User interface software and technology - UIST '00*. p. 129. doi:10.1145/354401.354427. ISBN 1581132123.

- "Rate Enhancement,Augmentative and Alternative Communication at the University of Washington, Seattle". Retrieved 19 March 2009.

- Zangari, C.; Lloyd, L.; Vicker, B. (1994). "Augmentative and alternative communication: An historic perspective". *Augmentative and Alternative Communication* **10** (1): 27–59. doi:10.1080/07434619412331276740.

Chapter 71

Speech synthesis

See also: Speech generating device

Speech Synthesis is the artificial production of human

Stephen Hawking is one of the most famous people using a speech computer to communicate

speech. A computer system used for this purpose is called a **speech computer** or **speech synthesizer**, and can be implemented in software or hardware products. A **text-to-speech (TTS)** system converts normal language text into speech; other systems render symbolic linguistic representations like phonetic transcriptions into speech.[1]

Synthesized speech can be created by concatenating pieces of recorded speech that are stored in a database. Systems

differ in the size of the stored speech units; a system that stores phones or diphones provides the largest output range, but may lack clarity. For specific usage domains, the storage of entire words or sentences allows for high-quality output. Alternatively, a synthesizer can incorporate a model of the vocal tract and other human voice characteristics to create a completely "synthetic" voice output.[2]

The quality of a speech synthesizer is judged by its similarity to the human voice and by its ability to be understood clearly. An intelligible text-to-speech program allows people with visual impairments or reading disabilities to listen to written works on a home computer. Many computer operating systems have included speech synthesizers since the early 1990s.

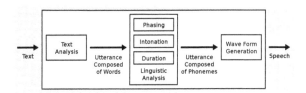

Overview of a typical TTS system

A text-to-speech system (or "engine") is composed of two parts:[3] a front-end and a back-end. The front-end has two major tasks. First, it converts raw text containing symbols like numbers and abbreviations into the equivalent of written-out words. This process is often called *text normalization*, *pre-processing*, or *tokenization*. The front-end then assigns phonetic transcriptions to each word, and divides and marks the text into prosodic units, like phrases, clauses, and sentences. The process of assigning phonetic transcriptions to words is called *text-to-phoneme* or *grapheme-to-phoneme* conversion. Phonetic transcriptions and prosody information together make up the symbolic linguistic representation that is output by the front-end. The back-end—often referred to as the *synthesizer*—then converts the symbolic linguistic representation into sound. In certain systems, this part includes the computation of the *target prosody* (pitch contour, phoneme durations),[4] which is then imposed on the output speech.

71.1 History

Long before electronic signal processing was invented, there were those who tried to build machines to create human speech. Some early legends of the existence of "Brazen Heads" involved Pope Silvester II (d. 1003 AD), Albertus Magnus (1198–1280), and Roger Bacon (1214–1294).

In 1779, the Danish scientist Christian Kratzenstein, working at the Russian Academy of Sciences, built models of the human vocal tract that could produce the five long vowel sounds (in International Phonetic Alphabet notation, they are [aː], [eː], [iː], [oː] and [uː]).[5] This was followed by the bellows-operated "acoustic-mechanical speech machine" by Wolfgang von Kempelen of Pressburg, Hungary, described in a 1791 paper.[6] This machine added models of the tongue and lips, enabling it to produce consonants as well as vowels. In 1837, Charles Wheatstone produced a "speaking machine" based on von Kempelen's design, and in 1857, M. Faber built the "Euphonia". Wheatstone's design was resurrected in 1923 by Paget.[7]

In the 1930s, Bell Labs developed the vocoder, which automatically analyzed speech into its fundamental tone and resonances. From his work on the vocoder, Homer Dudley developed a keyboard-operated voice synthesizer called The Voder (Voice Demonstrator), which he exhibited at the 1939 New York World's Fair.

The Pattern playback was built by Dr. Franklin S. Cooper and his colleagues at Haskins Laboratories in the late 1940s and completed in 1950. There were several different versions of this hardware device but only one currently survives. The machine converts pictures of the acoustic patterns of speech in the form of a spectrogram back into sound. Using this device, Alvin Liberman and colleagues were able to discover acoustic cues for the perception of phonetic segments (consonants and vowels).

Dominant systems in the 1980s and 1990s were the MITalk system, based largely on the work of Dennis Klatt at MIT, and the Bell Labs system;[8] the latter was one of the first multilingual language-independent systems, making extensive use of natural language processing methods.

Early electronic speech synthesizers sounded robotic and were often barely intelligible. The quality of synthesized speech has steadily improved, but output from contemporary speech synthesis systems is still clearly distinguishable from actual human speech.

As the cost-performance ratio causes speech synthesizers to become cheaper and more accessible to the people, more people will benefit from the use of text-to-speech

programs.[9]

71.1.1 Electronic devices

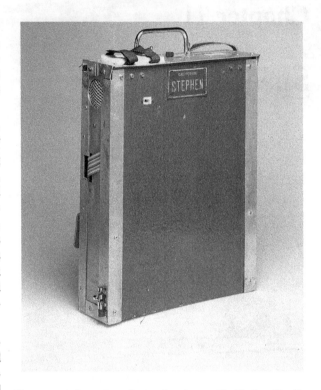

Computer and speech synthesiser housing used by Stephen Hawking in 1999

The first computer-based speech synthesis systems were created in the late 1950s. The first general English text-to-speech system was developed by Noriko Umeda *et al.* in 1968 at the Electrotechnical Laboratory, Japan.[10] In 1961, physicist John Larry Kelly, Jr and colleague Louis Gerstman[11] used an IBM 704 computer to synthesize speech, an event among the most prominent in the history of Bell Labs. Kelly's voice recorder synthesizer (vocoder) recreated the song "Daisy Bell", with musical accompaniment from Max Mathews. Coincidentally, Arthur C. Clarke was visiting his friend and colleague John Pierce at the Bell Labs Murray Hill facility. Clarke was so impressed by the demonstration that he used it in the climactic scene of his screenplay for his novel *2001: A Space Odyssey*,[12] where the HAL 9000 computer sings the same song as it is being put to sleep by astronaut Dave Bowman.[13] Despite the success of purely electronic speech synthesis, research is still being conducted into mechanical speech synthesizers.[14]

Handheld electronics featuring speech synthesis began emerging in the 1970s. One of the first was the Telesensory Systems Inc. (TSI) *Speech+* portable calculator for the blind in 1976.[15][16] Other devices were produced primarily for educational purposes, such as Speak & Spell, produced by Texas Instruments in 1978.[17] Fidelity released a speaking version of its electronic chess computer in 1979.[18] The first video game to feature speech synthesis was the 1980 shoot 'em up arcade game, *Stratovox*, from Sun Electronics.[19] Another early example was the arcade version of *Berzerk*, released that same year. The first multi-player electronic game using voice synthesis was *Milton* from Milton Bradley Company, which produced the device in 1980.

71.2   Synthesizer technologies

The most important qualities of a speech synthesis system are *naturalness* and *intelligibility*.[20] Naturalness describes how closely the output sounds like human speech, while intelligibility is the ease with which the output is understood. The ideal speech synthesizer is both natural and intelligible. Speech synthesis systems usually try to maximize both characteristics.

The two primary technologies generating synthetic speech waveforms are *concatenative synthesis* and *formant synthesis*. Each technology has strengths and weaknesses, and the intended uses of a synthesis system will typically determine which approach is used.

71.2.1   Concatenation synthesis

Main article: Concatenative synthesis

Concatenative synthesis is based on the concatenation (or stringing together) of segments of recorded speech. Generally, concatenative synthesis produces the most natural-sounding synthesized speech. However, differences between natural variations in speech and the nature of the automated techniques for segmenting the waveforms sometimes result in audible glitches in the output. There are three main sub-types of concatenative synthesis.

Unit selection synthesis

Unit selection synthesis uses large databases of recorded speech. During database creation, each recorded utterance is segmented into some or all of the following: individual phones, diphones, half-phones, syllables, morphemes, words, phrases, and sentences. Typically, the division into segments is done using a specially modified speech recognizer set to a "forced alignment" mode with some manual correction afterward, using visual representations such as the waveform and spectrogram.[21] An index of the units in the speech database is then created based on the segmen-

tation and acoustic parameters like the fundamental frequency (pitch), duration, position in the syllable, and neighboring phones. At run time, the desired target utterance is created by determining the best chain of candidate units from the database (unit selection). This process is typically achieved using a specially weighted decision tree.

Unit selection provides the greatest naturalness, because it applies only a small amount of digital signal processing (DSP) to the recorded speech. DSP often makes recorded speech sound less natural, although some systems use a small amount of signal processing at the point of concatenation to smooth the waveform. The output from the best unit-selection systems is often indistinguishable from real human voices, especially in contexts for which the TTS system has been tuned. However, maximum naturalness typically require unit-selection speech databases to be very large, in some systems ranging into the gigabytes of recorded data, representing dozens of hours of speech.[22] Also, unit selection algorithms have been known to select segments from a place that results in less than ideal synthesis (e.g. minor words become unclear) even when a better choice exists in the database.[23] Recently, researchers have proposed various automated methods to detect unnatural segments in unit-selection speech synthesis systems.[24]

Diphone synthesis

Diphone synthesis uses a minimal speech database containing all the diphones (sound-to-sound transitions) occurring in a language. The number of diphones depends on the phonotactics of the language: for example, Spanish has about 800 diphones, and German about 2500. In diphone synthesis, only one example of each diphone is contained in the speech database. At runtime, the target prosody of a sentence is superimposed on these minimal units by means of digital signal processing techniques such as linear predictive coding, PSOLA[25] or MBROLA.[26] or more recent techniques such as pitch modification in the source domain using discrete cosine transform[27] Diphone synthesis suffers from the sonic glitches of concatenative synthesis and the robotic-sounding nature of formant synthesis, and has few of the advantages of either approach other than small size. As such, its use in commercial applications is declining, although it continues to be used in research because there are a number of freely available software implementations.

Domain-specific synthesis

Domain-specific synthesis concatenates prerecorded words and phrases to create complete utterances. It is used in applications where the variety of texts the system will output is limited to a particular domain, like transit schedule announcements or weather reports.[28] The technology is very simple to implement, and has been in commercial use for a long time, in devices like talking clocks and calculators. The level of naturalness of these systems can be very high because the variety of sentence types is limited, and they closely match the prosody and intonation of the original recordings.

Because these systems are limited by the words and phrases in their databases, they are not general-purpose and can only synthesize the combinations of words and phrases with which they have been preprogrammed. The blending of words within naturally spoken language however can still cause problems unless the many variations are taken into account. For example, in non-rhotic dialects of English the "*r*" in words like *"clear"* /ˈklɪə/ is usually only pronounced when the following word has a vowel as its first letter (e.g. *"clear out"* is realized as /ˌklɪəɾˈʌʊt/). Likewise in French, many final consonants become no longer silent if followed by a word that begins with a vowel, an effect called liaison. This alternation cannot be reproduced by a simple word-concatenation system, which would require additional complexity to be context-sensitive.

71.2.2 Formant synthesis

Formant synthesis does not use human speech samples at runtime. Instead, the synthesized speech output is created using additive synthesis and an acoustic model (physical modelling synthesis).[29] Parameters such as fundamental frequency, voicing, and noise levels are varied over time to create a waveform of artificial speech. This method is sometimes called *rules-based synthesis*; however, many concatenative systems also have rules-based components. Many systems based on formant synthesis technology generate artificial, robotic-sounding speech that would never be mistaken for human speech. However, maximum naturalness is not always the goal of a speech synthesis system, and formant synthesis systems have advantages over concatenative systems. Formant-synthesized speech can be reliably intelligible, even at very high speeds, avoiding the acoustic glitches that commonly plague concatenative systems. High-speed synthesized speech is used by the visually impaired to quickly navigate computers using a screen reader. Formant synthesizers are usually smaller programs than concatenative systems because they do not have a database of speech samples. They can therefore be used in embedded systems, where memory and microprocessor power are especially limited. Because formant-based systems have complete control of all aspects of the output speech, a wide variety of prosodies and intonations can be output, conveying not just questions and statements, but a variety of emotions and tones of voice.

Examples of non-real-time but highly accurate intonation control in formant synthesis include the work done in the late 1970s for the Texas Instruments toy Speak & Spell, and in the early 1980s Sega arcade machines[30] and in many Atari, Inc. arcade games[31] using the TMS5220 LPC Chips. Creating proper intonation for these projects was painstaking, and the results have yet to be matched by real-time text-to-speech interfaces.[32]

71.2.3 Articulatory synthesis

Articulatory synthesis refers to computational techniques for synthesizing speech based on models of the human vocal tract and the articulation processes occurring there. The first articulatory synthesizer regularly used for laboratory experiments was developed at Haskins Laboratories in the mid-1970s by Philip Rubin, Tom Baer, and Paul Mermelstein. This synthesizer, known as ASY, was based on vocal tract models developed at Bell Laboratories in the 1960s and 1970s by Paul Mermelstein, Cecil Coker, and colleagues.

Until recently, articulatory synthesis models have not been incorporated into commercial speech synthesis systems. A notable exception is the NeXT-based system originally developed and marketed by Trillium Sound Research, a spin-off company of the University of Calgary, where much of the original research was conducted. Following the demise of the various incarnations of NeXT (started by Steve Jobs in the late 1980s and merged with Apple Computer in 1997), the Trillium software was published under the GNU General Public License, with work continuing as gnuspeech. The system, first marketed in 1994, provides full articulatory-based text-to-speech conversion using a waveguide or transmission-line analog of the human oral and nasal tracts controlled by Carré's "distinctive region model".

More recent synthesizers, developed by Jean Schoentgen, Jorge C. Lucero and colleagues, incorporate models of vocal fold biomechanics, glottal aerodynamics and acoustic wave propagation in the bronqui, traquea, nasal and oral cavities, and thus constitute full systems of physics-based speech simulation.[33][34]

71.2.4 HMM-based synthesis

HMM-based synthesis is a synthesis method based on hidden Markov models, also called Statistical Parametric Synthesis. In this system, the frequency spectrum (vocal tract), fundamental frequency (voice source), and duration (prosody) of speech are modeled simultaneously by HMMs. Speech waveforms are generated from HMMs themselves based on the maximum likelihood criterion.[35]

71.2.5 Sinewave synthesis

Sinewave synthesis is a technique for synthesizing speech by replacing the formants (main bands of energy) with pure tone whistles.[36]

71.3 Challenges

71.3.1 Text normalization challenges

The process of normalizing text is rarely straightforward. Texts are full of heteronyms, numbers, and abbreviations that all require expansion into a phonetic representation. There are many spellings in English which are pronounced differently based on context. For example, "My latest project is to learn how to better project my voice" contains two pronunciations of "project".

Most text-to-speech (TTS) systems do not generate semantic representations of their input texts, as processes for doing so are unreliable, poorly understood, and computationally ineffective. As a result, various heuristic techniques are used to guess the proper way to disambiguate homographs, like examining neighboring words and using statistics about frequency of occurrence.

Recently TTS systems have begun to use HMMs (discussed above) to generate "parts of speech" to aid in disambiguating homographs. This technique is quite successful for many cases such as whether "read" should be pronounced as "red" implying past tense, or as "reed" implying present tense. Typical error rates when using HMMs in this fashion are usually below five percent. These techniques also work well for most European languages, although access to required training corpora is frequently difficult in these languages.

Deciding how to convert numbers is another problem that TTS systems have to address. It is a simple programming challenge to convert a number into words (at least in English), like "1325" becoming "one thousand three hundred twenty-five." However, numbers occur in many different contexts; "1325" may also be read as "one three two five", "thirteen twenty-five" or "thirteen hundred and twenty five". A TTS system can often infer how to expand a number based on surrounding words, numbers, and punctuation, and sometimes the system provides a way to specify the context if it is ambiguous.[37] Roman numerals can also be read differently depending on context. For example, "Henry VIII" reads as "Henry the Eighth", while "Chapter VIII" reads as "Chapter Eight".

Similarly, abbreviations can be ambiguous. For example, the abbreviation "in" for "inches" must be differentiated from the word "in", and the address "12 St John St." uses the same abbreviation for both "Saint" and "Street". TTS systems with intelligent front ends can make educated guesses about ambiguous abbreviations, while others provide the same result in all cases, resulting in nonsensical (and sometimes comical) outputs, such as "co-operation" being rendered as "company operation".

71.3.2 Text-to-phoneme challenges

Speech synthesis systems use two basic approaches to determine the pronunciation of a word based on its spelling, a process which is often called text-to-phoneme or grapheme-to-phoneme conversion (phoneme is the term used by linguists to describe distinctive sounds in a language). The simplest approach to text-to-phoneme conversion is the dictionary-based approach, where a large dictionary containing all the words of a language and their correct pronunciations is stored by the program. Determining the correct pronunciation of each word is a matter of looking up each word in the dictionary and replacing the spelling with the pronunciation specified in the dictionary. The other approach is rule-based, in which pronunciation rules are applied to words to determine their pronunciations based on their spellings. This is similar to the "sounding out", or synthetic phonics, approach to learning reading.

Each approach has advantages and drawbacks. The dictionary-based approach is quick and accurate, but completely fails if it is given a word which is not in its dictionary. As dictionary size grows, so too does the memory space requirements of the synthesis system. On the other hand, the rule-based approach works on any input, but the complexity of the rules grows substantially as the system takes into account irregular spellings or pronunciations. (Consider that the word "of" is very common in English, yet is the only word in which the letter "f" is pronounced [v].) As a result, nearly all speech synthesis systems use a combination of these approaches.

Languages with a phonemic orthography have a very regular writing system, and the prediction of the pronunciation of words based on their spellings is quite successful. Speech synthesis systems for such languages often use the rule-based method extensively, resorting to dictionaries only for those few words, like foreign names and borrowings, whose pronunciations are not obvious from their spellings. On the other hand, speech synthesis systems for languages like English, which have extremely irregular spelling systems, are more likely to rely on dictionaries, and to use rule-based methods only for unusual words, or words that aren't in their dictionaries.

71.3.3 Evaluation challenges

The consistent evaluation of speech synthesis systems may be difficult because of a lack of universally agreed objective evaluation criteria. Different organizations often use different speech data. The quality of speech synthesis systems also depends to a large degree on the quality of the production technique (which may involve analogue or digital recording) and on the facilities used to replay the speech. Evaluating speech synthesis systems has therefore often been compromised by differences between production techniques and replay facilities.

Since 2005, however, some researchers have started to evaluate speech synthesis systems using a common speech dataset.[38]

71.3.4 Prosodics and emotional content

See also: Prosody (linguistics)

A study in the journal *Speech Communication* by Amy Drahota and colleagues at the University of Portsmouth, UK, reported that listeners to voice recordings could determine, at better than chance levels, whether or not the speaker was smiling.[39][40][41] It was suggested that identification of the vocal features that signal emotional content may be used to help make synthesized speech sound more natural. One of the related issues is modification of the pitch contour of the sentence, depending upon whether it is an affirmative, interrogative or exclamatory sentence. One of the techniques for pitch modification[42] uses discrete cosine transform in the source domain (linear prediction residual). Such pitch synchronous pitch modification techniques need a priori pitch marking of the synthesis speech database using techniques such as epoch extraction using dynamic plosion index applied on the integrated linear prediction residual of the voiced regions of speech.[43]

71.4 Dedicated hardware

Early Technology (not available anymore)

- Icophone
- Votrax
  - SC-01A (analog formant)
  - SC-02 / SSI-263 / "Artic 263"
- General Instrument SP0256-AL2 (CTS256A-AL2)
- National Semiconductor DT1050 Digitalker (Mozer - Forrest Mozer)

- Silicon Systems SSI 263 (analog formant)
- Texas Instruments LPC Speech Chips
  - TMS5110A
  - TMS5200
  - MSP50C6XX - Sold to Sensory, Inc. in 2001[44]

Current (as of 2013)

- Magnevation SpeakJet (www.speechchips.com) TTS256 Hobby and experimenter.
- Epson S1V30120F01A100 (www.epson.com) IC DECTalk Based voice, Robotic, Eng/Spanish
- Textspeak TTS-EM (www.textspeak.com) ICs, Modules and Industrial enclosures in 24 languages. Human sounding, Phoneme based.

71.5 Hardware and software systems

Popular systems offering speech synthesis as a built-in capability.

71.5.1 Mattel

The Mattel Intellivision game console, which is a computer that lacks a keyboard, offered the Intellivoice Voice Synthesis module in 1982. It included the SP0256 Narrator speech synthesizer chip on a removable cartridge. The Narrator had 2kB of Read-Only Memory (ROM), and this was utilized to store a database of generic words that could be combined to make phrases in Intellivision games. Since the Orator chip could also accept speech data from external memory, any additional words or phrases needed could be stored inside the cartridge itself. The data consisted of strings of analog-filter coefficients to modify the behavior of the chip's synthetic vocal-tract model, rather than simple digitized samples.

71.5.2 SAM

Also released in 1982, Software Automatic Mouth was the first commercial all-software voice synthesis program. It was later used as the basis for Macintalk. The program was available for non-Macintosh Apple computers (including the Apple II, and the Lisa), various Atari models and the Commodore 64. The Apple version preferred additional hardware that contained DACs, although it could instead use the computer's one-bit audio output (with the addition of much distortion) if the card was not present. The Atari made use of the embedded POKEY audio chip. Speech playback on the Atari normally disabled interrupt requests and shut down the ANTIC chip during vocal output. The audible output is extremely distorted speech when the screen is on. The Commodore 64 made use of the 64's embedded SID audio chip.

71.5.3   Atari

Arguably, the first speech system integrated into an operating system was the 1400XL/1450XL personal computers designed by Atari, Inc. using the Votrax SC01 chip in 1983. The 1400XL/1450XL computers used a Finite State Machine to enable World English Spelling text-to-speech synthesis.[45] Unfortunately, the 1400XL/1450XL personal computers never shipped in quantity.

The Atari ST computers were sold with "stspeech.tos" on floppy disk.

71.5.4   Apple

The first speech system integrated into an operating system that shipped in quantity was Apple Computer's MacInTalk. The software was licensed from 3rd party developers Joseph Katz and Mark Barton (later, SoftVoice, Inc.) and was featured during the 1984 introduction of the Macintosh computer. This January demo required 512 kilobytes of RAM memory. As a result, it could not run in the 128 kilobytes of RAM the first Mac actually shipped with.[46] So, the demo was accomplished with a prototype 512k Mac, although those in attendance were not told of this and the synthesis demo created considerable excitement for the Macintosh. In the early 1990s Apple expanded its capabilities offering system wide text-to-speech support. With the introduction of faster PowerPC-based computers they included higher quality voice sampling. Apple also introduced speech recognition into its systems which provided a fluid command set. More recently, Apple has added sample-based voices. Starting as a curiosity, the speech system of Apple Macintosh has evolved into a fully supported program, PlainTalk, for people with vision problems. VoiceOver was for the first time featured in Mac OS X Tiger (10.4). During 10.4 (Tiger) & first releases of 10.5 (Leopard) there was only one standard voice shipping with Mac OS X. Starting with 10.6 (Snow Leopard), the user can choose out of a wide range list of multiple voices. VoiceOver voices feature the taking of realistic-sounding breaths between sentences, as well as improved clarity at high read rates over PlainTalk. Mac OS X also includes say, a command-line based application that converts text to audible speech. The AppleScript Standard Additions includes a say verb that allows a script to use any of the installed voices and to control the pitch, speaking rate and modulation of the spoken text.

The Apple iOS operating system used on the iPhone, iPad and iPod Touch uses VoiceOver speech synthesis for accessibility.[47] Some third party applications also provide speech synthesis to facilitate navigating, reading web pages or translating text.

71.5.5   AmigaOS

The second operating system to feature advanced speech synthesis capabilities was AmigaOS, introduced in 1985. The voice synthesis was licensed by Commodore International from SoftVoice, Inc., who also developed the original MacinTalk text-to-speech system. It featured a complete system of voice emulation for American English, with both male and female voices and "stress" indicator markers, made possible through the Amiga's audio chipset.[48] The synthesis system was divided into a translator library which converted unrestricted English text into a standard set of phonetic codes and a narrator device which implemented a formant model of speech generation.. AmigaOS also featured a high-level "Speak Handler", which allowed command-line users to redirect text output to speech. Speech synthesis was occasionally used in third-party programs, particularly word processors and educational software. The synthesis software remained largely unchanged from the first AmigaOS release and Commodore eventually removed speech synthesis support from AmigaOS 2.1 onward.

Despite the American English phoneme limitation, an unofficial version with multilingual speech synthesis was developed. This made use of an enhanced version of the translator library which could translate a number of languages, given a set of rules for each language.[49]

71.5.6   Microsoft Windows

See also: Microsoft Agent

Modern Windows desktop systems can use SAPI 4 and SAPI 5 components to support speech synthesis and speech recognition. SAPI 4.0 was available as an optional add-on for Windows 95 and Windows 98. Windows 2000 added Narrator, a text–to–speech utility for people who have visual impairment. Third-party programs such as CoolSpeech, Textaloud and Ultra Hal can perform various text-to-speech tasks such as reading text aloud from a specified website, email account, text document, the Windows clipboard, the user's keyboard typing, etc. Not all programs can use speech synthesis directly.[50] Some programs can use plug-ins, extensions or add-ons to read text aloud. Third-party programs are available that can read text from the system clipboard.

Microsoft Speech Server is a server-based package for voice synthesis and recognition. It is designed for network use with web applications and call centers.

71.6 Text-to-speech systems

Text-to-Speech (**TTS**) refers to the ability of computers to read text aloud. A **TTS Engine** converts written text to a phonemic representation, then converts the phonemic representation to waveforms that can be output as sound. TTS engines with different languages, dialects and specialized vocabularies are available through third-party publishers.[51]

71.6.1 Android

Version 1.6 of Android added support for speech synthesis (TTS).[52]

71.6.2 Internet

Currently, there are a number of applications, plugins and gadgets that can read messages directly from an e-mail client and web pages from a web browser or Google Toolbar such as Text-to-voice which is an add-on to Firefox. Some specialized software can narrate RSS-feeds. On one hand, online RSS-narrators simplify information delivery by allowing users to listen to their favourite news sources and to convert them to podcasts. On the other hand, on-line RSS-readers are available on almost any PC connected to the Internet. Users can download generated audio files to portable devices, e.g. with a help of podcast receiver, and listen to them while walking, jogging or commuting to work.

A growing field in Internet based TTS is web-based assistive technology, e.g. 'Browsealoud' from a UK company and Readspeaker. It can deliver TTS functionality to anyone (for reasons of accessibility, convenience, entertainment or information) with access to a web browser. The non-profit project Pediaphon was created in 2006 to provide a similar web-based TTS interface to the Wikipedia.[53]

Other work is being done in the context of the W3C through the W3C Audio Incubator Group with the involvement of The BBC and Google Inc.

71.6.3 Open source

Systems that operate on free and open source software systems including Linux are various, and include open-source programs such as the Festival Speech Synthesis System which uses diphone-based synthesis, as well as more modern and better-sounding techniques, eSpeak, which supports a broad range of languages, and gnuspeech which uses articulatory synthesis[54] from the Free Software Foundation.

71.6.4 Others

- Following the commercial failure of the hardware-based Intellivoice, gaming developers sparingly used software synthesis in later games. A famous example is the introductory narration of Nintendo's Super Metroid game for the Super Nintendo Entertainment System. Earlier systems from Atari, such as the Atari 5200 (Baseball) and the Atari 2600 (Quadrun and Open Sesame), also had games utilizing software synthesis.

- Some e-book readers, such as the Amazon Kindle, Samsung E6, PocketBook eReader Pro, enTourage eDGe, and the Bebook Neo.

- The BBC Micro incorporated the Texas Instruments TMS5220 speech synthesis chip,

- Some models of Texas Instruments home computers produced in 1979 and 1981 (Texas Instruments TI-99/4 and TI-99/4A) were capable of text-to-phoneme synthesis or reciting complete words and phrases (text-to-dictionary), using a very popular Speech Synthesizer peripheral. TI used a proprietary codec to embed complete spoken phrases into applications, primarily video games.[55]

- IBM's OS/2 Warp 4 included VoiceType, a precursor to IBM ViaVoice.

- GPS Navigation units produced by Garmin, Magellan, TomTom and others use speech synthesis for automobile navigation.

- Yamaha produced a music synthesizer in 1999, the Yamaha FS1R which included a Formant synthesis capability. Sequences of up to 512 individual vowel and consonant formants could be stored and replayed, allowing short vocal phrases to be synthesized.

71.7 Speech synthesis markup languages

A number of markup languages have been established for the rendition of text as speech in an XML-compliant format. The most recent is Speech Synthesis Markup Language (SSML), which became a W3C recommendation in 2004. Older speech synthesis markup languages include Java Speech Markup Language (JSML) and SABLE. Although each of these was proposed as a standard, none of them have been widely adopted.

Speech synthesis markup languages are distinguished from dialogue markup languages. VoiceXML, for example, includes tags related to speech recognition, dialogue management and touchtone dialing, in addition to text-to-speech markup.

71.8 Applications

Speech synthesis has long been a vital assistive technology tool and its application in this area is significant and widespread. It allows environmental barriers to be removed for people with a wide range of disabilities. The longest application has been in the use of screen readers for people with visual impairment, but text-to-speech systems are now commonly used by people with dyslexia and other reading difficulties as well as by pre-literate children. They are also frequently employed to aid those with severe speech impairment usually through a dedicated voice output communication aid.

Speech synthesis techniques are also used in entertainment productions such as games and animations. In 2007, Animo Limited announced the development of a software application package based on its speech synthesis software FineSpeech, explicitly geared towards customers in the entertainment industries, able to generate narration and lines of dialogue according to user specifications.[56] The application reached maturity in 2008, when NEC Biglobe announced a web service that allows users to create phrases from the voices of Code Geass: Lelouch of the Rebellion R2 characters.[57]

In recent years, Text to Speech for disability and handicapped communication aids have become widely deployed in Mass Transit. Text to Speech is also finding new applications outside the disability market. For example, speech synthesis, combined with speech recognition, allows for interaction with mobile devices via natural language processing interfaces.

Text-to speech is also used in second language acquisition. Voki, for instance, is an educational tool created by Odd-cast that allows users to create their own talking avatar, using different accents. They can be emailed, embedded on websites or shared on social media.

In addition, speech synthesis is a valuable computational aid for the analysis and assessment of speech disorders. A voice quality synthesizer, developed by Jorge C. Lucero et al. at University of Brasilia, simulates the physics of phonation and includes models of vocal frequency jitter and tremor, airflow noise and laryngeal asymmetries.[34] The synthesizer has been used to mimic the timbre of dysphonic speakers with controlled levels of roughness, breathiness and strain.[58]

71.9 APIs

Multiple companies offer TTS APIs to their customers to accelerate development of new applications utilizing TTS technology. Companies offering TTS APIs include AT&T, IVONA, Neospeech, Readspeaker, SYNVO and YAKiToMe!. For mobile app development, Android operating system has been offering text to speech API for a long time. Most recently, with iOS7, Apple started offering an API for text to speech.

71.10 See also

- CereProc

- Chinese speech synthesis

- Comparison of speech synthesizers

- Google Text-to-Speech

- Loquendo

- Neospeech

- Cepstral (company)

- IVONA

- LumenVox

- Microsoft text-to-speech voices

- accessaphone

- Paperless office

- Comparison of screen readers

- Speech processing

- Silent speech interface

- SYNVO

- Text to Voice — Mozilla Firefox extension

- Cantor (music software)

- Vocaloid (singing synthesis)

- Voxygen

- Text to Speech in Digital Television

71.11 References

[1] Allen, Jonathan; Hunnicutt, M. Sharon; Klatt, Dennis (1987). *From Text to Speech: The MITalk system. Cambridge University Press. ISBN 0-521-30641-8.*

[2] Rubin, P.; Baer, T.; Mermelstein, P. (1981). "An articulatory synthesizer for perceptual research". *Journal of the Acoustical Society of America* **70** (2): 321–328. doi:10.1121/1.386780.

[3] van Santen, Jan P. H.; Sproat, Richard W.; Olive, Joseph P.; Hirschberg, Julia (1997). *Progress in Speech Synthesis.* Springer. ISBN 0-387-94701-9.

[4] Van Santen, J. (April 1994). "Assignment of segmental duration in text-to-speech synthesis". *Computer Speech & Language* **8** (2): 95–128. doi:10.1006/csla.1994.1005.

[5] History and Development of Speech Synthesis, Helsinki University of Technology, Retrieved on November 4, 2006

[6] *Mechanismus der menschlichen Sprache nebst der Beschreibung seiner sprechenden Maschine* ("Mechanism of the human speech with description of its speaking machine," J. B. Degen, Wien). (German)

[7] Mattingly, Ignatius G. (1974). Sebeok, Thomas A., ed. "Speech synthesis for phonetic and phonological models" (PDF). *Current Trends in Linguistics* (Mouton, The Hague) **12**: 2451–2487.

[8] Sproat, Richard W. (1997). *Multilingual Text-to-Speech Synthesis: The Bell Labs Approach.* Springer. ISBN 0-7923-8027-4.

[9] Kurzweil, Raymond (2005). *The Singularity is Near.* Penguin Books. ISBN 0-14-303788-9.

[10] Klatt, D. (1987) "Review of Text-to-Speech Conversion for English" *Journal of the Acoustical Society of America* **82**(3):737-93

[11] Lambert, Bruce (March 21, 1992). "Louis Gerstman, 61, a Specialist In Speech Disorders and Processes". *New York Times.*

[12] Arthur C. Clarke Biography at the Wayback Machine (archived December 11, 1997)

[13] "Where "HAL" First Spoke (Bell Labs Speech Synthesis website)". Bell Labs. Retrieved 2010-02-17.

[14] Anthropomorphic Talking Robot Waseda-Talker Series

[15] TSI Speech+ & other speaking calculators

[16] Gevaryahu, Jonathan, "TSI S14001A Speech Synthesizer LSI Integrated Circuit Guide"

[17] Breslow, et al. United States Patent 4326710: "Talking electronic game" April 27, 1982

[18] Voice Chess Challenger

[19] Gaming's Most Important Evolutions, GamesRadar

[20] Taylor, Paul (2009). *Text-to-speech synthesis.* Cambridge, UK: Cambridge University Press. p. 3. ISBN 9780521899277.

[21] Alan W. Black, Perfect synthesis for all of the people all of the time. IEEE TTS Workshop 2002.

[22] John Kominek and Alan W. Black. (2003). CMU ARCTIC databases for speech synthesis. CMU-LTI-03-177. Language Technologies Institute, School of Computer Science, Carnegie Mellon University.

[23] Julia Zhang. Language Generation and Speech Synthesis in Dialogues for Language Learning, masters thesis, Section 5.6 on page 54.

[24] William Yang Wang and Kallirroi Georgila. (2011). Automatic Detection of Unnatural Word-Level Segments in Unit-Selection Speech Synthesis, IEEE ASRU 2011.

[25] Pitch-Synchronous Overlap and Add (PSOLA) Synthesis at the Wayback Machine (archived February 22, 2007)

[26] T. Dutoit, V. Pagel, N. Pierret, F. Bataille, O. van der Vrecken. The MBROLA Project: Towards a set of high quality speech synthesizers of use for non commercial purposes. *ICSLP Proceedings*, 1996.

[27] R Muralishankar, A.G.Ramakrishnan and P Prathibha. Modification of Pitch using DCT in the Source Domain. "Speech Communication", 2004, Vol. 42/2, pp. 143-154.

[28] L.F. Lamel, J.L. Gauvain, B. Prouts, C. Bouhier, R. Boesch. Generation and Synthesis of Broadcast Messages, *Proceedings ESCA-NATO Workshop and Applications of Speech Technology*, September 1993.

[29] Dartmouth College: *Music and Computers*, 1993.

[30] Examples include Astro Blaster, Space Fury, and Star Trek: Strategic Operations Simulator

[31] Examples include Star Wars, Firefox, Return of the Jedi, Road Runner, The Empire Strikes Back, Indiana Jones and the Temple of Doom, 720°, Gauntlet, Gauntlet II, A.P.B., Paperboy, RoadBlasters, Vindicators Part II, Escape from the Planet of the Robot Monsters.

[32] John Holmes and Wendy Holmes (2001). *Speech Synthesis and Recognition* (2nd ed.). CRC. ISBN 0-7484-0856-8.

[33] Schoentgen, Jean; Fraj, Samia; Lucero, Jorge C. (2015-01-02). "Testing the reliability of Grade, Roughness and Breathiness scores by means of synthetic speech stimuli". *Logopedics Phoniatrics Vocology* **40** (1): 5–13. doi:10.3109/14015439.2013.837502. ISSN 1401-5439. PMID 24117123.

[34] Lucero, J. C.; Schoentgen, J.; Behlau, M. (2013). "Physics-based synthesis of disordered voices" (PDF). *Interspeech 2013* (Lyon, France: International Speech Communication Association). Retrieved Aug 27, 2015.

[35] "The HMM-based Speech Synthesis System". Hts.sp.nitech.ac.j. Retrieved 2012-02-22.

[36] Remez, R.; Rubin, P.; Pisoni, D.; Carrell, T. (22 May 1981). "Speech perception without traditional speech cues" (PDF). *Science* **212** (4497): 947–949. doi:10.1126/science.7233191. PMID 7233191.

[37] "Speech synthesis". World Wide Web Organization.

[38] "Blizzard Challenge". Festvox.org. Retrieved 2012-02-22.

[39] "Smile -and the world can hear you". University of Portsmouth. January 9, 2008. Archived from the original on 2008-05-17.

[40] "Smile - And The World Can Hear You, Even If You Hide". *Science Daily*. January 2008.

[41] Drahota, A. (2008). "The vocal communication of different kinds of smile" (PDF). *Speech Communication* **50** (4): 278–287. doi:10.1016/j.specom.2007.10.001.

[42] Muralishankar, R.; Ramakrishnan, A. G.; Prathibha, P. (February 2004). "Modification of pitch using DCT in the source domain". *Speech Communication* **42** (2): 143–154. doi:10.1016/j.specom.2003.05.001. Retrieved 7 December 2014.

[43] Prathosh, A. P.; Ramakrishnan, A. G.; Ananthapadmanabha, T. V. (December 2013). "Epoch extraction based on integrated linear prediction residual using plosion index". *IEEE Trans. Audio Speech Language Processing* **21** (12): 2471–2480. doi:10.1109/TASL.2013.2273717. Retrieved 19 December 2014.

[44] EE Times. "TI will exit dedicated speech-synthesis chips, transfer products to Sensory." June 14, 2001.

[45] "1400XL/1450XL Speech Handler External Reference Specification" (PDF). Retrieved 2012-02-22.

[46] "It Sure Is Great To Get Out Of That Bag!". folklore.org. Retrieved 2013-03-24.

[47] "iPhone: Configuring accessibility features (Including VoiceOver and Zoom)". Apple. Retrieved 2011-01-29.

[48] Miner, Jay; et al. (1991). *Amiga Hardware Reference Manual* (3rd ed.). Addison-Wesley Publishing Company, Inc. ISBN 0-201-56776-8.

[49] Devitt, Francesco (30 June 1995). "Translator Library (Multilingual-speech version)". Retrieved 9 April 2013.

[50] "Accessibility Tutorials for Windows XP: Using Narrator". Microsoft. 2011-01-29. Retrieved 2011-01-29.

[51] "How to configure and use Text-to-Speech in Windows XP and in Windows Vista". Microsoft. 2007-05-07. Retrieved 2010-02-17.

[52] Jean-Michel Trivi (2009-09-23). "An introduction to Text-To-Speech in Android". Android-developers.blogspot.com. Retrieved 2010-02-17.

[53] Andreas Bischoff, The Pediaphon - Speech Interface to the free Wikipedia Encyclopedia for Mobile Phones, PDA's and MP3-Players, Proceedings of the 18th International Conference on Database and Expert Systems Applications, Pages: 575-579 ISBN 0-7695-2932-1, 2007

[54] "gnuspeech". Gnu.org. Retrieved 2010-02-17.

[55] "Smithsonian Speech Synthesis History Project (SSSHP) 1986-2002". Mindspring.com. Retrieved 2010-02-17.

[56] "Speech Synthesis Software for Anime Announced". Anime News Network. 2007-05-02. Retrieved 2010-02-17.

[57] "Code Geass Speech Synthesizer Service Offered in Japan". Animenewsnetwork.com. 2008-09-09. Retrieved 2010-02-17.

[58] M. Englert, G. Madazio, I. Gielow, J. C. Lucero and M. Behlau. "Perceptual error identification of human and synthesized voices", 44th Annual Symposium of the Voice Foundation (Philadelphia, 2015). Abstract.

71.12   External links

- Tool for Speech Synthesis in the Browsers via Google Chrome

- Whole Articles Reader using Speech Synthesis via Google Chrome

- Text to Speech Synthesis in the Web Browser with JavaScript

- Speech synthesis at DMOZ

- Synthesis of disordered voices, at University of Brasilia.

- Text to Voice or Text to Speech Firefox Addon

- Dennis Klatt's History of Speech Synthesis

- Verbose Text-To-Speech.

- TextSpeak Multi-Lingual Text-To-Speech.

- Simulated singing with the singing robot Pavarobotti or a description from the BBC on how the robot synthesized the singing.

- 'Klatt's Last Tapes' a BBC Radio 4 programme on the history of speech synthesis with many examples of electronic speech included.

- Tamil and Kannada TTS demo by Medical intelligence and language engineering lab, Indian Institute of Science.

- What is Text-to-Speech and How Does it Work? A basic explanation of TTS and USS Synthesis by Neospeech.

Chapter 72

Statistical semantics

Statistical semantics is the study of "how the statistical patterns of human word usage can be used to figure out what people mean, at least to a level sufficient for information access" . How can we figure out what words mean, simply by looking at patterns of words in huge collections of text? What are the limits to this approach to understanding words?

72.1 History

The term *Statistical Semantics* was first used by Warren Weaver in his well-known paper on machine translation.[1] He argued that word sense disambiguation for machine translation should be based on the co-occurrence frequency of the context words near a given target word. The underlying assumption that "a word is characterized by the company it keeps" was advocated by J.R. Firth.[2] This assumption is known in Linguistics as the Distributional Hypothesis.[3] Emile Delavenay defined *Statistical Semantics* as "Statistical study of meanings of words and their frequency and order of recurrence."[4] "Furnas *et al.* 1983" is frequently cited as a foundational contribution to Statistical Semantics.[5] An early success in the field was Latent Semantic Analysis.

72.2 Applications of statistical semantics

Research in Statistical Semantics has resulted in a wide variety of algorithms that use the Distributional Hypothesis to discover many aspects of semantics, by applying statistical techniques to large corpora:

- Measuring the similarity in word meanings [6][7][8][9]

- Measuring the similarity in word relations [10]

- Modeling similarity-based generalization [11]

- Discovering words with a given relation [12]

- Classifying relations between words [13]

- Extracting keywords from documents [14][15]

- Measuring the cohesiveness of text [16]

- Discovering the different senses of words [17]

- Distinguishing the different senses of words [18]

- Subcognitive aspects of words [19]

- Distinguishing praise from criticism [20]

72.3 Related fields

Statistical Semantics focuses on the meanings of common words and the relations between common words, unlike text mining, which tends to focus on whole documents, document collections, or named entities (names of people, places, and organizations). Statistical Semantics is a subfield of computational semantics, which is in turn a subfield of computational linguistics and natural language processing.

Many of the applications of Statistical Semantics (listed above) can also be addressed by lexicon-based algorithms, instead of the corpus-based algorithms of Statistical Semantics. One advantage of corpus-based algorithms is that they are typically not as labour-intensive as lexicon-based algorithms. Another advantage is that they are usually easier to adapt to new languages than lexicon-based algorithms. However, the best performance on an application is often achieved by combining the two approaches.[21]

72.4 See also

- Latent semantic analysis

- Latent semantic indexing

- Text mining

- Information retrieval

- Natural language processing

- Computational linguistics

- Web mining

- Semantic similarity

- Co-occurrence

- Text corpus

- Semantic Analytics

72.5 References

[1] Weaver 1955

[2] Firth 1957

[3] Sahlgren 2008

[4] Delavenay 1960

[5] Furnas et al. 1983

[6] Lund, Burgess & Atchley 1995

[7] Landauer & Dumais 1997

[8] McDonald & Ramscar 2001

[9] Terra & Clarke 2003

[10] Turney 2006

[11] Yarlett 2008

[12] Hearst 1992

[13] Turney & Littman 2005

[14] Frank et al. 1999

[15] Turney 2000

[16] Turney 2003

[17] Pantel & Lin 2002

[18] Turney 2004

[19] Turney 2001

[20] Turney & Littman 2003

[21] Turney et al. 2003

72.5.1 Sources

- Delavenay, Emile (1960). *An Introduction to Machine Translation*. New York, NY: Thames and Hudson. OCLC 1001646.

- Firth, John R. (1957). "A synopsis of linguistic theory 1930-1955". *Studies in Linguistic Analysis* (Oxford: Philological Society): 1–32.

   Reprinted in Palmer, F.R., ed. (1968). *Selected Papers of J.R. Firth 1952-1959*. London: Longman. OCLC 123573912.

- Frank, Eibe; Paynter, Gordon W.; Witten, Ian H.; Gutwin, Carl; Nevill-Manning, Craig G. (1999). "Domain-specific keyphrase extraction". *Proceedings of the Sixteenth International Joint Conference on Artificial Intelligence*. IJCAI-99 **2**. California: Morgan Kaufmann. pp. 668–673. ISBN 1-55860-613-0. CiteSeerX: 10.1.1.43.9100 CiteSeerX: 10.1.1.148.3598.

- Furnas, George W.; Landauer, T. K.; Gomez, L. M.; Dumais, S. T. (1983). "Statistical semantics: Analysis of the potential performance of keyword information systems" (PDF). *Bell System Technical Journal* **62** (6): 1753–1806. doi:10.1002/j.1538-7305.1983.tb03513.x.

- Hearst, Marti A. (1992). "Automatic Acquisition of Hyponyms from Large Text Corpora" (PDF). *Proceedings of the Fourteenth International Conference on Computational Linguistics*. COLING '92. Nantes, France. pp. 539–545. doi:10.3115/992133.992154. CiteSeerX: 10.1.1.36.701.

- Landauer, Thomas K.; Dumais, Susan T. (1997). "A solution to Plato's problem: The latent semantic analysis theory of the acquisition, induction, and representation of knowledge". *Psychological Review* **104** (2): 211–240. doi:10.1037/0033-295x.104.2.211. CiteSeerX: 10.1.1.184.4759.

- Lund, Kevin; Burgess, Curt; Atchley, Ruth Ann (1995). "Semantic and associative priming in high-dimensional semantic space" (PDF). *Proceedings of the 17th Annual Conference of the Cognitive Science Society*. Cognitive Science Society. pp. 660–665.

- McDonald, Scott; Ramscar, Michael (2001). "Testing the distributional hypothesis: The influence of context

- on judgements of semantic similarity" (PDF). *Proceedings of the 23rd Annual Conference of the Cognitive Science Society*. pp. 611–616. CiteSeerX: 10.1.1.104.7535.

- Pantel, Patrick; Lin, Dekang (2002). "Discovering word senses from text". *Proceedings of ACM SIGKDD Conference on Knowledge Discovery and Data Mining*. KDD '02. pp. 613–619. doi:10.1145/775047.775138. ISBN 1-58113-567-X. CiteSeerX: 10.1.1.12.6771.

- Sahlgren, Magnus (2008). "The Distributional Hypothesis" (PDF). *Rivista di Linguistica* **20** (1): 33–53.

- Terra, Egidio L.; Clarke, Charles L. A. (2003). "Frequency estimates for statistical word similarity measures" (PDF). *Proceedings of the Human Language Technology and North American Chapter of Association of Computational Linguistics Conference 2003*. HLT/NAACL 2003. pp. 244–251. doi:10.3115/1073445.1073477. CiteSeerX: 10.1.1.12.9041.

- Turney, Peter D. (May 2000). "Learning algorithms for keyphrase extraction". *Information Retrieval* **2** (4): 303–336. arXiv:cs/0212020. doi:10.1023/A:1009976227802. CiteSeerX: 10.1.1.11.1829.

- Turney, Peter D. (2001). "Answering subcognitive Turing Test questions: A reply to French". *Journal of Experimental and Theoretical Artificial Intelligence* **13** (4): 409–419. arXiv:cs/0212015. doi:10.1080/09528130110100270. CiteSeerX: 10.1.1.12.8734.

- Turney, Peter D. (2003). "Coherent keyphrase extraction via Web mining". *Proceedings of the Eighteenth International Joint Conference on Artificial Intelligence*. IJCAI-03. Acapulco, Mexico. pp. 434–439. arXiv:cs/0308033. CiteSeerX: 10.1.1.100.3751.

- Turney, Peter D. (2004). "Word sense disambiguation by Web mining for word co-occurrence probabilities". *Proceedings of the Third International Workshop on the Evaluation of Systems for the Semantic Analysis of Text*. SENSEVAL-3. Barcelona, Spain. pp. 239–242. arXiv:cs/0407065.

- Turney, Peter D. (2006). "Similarity of semantic relations". *Computational Linguistics* **32** (3): 379–416. arXiv:cs/0608100. doi:10.1162/coli.2006.32.3.379. CiteSeerX: 10.1.1.75.8007.

- Turney, Peter D.; Littman, Michael L. (October 2003). "Measuring praise and criticism: Inference of semantic orientation from association". *ACM Transactions on Information Systems (TOIS)* **21** (4): 315–346. arXiv:cs/0309034. doi:10.1145/944012.944013. CiteSeerX: 10.1.1.9.6425.

- Turney, Peter D.; Littman, Michael L. (2005). "Corpus-based Learning of Analogies and Semantic Relations". *Machine Learning* **60** (1–3): 251–278. arXiv:cs/0508103. doi:10.1007/s10994-005-0913-1. CiteSeerX: 10.1.1.90.9819.

- Turney, Peter D.; Littman, Michael L.; Bigham, Jeffrey; Shnayder, Victor (2003). "Combining Independent Modules to Solve Multiple-choice Synonym and Analogy Problems". *Proceedings of the International Conference on Recent Advances in Natural Language Processing*. RANLP-03. Borovets, Bulgaria. pp. 482–489. arXiv:cs/0309035. CiteSeerX: 10.1.1.5.2939.

- Weaver, Warren (1955). "Translation" (PDF). In Locke, W.N.; Booth, D.A. *Machine Translation of Languages*. Cambridge, Massachusetts: MIT Press. pp. 15–23. ISBN 0-8371-8434-7.

- Yarlett, Daniel G. (2008). *Language Learning Through Similarity-Based Generalization* (PDF) (PhD thesis). Stanford University.

72.6 External links

- "George Furnas". *Faculty Profile*. University of Michigan, School of Information. Retrieved 2010-07-12.
- Susan Dumais
- Thomas Landauer
- Peter Turney
- Michael Ramscar
- Dekang Lin's Demos
- Patrick Pantel's Demos
- Kea keyphrase extraction
- Online keyphrase extractor

Chapter 73

Text mining

Text mining, also referred to as *text data mining*, roughly equivalent to **text analytics**, refers to the process of deriving high-quality information from text. High-quality information is typically derived through the devising of patterns and trends through means such as statistical pattern learning. Text mining usually involves the process of structuring the input text (usually parsing, along with the addition of some derived linguistic features and the removal of others, and subsequent insertion into a database), deriving patterns within the structured data, and finally evaluation and interpretation of the output. 'High quality' in text mining usually refers to some combination of relevance, novelty, and interestingness. Typical text mining tasks include text categorization, text clustering, concept/entity extraction, production of granular taxonomies, sentiment analysis, document summarization, and entity relation modeling (*i.e.*, learning relations between named entities).

Text analysis involves information retrieval, lexical analysis to study word frequency distributions, pattern recognition, tagging/annotation, information extraction, data mining techniques including link and association analysis, visualization, and predictive analytics. The overarching goal is, essentially, to turn text into data for analysis, via application of natural language processing (NLP) and analytical methods.

A typical application is to scan a set of documents written in a natural language and either model the document set for predictive classification purposes or populate a database or search index with the information extracted.

73.1   Text mining and text analytics

The term **text analytics** describes a set of linguistic, statistical, and machine learning techniques that model and structure the information content of textual sources for business intelligence, exploratory data analysis, research, or investigation.[1] The term is roughly synonymous with text mining; indeed, Ronen Feldman modified a 2000 description of "text mining"[2] in 2004 to describe "text analytics."[3] The latter term is now used more frequently in business settings while "text mining" is used in some of the earliest application areas, dating to the 1980s,[4] notably life-sciences research and government intelligence.

The term text analytics also describes that application of text analytics to respond to business problems, whether independently or in conjunction with query and analysis of fielded, numerical data. It is a truism that 80 percent of business-relevant information originates in unstructured form, primarily text.[5] These techniques and processes discover and present knowledge – facts, business rules, and relationships – that is otherwise locked in textual form, impenetrable to automated processing.

73.2   History

Labor-intensive manual text mining approaches first surfaced in the mid-1980s,[6] but technological advances have enabled the field to advance during the past decade. Text mining is an interdisciplinary field that draws on information retrieval, data mining, machine learning, statistics, and computational linguistics. As most information (common estimates say over 80%)[5] is currently stored as text, text mining is believed to have a high commercial potential value. Increasing interest is being paid to multilingual data mining: the ability to gain information across languages and cluster similar items from different linguistic sources according to their meaning.

The challenge of exploiting the large proportion of enterprise information that originates in "unstructured" form has been recognized for decades.[7] It is recognized in the earliest definition of business intelligence (BI), in an October 1958 IBM Journal article by H.P. Luhn, A Business Intelligence System, which describes a system that will:

> "...utilize data-processing machines for auto-abstracting and auto-encoding of documents and

for creating interest profiles for each of the 'action points' in an organization. Both incoming and internally generated documents are automatically abstracted, characterized by a word pattern, and sent automatically to appropriate action points."

Yet as management information systems developed starting in the 1960s, and as BI emerged in the '80s and '90s as a software category and field of practice, the emphasis was on numerical data stored in relational databases. This is not surprising: text in "unstructured" documents is hard to process. The emergence of text analytics in its current form stems from a refocusing of research in the late 1990s from algorithm development to application, as described by Prof. Marti A. Hearst in the paper Untangling Text Data Mining:[8]

> For almost a decade the computational linguistics community has viewed large text collections as a resource to be tapped in order to produce better text analysis algorithms. In this paper, I have attempted to suggest a new emphasis: the use of large online text collections to discover new facts and trends about the world itself. I suggest that to make progress we do not need fully artificial intelligent text analysis; rather, a mixture of computationally-driven and user-guided analysis may open the door to exciting new results.

Hearst's 1999 statement of need fairly well describes the state of text analytics technology and practice a decade later.

73.3   Text analysis processes

Subtasks — components of a larger text-analytics effort — typically include:

- Information retrieval or identification of a corpus is a preparatory step: collecting or identifying a set of textual materials, on the Web or held in a file system, database, or content corpus manager, for analysis.

- Although some text analytics systems apply exclusively advanced statistical methods, many others apply more extensive natural language processing, such as part of speech tagging, syntactic parsing, and other types of linguistic analysis.

- Named entity recognition is the use of gazetteers or statistical techniques to identify named text features: people, organizations, place names, stock ticker symbols, certain abbreviations, and so on. Disambiguation

— the use of contextual clues — may be required to decide where, for instance, "Ford" can refer to a former U.S. president, a vehicle manufacturer, a movie star, a river crossing, or some other entity.

- Recognition of Pattern Identified Entities: Features such as telephone numbers, e-mail addresses, quantities (with units) can be discerned via regular expression or other pattern matches.

- Coreference: identification of noun phrases and other terms that refer to the same object.

- Relationship, fact, and event Extraction: identification of associations among entities and other information in text

- Sentiment analysis involves discerning subjective (as opposed to factual) material and extracting various forms of attitudinal information: sentiment, opinion, mood, and emotion. Text analytics techniques are helpful in analyzing, sentiment at the entity, concept, or topic level and in distinguishing opinion holder and opinion object.[9]

- Quantitative text analysis is a set of techniques stemming from the social sciences where either a human judge or a computer extracts semantic or grammatical relationships between words in order to find out the meaning or stylistic patterns of, usually, a casual personal text for the purpose of psychological profiling etc.[10]

73.4   Applications

The technology is now broadly applied for a wide variety of government, research, and business needs. Applications can be sorted into a number of categories by analysis type or by business function. Using this approach to classifying solutions, application categories include:

- Enterprise   Business   Intelligence/Data   Mining, Competitive Intelligence

- E-Discovery, Records Management

- National Security/Intelligence

- Scientific discovery, especially Life Sciences

- Sentiment Analysis Tools, Listening Platforms

- Natural Language/Semantic Toolkit or Service

- Publishing

- Automated ad placement

- Search/Information Access

- Social media monitoring

73.4.1 Security applications

Many text mining software packages are marketed for security applications, especially monitoring and analysis of online plain text sources such as Internet news, blogs, etc. for national security purposes.[11] It is also involved in the study of text encryption/decryption.

73.4.2 Biomedical applications

Main article: Biomedical text mining

A range of text mining applications in the biomedical literature has been described.[12]

One online text mining application in the biomedical literature is PubGene that combines biomedical text mining with network visualization as an Internet service.[13][14] TPX is a concept-assisted search and navigation tool for biomedical literature analyses[15] - it runs on PubMed/PMC and can be configured, on request, to run on local literature repositories too.

GoPubMed is a knowledge-based search engine for biomedical texts.

73.4.3 Software applications

Text mining methods and software is also being researched and developed by major firms, including IBM and Microsoft, to further automate the mining and analysis processes, and by different firms working in the area of search and indexing in general as a way to improve their results. Within public sector much effort has been concentrated on creating software for tracking and monitoring terrorist activities.[16]

73.4.4 Online media applications

Text mining is being used by large media companies, such as the Tribune Company, to clarify information and to provide readers with greater search experiences, which in turn increases site "stickiness" and revenue. Additionally, on the back end, editors are benefiting by being able to share, associate and package news across properties, significantly increasing opportunities to monetize content.

73.4.5 Marketing applications

Text mining is starting to be used in marketing as well, more specifically in analytical customer relationship management.[17] Coussement and Van den Poel (2008)[18][19] apply it to improve predictive analytics models for customer churn (customer attrition).[18]

73.4.6 Sentiment analysis

Sentiment analysis may involve analysis of movie reviews for estimating how favorable a review is for a movie.[20] Such an analysis may need a labeled data set or labeling of the affectivity of words. Resources for affectivity of words and concepts have been made for WordNet[21] and ConceptNet,[22] respectively.

Text has been used to detect emotions in the related area of affective computing.[23] Text based approaches to affective computing have been used on multiple corpora such as students evaluations, children stories and news stories.

73.4.7 Academic applications

The issue of text mining is of importance to publishers who hold large databases of information needing indexing for retrieval. This is especially true in scientific disciplines, in which highly specific information is often contained within written text. Therefore, initiatives have been taken such as Nature's proposal for an Open Text Mining Interface (OTMI) and the National Institutes of Health's common Journal Publishing Document Type Definition (DTD) that would provide semantic cues to machines to answer specific queries contained within text without removing publisher barriers to public access.

Academic institutions have also become involved in the text mining initiative:

- The National Centre for Text Mining (NaCTeM), is the first publicly funded text mining centre in the world. NaCTeM is operated by the University of Manchester[24] in close collaboration with the Tsujii Lab,[25] University of Tokyo.[26] NaCTeM provides customised tools, research facilities and offers advice to the academic community. They are funded by the Joint Information Systems Committee (JISC) and two of the UK Research Councils (EPSRC & BBSRC). With an initial focus on text mining in the biological and biomedical sciences, research has since expanded into the areas of social sciences.

- In the United States, the School of Information at University of California, Berkeley is developing a program called BioText to assist biology researchers in text mining and analysis.

73.4.8   Digital Humanities and Computational Sociology

The automatic analysis of vast textual corpora has created the possibility for scholars to analyse millions of documents in multiple languages with very limited manual intervention. Key enabling technologies have been Parsing, Machine Translation, Topic categorization, Machine Learning.

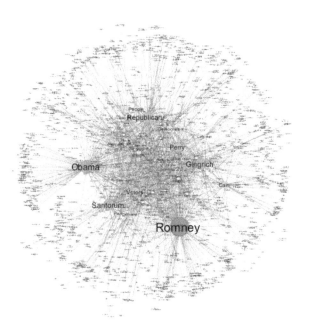

Narrative network of US Elections 2012[27]

The automatic parsing of textual corpora has enabled the extraction of actors and their relational networks on a vast scale, turning textual data into network data. The resulting networks, which can contain thousands of nodes, are then analysed by using tools from Network theory to identify the key actors, the key communities or parties, and general properties such as robustness or structural stability of the overall network, or centrality of certain nodes.[28] This automates the approach introduced by Quantitative Narrative Analysis,[29] whereby subject-verb-object triplets are identified with pairs of actors linked by an action, or pairs formed by actor-object.[27]

Content analysis has been a traditional part of social sciences and media studies for a long time. The automation of content analysis has allowed a "big data" revolution to take place in that field, with studies in social media and newspaper content that include millions of news items. Gender bias, readability, content similarity, reader preferences, and

even mood have been analyzed based on text mining methods over millions of documents. [30] [31] [32] [33] The analysis of readability, gender bias and topic bias was demonstrated in [34] showing how different topics have different gender biases and levels of readability; the possibility to detect mood shifts in a vast population by analysing Twitter content was demonstrated as well.[35]

73.5   Software

Text mining computer programs are available from many commercial and open source companies and sources. See List of text mining software.

73.6   Intellectual Property Law and Text Mining

73.6.1   Situation in Europe

Due to a lack of flexibilities in European copyright and database law, the mining of in-copyright works such as web mining without the permission of the copyright owner is not legal. In the UK in 2014, on the recommendation of the Hargreaves review the government amended copyright law[36] to allow text mining as a limitation and exception. Only the second country in the world to do so after Japan, which introduced a mining specific exception in 2009. However, due to the restriction of the Copyright Directive, the UK exception only allows content mining for non-commercial purposes. UK copyright law does not allow this provision to be overridden by contractual terms and conditions.

The European Commission facilitated stakeholder discussion on text and data mining in 2013, under the title of Licences for Europe.[37] The focus on the solution to this legal issue being licences and not limitations and exceptions to copyright law led to representatives of universities, researchers, libraries, civil society groups and open access publishers to leave the stakeholder dialogue in May 2013.[38]

73.6.2   Situation in United States

By contrast to Europe, the flexible nature of US copyright law, and in particular fair use means that text mining in America, as well as other fair use countries such as Israel, Taiwan and South Korea is viewed as being legal. As text mining is transformative, meaning that is it does not supplant the original work, it is viewed as being lawful under fair use. For example, as part of the Google Book settlement the presiding judge on the case ruled that Google's digitisation project of in-copyright books was lawful, in part because of the transformative uses that the digitisation project displayed - one such use being text and data mining.[39]

73.7 Implications

Until recently, websites most often used text-based searches, which only found documents containing specific user-defined words or phrases. Now, through use of a semantic web, text mining can find content based on meaning and context (rather than just by a specific word). Additionally, text mining software can be used to build large dossiers of information about specific people and events. For example, large datasets based on data extracted from news reports can be built to facilitate social networks analysis or counter-intelligence. In effect, the text mining software may act in a capacity similar to an intelligence analyst or research librarian, albeit with a more limited scope of analysis. Text mining is also used in some email spam filters as a way of determining the characteristics of messages that are likely to be advertisements or other unwanted material.

73.8 See also

- Approximate nonnegative matrix factorization, an algorithm used for text mining

- BioCreative text mining evaluation in biomedical literature

- Meta (academic company) text mining in scientific literature

- Concept Mining

- Full text search

- List of text mining software

- Name resolution (semantics and text extraction)

- Stop words

- Text classification sometimes is considered a (sub)task of text mining.

- Web mining, a task that may involve text mining (e.g. first find appropriate web pages by classifying crawled web pages, then extract the desired information from the text content of these pages considered relevant).

- w-shingling

- Sequence mining: String and Sequence Mining

- Noisy text analytics

- Named entity recognition

- Identity resolution

- News analytics

- Spam detection

73.9 Notes

[1] Archived November 29, 2009 at the Wayback Machine

[2] "KDD-2000 Workshop on Text Mining - Call for Papers". Cs.cmu.edu. Retrieved 2015-02-23.

[3]

[4] Hobbs, Jerry R.; Walker, Donald E.; Amsler, Robert A. (1982). "Proceedings of the 9th conference on Computational linguistics" **1**. pp. 127–32. doi:10.3115/991813.991833.

[5] "Unstructured Data and the 80 Percent Rule". Breakthrough Analysis. Retrieved 2015-02-23.

[6] "Content Analysis of Verbatim Explanations". Ppc.sas.upenn.edu. Retrieved 2015-02-23.

[7] "A Brief History of Text Analytics by Seth Grimes". Beyenetwork. 2007-10-30. Retrieved 2015-02-23.

[8] Hearst, Marti A. (1999). "Proceedings of the 37th annual meeting of the Association for Computational Linguistics on Computational Linguistics". pp. 3–10. doi:10.3115/1034678.1034679. ISBN 1-55860-609-2.

[9] "Full Circle Sentiment Analysis". Breakthrough Analysis. Retrieved 2015-02-23.

[10] Mehl, Matthias R. (2006). "Handbook of multimethod measurement in psychology". p. 141. doi:10.1037/11383-011. ISBN 1-59147-318-7.

[11] Zanasi, Alessandro (2009). "Proceedings of the International Workshop on Computational Intelligence in Security for Information Systems CISIS'08". Advances in Soft Computing **53**. p. 53. doi:10.1007/978-3-540-88181-0_7. ISBN 978-3-540-88180-3.

[12] Cohen, K. Bretonnel; Hunter, Lawrence (2008). "Getting Started in Text Mining". *PLoS Computational Biology* **4** (1): e20. doi:10.1371/journal.pcbi.0040020. PMC 2217579. PMID 18225946.

[13] Jenssen, Tor-Kristian; Lægreid, Astrid; Komorowski, Jan; Hovig, Eivind (2001). "A literature network of human genes for high-throughput analysis of gene expression". *Nature Genetics* **28** (1): 21–8. doi:10.1038/ng0501-21. PMID 11326270.

[14] Masys, Daniel R. (2001). "Linking microarray data to the literature". *Nature Genetics* **28** (1): 9–10. doi:10.1038/ng0501-9. PMID 11326264.

[15] Joseph, Thomas; Saipradeep, Vangala G; Venkat Raghavan, Ganesh Sekar; Srinivasan, Rajgopal; Rao, Aditya; Kotte, Sujatha; Sivadasan, Naveen (2012). "TPX: Biomedical literature search made easy". *Bioinformation* **8** (12): 578–80. doi:10.6026/97320630008578. PMC 3398782. PMID 22829734.

[16]

[17] "Text Analytics". Medallia. Retrieved 2015-02-23.

[18] Coussement, Kristof; Van Den Poel, Dirk (2008). "Integrating the voice of customers through call center emails into a decision support system for churn prediction". *Information & Management* **45** (3): 164–74. doi:10.1016/j.im.2008.01.005.

[19] Coussement, Kristof; Van Den Poel, Dirk (2008). "Improving customer complaint management by automatic email classification using linguistic style features as predictors". *Decision Support Systems* **44** (4): 870–82. doi:10.1016/j.dss.2007.10.010.

[20] Pang, Bo; Lee, Lillian; Vaithyanathan, Shivakumar (2002). "Proceedings of the ACL-02 conference on Empirical methods in natural language processing" **10**. pp. 79–86. doi:10.3115/1118693.1118704.

[21] Alessandro Valitutti, Carlo Strapparava, Oliviero Stock (2005). "Developing Affective Lexical Resources" (PDF). *Psychology Journal* **2** (1): 61–83.

[22] Erik Cambria; Robert Speer; Catherine Havasi; Amir Hussain (2010). "SenticNet: a Publicly Available Semantic Resource for Opinion Mining" (PDF). *Proceedings of AAAI CSK*. pp. 14–18.

[23] Calvo, Rafael A; d'Mello, Sidney (2010). "Affect Detection: An Interdisciplinary Review of Models, Methods, and Their Applications". *IEEE Transactions on Affective Computing* **1** (1): 18–37. doi:10.1109/T-AFFC.2010.1.

[24] "The University of Manchester". Manchester.ac.uk. Retrieved 2015-02-23.

[25] "Tsujii Laboratory". Tsujii.is.s.u-tokyo.ac.jp. Retrieved 2015-02-23.

[26] "The University of Tokyo". UTokyo. Retrieved 2015-02-23.

[27] Automated analysis of the US presidential elections using Big Data and network analysis; S Sudhahar, GA Veltri, N Cristianini; Big Data & Society 2 (1), 1-28, 2015

[28] Network analysis of narrative content in large corpora; S Sudhahar, G De Fazio, R Franzosi, N Cristianini; Natural Language Engineering, 1-32, 2013

[29] Quantitative Narrative Analysis; Roberto Franzosi; Emory University © 2010

[30] I. Flaounas, M. Turchi, O. Ali, N. Fyson, T. De Bie, N. Mosdell, J. Lewis, N. Cristianini, The Structure of EU Mediasphere, PLoS ONE, Vol. 5(12), pp. e14243, 2010.

[31] Nowcasting Events from the Social Web with Statistical Learning V Lampos, N Cristianini; ACM Transactions on Intelligent Systems and Technology (TIST) 3 (4), 72

[32] NOAM: news outlets analysis and monitoring system; I Flaounas, O Ali, M Turchi, T Snowsill, F Nicart, T De Bie, N Cristianini Proc. of the 2011 ACM SIGMOD international conference on Management of data

[33] Automatic discovery of patterns in media content, N Cristianini, Combinatorial Pattern Matching, 2-13, 2011

[34] I. Flaounas, O. Ali, T. Lansdall-Welfare, T. De Bie, N. Mosdell, J. Lewis, N. Cristianini, RESEARCH METHODS IN THE AGE OF DIGITAL JOURNALISM, Digital Journalism, Routledge, 2012

[35] Effects of the Recession on Public Mood in the UK; T Lansdall-Welfare, V Lampos, N Cristianini; Mining Social Network Dynamics (MSND) session on Social Media Applications

[36] Archived June 9, 2014 at the Wayback Machine

[37] "Licences for Europe - Structured Stakeholder Dialogue 2013". *European Commission*. Retrieved 14 November 2014.

[38] "Text and Data Mining:Its importance and the need for change in Europe". *Association of European Research Libraries*. Retrieved 14 November 2014.

[39] "Judge grants summary judgment in favor of Google Books — a fair use victory". *Lexology.com*. Antonelli Law Ltd. Retrieved 14 November 2014.

73.10   References

- Ananiadou, S. and McNaught, J. (Editors) (2006). *Text Mining for Biology and Biomedicine*. Artech House Books. ISBN 978-1-58053-984-5

- Bilisoly, R. (2008). *Practical Text Mining with Perl*. New York: John Wiley & Sons. ISBN 978-0-470-17643-6

- Feldman, R., and Sanger, J. (2006). *The Text Mining Handbook*. New York: Cambridge University Press. ISBN 978-0-521-83657-9

- Indurkhya, N., and Damerau, F. (2010). *Handbook Of Natural Language Processing*, 2nd Edition. Boca Raton, FL: CRC Press. ISBN 978-1-4200-8592-1

- Kao, A., and Poteet, S. (Editors). *Natural Language Processing and Text Mining*. Springer. ISBN 1-84628-175-X

- Konchady, M. *Text Mining Application Programming (Programming Series)*. Charles River Media. ISBN 1-58450-460-9

- Manning, C., and Schutze, H. (1999). *Foundations of Statistical Natural Language Processing*. Cambridge, MA: MIT Press. ISBN 978-0-262-13360-9

- Miner, G., Elder, J., Hill. T, Nisbet, R., Delen, D. and Fast, A. (2012). *Practical Text Mining and Statistical Analysis for Non-structured Text Data Applications*. Elsevier Academic Press. ISBN 978-0-12-386979-1

- McKnight, W. (2005). "Building business intelligence: Text data mining in business intelligence". *DM Review*, 21-22.

- Srivastava, A., and Sahami. M. (2009). *Text Mining: Classification, Clustering, and Applications*. Boca Raton, FL: CRC Press. ISBN 978-1-4200-5940-3

- Zanasi, A. (Editor) (2007). *Text Mining and its Applications to Intelligence, CRM and Knowledge Management*. WIT Press. ISBN 978-1-84564-131-3

73.11   External links

- Marti Hearst: What Is Text Mining? (October, 2003)

- Automatic Content Extraction, Linguistic Data Consortium

- Automatic Content Extraction, NIST

- Research work and applications of Text Mining (for instance AgroNLP)

Chapter 74

TuVox

TuVox is a company that produces VXML-based telephone speech-recognition applications to replace DTMF touchtone systems for their clients.

74.1 History

TuVox was founded in 2001 by Steven S. Pollock and Ashok Khosla, formerly of Apple Computer Corporation and Claris Corporation. Since then, TuVox has grown to over 40 employees and has US offices in Cupertino, California and Boca Raton, Florida as well as international offices in London, Vancouver and Sydney. In 2005, TuVox acquired the customers and hosting facilities of Net-By-Tel.

On July 22, 2010, West Interactive—a subsidiary of West Corporation—announced its acquisition of TuVox.

74.2 Customers

TuVox clients include 1-800-Flowers.com, AMC Entertainment, American Airlines, British Airways, M&T Bank, Canon Inc., Gateway, Inc., Motorola, Progress Energy Inc., Telecom New Zealand, Time, Inc., BECU, Virgin America and USAA.

74.3 References

- Destination CRM, April 1, 2007: Winnowing Customer Care Woes. by Coreen Bailor, Destination CRM

- ZDNet News, September 28, 2004: TuVox calls for the 'perfect' app. By Nadia Ilyin, ZDNet News

- TMCnet. September 29, 2005. TuVox Acquires Net-ByTel's Hosted Speech. By David Sims, TMCnet CRM Alert Columnist

- Speech Technology Magazine's 2006 Most Innovative Solutions Awards.Canon's speech application from TuVox named "Most Innovative Solution". Speech Technology Magazine recognizes Canon's deployment of TuVox Perfect Router as most creative in the industry.

- Speech Technology Magazine NewsBlast May 24, 2006 - Speech Technology Magazine's Q&A with Steve Pollock, Co-founder and EVP of TuVox

- San Jose Mercury News, March 21, 2005 - 1E Tech Monday "They speak, thereby they brand. Speech recognition systems that converse with you give companies a new way to say who they are"

- Red Herring (magazine) July 18, 2005 - TuVox: Anatomy of a Deal, The inside story of how TuVox raised the cash to become an international player.

- Call Center Magazine April 1, 2006 - Is Hosting the Future of Speech?

- The Wall Street Journal June 5, 2006 - Big Tech Companies Shop for Tiny Ventures

- Press Release: West Interactive Acquires TuVox

Chapter 75

Validis

Validis is a web based service which detects anomalies in accounting data in very much the same manner as a spell checker finds errors in a text document. The word itself is derived from a concatenation of Validate and Discover. The primary user base is among accounting professionals both within the financial community of corporate and SME business and across professional accounting practice. It provides a means to identify out of line data that is incomplete, invalid, inconsistent, or inaccurate, an analysis collectively tagged the 'Four Is'.

75.1 Technology

The service, offered by **Validis** is based on IP owned and patent protected by **Future Route**.

Validis presents their service through a web-based interface. On the server side the system uses a number of sophisticated techniques to analyse data for quality problems.

Underlying the system is an abstract representation of accounting data, in the form of an ontology of accounting concepts. In an initial setup step the users accounts are automatically mapped into this representation by analysing the Chart of Accounts.

The system maintains an Expert System in the form of a body of rules that describe valid, and invalid states for individual transactions, accounts, and other elements of the accounting ontology. Validis employs a specialised rule language developed in house, similar to Prolog and SQL, to create these rules. The rules are written in terms of elements of the accounting ontology, and therefore once a set of accounts has been mapped into it, the rules can immediately be applied to that set of accounts.

Validis also uses Information Theory to discover records in the data that are inconsistent with the typical behaviour exhibited in the data. By finding records which have excess information bits relative to the information bits of the individual field values in that record, Validis is able to identify unusual combinations of field values. It presents these un-

usual combinations to the user in the form of easily understood propositional rules.

Numerical values in the data are also subjected to outlier analysis, individually, and agglomerated over time periods and over elements of the accounting ontology. Records with values that are outliers in absolute value terms, or that deviate from patterns identified in the data, are shown to the user.

Accounting data uploaded to Validis is also analysed and compared to the Benford Distribution (see Benford's Law), to check that the data has not been artificially generated or manipulated. The user is alerted if the data deviates from the expected distribution.

75.2 Reporting

Output is presented in graphical form via a web interface. Underlying report data may be downloaded into excel for further analysis and manipulation. A presentable drill down analytical review may be manipulated across user selected time periods.

75.3 Timeline

While the parent business Future Route has been developing and deploying machine learning solutions since 2002. The service is due to enter beta release during March 2007 within a selected community of UK accountants, with full market availability soon thereafter. Initial deployments are compatible with SAGE (line 50), it is understood that further versions will be available shortly covering other versions of SAGE then MYOB, Intuit Quickbooks, Microsoft Dynamics GP and AX, Oracle, SAP, Sun Accounts,

An alpha test period operating throughout January and February 2007 resulted in user interface modifications and adaptations to bring the service in line with UK accounting industry expectations. Initial deployments are based on

Sage Line 50 accounting data.

Following release of an initial library of business rules, capturing local legislative guidelines for accounts preparation, and typical accounting errors, such as missposts, omissions the service is expected to extend to include industry specific rule packs and advanced analytic functions and to support additional accounting packages throughout 2007.

75.4   External links

- **Future Route**

- **Validis**

Chapter 76

Vehicle infrastructure integration

Vehicle Infrastructure Integration (**VII**) is an initiative fostering research and applications development for a series of technologies directly linking road vehicles to their physical surroundings, first and foremost in order to improve road safety. The technology draws on several disciplines, including transport engineering, electrical engineering, automotive engineering, and computer science. VII specifically covers road transport although similar technologies are in place or under development for other modes of transport. Planes, for example, use ground-based beacons for automated guidance, allowing the autopilot to fly the plane without human intervention. In highway engineering, improving the safety of a roadway can enhance overall efficiency. VII targets improvements in both safety and efficiency.

Vehicle infrastructure integration is that branch of engineering, which deals with the study and application of a series of techniques directly linking road vehicles to their physical surroundings in order to improve road safety.

76.1 Goals

The goal of VII is to provide a communications link between vehicles on the road (via On-Board Equipment, OBE), and between vehicles and the roadside infrastructure (via Roadside Equipment, RSE), in order to increase the safety, efficiency, and convenience of the transportation system. It is based on widespread deployment of a dedicated short-range communications (DSRC) link, incorporating IEEE 802.11p. VII's development relies on a business model supporting the interests of all parties concerned: industry, transportation authorities and professional organisations. The initiative has three priorities:

- evaluation of the business model (including deployment scheduling) and acceptance by the stakeholders;

- validation of the technology (in particular the communications systems) in the light of deployment costs; and

- development of legal structures and policies (particularly in regard to privacy) to enhance the system's potential for success over the longer term.

76.1.1 Safety

Current active safety technology relies on vehicle-based radar and vision systems. For example, this technology can reduce rear-end collisions by tracking obstructions in front or behind the vehicle, automatically applying brakes when needed. This technology is somewhat limited in that it senses only the distance and speed of vehicles within the direct line of sight. It is almost completely ineffective for angled and left-turn collisions . It may even cause a motorist to lose control of the vehicle in the event of an impending head-on collision. The rear-end collisions covered by today's technology are typically less severe than angle, left-turn, or head-on collisions. Existing technology is therefore inadequate for the overall needs of the roadway system.

VII would provide a direct link between a vehicle on the road and all vehicles within a defined vicinity. The vehicles would be able to communicate with each other, exchanging data on speed, orientation, perhaps even on driver awareness and intent. This could increase safety for nearby vehicles, while enhancing the overall sensitivity of the VII system, for example, by performing an automated emergency maneuver (steering, decelerating, braking) more effectively. In addition, the system is designed to communicate with the roadway infrastructure, allowing for complete, real-time traffic information for the entire network, as well as better queue management and feedback to vehicles. It would ultimately close the feedback loops on what is now an open-loop transportation system.

Through VII, roadway markings and road signs could become obsolete. Existing VII applications use sensors within vehicles which can identify markings on the roadway or signing along the side of the road, automatically adjusting vehicle parameters as necessary. Ultimately, VII aims to treat such signs and markings as little more than stored data within the system. This could be in the form of data acquired via beacons along a roadway or stored at a centralised database and distributed to all VII-equipped vehicles.

76.1.2 Efficiency

All the above factors are largely in response to safety but VII could lead to noticeable gains in the operational efficiency of a transportation network. As vehicles will be linked together with a resulting decrease in reaction times, the headway between vehicles could be reduced so that there is less empty space on the road. Available capacity for traffic would therefore be increased. More capacity per lane will in turn mean fewer lanes in general, possibly satisfying the community's concerns about the impact of roadway widening. VII will enable precise traffic-signal coordination by tracking vehicle platoons and will benefit from accurate timing by drawing on real-time traffic data covering volume, density and turning movements.

Real-time traffic data can also be used in the design of new roadways or modification of existing systems as the data could be used to provide accurate origin-destination studies and turning-movement counts for uses in transportation forecasting and traffic operations. Such technology would also lead to improvements for transport engineers to address problems whilst reducing the cost of obtaining and compiling data. Tolling is another prospect for VII technology as it could enable roadways to be automatically tolled. Data could be collectively transmitted to road users for in-vehicle display, outlining the lowest cost, shortest distance, and/or fastest route to a destination on the basis of real-time conditions.

76.1.3 Existing applications

To some extent, results along these lines have been achieved in trials performed around the globe, making use of GPS, mobile phone signals, and vehicle registration plates. GPS is becoming standard in many new high-end vehicles and is an option on most new low- and mid-range vehicles. In addition, many users also have mobile phones which transmit trackable signals (and may also be GPS-enabled). Mobile phones can already be traced for purposes of emergency response. GPS and mobile phone tracking, however, do not provide fully reliable data. Furthermore, integrating mobile phones in vehicles may be prohibitively difficult. Data from mobile phones, though useful, might even increase risks to motorists as they tend to look at their phones rather than concentrate on their driving. Automatic registration plate recognition can provide high levels of data, but continuously tracking a vehicle through a corridor is a difficult task with existing technology. Today's equipment is designed for data

acquisition and functions such as enforcement and tolling, not for returning data to vehicles or motorists for response. GPS will nevertheless be one of the key components in VII systems.[1]

76.2 Limitations

There are numerous limitations to the development of VII. A common misconception is that the biggest challenge to VII technology is the computing power that can be fitted inside a vehicle. While this is indeed a challenge, the technology for computers has been advancing rapidly and is not a particular concern for VII researchers. Given the fact that technologies already exist for the most basic of forms of VII, perhaps the greatest hurdle to the deployment of VII technology is public acceptance.

76.2.1 Privacy

The most common myth about VII is that it includes tracking technology; however, this is not the case.[2] The architecture is designed to prevent identification of individual vehicles, with all data exchange between the vehicle and the system occurring anonymously. Exchanges between the vehicles and third parties such as OEMs and toll collectors will occur, but the network traffic will be sent via encrypted tunnels and will therefore not be decipherable by the VII system.

Although the system will be able to detect signal and speed violations, it will not have the capability to identify the violator and report them. The detection is for the purpose of alerting the violator and/or approaching vehicles, to prevent collisions.

76.2.2 Other public concerns

Other public acceptance concerns come from advocates of recreational driving as well as from critics of tolling. The former argue that VII will increase the automation of the vehicle, reducing the driver's enjoyment. Recreational driving concerns are particularly prevalent among owners of sports cars. They could be attenuated by compensating for the presence of vehicles without VII or perhaps by maintaining roadways where vehicles without VII are permitted to travel.

Those opposed to tolling believe it will make driving prohibitively expensive for motorists in the lower-income bracket, conflicting with the general wish to provide equal services for all. In response, public transit discounts or road use discounts can be considered for qualifying individuals and/or families. Such provisions currently exist for numerous tolled roadways and could be applicable to roadways that are tolled via VII. However, as VII could allow for the tolling of *every* VII-enabled roadway, the provisions may be ineffective in view of the increased need to provide user-efficient transit services to every area.

76.2.3 Technical issues

Coordination

A major issue facing the deployment of VII is the problem of how to stand up the system initially. The costs associated with installing the technology in vehicles and providing communications and power at every intersection are significant. Building out the infrastructure along the roadside without the auto manufacturers' cooperation would be disastrous, as would the reverse situation; therefore, the two parties will need to work together to make the VII concept work.

There are proof of concept tests being performed in Michigan and California that will be evaluated by the US DOT and the auto manufacturers, and a decision will be made, jointly, about whether or not to move forward with implementation of the system at that time.

Maintenance

Another factor for consideration in regard to the technology's distribution is how to update and maintain the units. Traffic systems are highly dynamic, with new traffic controls implemented every day and roadways constructed or repaired every year. The vehicle-based option could be updated via the internet (preferably wireless), but may subsequently require all users to have access to internet technology. Many local government agencies have been testing deployment of internet facilities in cities and along roadways, for example at rest-stops. These systems could be used for VII updating.

An additional option is to provide updates whenever a vehicle is brought in for inspection or servicing. A major limitation here is that updating would be in the hands of the user. Some vehicle owners maintain their vehicles themselves, and periodic inspections or servicing are considered too infrequent for updating VII. Motorists might also be reluctant to stop at rest-stops for an update if they do not have the possibility of driving in an internet-enabled city.

Alternatively, if receivers were placed in all vehicles and the VII system was primarily located along the roadside, information could be stored in a centralised database. This would allow the agency responsible to issue updates at any time. These would then be disseminated to the roadside units for passing motorists. Operationally, this method is currently considered to provide the greatest effectiveness but at a high cost to the authorities.

Security

Security of the units is another concern, especially in the light of the public acceptance issue. Criminals could tamper with VII units, or remove and/or destroy them regardless of whether they are installed inside vehicles or along the roadside. If they are placed inside vehicles, laws similar to those for tampering with an odometer could be enacted; and the units could be examined during inspections or services for signs of tampering. This method has many of the limitations mentioned in relation to the frequency of inspection and motorists who perform their own servicing. It also raises concerns regarding the honesty of vehicle technicians performing the inspections. The ability of technicians to identify signs of tampering would be dependent on their knowledge of the VII systems themselves.

Magnets, electric shocks, and malicious software (viruses, hacking, or jamming) could be used to damage VII systems - regardless of whether units are located inside vehicle or along the roadside. Extensive training and certification would be required for technicians to inspect VII units within a vehicle. Along the roadside, a high degree of security would be required to ensure that the equipment is not damaged and to increase its durability. However, as roadside units could well be placed on the public right-of-way - which is often close to the edge of the roadway - there could be concerns about vehicles hitting them (whether on purpose or by accident). The units would either have to be built so that they do not provide a threat to motorists: perhaps in the form of a low-profile and/or low-mass object designed to be run over or to break apart (which would entail a relatively inexpensive unit); or the unit would have to be shielded by a device such as a guardrail, raising safety concerns of its own.

Data input

Yet another limitation is in digitizing the inputs for the VII system. VII systems will probably continue to sense existing signs and roadway markings but one of the goals is to eliminate such signs and markings altogether. This would require converting the locations and messages of each item into the VII system's format. Responsibility for this work would probably fall on the highway agencies which nearly all face difficulties in funding, manpower, and available time. Implementing and maintaining VII systems may therefore require support at the national level.

Communications and authorization

While VII is largely being developed as a joint research enterprise involving numerous transport agencies, it is likely initial products will be tailored to individual applications. As a result, compatibility and formatting issues could well arise as systems expand. Overcoming these difficulties could require complicated translation programs between different systems or possibly a complete overhaul of existing VII systems in order to develop a more comprehensive approach. In either case, the costs and potential for bugs in the software will likely be high.

Legislation will be required to set in place access to the VII data and communications between applicable agencies. In the USA, for example, an Interstate is a Federal roadway that is often maintained by the State, but the local county or municipal authorities may be involved too. The legislation would need to set the levels of authority of each agency. In Pennsylvania, for example, municipalities tend to have greater authority than counties and sometimes even the State whereas neighboring Maryland has more authority at the county level than at municipal level; and State roads are almost exclusively controlled by the State. It would also have to be determined which other agencies can use the data (i.e. law enforcement, Census, etc.) and to what degree it is permissible to use the information. Law enforcement would be needed to minimise data misuse. The various levels of authority could also increase incompatibility.

76.3 Recent developments

Much of the current research and experimentation is conducted in the United States[3] where coordination is ensured through the Vehicle Infrastructure Integration Consortium, consisting of automobile manufacturers (Ford, General Motors, DaimlerChrysler, Toyota, Nissan, Honda, Volkswagen, BMW), IT suppliers, U.S. Federal and state transportation departments, and professional associations.[4] Trialling is taking place in Michigan[5] and California.[6]

The specific applications now being developed under the U.S. initiative[7] are:

- Warning drivers of unsafe conditions or imminent collisions.

- Warning drivers if they are about to run off the road or speed around a curve too fast.

- Informing system operators of real-time congestion, weather conditions and incidents.

- Providing operators with information on corridor capacity for real-time management, planning and provi-

sion of corridor-wide advisories to drivers.

In mid-2007, a VII environment covering some 20 square miles ($52 \, km^2$) near Detroit will be used to test 20 prototype VII applications. Several automobile manufacturers are also conducting their own VII research and trialling.

76.4 See also

- Intelligent transportation system

- Tracking

  - Vehicle tracking system

  - GPS tracking

  - Automatic number plate recognition

- Automated highway system

- Driverless car

76.5 References

[1] GPS Drives Vehicle Infrastructure Integration, GPS World, October 2006.

[2] http://www-nrd.nhtsa.dot.gov/pdf/nrd-01/NRDmtgs/ 2005Honda/Resendes_VII.pdf

[3] U.S. DOT VII. Retrieved 21 February 2007.

[4] Full speed ahead for intelligent car design, Financial Times, 20 February 2007

[5] Michigan DOT VII Program. Retrieved 21 February 2007.

[6] Expediting Vehicle Infrastructure Integration. Retrieved 21 February 2007

[7] Vehicle Infrastructure Integration from U.S. DOT. Retrieved 21 February 2007.

76.6 External links

- VII Coalition Website

- ITS Website of the USDOT

- FHWA Powerpoint Presentation

- Michigan DOT VII Development Site

- GPS World article on GPS-based VII

- eSafety

Chapter 77

Verbot

This article is about the chatterbot software. For the 1980s toy robot, see Omnibot#Verbot.2FKI.2AKU.2AZO.

The **Verbot** (Verbal-Robot) was a popular[1] chatterbot program and Artificial Intelligence Software Development Kit (SDK) for the Windows platform and for the web.

77.1 Early beginning

Virtual Personalities, Inc. traces its technology back to Dr. Michael Mauldin's work as a graduate student and post doctoral fellow at Carnegie Mellon University; and its artistry back to Peter Plantec's work in personality psychology and art direction.

77.1.1 Historic outline

In 1994, Dr. Mauldin, Founder of Lycos, Inc., developed a prototype Chatterbot, Julia, which competed in the internationally known Turing test, for the coveted Loebner Prize. The Turing Test matches computer scientist judges against machines to see if they can distinguish a computer from a real human. This prototype version was refined and developed, and in 1997, Dr. Mauldin and Peter Plantec, a clinical psychologist, and animator, formed Virtual Personalities, Inc. (now Conversive, Inc.) in order to create a virtual human interface that would incorporate real-time animation as well as speech and natural language processing. The initial release, a stand-alone virtual person called Sylvie, was beta-tested to the public. This release was well received, and finally, after several versions, the production release (deemed version 3) of the Verbally Enhanced Software Robot—or, Verbot was deployed in the Fall 2000.

- The grandfather of all Verbots is Rog-O-Matic, which although it could not talk, could and did explore a virtual world.

- Julia has been active on the internet in one form or another since 1989.

- A close cousin of Julia is Lycos, a robot that explores the World Wide Web and answers questions about it.

- Sylvie was the first Verbot with a face and a voice.

- Sylvie was the first Virtual Human with advanced, flexible interfacing capability.

77.1.2 Beginnings

The Virtual Personalities story goes back to 1978, where Mauldin was attending Rice University. Fascinated by the idea of ELIZA, he proceeded to write a program called "PET" for his 8 kilobyte Commodore PET Computer. PET included simple induction as a way to post new information, and once managed the following deep observation: Meanwhile, Plantec was separately designing a personality for "Entity", a theoretical virtual human that would interact comfortably with humans without pretending to be one. At that time the technology was not advanced enough to bring Entity to life, however, Mauldin was working on that.

Subject: I like my friend (later) Subject: I like food. PET: I have heard that food is your friend.

Mauldin got so involved with this, that he majored in Computer Science and minored in Linguistics.

77.1.3 Rogue

In the late seventies and early eighties, a popular computer game at Universities was Rogue, an implementation of Dungeons and Dragons where the player would descend 26 levels in a randomly created dungeon, fighting monsters, gathering treasure, and searching for the elusive "Amulet of Yendor". Mauldin was one of four grad students who devoted a large amount of time to building a program called "Rog-O-Matic" that could and on several occasions did

217

manage to retrieve the amulet and emerge victorious from the dungeon.

77.1.4 TinyMUD

So when in 1989, James Aspnes at Carnegie Mellon created the first TinyMUD (a descendent of MUD and AberMUD), Mauldin was one of the first to create a computer player that would explore the text-based world of TinyMUD. But his first robot, Gloria, gradually accreted more and more linguistic ability, to the point that it could pass the "unsuspecting" Turing Test. In this version of the test, the human has no reason to suspect that one of the other occupants of the room is controlled by a computer, and so is more polite and asks fewer probing questions. The second generation of Mauldin's TinyMUD robots was Julia, created on Jan. 8, 1990. Julia slowly developed into a more and more capable conversational agent, and assumed useful duties in the TinyMUD world, including tour guide, information assistant, note-taker, message-relayer, and even could play the card game hearts along with the other human players.

In 1991, the first Loebner Prize contest was held in Boston, Mass., and Julia was there. Although she only finished third, she was ranked by one judge as more human than one of the human confederates, winning a coveted certificate of humanness in the world's first restricted Turing test.

Julia continued to log into to various TinyMUD's and TinyMucks for the next seven years, and also chats with hundreds of people a month over the internet.

77.1.5 Lycos

Julia's job was to explore a virtual world consisting of pages of textual descriptions, with links between them, and to construct an internal map of that world and answer questions about it (including path information such as the shortest route from one room to another, and matching information, such as which rooms contained a certain kind of object or textual description).

It was therefore only a very short cognitive leap from Julia to Lycos, another robotic agent that explores a virtual world made of hyperlinked pages of text, and which answers questions about those pages. Sylvie was born and her abilities were expanded greatly to include interfacing with computers and control systems via her serial ports.

77.1.6 Sylvie

Sylvie was the first intelligent animated virtual human. She was designed both as a conversation agent and as a virtual

human interface that would form a bridge between the two. She became more popular as a conversation agent, but her designers believe she serves as a prototype for future virtual human interface design that will help us all cope with the increasing complexity of technology.

As and aside, Plantec noticed that an inordinately large number of Sylvies were being sold in Southeast Asia. Upon investigation he discovered that students had discovered a "test" mode that would allow them to type in English sentences that Sylvie would pronounce in her somewhat stylized English. Sylvie was teaching them English ... her style of English.

77.2 Ownership

In 1997, Dr. Mauldin and Peter Plantec, formed Virtual Personalities, Inc. to create Natural Language Processing solutions for companies. In 2001 Virtual Personalities, Inc. became Conversive, Inc. to reflect the focus on providing Customer Service and Marketing to the Enterprise Market. In late 2012 Avaya, Inc. acquired Conversive's assets including Verbots. [2]

77.3 Verbot versions

The Verbot 4 version was created and released in 2004. In 2005 Version 4.1 of the Verbot Software was released with many feature enhancements and bug fixes, including built-in support for embedding C# code in outputs and conditionals. In Early 2006 Conversive launched Verbots Online allowing Verbot 4 users to upload their knowledge and show off their bots to the world. In 2009 Version 5 was released, completely free and fully featured. In early 2012 the last version of Verbot, 5.0.1.2, was released to the general public with support for Windows 7. Also in 2012 Verbots Online completely shutdown. [3]

77.4 Verbots today

Verbots.com, its community of users and its forums no longer exist but the software and users can still be found. There has been no active development since the early 2012 release of Verbot 5.0.1.2. [4]

77.5 See also

• Turing test

- Loebner prize
- Chatterbot
- List of Chatterbots

77.6 Notes

[1] Joshua, Quittner (1997-12-08). "WHAT'S HOT IN BOTS". Time Magazine.

[2] "A little history: Chatterbots and Conversive". Retrieved Feb 27, 2014.

[3] "Verbots Online shut down". Retrieved Feb 27, 2014.

[4] "Verbot Permanently Shutdown". Retrieved Feb 27, 2014.

77.7 External links

- Julia
- Conversive
- Verbots
- Open Source (GPL) Verbots SDK
- Open Source (GPL) Knowedgebase Editor

Chapter 78

VoiceWeb

VoiceWeb is a privately held company that sells speech enabled products and applications to replace the now obsolete DTMF systems. The company specializes in highly interactive voice user interfaces with natural language understanding and several degrees of freedom.

78.1 History

The company was founded in March 2001 by Dr. Nikos Patsis & Dr. Damianos Chatziantoniou and launched the first Greek Voice Portal in May 2001. Since then, the company has opened offices in Athens, Greece and Guatemala City, Guatemala. Amongst the major stockholders are In-QLab, the 1st Greek incubator of technology startups and SETE Ventures, a Venture Capital located in Geneva.

78.2 Products

VoiceWeb offers a variety of speech enabled products in the following areas:

- Ticketing applications for
  - Entertainment
  - Transportation
  - Sports
- Voice Portals
- Automated Ordering Systems
- Value Added Services
- Call Center Automation
- Computer Telephony Integration
- Integrated Voice Banking Systems
- Embedded Voice Systems

- Interactive Voice and Video Response (IVVR) systems and other multimodal applications

The company also sells SMS systems and applications as well as complete web based control and administration panels for their products.

VoiceWeb is a supporter member of the VXML Forum, and a partner of Envox Worldwide.

78.3 Customers

VoiceWeb's customers include WIND Hellas (ex TIM Hellas), Vodafone Hellas, Q-Telecom, Village Cinemas, Hellenic Ministry of Finance, Ministry of Labour, First Data, Tellas, Emporiki Bank and many others.

78.4 References and Links

1. VoiceWeb Voice Ticketing for Village Cinemas, case study at envox.com

2. Village Cinemas VoiceWeb Voice Ticketing Solution at speechtechmag.com

3. The Pythia Taxi Dispatching System in Greece by VoiceWeb and Loquendo

Chapter 79

WebCrow

The **WebCrow** is a research project carried out at the Information Engineering of the University of Siena with the purpose of automatically solving crosswords.

79.1 The Project

The scientific relevance of the project can be understood considering that cracking crosswords requires human-level knowledge. Unlike chess and related games and there is no closed world configuration space. Interestingly, a first nucleus of technology, such as search engines, information retrieval, and machine learning techniques enable computers to enfold with semantics real-life concepts. The project is based on a software system whose major assumption is to attack crosswords making use of the Web as its primary source of knowledge.

WebCrow is very fast and often thrashes human challengers in competitions,[1] especially on multi language crossword schemes. A distinct feature of the WebCrow software system is to combine properly natural language processing (NLP) techniques, the Google web search engine, and constraint satisfaction algorithms from artificial intelligence to acquire knowledge and to fill the schema. The most important component of WebCrow is the Web Search Module (WSM), which implements a domain specific web based question answering algorithm.

The way WebCrow approaches crosswords solving is quite with respect to humans:[2] Whereas we tend to first answer clues we are sure of and then proceed filling the schema by exploiting the already answered clues as hints, WebCrow uses two clearly distinct stages. In the first one, it processes all the clues and tries to answer them all: For each clue it finds many possible candidates and sorts them according to complex ranking models mainly based on a probability criteria. In the second stage, WebCrow uses constraint satisfaction algorithms to fill the grid with the overall most likely combination of clue answers.

In order to interact with Google, first of all, WebCrow needs to compose queries on the basis of the given clues. This is done by query expansion, whose purpose is to convert the clue into a query expressed by a simplified and more appropriate language for Google. The retrieved documents are parsed so as to extract a list of word candidates that are congruent with the crossword length constraints. Crosswords can hardly be faced by using encyclopedic knowledge only, since many clues are wordplays or are otherwise purposefully very ambiguous. This enigmatic component of crosswords is faced by a massive use of database of solved crosswords, and by automatic reasoning on a properly organized knowledge base of wired rules. Last but not the least, the final constraint satisfaction step is very effective to fill the correct candidate, even though, unlike humans, the system can not rely on very high confidence on the correctness of the answer.

79.2 Competitions

WebCrow speed and effectiveness [3] has been tested many times in man-machine competitions [1] on Italian, English and multi-language crosswords The outcome of the tests is that WebCrow can successfully compete with average human players on single language schemes and reaches expert level performance in multi-language crosswords. However, WebCrow has not reached expert level in single-language crosswords, yet.

79.2.1 ECAI-06 Competition

On August 30, 2006, at the European Conference on Artificial Intelligence (ECAI2006), 25 conference attendees and 53 internet connected crosswords lovers, competed with WebCrow in an official challenge organized within the conference program. The challenge consisted in 5 different crosswords (2 in Italian, 2 in English and one multi-language in Italian and English) and 15 minutes were assigned for each crossword. WebCrow ranked 21 out of 74 participants in the Italian competition, and won both the bilingual and English competitions.

79.2.2   Other Competitions

Several competitions have been held in Florence, Italy within the Creativity Festival in December 2006, and another official conference competition took place in Hyderabad, India in January 2007, within the International Conference of Artificial Intelligence, where it ranked second out of 25 participants.

79.3   References

[1] G.Angelini, M. Ernandes, E. Di Iorio, "WebCrow: Previous competitions"

[2] John S. Quarterman,"Google as AI"

[3] Tom Simonite, "Crossword Software Thrashes Human Challengers", *New Scientist*

79.4   External links

- The WebCrow Website

- Google as AI

- I'm puzzled, Dr. Dobbs portal

- Crossword-solving system strikes a blow for AI, by Simon Aughton

- Crosswords at the crossroads with "il computer enigmista?", Blogos - news and views on languages and technologies

- cbc.ca radio

- cruciverb.com

- Crossword Software Thrashes Human Challengers, The New Scientist

Chapter 80

Xaitment

xaitment is a German-based company that develops and sells artificial intelligence (AI) software to video game developers and simulation developers. The company was founded in 2004 by Dr. Andreas Gerber,[1] and is a spin-off of the German Research Centre for Artificial Intelligence, or DFKI. **xaitment** has its main office in Quierschied, Germany, and field offices in San Francisco and China.

80.1 Products

xaitment currently sells two AI software modules: xaitMap and xaitControl. xaitMap provides runtime libraries and graphical tools for navigation mesh generation (also called NavMesh generation), pathfinding, dynamic collision avoidance, and individual and crowd movement. xaitControl is a finite-state machine for game logic and character behavior modeling that also includes a real-time debugger. On January 11, 2012, xaitment announced that it making its source code for these modules available to "all current and future US and European licensees".

On February 22, 2012 **xaitment** released two new plug-ins, xaitMap and xaitControl for the Unity Game Engine.[2]

The full versions are available for PC (Windows and Linux), PlayStation 3, Xbox 360 and Wii. The pathfinding plug-in is available with a Windows dev environment, but can deployed on iOS, Mac, Android and the Unity Web Player.

80.2 Partners

xaitment's AI software is currently integrated into the Unity game engine, Havok's Vision Engine, Bohemia Interactive's VBS2 Simulation Engine, GameBase's Gamebryo game engine.[3]

80.3 Customers

xaitment sells its AI software products to video game developers and military and civil simulation developers. Current customers include Tencent, gamania, TML Studios, Emobi Games, IP Keys and others. A full list of customers can be found on **xaitment's** website.

80.4 References

[1] "xaitment Company Profile on Develop". Develop. 2005.

[2] "xaitment Launches Smart AI for Unity". xaitment. February 22, 2012.

[3] "Emergent, Xaitment Integrate xaitEngine AI With Gamebryo". gamasutra. July 21, 2009.

80.5 External links

- xaitment.com

Chapter 81

YouNoodle

YouNoodle is a San Francisco-based company, founded in 2010, building a platform for entrepreneurship competitions all over the world. YouNoodle matches entrepreneurs with competitions, accelerators, and startup programs, and provides a judging and voting SaaS platform to university, non-profit, government and enterprise clients organizing innovation challenges and competitions. Stanford's BASES, UC Berkeley's B-Plan, Start-Up Chile, Amazon Startup Challenge, and NASA are all running one or more competitions on YouNoodle's platform.

81.1 History and structure

YouNoodle was founded by Rebeca Hwang and Torsten Kolind in 2010. The company was spun off a project started by Bob Goodson and Kirill Makharinsky in 2007 with support from Peter Thiel (Founders Fund), Max Levchin (PayPal) and Charles Lho (Amicus Group), founding investor and Chairman of YouNoodle today. This project also spawned Quid (Goodson) and indirectly Ostrovok (Makharinsky). Although also named YouNoodle, this project/company was discontinued in 2010, when the three new entities started operations.

The founders of the 2007-2010 entity were Bob Goodson and Kirill Makharinsky, both former students of the University of Oxford.[1] Goodson had studied medieval English literature before moving from Oxford to California when Max Levchin, the co-founder of Paypal, invited him to join a start-up there.[2][3] Makharinsky's degree was in applied mathematics,[4] and he was also encouraged to pursue opportunities in the United States by Levchin.[5] Other significant employees included Rebeca Hwang (co-founder of today's YouNoodle), a Stanford University doctoral student whose research is into social network theory.[6]

81.2 Startup predictor

YouNoodle's now discontinued "Startup predictor", part of the 2007-2010 entity and developed by Makharinsky and Hwang, uses mathematical models to predict the success of new businesses.[4] The user fills in a questionnaire, which takes about half an hour to complete and concentrates on the business' concept, finances, founders and advisers.[7][8] Because the procedure is designed for very new companies, questions on revenue and traffic are not included.[6] The site then provides an estimate of what the company's value will be after three years and a score from 1 to 1000 representing its value as an investment.[7] The service is free for the startups themselves, but YouNoodle intends to charge third parties for access to the results.[9] (The level of detail required by the questionnaire makes it difficult for people without inside knowledge of a company to provide the data for a prediction on their own.[10])

The company's founders have declined to explain the algorithm in detail, but state that it takes into account the entrepreneurs' experience, networks and mutual relations. Information provided by companies which use the site's networking features is used to improve the algorithm.[1] As of August 2008, the algorithm was based on data from 3,000 startups.[9] In the same month the company had four patents pending on the technology.[4]

81.3 References

[1] Matt Richtel (February 18, 2008). "A Start-Up Says It Can Predict Others' Fate". *The New York Times*. Retrieved 2008-08-13.

[2] Richard Tyler (August 7, 2008). "YouNoodle takes its own test". *Telegraph.co.uk*. Retrieved 2008-08-13.

[3] Richard Tyler (May 1, 2008). "Oxford's brightest head to Silicon Valley for dotcom riches". *Telegraph.co.uk*. Retrieved 2008-08-13.

[4] Richard Tyler (August 7, 2008). "YouNoodle: The startup valuation tool that claims to outguess gut instinct". *Telegraph.co.uk*. Retrieved 2008-08-13.

[5] Matt Marshal (February 18, 2008). "YouNoodle offers investors a "start-up predictor"". *VentureBeat*. Retrieved 2008-08-13.

[6] Anthony Ha (August 7, 2008). "YouNoodle's startup predictor wants to tell you how much your company is worth". *VentureBeat*. Retrieved 2008-08-13.

[7] Liz Gunnison (August 7, 2008). "A Crystal Ball for Startups". *Condé Nast Portfolio*. Retrieved 2008-08-13.

[8] Rico Gagliano (August 7, 2008). "Site lets you peek at a startup's future". *Marketplace* (American Public Media). Retrieved 2008-08-13.

[9] Michael Arrington (August 5, 2008). "The (Highly Controversial) YouNoodle Startup Valuation Predictor Is Coming". *TechCrunch*. Retrieved 2008-08-13.

[10] Jessica Vascellaro (August 6, 2008). "Noodling Around On Startup Valuations". *WSJ.com*. Retrieved 2008-08-13.

81.4 External links

- YouNoodle (company website)

81.5 Text and image sources, contributors, and licenses

81.5.1 Text

- **Applications of artificial intelligence** *Source:* https://en.wikipedia.org/wiki/Applications_of_artificial_intelligence?oldid=686994254 *Contributors:* Auric, HaeB, Beland, Rich Farmbrough, Kesara, Guy Harris, Wtmitchell, Velella, Woohookitty, Rjwilmsi, Wavelength, Markicus, Chase me ladies, I'm the Cavalry, Arthur Rubin, SmackBot, Vasiliy Faronov, MilborneOne, Robofish, JHP, Pgr94, Countchoc, The Transhumanist, RebelRobot, Magioladitis, Jiuguang Wang, Mikael Häggström, Llorenzi, Steel1943, Philip Trueman, Wassname, 1337pino, LeadSongDog, Soler97, JamesKotecki, Jdaloner, Svick, CharlesGillingham, Fuddle, XLinkBot, Nepenthes, PL290, HarlandQPitt, SuperSmashBros.Brawl777, Landon1980, Elperzon, Tnordlan, Yobot, Materialscientist, Fathomer, Ayomawdb, ReformatMe, Csc300student, IO Device, Gh23, Citation bot 1, John of Reading, Xamuel, GraffDecors, Makecat, Thine Antique Pen, Brandmeister, Rangoon11, Rocketrod1960, ClueBot NG, Canzhiye, Cresdajv, Helpful Pixie Bot, Compfreak7, A*-search, Achowat, Quipa, IjonTichyIjonTichy, Dexbot, Cpgupta9460, Telfordbuck, Randykitty, Comp.arch, Ugog Nizdast, Julaei, Rikki233752, Skr15081997, APMcM, Lizfarabee, Ashleytway, TheEducatedPlatypus, Kvsbharath, JamieWilson99, Hestelars, JeremiahY and Anonymous: 69

- **Activity recognition** *Source:* https://en.wikipedia.org/wiki/Activity_recognition?oldid=666951753 *Contributors:* Edward, Ronz, Rich Farmbrough, Rjwilmsi, Stephenb, Malcolma, Paxse, Colonies Chris, CmdrObot, Gregbard, Dancter, Panjunfeng, The Transhumanist, Leolaursen, TAnthony, David Eppstein, Phoenixinter, Cobi, Guillaume2303, Robennals, JL-Bot, Sun Creator, Yobot, AnomieBOT, Gutao, J04n, Aaron Kauppi, FrescoBot, Jonesey95, Gutao98, Dewritech, Dawooga, Chire, Caddy68, Atiqahad, BG19bot, Vhoom2002, Ytianhui~enwiki, ChrisGualtieri, Khazar2, Sebowsky, Timvankasteren, Ubicomper, Interstela and Anonymous: 41

- **AForge.NET** *Source:* https://en.wikipedia.org/wiki/AForge.NET?oldid=664877779 *Contributors:* W3bbo, SmackBot, Cydebot, Gioto, R'n'B, Aleks-eng, Eeekster, Addbot, Dawynn, Ben Ben, Frank.nagl, Uzma Gamal, HardyVeles, Alexwho314, Samratsubedi, Woderkant and Anonymous: 8

- **Akinator** *Source:* https://en.wikipedia.org/wiki/Akinator?oldid=689175034 *Contributors:* Bearcat, Xanzzibar, Valenciano, IronGargoyle, Ishdarian, Silver seren, PresN, NapoliRoma, Skomorokh, Twsx, Pikolas, Tgeairn, Trusilver, Khullah~enwiki, Wagg4, Jean-Frédéric, Bfpage, Trivialist, Johnuniq, Addbot, MrOllie, Download, LaaknorBot, Luckas-bot, Yobot, Jamian45, Fraggle81, AnomieBOT, JackieBot, Materialscientist, Xqbot, I dream of horses, Actarus Prince d'Euphor, Sultan11, Lightlowemon, Sternenmeer, Clarkcj12, Vinnyzz, Tuankiet65, Myyuri, K6ka, ZéroBot, Speedbird536, ClueBot NG, Mr Sheep Measham, Brez93, Calabe1992, MolSno, Dynamicwork, Mark Arsten, Supernerd11, Shreyashubam, The1337gamer, KhabarNegar, The Illusive Man, Tentinator, EvergreenFir, Googap33, Thatweirdcreepydudeonthecorner, Nextinwire, Folded melon, Wtfguy123, Koosta, KickItRootDown, Santhosh139, Mplou6, Itslevanessa, Awesomeyveltal, SIDFAGOT and Anonymous: 73

- **Artificial imagination** *Source:* https://en.wikipedia.org/wiki/Artificial_imagination?oldid=580670992 *Contributors:* BRW, GregorB, TestPilot, Loukinho, Blanchardb, Tommosimmo, Cocolee2, Mitch Ames, Yobot, The Evil IP address, J04n, Compfun, Gregman2, ClaretAsh and Anonymous: 2

- **Artificial Intelligence Applications Institute** *Source:* https://en.wikipedia.org/wiki/Artificial_Intelligence_Applications_Institute?oldid=476983692 *Contributors:* BanyanTree, Xoloz, SmackBot, Twelsht, Austintate, Stephen potter, CharlesGillingham, 718 Bot, ZooFari, Addbot, Anubhab91 and Anonymous: 2

- **Artificial intuition** *Source:* https://en.wikipedia.org/wiki/Artificial_intuition?oldid=685020857 *Contributors:* Topbanana, Neko-chan, Rjwilmsi, Nick Number, Magioladitis, Jojalozzo, Stfg, Dthomsen8, ERK, John of Reading, Uploadvirus, Helpful Pixie Bot, Drift chambers, Churchgoer251, CS2012, BattyBot, DietFoodstamp, Cerberusrex, RichardKPSun, Venomzx, Yukio22 and Anonymous: 2

- **Artificial Solutions** *Source:* https://en.wikipedia.org/wiki/Artificial_Solutions?oldid=666860605 *Contributors:* Beland, Back ache, Derek R Bullamore, MurrayMunch, MatthewVanitas, Jujutacular, BG19bot, Barney the barney barney, Acalycine and Anonymous: 2

- **Automatic image annotation** *Source:* https://en.wikipedia.org/wiki/Automatic_image_annotation?oldid=635986456 *Contributors:* Sam Hocevar, Drbreznjev, Ligulem, Msbmsb, Shyam, Sharat sc, Kipmaster, KYN, Chris the speller, Barticus88, Guy Macon, Schmloof, Onun, Mr. Granger, Yohan.jin, Addbot, DOI bot, Fraggle81, Twri, Citation bot 1, Trappist the monk, RjwilmsiBot, John of Reading, Cogiati, Ibartolini, KritzAT, Mark viking, I am One of Many, Monkbot and Anonymous: 22

- **Automatic number plate recognition** *Source:* https://en.wikipedia.org/wiki/Automatic_number_plate_recognition?oldid=684516297 *Contributors:* Rbrwr, Edward, Michael Hardy, Pnm, Delirium, Ahoerstemeier, Ronz, Kingturtle, Ehn, Timwi, Dcoetzee, Snickerdo, Tpbradbury, דוד, Shantavira, Phil Boswell, Jeff8765, Kadin2048, Auric, Hadal, Alan Liefting, Yama, Hylaride, Lupin, Bobblewik, Tagishsimon, Gadfium, John Foley, Necrothesp, Elwell, Picapica, Corti, Grstain, Discospinster, Shermozle, Neko-chan, Violetriga, Tooto, Pmcm, Vinsci, Chairboy, Shanes, Webgeer, Brendansa, Cavrdg, Slambo, Licon, Alansohn, Thebeginning, 119, Jeltz, SlimVirgin, Kocio, Mailer diablo, Dark Shikari, GL, Danhash, Dtcdthingy, Jheald, Geraldshields11, Henry W. Schmitt, Ericl234, Jef-Infojef, Ukulele~enwiki, Tckma, Tabletop, Torqueing, Gimboid13, Mandarax, Stefan h~enwiki, Yurik, Jyran, Rjwilmsi, Harry491, Ashuttleworth, Alaney2k, Rillian, Oblivious, Renaissance Man, Sapient, RobertG, Musser, Josh~enwiki, Gurch, Zotel, Reetep, Duckypedia, Gwernol, YurikBot, Assawyer, MarkH, Rsrikanth05, Bovineone, Ugur Basak, Maylett, ENeville, Tgsh2005, Orioneight, Tony1, Ckamaeleon, Rwxrwxrwx, YEPPOON, Zzuuzz, Pb30, Lynbarn, BorgQueen, Shyam, Thomas Blomberg, SmackBot, Londonlinks, Video99, KYN, Saros136, Chris the speller, Master Jay, Bluebot, Cryngo, Robth, Chendy, Frap, DeFacto, Chainz, Dev1n, JonHarder, Thisisbossi, Kittybrewster, Zvar, Mrt doulaty, BIL, Downwards, B jonas, MichaelBillington, Wkerney, Ryan Roos, Kc2idf, ALR, JackLumber, Kricket~enwiki, Makyen, Beetstra, Erwin, Dl2000, 08-15, Iridescent, Chris55, CmdrObot, Stevo1000, MeekMark, Ravensfan5252, CompRhetoric, Cydebot, Khatru2, Mindjuicer, BMG~enwiki, Greatderren, Kozuch, NorthernThunder, Christonard, Mark tb, Mojo Hand, Moulder, Tapir Terrific, FearedInLasVegas, Ladybirdintheuk, RichardVeryard, LionFlyer, Mentifisto, AntiVandalBot, Luna Santin, Ndorr, Rlucena, Leuqarte, The Transhumanist, Albany NY, Zorro CX, Haku8645, JamesBWatson, CS46, Bubba hotep, Tandras, Rlucenatalavera, Cropredy, R'n'B, CommonsDelinker, Nono64, AtholM, Dispenser, Innovationinsight, Ondrejmartinsky, Pandaplodder, Fullmetal2887, Something Original, GS3, Lexein, GimmeBot, BuickCenturyDriver, Kiranwashindkar, Pawanrh, Davin, Billinghurst, Haseo9999, D053, TML, Soyboyrama, Asiavision01, Zatoichi1564, Radon210, Lightmouse, Flightman123, Byeshaswi, SallyForth123, Zandorgreb, Rumping, Binksternet, Francis45, Mild Bill Hiccup, Saboorian, Gu1dry, Kitchen Knife, Alexbot, John Nevard, Sun Creator, Arjayay,

Night-vision-guru, Codumon, Versus22, Jammmie999, XLinkBot, Afpre, Sponsion, Silvia20, Paperboyz, C.n.anag, Addbot, PahaOlo, Harrymph, MrOllie, Debresser, LinkFA-Bot, Splodgeness, Tassedethe, Muyagi~enwiki, Peridon, Wireless friend, Luckas-bot, Yobot, Fraggle81, AnomieBOT, Anthony 1l, Thiagoa1, Elsagna, Materialscientist, Citation bot, Quebec99, LilHelpa, Mononomic, Shirik, Adrignola, Ashematian, Thehelpfulbot, FrescoBot, Devnullnor, Kennedia, PeterEastern, HamburgerRadio, Pinethicket, Codebum2000, Lprguru, Lotje, Connelly90, J-Georg, MegaSloth, RjwilmsiBot, TankMiche, Lyne9854, DASHBot, EmausBot, John of Reading, Idgs78, GoingBatty, Illegitimate Barrister, RaptureBot, Casia wyq, Ego White Tray, Lilinjing cas, Russianbill, Anpr expert, Rhollis7, ClueBot NG, Driver8888, Widr, Carnetnoir, Strike Eagle, BG19bot, Jay8g, BattyBot, NWRGeek, Kunio toba, Dexbot, Mogism, Mparlione, Lagoset, Erdvid01, Ben89129, Hants.romanse, Surfhun, Neiljdillon, Zorak03 and Anonymous: 295

- **Big mechanism** *Source:* https://en.wikipedia.org/wiki/Big_mechanism?oldid=684967260 *Contributors:* ONUnicorn, Lfstevens, I dream of horses, Wgolf, Dexbot and Anonymous: 1

- **Braina** *Source:* https://en.wikipedia.org/wiki/Braina?oldid=688835713 *Contributors:* Rankersbo, Wikiuser13, Nickjames90, SmackoVector, Some Gadget Geek and Anonymous: 7

- **Chinese speech synthesis** *Source:* https://en.wikipedia.org/wiki/Chinese_speech_synthesis?oldid=683202167 *Contributors:* Cncs wikipedia, D6, Kwamikagami, Hgneng~enwiki, XP1, Wavelength, Canley, SmackBot, Writtenonsand, Iridescent, Vanisaac, Torchiest, Stephenchou0722, Jiuguang Wang, Silas S. Brown, Metal.lunchbox, Sintaku, Kockgunner, Mlaffs, DumZiBoT, Addbot, Yobot, ChristopheS, L736E, DARTH SIDIOUS 2, WeijiBaikeBianji, Helpful Pixie Bot, Technical 13, Markgavin pa, Tvo05, BostonRed26 and Anonymous: 12

- **Cleverbot** *Source:* https://en.wikipedia.org/wiki/Cleverbot?oldid=686874118 *Contributors:* Bearcat, Ruakh, Jason Quinn, Node ue, Gadfium, Jokestress, Discospinster, Smalljim, Wtmitchell, Velella, WadeSimMiser, Sjö, The wub, Cjdyer, Rsrikanth05, Moe Epsilon, Alpha 4615, Nikkimaria, Arthur Rubin, Back ache, Allens, SmackBot, InverseHypercube, McGeddon, Canthusus, Gilliam, Ohnoitsjamie, Deli nk, Sadads, Tommyjb, Microchip08, IronGargoyle, Lim Wei Quan, Az1568, Morganfitzp, MarsRover, Gogo Dodo, Islander, DumbBOT, Cubfanpgh, Epbr123, OrenBochman, Dqd, Seaphoto, Lfstevens, Golgofrinchian, Bongwarrior, Pikolas, Anaxial, Tgeairn, NewEnglandYankee, Ljgua124, Bonadea, SoCalSuperEagle, VolkovBot, Philip Trueman, Oshwah, Oxfordwang, The Devil's Advocate, Insanity Incarnate, K69, S8333631, OsamaK, Happysailor, Flyer22 Reborn, OKBot, Mr. Stradivarius, Narom, The Thing That Should Not Be, Quinxorin, Turbo566, Eeekster, Tnxman307, Jivadent, Jwpat7, XLinkBot, AgnosticPreachersKid, WikHead, Addbot, RPHv, Some jerk on the Internet, TutterMouse, KorinoChikara, CanadianLinuxUser, Download, Tide rolls, LuK3, Luckas-bot, AnomieBOT, Rubinbot, Booth789, Materialscientist, The High Fin Sperm Whale, ArthurBot, Hyperdieter, CXCV, Amaury, Thehelpfulbot, Edgars2007, Xiphoidp, Pinethicket, I dream of horses, MJ94, Robo Cop, SkyMachine, Gabrasca, Callanecc, Vrenator, Brian the Editor, John of Reading, RenamedUser01302013, Wikipelli, K6ka, ZéroBot, Érico, A930913, Rails, AlphaPikachu578, Axxonnfire, Thine Antique Pen, Rcsprinter123, APTEM, Moshi Monster Fan303, Ajstov, TYelliot, Helpsome, ClueBot NG, Gareth Griffith-Jones, Loba mal, Rtucker913, Gilderien, Hio568, Jcr211, Jdcollins13, The Master of Mayhem, Anandkulkarni64, Cntras, ScottSteiner, Adwiii, Marechal Ney, Kiara99miles, Widr, Levilucas, Blizzblast, Sassiesam, Theopolisme, Garythecoconut, Deltadawgs, Myskoxen, Titodutta, Lowercase sigmabot, BG19bot, Welcometogoodburger, Loveiseverything, Krenair, Jordan james elder, TetraEleven, GATJREMAT, Empendium, Cleverbotgenious, Super Fat Crap, Quality wikipedian, MusikAnimal, Stelpa, Andrei.smolnikov, Mark Arsten, James.mansell, Existor~enwiki, XxSullyMan, JessR11, Anbu121, Dacarroll1999, Riley Huntley, If:sasuke=awesome, Esco2878, JoshuSasori, ChrisGualtieri, TheJJJunk, ShadowMarioBoy, HerDeadNation, Mehedi Arora, E4024, Dexbot, Gibbles96, Webclient101, Lugia2453, Radianttoe, Vanished User 378492adskljfl, Roguerocket, Parabola andtheright, Epicgenius, Equilibrium Allure, Zeke1324, Qwertyqwertyqwerty12345, Melonkelon, Sosthenes12, Apazon, BeEpic, Cobrien17, SilverMonoceros, Mebesee123, Ugog Nizdast, Andrew Stiff, Mtkillajr, MichaelDomingues, ShutDownCleverBot, Messaboutaccount, MARTIN REVELLO, Fixuture, JaconaFrere, G S Palmer, Looncrown, Katastasi, Eclairs cadbury, Ailankhar, Skullzgamers101, Lor, Dog72910, I love porn so so so much, Lexieboo411, Orduin, P!nkc00kie, Benny thekidd, Thetextediter, User000name, Biscuitboy1211, Jertjeru, RizwanRzaKhan, SalSailor and Anonymous: 285

- **Clinical decision support system** *Source:* https://en.wikipedia.org/wiki/Clinical_decision_support_system?oldid=687678708 *Contributors:* Rsabbatini, Michael Hardy, Kku, Ronz, Greenrd, Jfdwolff, Rich Farmbrough, Xezbeth, Femto, Sole Soul, Mandarax, Rjwilmsi, MZMcBride, Ucucha, Shaggyjacobs, Jlittlet, Deanforrest, Jugander, Supten, Vojtech huser, Kkmurray, Closedmouth, SmackBot, DXBari, Amatulic, Chris the speller, Bluebot, OrangeDog, JonHarder, Codish, Springnuts, ArglebargleIV, Kuru, Khazar, John, Hmbr, Mcstrother, Pgr94, Cydebot, Widefox, Obiwankenobi, The Transhumanist, Ph.eyes, Magioladitis, WhatamIdoing, Reedy Bot, Mikael Häggström, Bonadea, Llorenzi, Sirrtoby, Dr Ramon Simon-Lopez, Ashdamle, Michaeldsuarez, Fcnorman, Doc James, Pdfpdf, Hirohisat, Jsfouche, Pattigustafson, CharlesGillingham, Phelfe, Excirial, Apparition11, Jytdog, Rror, Rich Tullie, Addbot, Quercus solaris, Waghsk, Yobot, Bunnyhop11, In7sky, AnomieBOT, Quebec99, LilHelpa, Cervelo58, Stephen.a.fox, KMPreston, Th3void, Iron007, MSUDrew84, FrescoBot, Cjlederer, BMDampbellc, Trappist the monk, Tofutwitch11, Specs112, RjwilmsiBot, Beowulf779, Splmko, John 14:23, Lingmac, Ccricco, CDDSFan, 503betty, Brandmeister, DoctorN-Nam, Sarah Taj Khan, EdoBot, Bchaiken, ClueBot NG, Rburkhal, Helpful Pixie Bot, BG19bot, BattyBot, Martinsw6, ChrisGualtieri, Eatsea, Jmaude, Dexbot, Pgalinanes, JakobSteenberg, SomeFreakOnTheInternet, Tentinator, Shaunamcegan, LT910001, Bitrut, Monkbot, 27crafts, Bitzleon, RamiRandell, EccentricZ, 115ash, LiberumConsilium, EoRdE6, Hitman181990, Abx stew and Anonymous: 94

- **Concept mining** *Source:* https://en.wikipedia.org/wiki/Concept_mining?oldid=633227839 *Contributors:* Angelo.romano, Beland, Aaronbrick, John Vandenberg, Konetidy, Bkkbrad, GregorB, Cmouse, Ste1n, GraemeL, Thelb4, Paul D. Anderson, SmackBot, Harryboyles, Iridescent, Scientio, MarshBot, Alphachimpbot, The Transhumanist, David Eppstein, Jfroelich, Roee, CharlesGillingham, JBrookeAker, DFRussia, Oletorp, Seanbair, Rankiri, Pateyl, Texterp, Johnchallis, Yobot, Tiffany9027, Fortdj33, Kallikanzarid, Ngocminh.oss, YuenHsienTseng and Anonymous: 22

- **Content-based image retrieval** *Source:* https://en.wikipedia.org/wiki/Content-based_image_retrieval?oldid=680214585 *Contributors:* Zundark, Edward, DopefishJustin, Fuzzie, Haakon, Ronz, Hike395, Omegatron, Hobbes~enwiki, ZimZalaBim, DocWatson42, Akadruid, ShaunMacPherson, AlistairMcMillan, Rich Farmbrough, NeuronExMachina, Mani1, Bender235, Thinkgeek, Alxndr, Ajay Joglekar, Apoc2400, Wtmitchell, Here, Stephan Leeds, GregorB, Mandarax, Zzedar, Mendaliv, Rjwilmsi, Nowa, Femmina, Shyam, Allens, Nicolas Barbier, Laserlasse~enwiki, Kipmaster, KYN, MalafayaBot, Derek R Bullamore, Ckatz, Optimale, Lajm, Tpl, Gnome (Bot), Raysonho, StaceyK, Lennylk, Modernist, Hayesgm, MER-C, Gwern, Kiore, RGS1510, JohnEklund, Jeff G., Rnc000, Jonnypolite, Qtian~enwiki, Ravanacker, Onun, Svante1, EoGuy, Xiawi, Lamberto.ballan, Auntof6, Algomaster, BirgerH, Noteremote, DumZiBoT, XLinkBot, Lhenriquez, Addbot, Deselaers, DOI bot, MrOllie, Lightbot, Luckas-bot, Yobot, JackCoke, Sivamskr, AnomieBOT, Citation bot, Devantheryv, LilHelpa, Xqbot, Einfach Toll, Jayhawk of Justice, Cydral, GrouchoBot, Nancyshapira50, FrescoBot, Vidico18, Citation bot 1, DrilBot, Hereñu, RedBot, Trappist the monk,

Lotje, Rentzepopoulos, Jbonduk, Gregman2, Sf228, RjwilmsiBot, HappyFlappy, EmausBot, Techmatters, Thescreamer, Jashansd, SBaker43, ClueBot NG, Shashwat.goel, Ibartolini, Helpful Pixie Bot, MusikAnimal, Garydoranjr, Eidenberger, Benoit.lebonhomme, Akbkgroup, Urilavi, Neoberserker, Kurtdressel, Maurèn, Faizan, Janiejones81, Monkbot, Bencss1, Sdxu, Ajolyinria and Anonymous: 140

- **Context-sensitive user interface** *Source:* https://en.wikipedia.org/wiki/Context-sensitive_user_interface?oldid=640299657 *Contributors:* MSGJ, Mike Rosoft, Alison9, Diego Moya, Mandarax, Rjwilmsi, SmackBot, Frap, John, Euchiasmus, Antonielly, Cydebot, JustAGal, Squids and Chips, Wonchop, Robenel, Yobot, AnomieBOT, Citation bot, Citation bot 1, Jonesey95, Trappist the monk, Jcubic and Anonymous: 4
- **DialogOS** *Source:* https://en.wikipedia.org/wiki/DialogOS?oldid=633447798 *Contributors:* TakuyaMurata, Dialectric, SmackBot, Angel Emfrbl, Iridescent, Hroðulf, Jiuguang Wang, DanielBe, Addbot, LePassant12, AnomieBOT, Full-date unlinking bot, Danim, BattyBot, 602p, Filedelinkerbot and Anonymous: 3
- **Document capture software** *Source:* https://en.wikipedia.org/wiki/Document_capture_software?oldid=680493879 *Contributors:* Ahunt, NeilN, BoKu, Gbenga Olayiwola, Fabrictramp, Katharineamy, Wikiisawesome, Jimhill10, Biscuittin, Jsfouche, JL-Bot, Martarius, MrOllie, Yobot, Erik9bot, Oashi, Sboals, Sameer9812, MainFrame, Deejmer, Vider73, BG19bot, BattyBot, Carefreecapture, Abaileycng, Ankifor, Arpitkhurana155, Mchartr99, Milan Suchy and Anonymous: 10
- **Document processing** *Source:* https://en.wikipedia.org/wiki/Document_processing?oldid=559860626 *Contributors:* Kku, Jnc, SmackBot, BetacommandBot, Jodi.a.schneider, J.delanoy, Katharineamy, Cerebellum, Outprosys, TheAMmollusc, Erik9bot, MainFrame and Anonymous: 2
- **Dr. Sbaitso** *Source:* https://en.wikipedia.org/wiki/Dr._Sbaitso?oldid=679288028 *Contributors:* Sbisolo, Fastfission, Thetorpedodog, Duncharris, Karol Langner, Fuffzsch, Tgies, Hooperbloob, Kenyon, Quuxplusone, Spencerk, The Rambling Man, WhatDoesKoshDoAllDay, Brandon, Pegship, SmackBot, Angel Emfrbl, Bando26, KingRyu, Djp27, JustAGal, Czj, BobTheMad, Termo~enwiki, Truthanado, ImageRemovalBot, Sfan00 IMG, M4gnum0n, Addbot, Download, Lightbot, AnomieBOT, Mortimer452, Matthiaspaul, AdventurousSquirrel, Hmainsbot1, Dutral and Anonymous: 22
- **Eccky** *Source:* https://en.wikipedia.org/wiki/Eccky?oldid=628359553 *Contributors:* Delirium, Gtrmp, Quarl, SteinbDJ, Marasmusine, Woohookitty, Tangotango, Lyo, RexNL, Intgr, RussBot, Sandstein, Pb30, SmackBot, Betacommand, Chris the speller, OrphanBot, Nakon, Funky Monkey, Ck lostsword, Ex nihil, AndrewHowse, Alfirin, Ginaeccky, Expatdc, Booshakla, MarshBot, WinBot, Eckkygina, Dekimasu, J.delanoy, SharkD, Yifanzhang, Strangerer, Dravecky, The Thing That Should Not Be, EoGuy, 718 Bot, Resoru, Classicrockfan42, Fastily, MystBot, LilHelpa, DivineAlpha, Full-date unlinking bot, Xoxokimberlymariexoxo, Tribeplay, John of Reading, Richardschieberg, Richardschieberg2, Bamyers99, ClueBot NG, O.Koslowski and Anonymous: 18
- **ESTAR project** *Source:* https://en.wikipedia.org/wiki/ESTAR_project?oldid=617260449 *Contributors:* Timrollpickering, Dbenbenn, Utcursch, Ire and curses, Eptin, SmackBot, Commander Keane bot, Gilliam, Bluebot, Neo-Jay, Blehfu, Jiuguang Wang, Bentogoa, Chaosdruid, John of Reading, Danim, Mogism, Mktandpr and Anonymous: 7
- **ETAP-3** *Source:* https://en.wikipedia.org/wiki/ETAP-3?oldid=626595099 *Contributors:* Bearcat, Menelik3, Mendicott, Derek R Bullamore, Soshial, Cnilep, ImageRemovalBot, Sun Creator, AnomieBOT, Tschäfer, BG19bot, Ramesh Ramaiah, Vanishingcattle, Jodosma and Anonymous: 2
- **EuResist** *Source:* https://en.wikipedia.org/wiki/EuResist?oldid=642889333 *Contributors:* Bearcat, Number 57, Cydebot, Obiwankenobi, Ph.eyes, CMBJ, Udirock, Addbot, אריה ה., MerlIwBot, PhnomPencil and Anonymous: 1
- **Eurisko** *Source:* https://en.wikipedia.org/wiki/Eurisko?oldid=689800755 *Contributors:* Derek Ross, The Anome, Wik, HappyDog, Cyberia23, Wolfkeeper, GL7, Sukael, Canterbury Tail, Ben-Arba, CyberSkull, Ynhockey, Bhn781, BlankVerse, Jok2000, Josh Parris, Rjwilmsi, Kri, Gaius Cornelius, Natmaka, Draicone, Hide&Reason, SmackBot, Thumperward, Outlawpoet, CmdrObot, Lance McCord, Ntsimp, Omicronpersei8, Hilgerdenaar, Rhwawn, Gwern, Don Quixote de la Mancha, Paradoctor, Phe-bot, Classicalecon, C. A. Russell, Addbot, Dawynn, LaaknorBot, Debresser, Lightbot, Citation bot, Citation bot 1, RjwilmsiBot, BattyBot, Monkbot, BlackCat1978 and Anonymous: 17
- **FatKat (investment software)** *Source:* https://en.wikipedia.org/wiki/FatKat_(investment_software)?oldid=626136458 *Contributors:* Edward, CaribDigita, Hmains, Chris the speller, Tim333, Cander0000, WOSlinker, Urbanrenewal, Jerryobject, ColdPopTart, Trappist the monk, Alpha Quadrant, Y.golovko and BattyBot
- **GestureTek** *Source:* https://en.wikipedia.org/wiki/GestureTek?oldid=666833441 *Contributors:* Orangemike, Pascal666, Rjwilmsi, Malcolma, SmackBot, Stifle, Chris the speller, Ohconfucius, BeenAroundAWhile, Shawn in Montreal, Dawn Bard, Wuhwuzdat, Auntof6, SchreiberBike, Addbot, Download, Kyle1278, Yobot, Citation bot, Erik9bot, Gesturetek, KristinMiller, Hamiltha, Simplefishman, BattyBot, Nloeillot, GesturetekSystemsInc, MegRabbit and Anonymous: 3
- **GNOME Chess** *Source:* https://en.wikipedia.org/wiki/GNOME_Chess?oldid=686095301 *Contributors:* KAMiKAZOW, D6, Bubba73, FlaBot, SmackBot, Frap, Jinnai, Aljullu, Cydebot, Shirulashem, VolkovBot, Comrade Graham, Voorlandt, CMBJ, Niceguyedc, Dthomsen8, Ost316, Id1337x, Addbot, LaaknorBot, EnBob08, Double sharp, Haaninjo, Lotje, Primefac, Staszek Lem, Pauloslomp, GBRV, GioGziro95, IusedtobecalledAndrea, Nachouve, Максим Пе, Ghostsarememories, ChrisGualtieri, Chrisgerbo, Izzyvp, ScotXW, Lucrus and Anonymous: 5
- **Grandmaster Chess** *Source:* https://en.wikipedia.org/wiki/Grandmaster_Chess?oldid=677852436 *Contributors:* Ylee, SMC, Bgwhite, Quentin X, Arbitrarily0, The1337gamer, Samwalton9 and Chrisgerbo
- **Handwriting recognition** *Source:* https://en.wikipedia.org/wiki/Handwriting_recognition?oldid=687333788 *Contributors:* Heron, Edward, Patrick, Nixdorf, Yaronf, LittleDan, Kimiko, Hike395, Wik, Skyfire, Fredrik, Tobias Bergemann, Chowbok, Beland, Piotrus, Gene s, Ilya-Haykinson, Hhielscher, Thebrid, Giraffedata, LostLeviathan, Hu, Woohookitty, RHaworth, Aperezbios, Mandarax, Rjwilmsi, Swirsky, Vegaswikian, Yug, Richdiesal, Skierpage, YurikBot, Wavelength, Semperf, StealthFox, SmackBot, Onorem, Matthew, Kcordina, Dl2000, Greg Hullender, Hakunio, Houat, Dancter, B, Tawkerbot4, Aiko, The Transhumanist, R'n'B, Steve@brunmedinc, Mrh30, Lifeisfun, Clarince63, NinjaRobotPirate, Computerwguy, Nopetro, Bemus, Srig, Phatware, Martarius, Ahmadab, Techguy95, Sakiemiri, A2iA, Hieuletrung, PenComputingPerson, YrPolishUncle, Addbot, Claudetteallingham, Binary TSO, MrOllie, Prabhupritam, Lightbot, Yobot, Themfromspace, Paultaele, Noq, Materialscientist, Citation bot, Devantheryv, 4twenty42o, Tuba.terry, Jaleks, Mxp de, FrescoBot, Nicolas Perrault III, Thumbmaster021, 01000100 W 01000010, Oscar1905, Michael Malloy, A7N8X, Slon02, EmausBot, John of Reading, Rockin291, Erianna, Donner60, ClueBot NG, Lawrence87, Andrewsailer, Ronjon123, Widr, Tr00rle, BG19bot, Leka99, Oleg-ch, Shrutzy, Cyberbot II, MFZBCN, Deeper Learning, Deltaco17, Ramkiag, 1appleaday, Golopotw, Sofia Koutsouveli, Sguberman and Anonymous: 97

- **Human-centered computing (NASA)** *Source:* https://en.wikipedia.org/wiki/Human-centered_computing_(NASA)?oldid=587342163 *Contributors:* Bearcat, Andicat, MaxVeers, Feureau, John254, Magioladitis, Addbot and Alvin Seville

- **Imense** *Source:* https://en.wikipedia.org/wiki/Imense?oldid=603805056 *Contributors:* Wavelength, KYN, Katharineamy, Yobot, Jamesrnorwood, Vidico18, SciHalo, Khazar2 and Anonymous: 2

- **Intelligent character recognition** *Source:* https://en.wikipedia.org/wiki/Intelligent_character_recognition?oldid=630402175 *Contributors:* Leandrod, Kku, Thorwald, Robert K S, FlaBot, Gurch, YurikBot, Borgx, Baseballnut, SmackBot, Dweller, Chris the speller, Thumperward, MaxSem, FelisLeo, Danieled, CmdrObot, ShelfSkewed, Mike Hayesman, B, Biblbroks, Mattisse, JAnDbot, Joeafp, AlanIngram, Atama, MariaLD, Wickedpede, Flyer22 Reborn, Iain99, Srig, Iohannes Animosus, Rror, PenComputingPerson, Addbot, Dawynn, Symac, MrOllie, SpBot, AnomieBOT, DanielZhang27, Erik9bot, Onsyu03, HJ Mitchell, Slham1972, Kenrick95, Megapus, Onel5969, Wikipelli, Gregtheross, ClueBot NG, Braincricket, SAPryor, Parascript, GRa2ia, 1appleaday, M.i.ivanov and Anonymous: 33

- **Intelligent software assistant** *Source:* https://en.wikipedia.org/wiki/Intelligent_personal_assistant?oldid=689868157 *Contributors:* Bender235, MONGO, Bgwhite, Whistler, Dennis.mortensen, McGeddon, Gilliam, Sturm, Nyq, Mainehaven, Zero Serenity, Jcs2006, Jerryobject, Cyfal, Martarius, Renzoy16, Addbot, LaaknorBot, Lipehauss~enwiki, Yobot, Rafaelbb, Biker Biker, LittleWink, Koi.lover, 420lex, Senator2029, Jeromesandilanico, Jjj84206, Ibmonty, Starship.paint, AldeyWahyuPutra, Falkirks, Mayast, NietzscheSpeaks, Mogism, Gottalovebrando, Tomajda8, Pdatnic, Dweberlj, Tango303, SmackoVector, Corti45, Kokopuffs1, Crystallizedcarbon, LasPo rocks, Shaun.R.M., Wrtr63, Tochni and Anonymous: 34

- **Interactions Corporation** *Source:* https://en.wikipedia.org/wiki/Interactions_Corporation?oldid=669473096 *Contributors:* Addbot, Tassedethe, Yobot, Bellerophon, A.amitkumar, Bioevolution, Rfsully, ChzzBot IV, ArticlesForCreationBot, BattyBot and Anonymous: 5

- **Kasparov's Gambit** *Source:* https://en.wikipedia.org/wiki/Kasparov'{}s_Gambit?oldid=678833153 *Contributors:* Frecklefoot, Neuromancien, Bgwhite, Rwalker, Cobblet, Gregbard, X201, Keith D, Mild Bill Hiccup, Sun Creator, Hahc21, Yobot, John of Reading, ClueBot NG, Moritz37, Malbakov Korkem Shamshievih, Chessbloke, Chrisgerbo, GravRidr, Tabloke, Vailedfoot68789 and Anonymous: 3

- **Language Acquisition Device (computer)** *Source:* https://en.wikipedia.org/wiki/Language_Acquisition_Device_(computer)?oldid=605227347 *Contributors:* SmackBot, Sm8900, R'n'B, Dpmuk, Looie496, Yobot, LilHelpa, I dream of horses, Chire, Llightex, Jeancey and Anonymous: 1

- **Language identification** *Source:* https://en.wikipedia.org/wiki/Language_identification?oldid=667166498 *Contributors:* The Anome, Greenrd, Silvonen, Babbage, Dupuy, Qwertyus, Wavelength, Sandstein, Allens, SmackBot, Chris the speller, Sjlewis, CmdrObot, Alaibot, Spencer, Erxnmedia, AtticusX, Francis Tyers, Otisg, Jon335, TXiKiBoT, Tlieu, Dcavar, Insanity Incarnate, Legoktm, Yerpo, TedDunning, Tnxman307, Diaa abdelmoneim, Unicoart, Addbot, PaterMcFly, AnomieBOT, ChristopheS, I dream of horses, Hannolans, Ycchew, LinguistManiac, WikitanvirBot, Ivan.akcheurov, Wikiyant, Concord hioz, Migueldc01, Dagoneye, Ocelot8, 1914sep and Anonymous: 32

- **Machine translation** *Source:* https://en.wikipedia.org/wiki/Machine_translation?oldid=688125779 *Contributors:* Bryan Derksen, The Anome, Youssefsan, SimonP, Boleslav Bobcik, Arj, Atlan, Stevertigo, DopefishJustin, Norm, Cyde, Karada, Mac, Nanshu, Yaronf, Glenn, Deisenbe, Schneelocke, Hike395, Nohat, Boson, Viajero, Dysprosia, Timc, Furrykef, Taxman, Bearcat, Robbot, Icestryke, 1984, Kiwibird, Altenmann, Kowey, Babbage, Zabek, Diderot, Hippietrail, Timrollpickering, Hadal, JesseW, Vikreykja, Dhodges, Giftlite, Cokoli, Haeleth, Bfinn, Everyking, Brona, Eequor, Solipsist, Khalid hassani, Brockert, Alvestrand, ALargeElk, Gyrofrog, Wmahan, Bacchiad, Woggly, Toytoy, Jossi, Irune Berdún, Karl-Henner, Migueldelval, Histrion, Pnot, Arezae, Grstain, D6, Freakofnurture, Jim Henry, Rich Farmbrough, Michal Jurosz, Saintswithin, Mani1, Kimbly, Nick Mulder, El C, Cmdrjameson, SpeedyGonsales, Nk, Flammifer, Sam Korn, Avian, Anthony Appleyard, Blahma, Logologist, Spinoza1111, JosebaAbaitua, Wdfarmer, Cookiemobsta, Marianocecowski, Melaen, KingTT, Knowledge Seeker, Ffbond, FrancisTyers, Angr, Woohookitty, Sandius, Apokrif, Sdelat, Tutmosis, Jon Harald Søby, Graham87, BD2412, Qwertyus, Tradnor, Hulagutten, JHMM13, Ligulem, Hathawayc, FlaBot, Sasanjan, Karel Anthonissen, Wastl23, Chobot, DVdm, Bgwhite, Mysekurity, Msbmsb, YurikBot, Wavelength, RobotE, Freerick, NTBot~enwiki, Dnik, Trondtr, DanMS, Jaxl, Catamorphism, RazorICE, Mccready, Edwardlalone, Tony1, BraneJ, User27091, Sandstein, CQ, Esprit15d, JuJube, Ulf Hermjakob, Eaefremov, Ásgeir IV.~enwiki, NeilN, GrinBot~enwiki, SmackBot, Henri de Solages, Prodego, KnowledgeOfSelf, Iopq, Davewild, Kintetsubuffalo, ActiveSelective, Fetofs, Chris the speller, Tsca.bot, Chlewbot, Matthew, Robdjun, Ged UK, Serein (renamed because of SUL), Autoterm, Thebt, Acidburn24m, MagnaMopus, Wtwilson3, Galilite, Transclick, Hvn0413, Erwin, Hu12, Ostreiter, Joseph Solis in Australia, IvanLanin, INkubusse, Mellery, FleetCommand, Aaron J Nicoli, Cxw, CBM, DavidCowhig, John Chandioux, Safalra, RenamedUser2, Kozuch, Cs california, Sagaciousuk, Seancron, Escarbot, AntiVandalBot, Wl219, Erxnmedia, JAnDbot, PhilKnight, SiobhanHansa, Magioladitis, EMLM, Pax:Vobiscum, Calltech, Hdt83, Jarcud, Glrx, R'n'B, Francis Tyers, Senu, Mike.lifeguard, Octopus-Hands, Tihanyi, Dispenser, Ignatzmice, Freemae, Tobias Kuhn, Chris Croy, Treisijs, Ajfweb, Squids and Chips, Idioma-bot, Malik Shabazz, VolkovBot, Sporti, Paulscho, TXiKiBoT, Mercy, Technopat, TwilligToves, JhsBot, Drewyan, Mazarin07, Yannis1962, Nazar, Altermike, LittleBenW, Legoktm, Brucewydner, SieBot, YonaBot, Nihil novi, Graham Beards, VVVBot, Soler97, Entropy In Hairdo, Masgatotkaca, Bguest, Stephen Shaw, Fleurka, Jennifer Jenner, Mr. Granger, Sfan00 IMG, Elassint, ClueBot, SummerWithMorons, GorillaWarfare, Fadesga, Vacio, Fr.ev, MadisonCloutier, Three-quarter-ten, PixelBot, Davidgrunwald, Estirabot, Arithmandar, Arjayay, SchreiberBike, Muro Bot, Stepheng3, 7, SF007, DumZiBoT, Camboxer, Gwandoya, BodhisattvaBot, PK2, Ost316, The Aviv, Addbot, Mortense, Betterusername, Rmalouf, Cloudflashes, Drbobpgh, MrOllie, KimmoSainio, Figarow, Amitabh216, Numbo3-bot, Zorrobot, Jarble, HerculeBot, Narrosse, Luckas-bot, Yobot, Una giornata uggiosa '94, Maxí, Fragaro2000, AnomieBOT, Rubinbot, Mfelkess, Jim1138, Citation bot, ArthurBot, Xqbot, Jsharpminor, Omnipaedista, RibotBOT, Goodwin-Brent, Nickruiz, Robykiwi~enwiki, FrescoBot, Dalai.lamia, Patelurology2, Blackdaz, Doctajohn, I dream of horses, MastiBot, Gabriel.cercel, Gwheeldon, Crabtownwiki, Mjs1991, TobeBot, SchreyP, Lotje, Fox Wilson, MT301, चंद्रकांत भुतडमल, WildBot, EmausBot, Dionwiggins, Lv 2010, Mlang.Finn, Rangoon11, Garcia-fm, Vmahalingam, Shaalank, DASHBotAV, Alvations, Bmw20, Will Beback Auto, ClueBot NG, Tillander, Jack Greenmaven, Movses-bot, 10k, Cntras, Gsanchis, Translategree, Brahim.aioun, Bojangles2011, Oddbodz, NoNamePizza, ProtextTranslations, BG19bot, AndrejsV, Hagiza121, Skybirdnomad, Farooqzaman20, BattyBot, Doherts2, Cyberbot II, Cpaw1, ChrisGualtieri, Shallowhai, Dexbot, Yakuta02, SoledadKabocha, S hp8azy, Mogism, OlenaUa, Kanahasta, Weeweeus, Safaba, Udih, Wieldthespade, JustAMuggle, CsDix, Narcheung2, Melodyyuan, Arencezzz, Csteinb, Loxleof, DennisWKonkel, Kijaw, Ahr2nd, PsyLingLG, Fabianvf, Spc2dg, Angl84, Stephnn, Hythy, Monkbot, Dtatsu, Zsl3m, Kellyhenderson7792, Morgan.m.mullen, Nvt9kh, Bethcarey, Alex24101987, Kira Xinyi, Jozefsanders, KasparBot, Akashdondo, Sylyle, Krz.wolk and Anonymous: 274

- **Machine translation software usability** *Source:* https://en.wikipedia.org/wiki/Machine_translation_software_usability?oldid=616311902 *Contributors:* Skysmith, Bearcat, Rjwilmsi, SmackBot, Od Mishehu, J Milburn, CmdrObot, Erxnmedia, Francis Tyers, Funandtrvl, SchreiberBike, Yobot, Canoe1967, BattyBot and Anonymous: 2

- **Marketing and artificial intelligence** *Source:* https://en.wikipedia.org/wiki/Marketing_and_artificial_intelligence?oldid=552054943 *Contributors:* Niceguyedc, SchreiberBike, John of Reading, Snotbot, Scopecreep, Arcandam, AK456, Mart431acr and Davidviele1

- **Mind's Eye (US military)** *Source:* https://en.wikipedia.org/wiki/Mind'{}s_Eye_(US_military)?oldid=619798015 *Contributors:* Gobonobo, InedibleHulk, Cydebot, Corvus cornix, Ng.j, BlueDevil, Claymorde, AnomieBOT, BabbaQ, Dainomite, Kumioko, Lennyshk and Anonymous: 2

- **Mobileye** *Source:* https://en.wikipedia.org/wiki/Mobileye?oldid=689381034 *Contributors:* Gidonb, Ukexpat, Rd232, Ynhockey, Drbreznjev, Qwertyus, Jclemens, Amire80, Ground Zero, Bgwhite, Arado, Malcolma, Scheinwerfermann, SmackBot, Alepik, KYN, Freewol, Hmbr, MottyGlix, CmdrObot, Kozuch, Marokwitz, MER-C, Magioladitis, DGG, Toon05, Zoharby, Typ932, Aspects, JL-Bot, Martarius, CorenSearchBot, Stypex, 7&6=thirteen, Stepheng3, Gnickett1, MystBot, Addbot, Yobot, AnomieBOT, Crecy99, Shirik, SassoBot, Aaditya 7, FrescoBot, Mobileye Vision Technologies, RjwilmsiBot, CarSafety, Pitlane02, John of Reading, GoingBatty, Werieth, Casia wyq, Ruddjason, ClueBot NG, Jasonrudd, VanishedUser sdu8asdasd, Widr, Nissomoyal, Wbm1058, Technical 13, BG19bot, Mobileye, Hucyeric, ExtrimDrive, Noa.mobileye, Whitearray, Wikimobileye, Binarysequence, RaphaelQS, ArmbrustBot, Sharmin.h, Bad Dryer, Jameskroberts, Anindakumars, Danielrose23wiki, Phm01, DenisChikunov, SirRanSirRan, Dimps25 and Anonymous: 22

- **Monitoring and Surveillance Agents** *Source:* https://en.wikipedia.org/wiki/Monitoring_and_Surveillance_Agents?oldid=532968990 *Contributors:* Versageek, SmackBot, Xyzzyplugh, Raysonho, B3rt0h, Mereda, MarshBot, Cleclair, Dmitry Skavish, Tom oursecret, MKS, Charles-Gillingham, Addbot and Anonymous: 6

- **Trenchard More** *Source:* https://en.wikipedia.org/wiki/Trenchard_More?oldid=548120361 *Contributors:* Felix Folio Secundus, Wrelwser43, FrescoBot, Helpful Pixie Bot and Drift chambers

- **Natachata** *Source:* https://en.wikipedia.org/wiki/Natachata?oldid=641409678 *Contributors:* Ahoerstemeier, Male1979, Kerowyn, SmackBot, Alksub, Paxse, Bluebot, Tkgd2007, WikHead, Yobot and Anonymous: 5

- **Natural language user interface** *Source:* https://en.wikipedia.org/wiki/Natural_language_user_interface?oldid=685763251 *Contributors:* Beland, Crouchingturbo, Spencerk, Bgwhite, Bhny, SmackBot, InverseHypercube, Timtrent, Cydebot, Guy Macon, Buguldey, CommonsDelinker, AKA MBG, Jerryobject, Bgalitsky, JL-Bot, De728631, GorillaWarfare, Apparition11, XLinkBot, Clive spenser, Addbot, Jarble, Yobot, Mission Fleg, AnomieBOT, Sdmonroe, Alvin Seville, Erik9bot, FrescoBot, Yossishani, Fresnocom, ClueBot NG, Kolibrical, Mghoffmann, BG19bot, Jordi.torras.manya, Akashshastri, Juan.manuel.gonzalez.gonzalez, Mogism, Darko.sancanin, GabeIglesia, SmackoVector, Razorenov, Ijdykeman, Martinwheatman and Anonymous: 35

- **Network Compartment** *Source:* https://en.wikipedia.org/wiki/Network_Compartment?oldid=591133837 *Contributors:* Kku, Bluebot, Robnick, Starionwolf, Shmlchr, Minnaert, CharlesGillingham, NintendoFan, Yobot, DoctorKubla, CBRT IT Mission and Anonymous: 1

- **Neural machine translation** *Source:* https://en.wikipedia.org/wiki/Neural_machine_translation?oldid=688129156 *Contributors:* Bearcat, Glrx, Largoplazo, AnomieBOT, BG19bot and Krz.wolk

- **Noisy text analytics** *Source:* https://en.wikipedia.org/wiki/Noisy_text_analytics?oldid=678750858 *Contributors:* Michael Hardy, Beland, OMouse, Clicketyclack, Barticus88, DuncanHill, Lvsubram, Carre, Melcombe, Jahub and Anonymous: 6

- **OpenNN** *Source:* https://en.wikipedia.org/wiki/OpenNN?oldid=684755697 *Contributors:* Leondz, Rjwilmsi, Tedickey, CommonsDelinker, Cnilep, MrOllie, AnomieBOT, PabloCastellano, BG19bot, Monkbot, Rober9876543210, Sergiointelnics, The Quixotic Potato and Anonymous: 6

- **Optical answer sheet** *Source:* https://en.wikipedia.org/wiki/Optical_answer_sheet?oldid=669824508 *Contributors:* Radiojon, Smurfix, YUL89YYZ, La goutte de pluie, Nesbit, NeilN, SmackBot, Chris the speller, Chris53516, Amalas, Avillia, R'n'B, Fratrep, Trivialist, SchreiberBike, Addbot, AnomieBOT, GB fan, GrouchoBot, Erik9bot, Jesse V., SensibleStuff, Roycekimmons, BG19bot, Kelvinsong, Avoids, Jayesh1990 and Anonymous: 4

- **Optical braille recognition** *Source:* https://en.wikipedia.org/wiki/Optical_braille_recognition?oldid=663422812 *Contributors:* Bearcat, Rjwilmsi, Chris the speller, GorillaWarfare, Dolescum, ChrisGualtieri, Charmlet, Getuabebe and Monkbot

- **Optical character recognition** *Source:* https://en.wikipedia.org/wiki/Optical_character_recognition?oldid=688253503 *Contributors:* Damian Yerrick, Peter Winnberg, Robert Merkel, Rjstott, Deb, Ben-Zin~enwiki, B4hand, Leandrod, Frecklefoot, Patrick, D, Michael Hardy, Gabbe, Karada, Rethunk, Alfio, Tregoweth, Ahoerstemeier, Mac, Ronz, Den fjättrade ankan~enwiki, Chrysalis, Netsnipe, TonyClarke, Hike395, Jid-Gom, Timwi, Dcoetzee, Tempshill, Fernkes, Wernher, Indefatigable, Warofdreams, UninvitedCompany, Denelson83, Robbot, Kizor, Chris 73, KellyCoinGuy, Hippietrail, Hadal, David Gerard, Tosha, Giftlite, Gwalla, DocWatson42, Christopher Parham, DavidCary, ShaunMacPherson, Seabhcan, Cobaltbluetony, Orangemike, Ds13, Jason Quinn, Eequor, Just Another Dan, Pne, Sonjaaa, Beland, Szajd, Salvadors, Creidieki, Peter bertok, Ohka-, Abdull, Grstain, Mormegil, Rfl, Imroy, JTN, Rich Farmbrough, Iainscott, Vapour, Chowells, Dbachmann, Mani1, Violetriga, Kaszeta, CanisRufus, Bookofjude, Mickeymousechen~enwiki, Gershwinrb, Pablo X, Martey, SpeedyGonsales, James Foster, Knucmo2, Alansohn, Quiggles, 119, Denoir, CyberSkull, Diego Moya, Andrewpmk, Sligocki, Batmanand, Velella, Rick Sidwell, Dhshepard, Versageek, Saxifrage, Distantbody, Woohookitty, Mindmatrix, RHaworth, Rocastelo, Miaow Miaow, Bkkbrad, Pol098, Winterdragon, Slike2, Terence, Havarhen, Gerbrant, Mandarax, RichardWeiss, Lawrence King, Graham87, FreplySpang, Sjö, Sjakkalle, Rjwilmsi, Hulagutten, Nneonneo, Mbutts, NeonMerlin, LjL, Dionyseus, FlaBot, SchuminWeb, Intgr, Predictor, Ahunt, Silversmith, Chobot, Krishnavedala, Bgwhite, YurikBot, Wavelength, Borgx, Hauskalainen, Iayork, Backburner001, Maxim Leyenson, C777, Gaius Cornelius, Bisqwit, Wimt, Thane, Hm2k, Wiki alf, Porthugh, Jpbowen, Matticus78, Emersoni, Cavan, User27091, Yabbadab, Rwxrwxrwx, Jonas Viper, Encephalon, Rlove, Shyam, Tobybuk, EtherealPurple, GrinBot~enwiki, Vanished user 99034jfoiasjq2oirhsf3, Matt Heard, Stalfur, SmackBot, Reedy, McGeddon, Vald, Xfreebird, Renesis, Delldot, Eskimbot, KYN, Gilliam, Chrisnewell, Thumperward, Conway71, DHN-bot~enwiki, Torzsmokus, Tarikash, Tsca.bot, Can't sleep, clown will eat me, Mulder416, Nakon, Shadow1, Dreadstar, Mwtoews, Wybot, Ricky@36, Deepred6502, Rory096, Kuru, Euchiasmus, NongBot~enwiki, PseudoSudo, Edwindreillyjr, Slakr, Beetstra, Bollinger, Erwin, Kiwipat, Davydog, Lee Carre, Shoeofdeath, Lakshmish, Joshua lee, Sunjan, Tawkerbot2, Vanisaac, PureFire, Artemgy, INkubusse, Raysonho, BeenAroundAWhile, MicahDCochran, Requestion, Affection~enwiki, Drone007, Alfirin, Kallerdis, Goldencako, B, Thijs!bot, Ultimus, Kablammo, Smile a While, PsychoInfiltrator, Drmccreedy, Rompe, Escarbot, AntiVandalBot, Joachimb~enwiki, Amoverload, Luna Santin, Just Chilling, Rsciaccio, Alphachimpbot, Fireice, Erxnmedia, Xiaofan Lin, The Transhumanist, Udayangahpur, Austinmurphy, BrotherE, Penubag, Celithemis, JPG-GR, Franzvm, Tandras, Ftiercel, Matthias

Röder, Brothaslide, Kuangc, MartinBot, Craigb81, R'n'B, Tgeairn, Saladinct, J.delanoy, Joshuaali, Diablonhn, Xris0, Laurusnobilis, Nemo bis, Gypsydoctor, (jarbarf), Girl2k, Robigus, Sarregouset, Bonadea, Youlivnlearn, VolkovBot, Kanakukk, Pierson's Puppeteer, Philip Trueman, Rhagerman, Sharareh 601, Leafyplant, Slysplace, Badly Bradley, Raryel, VR718, Wickedpede, Cnilep, NinjaRobotPirate, Gevans712, CVI-SION, Kbrose, Dvidby0, SieBot, BotMultichill, Paradoctor, Yintan, Asiavision01, Le Pied-bot~enwiki, OsamaBinLogin, Martinlc, Tesi1700, Dust Filter, ZorbaTheSwede, ClueBot, Ignacio Javier Igjav, The Thing That Should Not Be, Pwnvds, Marinazhao, Wikinoki, Blendenzo, Stopol, Blanchardb, PMDrive1061, Kitsunegami, M4gnum0n, Lartoven, ScanStoreAaron, Markk474, 7, WikiLyd, XLinkBot, Ivan Akira, Nardyca, SilvonenBot, PenComputingPerson, ZTebaykina, Addbot, Proofreader77, Orlando7777, Superduperpup, Betterusername, Gdommett, Ashton1983, Sharnden, MrOllie, LaaknorBot, ChenzwBot, ColinMB, Tide rolls, Lightbot, GJo, Zorrobot, Narayan, Luckas-bot, Yobot, Legobot II, Kzamir, Jbrox, Ytterbium3, Paultaele, Draney13, محبوب عالم, AnomieBOT, DemocraticLuntz, Noq, Otaviogood, TWWhiting, Kingpin13, Josehill, Materialscientist, Loveonearth, Ahlc, ArthurBot, AaB-ern, Xqbot, ParsaNikbin, S h i v a (Visnu), Umburana, Almabot, GrouchoBot, Omnipaedista, Backpackadam, RibotBOT, Ace111, Lafirel, DanielZhang27, D'Artagnol, LucienBOT, Abcde2, X7q, Dance1992, Spanthony, Ankit1 nagpal, Wifione, Igmat, Citation bot 1, Slham1972, Dataxprts, Rushbugled13, Skyerise, Mvcfalcon, MastiBot, Robert.Baruch, OCR-PDF, Mjs1991, AramediA, Compvis, North8000, Etincelles, MariaDR, Lotje, Vrenator, Morgan814, StorkenSture, MarkAnthony01, Mean as custard, Amaranthine J, Kyeung123, Jackehammond, चंद्रकांत धुतडमल, Archetypalsphere, EmausBot, John of Reading, WikitanvirBot, Mo ainm, Maximshulgin, Wikipelli, Ponydepression, HiW-Bot, Pgdyck, Gianmarcocastagna, Erianna, Icefable2010, Hamiltha, Иванк1, Orange Suede Sofa, Deejmer, JohnM.Farmer, Petrb, Mikhail Ryazanov, ClueBot NG, Vider73, RichardH.Lincoln, Gareth Griffith-Jones, RichardM.Zhang, Satellizer, Frietjes, Psubhashish, Widr, Ngocminh.oss, BG19bot, Gurt Posh, Wz0911, Metricopolus, Pgmail, Compfreak7, Glacialfox, Anbu121, Cyberbot II, ChrisGualtieri, APerson, Dexbot, Cerabot~enwiki, Lugia2453, Graphium, Jamesx12345, Hellotheretoby, PlanetEditor, Aaajaykumar83, Eyesnore, Ramkiag, Ugog Nizdast, Sam Sailor, Jianhui67, Manul, Golopotw, Mjul, Tjuchenqing, MSheshera, Nyashinski, Cnadak, Angelababy00, PaulRamone2, Ashubuntu, Diallord and Anonymous: 518

- **Optical mark recognition** *Source:* https://en.wikipedia.org/wiki/Optical_mark_recognition?oldid=681025191 *Contributors:* Deb, Minesweeper, Julesd, Charles Matthews, Jogloran, Petesm, Denelson83, KellyCoinGuy, Bkell, DavidCary, Xerxes314, Alexf, Beland, Ary29, Indolering, Canterbury Tail, Imroy, Rich Farmbrough, Smalljim, La goutte de pluie, Nsaa, Masums, Ricky81682, Snowolf, RHaworth, BD2412, Jorunn, Misternuvistor, Bhadani, Intgr, Chobot, Gaius Cornelius, Rsrikanth05, Saper, ScottyWZ, Zwobot, S. Neuman, DeadEyeArrow, Nlu, Zzuuzz, Closedmouth, Oscarcwk, ViperSnake151, NeilN, SmackBot, Gilliam, Hmains, Chris the speller, Bluebot, ZhongHan, J. Straub, Derek R Bullamore, Mwtoews, Wizardman, Henning Makholm, Gbrown@xmn.com, Aaditeshwar, BranStark, Tan90deg, IvanLanin, PRhyu, Requestion, Myasuda, Odie5533, Room101, Epbr123, Daa89563, James086, AntiVandalBot, Kmacdonald-mmeek, SummerPhD, The Transhumanist, Austinmurphy, Xeno, SimonFlummox, Nicolaasuni, VoABot II, Xeddy, 28421u2232nfenfcenc, Glrx, R'n'B, J.delanoy, Xris0, Kmmhasan, Drdanny, Lukebishop, Pegase~enwiki, Zidonuke, Anna Lincoln, Ssisurvey, Softtest123, Jimhill10, W.edelberg, AlleborgoBot, Gevans712, Hingram, Flyer22 Reborn, Jojalozzo, Randommuses, ترجمان05, Denisarona, Ratemonth, Martarius, ClueBot, DumZiBoT, WikiLyd, IsmaelLuceno, Addbot, Indiaoutsources, Orlando7777, Mentisock, AnomieBOT, Dinosauregg11, SassoBot, Poolisfun, Shadowjams, Patricius12, FrescoBot, Wiki episteme, Giuseb, Slham1972, A8UDI, Blackbaud, Vrenator, PleaseStand, Jfmantis, Sameer9812, Mean as custard, Archur1, Kubohiorya, MWOAP(AWB), CeStu, Hutchison de, SensibleStuff, Dewritech, Vipul6538, Goswami.kapil, Mbstern, ClueBot NG, This lousy T-shirt, Jbhunley, Esky.omrtest, ConconJondor, Amkou, Weekyer, 1996vishak, HMSSolent, BG19bot, GKFX, Darcio.pacifico, L888Y5, JD.Jack.Daniels.965, Anbu121, Dimasprabowo, TheMongoose38, Hellotheretoby, EthanRox123, Faizan, Wikiuser13, Pizzagreen, 1appleaday, Joe885, Wubc, Superalberto76, Tom.P cz23, ChadwickYoung and Anonymous: 172

- **Polyworld** *Source:* https://en.wikipedia.org/wiki/Polyworld?oldid=687171463 *Contributors:* Jeffrey Smith, Joy, Romanpoet, Pearle, Marudubshinki, Jeremybub, Dialectric, JonHarder, Mulder416sBot, TimMagic, Sm8900, Scarian, ClueBot, XLinkBot, Dawynn, Damiens.rf, AnomieBOT, Jfmantis, Northamerica1000, Larryy and Anonymous: 18

- **Pop music automation** *Source:* https://en.wikipedia.org/wiki/Pop_music_automation?oldid=660707777 *Contributors:* Hyacinth, Bender235, Spencerk, Esslk, Reedy, Kleinzach, Mgiganteus1, Skittleys, Reedy Bot, Fratrep, Yobot, Unara, LilHelpa, Citation bot 1, Helpful Pixie Bot, Mark viking, Besugo pikado and Anonymous: 8

- **Quack.com** *Source:* https://en.wikipedia.org/wiki/Quack.com?oldid=651975452 *Contributors:* Edward, Vegaswikian, Tijuana Brass, Chris the speller, Robofish, Magioladitis, Martarius, Stepheng3, Lightbot, Drservos, Sophus Bie, FrescoBot, W Nowicki, The Master of Mayhem, Mogism and Anonymous: 10

- **Question answering** *Source:* https://en.wikipedia.org/wiki/Question_answering?oldid=685822014 *Contributors:* Tarquin, Edward, Michael Hardy, Dcljr, Ronz, Hike395, Charles Matthews, Wik, Kowey, Dmolla, Bovlb, AskaLee, Michal Jurosz, Bender235, Here, Vak, Computerjoe, Brookie, Waldir, Mandarax, Qwertyus, Sjö, Rjwilmsi, Biederman, Peter.r.bailey, Spencerk, Msbmsb, YurikBot, Wavelength, Cpollett, Mendicott, HereToHelp, KnightRider~enwiki, SmackBot, McGeddon, Ed whittaker, Chris the speller, Snori, Chlewbot, Neshatian, SashatoBot, Srdjan Vesic, InedibleHulk, P199, Iridescent, CmdrObot, Pgr94, Spoxox, Pjvpjv, Suzanv, Sblohm, Fbahr, Lvsubram, Magioladitis, Wannabehacker, AskaE, R'n'B, Tgeairn, J.delanoy, Bonadea, Ummonk, VanishedUserABC, Turgan, VVVBot, Bgalitsky, Maybury, Charles-Gillingham, Maxschmelling, Shidzu, ClueBot, Alexbot, ClanCC, Dikisoccer, Addbot, LaaknorBot, Tide rolls, Lightbot, Jarble, Yobot, IW.HG, AnomieBOT, FrescoBot, Hobsonlane, Alxeedo, Cobetadeeper, MastiBot, Defender of torch, Gregman2, EmausBot, WikitanvirBot, Going-Batty, Thebestrebels, Fæ, ClueBot NG, MelbourneStar, Wdchk, Widr, Vqazvinian, Ngocminh.oss, BG19bot, Qinsoon, Buisman, Manohar reddy123123, Dawud87930, Beth Holmes 1, Chunliang Lyu, Webclient101, Andrey.a.mitin, Monkbot, Dai Pritchard, Ba.ofoghi, Newwikieditor678, Jameswroxham121654 and Anonymous: 113

- **Resistance Database Initiative** *Source:* https://en.wikipedia.org/wiki/Resistance_Database_Initiative?oldid=679034082 *Contributors:* Cydebot, Obiwankenobi, Wilhelmina Will, Yobot, RjwilmsiBot, Brycehughes, Danielcoe15, Danim, BG19bot and Monkbot

- **Roblog** *Source:* https://en.wikipedia.org/wiki/Roblog?oldid=656305354 *Contributors:* Calton, Computerjoe, Toussaint, SmackBot, Bwpach, Alaibot, Mafmafmaf, Cgingold, Jiuguang Wang, Funandtrvl, JhsBot, Spudzonatron, McM.bot, ClueBot, Wysprgr2005, Chaosdruid, Addbot, Something4756, FrescoBot, Mean as custard, ClueBot NG, Helpful Pixie Bot, Fraulein451, ChrisGualtieri, CoolDude0017, Waqob, Coolepikly, Hamoudafg, Hibrohi1 and Anonymous: 2

- **Sayre's paradox** *Source:* https://en.wikipedia.org/wiki/Sayre'{}s_paradox?oldid=633632304 *Contributors:* AnomieBOT, Ontyx and BG19bot

- **SCIgen** *Source:* https://en.wikipedia.org/wiki/SCIgen?oldid=680941052 *Contributors:* Perique des Palottes, Wwwwolf, EALacey, Mackensen, Phil Boswell, Rebrane, Peter L, Mbh, Alexander.stohr, GreenReaper, Brianhe, Rich Farmbrough, Pèrez, Pol098, Apokrif, Bluemoose, GregorB, Josh Parris, Leeyc0, NeonMerlin, Vsion, SpuriousQ, Chick Bowen, Roy Brumback, GMan552, SmackBot, Yuriy75, Gilliam, Frap, Tim

Pierce, Derek R Bullamore, LavosBaconsForgotHisPassword, Dl2000, Thijs!bot, VoABot II, Adrian J. Hunter, Jtbarr4, Oleolius, VolkovBot, Fences and windows, EvanCarroll, Arcfrk, Marashie, Curuxz, Alexbot, Tahmasp, Addbot, Fgnievinski, LaaknorBot, Verbal, Lightbot, Yobot, Pcap, Housecarl, Hairhorn, Gaswen, IRP, First-user, GrouchoBot, Hopebring-elpidoforous, Monaliza2010, Waltoncoyman, Bebel2009, Juliod-kgt, Zuffo-Oliveira, Chriss1980, Dlouismusic, WikiEditor10001, 3-ph-d-students, Zero Thrust, Steve Quinn, Citation bot 1, Adalbrecht, Al-labnixcomputers, Greenenergy20, Trappist the monk, Lolita-dolores, Afteread, Zujine, Dewritech, ZéroBot, Esmito, Tijfo098, ClueBot NG, BarrelProof, Hodeken, MrBill3, Comfr, Laberkiste, Platopete, TKreuz, Hmainsbot1, Fausto zonaro, Kephir, C5st4wr6ch, Randykitty, Wuzh, E8xE8, Monkbot, Scarajason and Anonymous: 73

- **Silent speech interface** *Source:* https://en.wikipedia.org/wiki/Silent_speech_interface?oldid=681645051 *Contributors:* The Transhumanist, Magioladitis, LittleHow, Martarius, Addbot, Queenmomcat, Bellelettron, Dinamik-bot, Rlarue1, CopperSquare, Widr, Starrysky2 and Anonymous: 7

- **SILVIA** *Source:* https://en.wikipedia.org/wiki/SILVIA?oldid=647042976 *Contributors:* Jonsafari, RussBot, Thnidu, Renzoy16, AnomieBOT, Eumolpo, Jeromesandilanico, Codename Lisa, WikiU2013, InsuranceAgentof Satan and Anonymous: 3

- **Sinewave synthesis** *Source:* https://en.wikipedia.org/wiki/Sinewave_synthesis?oldid=420057239 *Contributors:* The Anome, SteinbDJ, Gerstman ny, Voxsprechen and Anonymous: 2

- **SmartAction** *Source:* https://en.wikipedia.org/wiki/SmartAction?oldid=679188263 *Contributors:* SoWhy, GabrielF, BD2412, ApprenticeFan, CmdrObot, Spartaz, Magioladitis, Theroadislong, Coffeepusher, Btimeline, Yobot, ChildofMidnight, Cnwilliams, R001605, Foxegon, Akerans, Metawizard, Iloveitsf, Helpful Pixie Bot, Nmanos1986, Waters.Justin, Cschrier2009 and Anonymous: 4

- **Speech-generating device** *Source:* https://en.wikipedia.org/wiki/Speech-generating_device?oldid=687862728 *Contributors:* Pnm, Tobias Bergemann, Michael Devore, Quadell, Rich Farmbrough, Sladen, Stuartyeates, RHaworth, Graham87, BD2412, Tony1, SmackBot, Cs-wolves, Mirokado, Ohconfucius, Dl2000, Cryptic C62, K7aay, Danger, Jamesontai, Aesopos, Nosloc, Yintan, Dodger67, Chaosdruid, Vanished user uih38riiw4hjlsd, Mortense, Yobot, AnomieBOT, Citation bot, Poule, FrescoBot, Pinethicket, Tinton5, Fayedizard, John of Reading, GA bot, Oemengr, Rpalmquist, ClueBot NG, Pflat, Helpful Pixie Bot, BG19bot, Livingat45north, CitationCleanerBot, Msmousette, MathewTownsend, Khazar2, Dexbot, UnderstandingPotato, TobiiAAC, MHartHenry, Rauckit, Monkbot and Anonymous: 11

- **Speech synthesis** *Source:* https://en.wikipedia.org/wiki/Speech_synthesis?oldid=689363319 *Contributors:* Damian Yerrick, Brion VIBBER, Arvindn, Hhanke, Maury Markowitz, Caltrop, Heron, Arj, Patrick, Dcljr, Eurleif, Paul A, Ppareit, Mac, Jimfbleak, MarcS~enwiki, Glenn, Kwekubo, Smack, Hike395, Nohat, Viajero, Wik, Tpbradbury, Furrykef, Grendelkhan, Thue, Raul654, Scott Sanchez, TMC1221, RedWolf, Chocolateboy, Kuszi, Yosri, Auric, Thesilverbail, Pengo, Tobias Bergemann, David Gerard, Giftlite, Gwalla, Holizz, Lupin, Ds13, Everyking, Moyogo, Wesley crossman, Matt Crypto, Python eggs, W4HTX, Alexf, Sonjaaa, Quadell, Latitude0116, Tjwood, Bumm13, Satori, Aaronrp, Chmod007, Abdull, StephenPratt, Kate, Discospinster, Rich Farmbrough, Sladen, Michal Jurosz, JoeSmack, BjarteSorensen, CanisRufus, Pjrich, Shrike, Kwamikagami, Bootedcat, Bobo192, Koosh, Polluks, Photonique, MrTree, Calton, PAR, Wtshymanski, Suruena, SteinbDJ, Dwiki, Thoobik, Angr, Jimich~enwiki, Ruud Koot, Twthmoses, Marskell, BD2412, JIP, CortlandKlein, Rjwilmsi, Koavf, Roberto111199, Raffaele Megabyte, Ligulem, NeonMerlin, Husky, Cassowary, Yamamoto Ichiro, Chrysoula, RobertG, Brianreading, Gary Cziko, Intgr, GreyCat, Chobot, Dadu~enwiki, YurikBot, RobotE, Jlittlet, RussBot, Conscious, Nahitk, Gaius Cornelius, Bovineone, Yrithinnd, NawlinWiki, Jeff Henderson, Joelr31, Bobbo, Xdenizen, Stephanos Georgios John, Amakuha, Tony1, Trainra, Nlu, Pb30, Fram, Back ache, Palthrow, SigmaEpsilon, JLaTon-dre, GrinBot~enwiki, Crystallina, SmackBot, Thefreethinker, Jagged 85, Paxse, Thenickdude, Canderra, Naikrovek, MonteChristof, Amatulic, Chris the speller, Bluebot, Thumperward, Oli Filth, DHN-bot~enwiki, Srchvrs, E946, Jacob Poon, Kindall, Kcordina, GVnayR, Cybercobra, Doodle77, Pgillman, Dave w74, SashatoBot, Yiddophile, Harryboyles, Savetz, Stefan2, Tlesher, Backstabb, Beetstra, Ace Frahm, EdC~enwiki, Dr.K., H, Saxbryn, SubSeven, Politepunk, TheFarix, Lakshmish, Ziusudra, Dycedarg, KyraVixen, 67-21-48-122, Argon233, Requestion, Out-riggr (2006-2009), Neelix, Simeon, Charlie danger, Morfeuz, AndrewHowse, Dogman15, Supremeknowledge, Kaldosh, Tawkerbot4, Dennishc, Thijs!bot, Geothermal, Al Lemos, Invitatious, AntiVandalBot, Hamedkhoshakhlagh, K7aay, Fayenatic london, Dylan Lake, Shaneymac, Wolf grey, MER-C, ChuckOp, Cypher543, SiobhanHansa, PrimroseGuy, Pedro, Bongwarrior, VoABot II, Faizhaider, Nameless Voice, Smihael, Tim-Magic, Wikipodium, Chrischris349, Twistor, A3nm, David Eppstein, JoergenB, Wayne Miller, Calltech, Ftiercel, Gwern, Stephenchou0722, JohnMRye, Andreas Bischoff, R'n'B, Instine, Ddp224, Jiuguang Wang, Itzcuauhtli, Wizzard2006, Wayp123, Oznull, Silas S. Brown, Little-How, Parasane, Flatterworld, Uluboz, Gerstman ny, Bonadea, Fr33kman, ACSE, Chachou, Johnny Au, TobyDZ, Toddy1, SteveRenals, Mar-tinevans123, Technopat, Rmcguire, Voxsprechen, Oznux, Badly Bradley, Tommy Blueseed, Billinghurst, Michaeldsuarez, Altermike, Bradfuller, Chuck Sirloin, Twikir, SieBot, Santhosh.thottingal, MaltaGC, Xenobiologista, Bocharov, Shafferb1, Jerryobject, Rafalfa, Nopetro, Ellamosi, StaticGull, JJblack, Renaudforestie, Fishnet37222, Martarius, ClueBot, Justin W Smith, Serezniy, Lukeluke1978, Auntof6, Jimboradley, Speech-grl, Canis Lupus, Kwizy, 12 Noon, The Founders Intent, Preservation Guide, Weheh, 7, Versus22, Kayemel3, MelonBot, DumZiBoT, Escientist, InternetMeme, Eik Corell, XLinkBot, Crb136, Actam, MystBot, Addbot, Fractaler, Betterusername, MrOllie, 5 albert square, Redox12, Luckas-bot, Thw416, Yobot, Southpolekat, Rogerb67, Paulson74, Lksdfvbmwe, N1RK4UDSK714, Shaftesbury12, AnomieBOT, Rjanag, ValerieCh-ernek, Sinus Pi~enwiki, Bluerasberry, Materialscientist, Citation bot, MotherFerginPrincess, Xqbot, CHIPSpeaking, T33guy, Nige7, RibotBOT, MatthPeder, MaviAteş, Shadowjams, Jenliv2ryd, Agoubard, Matrixbob, FrescoBot, Surv1v4l1st, L736E, Thorenn, Darkspartan4121, Citation bot 1, BStrategic, Pinethicket, LittleWink, TextToSpeech, RedBot, MastiBot, Googly2006, Reichenbachj, Full-date unlinking bot, W9000, Knowledgerend, TobeBot, SchreyP, Jonkerz, Nanard, Benimation, Lalalele, PleaseStand, VmZH88AZQnCjhT40, Bikepunk2, DARTH SID-IOUS 2, RjwilmsiBot, Codehydro, चंद्रकांत धुतडमल, EmausBot, Singlebarrel, Dewritech, GoingBatty, Bigbubba954, Ladysmithrose, Clus-ternote, SlowByte, Oemengr, Quorncider, Wingman4l7, MaGa, Donner60, Jphvs, ChuispastonBot, DASHBotAV, Diamondland, ClueBot NG, Yourmomblah, Drivertodriver1, Jose Manuel Ortega Torres, Dustin astrong, Marechal Ney, Helpful Pixie Bot, Ngocminh.oss, BG19bot, Fim-bim, Forthepoeple, Hagiza121, Blk2006, Hero10all, Sahassagala, Statisfactions, Octavius SV, Kephir, Makecat-bot, Snappysnackshack, Phamn-hatkhanh, Silas Ropac, Chillijohn, Ramkiag, Cmagnollay, Tvo05, Param Mudgal, Pavamit, Monkbot, Jahid.Hamid, Dyjung130, Mohithbp, Amaiagl, Carbon1400, Oproot, Utsavullas33, Sitarooman, Cs104group17, AlishiaHolmes, KasparBot, Speech 33, Jxtps435, MustaphaHadeed, You better look out below! and Anonymous: 381

- **Statistical semantics** *Source:* https://en.wikipedia.org/wiki/Statistical_semantics?oldid=666779180 *Contributors:* Phil Boswell, Beland, Jon-safari, Thüringer, Rjwilmsi, SmackBot, Pdturney, Rcartic, Melcombe, DragonBot, Libcub, Addbot, AnomieBOT, LatentDrK, FrescoBot, Salthizar, RjwilmsiBot, Intervallic, BattyBot, Monkbot and Anonymous: 5

- **Text mining** *Source:* https://en.wikipedia.org/wiki/Text_mining?oldid=688928444 *Contributors:* Fnielsen, Lexor, Nixdorf, Kku, Ronz, An-gela, Hike395, Furrykef, Khym Chanur, Pigsonthewing, ZimZalaBim, TimothyPilgrim, Timrollpickering, Adam78, Fennec, Ds13, Alison,

Dmb000006, Nwynder, Utcursch, Alexf, Geni, Beland, Mike Rosoft, D6, Bender235, MBisanz, Shanes, Serapio, Comtebenoit, John Vandenberg, Alansohn, Thüringer, Stephen Turner, Woohookitty, Dallan, Macaddct1984, Joerg Kurt Wegner, GrundyCamellia, Rjwilmsi, FayssalF, Intgr, Eric.dane~enwiki, Adoniscik, Alexmorgan, Chris Capoccia, Dialectric, Ksteen~enwiki, Kawika, GraemeL, GrinBot~enwiki, Veinor, SmackBot, Object01, Nixeagle, JonHarder, Matthew, Mfalhon, Gokmop, Derek R Bullamore, Dr.faustus, Musidora, JzG, Fernando S. Aldado~enwiki, Agathoclea, Slakr, Beetstra, Tmcw, Hobbularmodule, Hu12, Iridescent, Dreftymac, Ralf Klinkenberg, IvanLanin, Tawkerbot2, Dlohcierekim, PhillyPartTwo, CmdrObot, Van helsing, Gogo Dodo, Firstauthor, Scientio, A3RO, Nick Number, Zang0, AntiVandalBot, JAndbot, Olaf, East718, Whayes, Magioladitis, Bubba hotep, Jodi.a.schneider, Shadesofgrey, Saganaki-, Infovarius, MartinBot, Anaxial, CalendarWatcher, Jfroelich, Textminer, Vision3001, Hdurina, AKA MBG, Jkwaran, KylieTastic, DarkSaber2k, Lalvers, VolkovBot, ABF, Maghnus, Rogerfgay, Valerie928, Slabbe, Sebastjanmm, EverGreg, Guyjones, Znmeb, K. Takeda~enwiki, Sonermanc, Louiseh, Periergeia, Jerryobject, Eikoku, Mkonchady, Alessandro.zanasi, CharlesGillingham, Disooqi, Shah1979, JBrookeAker, Drgarden, Dokkai, Kotsiantis, Dtunkelang, Wikimeyou, Mdehaaff, Ray3055, Jplehmann, Pixelpty, Ferzsamara, Atolf19, Johnuniq, SoxBot III, Justin Mauger, XLinkBot, Ubahat, Chickensquare, DamsonDragon, Dianeburley, Maximgr, Texterp, Addbot, DOI bot, Fgnievinski, MrOllie, Kq-hit, Yami0226, Lightbot, Sredmore, Luckas-bot, Yobot, Themfromspace, Xicouto, Paulbalas, Glentipton, Tiffany9027, IslandData, Lexisnexisamsterdam, AnomieBOT, 1exec1, JoshKirschner, Saustinwiki, Citation bot, Wileri, Drecute, FrescoBot, Citation bot 1, Bina2, Boxplot, MastiBot, Trappist the monk, Lam Kin Keung, 564dude, Wikri63, Mean as custard, RjwilmsiBot, Pangeaworld, NotAnonymous0, Waidanian, Jahub, AvicAWB, Chire, AManWithNoPlan, Yatsko, TyA, Mayko333, Stanislaw.osinski, Amzimti, Epheson, ClueBot NG, Researchadvocate, Babaifalola, Babakdarabi, Luke145, Lawsonstu, Debuntu, Helpful Pixie Bot, Andrewjsledge, Rgranich, BG19bot, Meshlabs, Martinef, Desildorf, TextAnalysisProf, Cyberbot II, Astaravista, Anonymous but Registered, Marie22446688, Stabylorus, Cerabot~enwiki, Davednh, Marketpsy, Bradhill14, Tomtcs, SCBerry, Gnust, Koichi home add, Semantria, Astigitana, RTNTD, Fabio.ruini, LegalResearch345 2, Cognie, Cbuyle, Monkbot, Java12389, Aasasd, KasparBot, Howardbm, Mroche.perso and Anonymous: 260

- **TuVox** *Source:* https://en.wikipedia.org/wiki/TuVox?oldid=647218377 *Contributors:* Pnm, Quadell, Bender235, VoiceOfReason, BanyanTree, Graham87, The wub, NawlinWiki, Zzuuzz, Bluebot, Sadads, Robth, Angel Emfrbl, TruthbringerToronto, Goldenrowley, Nezzo, Magioladitis, Calltech, 718 Bot, Stepheng3, Addbot, Andywiener and Anonymous: 6

- **Validis** *Source:* https://en.wikipedia.org/wiki/Validis?oldid=619352512 *Contributors:* Mdd, SmackBot, Kvng, Cydebot, Alaibot, Willlovatt, CharlesGillingham, Libcub, AnomieBOT, Serdar XoXo, Zollerriia and Anonymous: 1

- **Vehicle infrastructure integration** *Source:* https://en.wikipedia.org/wiki/Vehicle_infrastructure_integration?oldid=662015423 *Contributors:* Seraphimblade, Mukkakukaku, RussBot, Hobit, SmackBot, Thisisbossi, Ckatz, Neelix, Basar, Cydebot, Kozuch, Mausy5043, Trusilver, Ipigott, GrdnAngel, ILoveKnowledge, Andy Dingley, Typ932, Longobord, Lightmouse, Anakin101, Sfan00 IMG, Fyrael, II MusLiM HyBRiD II, Shirik, DessertRat, Casia wyq, Lilinjing cas, ArmbrustBot and Anonymous: 17

- **Verbot** *Source:* https://en.wikipedia.org/wiki/Verbot?oldid=681262624 *Contributors:* Skysmith, Christopherlin, Chowbok, Bender235, Giraffedata, Lkinkade, Marudubshinki, Anomalocaris, Nlu, Samuel Blanning, SmackBot, Bluebot, Mpalmerlee, Iridescent, SimonDeDanser, Matthew Proctor, Thenar, Stevefish, Telgo, ClueBot, XLinkBot, JBsupreme, Ckenst, Freikorp, AnomieBOT, DataWraith, PigFlu Oink, Gerolkae, OMPIRE, MZDemonRaven and Anonymous: 11

- **VoiceWeb** *Source:* https://en.wikipedia.org/wiki/VoiceWeb?oldid=685840119 *Contributors:* D6, Riana, SmackBot, Pgillman, Magioladitis, Costrat, Pgezerlis, JL-Bot, Pkoutsod~enwiki, Addbot, AnomieBOT, Mean as custard, MOSNUM Bot, Helpful Pixie Bot, BattyBot and Anonymous: 10

- **WebCrow** *Source:* https://en.wikipedia.org/wiki/WebCrow?oldid=542674253 *Contributors:* RussBot, SmackBot, Colonies Chris, Rror, Yobot, MuffledThud, Erik9bot, Full-date unlinking bot and VincenzoDiMassa

- **Xaitment** *Source:* https://en.wikipedia.org/wiki/Xaitment?oldid=647234698 *Contributors:* Bearcat, LadyofShalott, Magioladitis, ESchuey, Wilhelmina Will, Tassedethe, FrescoBot, Tuankiet65, Techschuey and Anonymous: 2

- **YouNoodle** *Source:* https://en.wikipedia.org/wiki/YouNoodle?oldid=685158929 *Contributors:* EALacey, Bender235, Stesmo, BD2412, KFP, SmackBot, Stevenmitchell, Lighthead, J.delanoy, Mercurywoodrose, Urbanrenewal, Niceguyedc, Auntof6, Cookiehead, XLinkBot, Yobot, LilHelpa, Bethalicecook, Napi'shite po'zhaluista, Full-date unlinking bot, Hugc, Tkolind and Anonymous: 10

81.5.2 Images

- **File:AIAI-logo-172x77.png** *Source:* https://upload.wikimedia.org/wikipedia/en/4/4b/AIAI-logo-172x77.png *License:* Fair use *Contributors:*

    - http://www.aiai.ed.ac.uk/img/logo/aiai-172x77.gif *Original artist:* ?

    - **File:ARH_CAM-S1.jpg** *Source:* https://upload.wikimedia.org/wikipedia/commons/e/e8/ARH_CAM-S1.jpg *License:* CC BY 4.0 *Contributors:* Own work *Original artist:* Cameramann

    - **File:ARH_TrafficSpot_Gantry_Data_Point_Front.jpg** *Source:* https://upload.wikimedia.org/wikipedia/commons/c/ca/ARH_TrafficSpot_Gantry_Data_Point_Front.jpg *License:* CC BY-SA 4.0 *Contributors:* Own work *Original artist:* Cameramann

    - **File:Address_Recognition.png** *Source:* https://upload.wikimedia.org/wikipedia/commons/7/7c/Address_Recognition.png *License:* CC0 *Contributors:* Sargur Srihari
    Original artist: lawrence87

    - **File:Aforgenet.jpg** *Source:* https://upload.wikimedia.org/wikipedia/commons/b/bb/Aforgenet.jpg *License:* Public domain *Contributors:* http://www.aforgenet.com/img/aforgenetf.jpg *Original artist:* Andrew Kirillov

    - **File:Alexandria_VA_Dodge_Charger_Police_Car_ANPR.JPG** *Source:* https://upload.wikimedia.org/wikipedia/commons/f/f6/Alexandria_VA_Dodge_Charger_Police_Car_ANPR.JPG *License:* CC BY-SA 3.0 *Contributors:* Transferred from en.wikipedia; transferred to Commons by User:Kafuffle using CommonsHelper.
    Original artist: Something Original (talk). Original uploader was Something Original at en.wikipedia

- **File:Ambox_current_red.svg** *Source:* https://upload.wikimedia.org/wikipedia/commons/9/98/Ambox_current_red.svg *License:* CC0 *Contributors:* self-made, inspired by Gnome globe current event.svg, using Information icon3.svg and Earth clip art.svg *Original artist:* Vipersnake151, penubag, Tkgd2007 (clock)

- **File:Ambox_important.svg** *Source:* https://upload.wikimedia.org/wikipedia/commons/b/b4/Ambox_important.svg *License:* Public domain *Contributors:* Own work, based off of Image:Ambox scales.svg *Original artist:* Dsmurat (talk · contribs)

- **File:Ambox_rewrite.svg** *Source:* https://upload.wikimedia.org/wikipedia/commons/1/1c/Ambox_rewrite.svg *License:* Public domain *Contributors:* self-made in Inkscape *Original artist:* penubag

- **File:Ambox_wikify.svg** *Source:* https://upload.wikimedia.org/wikipedia/commons/e/e1/Ambox_wikify.svg *License:* Public domain *Contributors:* Own work *Original artist:* penubag

- **File:Animation2.gif** *Source:* https://upload.wikimedia.org/wikipedia/commons/c/c0/Animation2.gif *License:* CC-BY-SA-3.0 *Contributors:* Own work *Original artist:* MG (talk · contribs)

- **File:Artificial_Solutions_Logo.png** *Source:* https://upload.wikimedia.org/wikipedia/en/7/78/Artificial_Solutions_Logo.png *License:* PD *Contributors:*

  Artificial Solutions

  Original artist:

  Artificial Solutions

- **File:Automated_online_assistant.png** *Source:* https://upload.wikimedia.org/wikipedia/commons/8/8b/Automated_online_assistant. png *License:* Attribution *Contributors:*

  The text is adapted from the Wikipedia merchandise page (this automated customer service itself, however, is fictional), and pasted into a page in Wikipedia:

  Original artist: Mikael Häggström

- **File:BE_license_plate.jpg** *Source:* https://upload.wikimedia.org/wikipedia/commons/d/de/BE_license_plate.jpg *License:* CC-BY-SA-3.0 *Contributors:* Own work *Original artist:* CNB

- **File:Braille_text.jpg** *Source:* https://upload.wikimedia.org/wikipedia/commons/e/ee/Braille_text.jpg *License:* CC BY 2.0 *Contributors:* Flickr *Original artist:* Ralph Aichinger

- **File:Braina-logo.png** *Source:* https://upload.wikimedia.org/wikipedia/commons/0/02/Braina-logo.png *License:* Public domain *Contributors:* http://www.brainasoft.com/media/ *Original artist:* Brainasoft

- **File:Brookyn_Bridge_ANPR.jpg** *Source:* https://upload.wikimedia.org/wikipedia/en/2/20/Brookyn_Bridge_ANPR.jpg *License:* CC-BY-SA-3.0 *Contributors:*

  Own work

  Original artist:

  Jammmie999 (talk) (Uploads)

- **File:California_license_plate_ANPR.png** *Source:* https://upload.wikimedia.org/wikipedia/commons/9/9c/California_license_plate_ ANPR.png *License:* CC-BY-SA-3.0 *Contributors:* ? *Original artist:* ?

- **File:Cheaptalk_and_switch.jpg** *Source:* https://upload.wikimedia.org/wikipedia/commons/a/af/Cheaptalk_and_switch.jpg *License:* CC BY-SA 3.0 *Contributors:* Transferred from en.wikipedia; transferred to Commons by User:Bobamnertiopsis using CommonsHelper. *Original artist:* Poule (talk). Original uploader was Poule at en.wikipedia

- **File:Cleverbot_website.png** *Source:* https://upload.wikimedia.org/wikipedia/en/3/39/Cleverbot_website.png *License:* Fair use *Contributors:*

  Cleverbot.com *Original artist:* ?

- **File:Closed.circuit.twocameras.arp.750pix.jpg** *Source:* https://upload.wikimedia.org/wikipedia/commons/8/80/Closed.circuit. twocameras.arp.750pix.jpg *License:* Public domain *Contributors:* Own work *Original artist:* Adrian Pingstone

- **File:Commons-logo.svg** *Source:* https://upload.wikimedia.org/wikipedia/en/4/4a/Commons-logo.svg *License:* ? *Contributors:* ? *Original artist:* ?

- **File:Computer_and_speech_synthesiser_housing,_19_(9663804888).jpg** *Source:* https://upload.wikimedia.org/wikipedia/ commons/e/ec/Computer_and_speech_synthesiser_housing%2C_19_%289663804888%29.jpg *License:* CC BY-SA 2.0 *Contributors:* Computer and speech synthesiser housing, 19 *Original artist:* Science Museum London / Science and Society Picture Library

- **File:Crystal_Clear_action_run.png** *Source:* https://upload.wikimedia.org/wikipedia/commons/5/5d/Crystal_Clear_action_run.png *License:* LGPL *Contributors:* All Crystal Clear icons were posted by the author as LGPL on kde-look; *Original artist:* Everaldo Coelho and YellowIcon;

- **File:Crystal_Clear_app_kedit.svg** *Source:* https://upload.wikimedia.org/wikipedia/commons/e/e8/Crystal_Clear_app_kedit.svg *License:* LGPL *Contributors:* Sabine MINICONI *Original artist:* Sabine MINICONI

- **File:Crystal_kchart.png** *Source:* https://upload.wikimedia.org/wikipedia/commons/2/28/Crystal_kchart.png *License:* LGPL *Contributors:* All Crystal icons were posted by the author as LGPL on kde-look *Original artist:* Everaldo Coelho and YellowIcon

- **File:CustomAAC.jpg** *Source:* https://upload.wikimedia.org/wikipedia/en/e/e9/CustomAAC.jpg *License:* CC-BY-3.0 *Contributors:* ? *Original artist:* ?

- **File:Dasher.png** *Source:* https://upload.wikimedia.org/wikipedia/commons/c/cc/Dasher.png *License:* GPL *Contributors:* Transferred from en.wikipedia; transferred to Commons by User:IngerAlHaosului using CommonsHelper. *Original artist:* Original uploader was Freyr at en.wikipedia

- **File:Decrease_Positive.svg** *Source:* https://upload.wikimedia.org/wikipedia/commons/9/92/Decrease_Positive.svg *License:* Public domain *Contributors:*

- Decrease2.svg *Original artist:* Decrease2.svg: Sarang

- **File:DialogOSLogo.jpg** *Source:* https://upload.wikimedia.org/wikipedia/en/d/dc/DialogOSLogo.jpg *License:* CC-BY-SA-3.0 *Contributors:* ? *Original artist:* ?

- **File:Direct_translation_and_transfer_translation_pyramind.svg** *Source:* https://upload.wikimedia.org/wikipedia/commons/a/af/Direct_translation_and_transfer_translation_pyramind.svg *License:* CC-BY-SA-3.0 *Contributors:* ? *Original artist:* ?

- **File:Dubai-anpr-camera.png** *Source:* https://upload.wikimedia.org/wikipedia/commons/d/d6/Dubai-anpr-camera.png *License:* Public domain *Contributors:* Own work *Original artist:* Driver8888

- **File:Dutch_license_plate_segment.jpg** *Source:* https://upload.wikimedia.org/wikipedia/commons/3/3c/Dutch_license_plate_segment.jpg *License:* Public domain *Contributors:* ? *Original artist:* ?

- **File:Dynawrite.jpg** *Source:* https://upload.wikimedia.org/wikipedia/commons/4/4b/Dynawrite.jpg *License:* CC BY-SA 3.0 *Contributors:* Transferred from en.wikipedia; transferred to Commons by User:Bobamnertiopsis using CommonsHelper. *Original artist:* Poule (talk). Original uploader was Poule at en.wikipedia

- **File:EW_206_full_LED_lightbar_and_ANPR_camera'{}s_-_Flickr_-_Highway_Patrol_Images.jpg** *Source:* https://upload.wikimedia.org/wikipedia/commons/c/c1/EW_206_full_LED_lightbar_and_ANPR_camera%27s_-_Flickr_-_Highway_Patrol_Images.jpg *License:* CC BY 2.0 *Contributors:* EW 206 full LED lightbar and ANPR camera's *Original artist:* Highway Patrol Images

- **File:Edit-clear.svg** *Source:* https://upload.wikimedia.org/wikipedia/en/f/f2/Edit-clear.svg *License:* Public domain *Contributors:* The Tango! Desktop Project. *Original artist:*

  The people from the Tango! project. And according to the meta-data in the file, specifically: "Andreas Nilsson, and Jakub Steiner (although minimally)."

- **File:Emoji_u1f4bb.svg** *Source:* https://upload.wikimedia.org/wikipedia/commons/d/d7/Emoji_u1f4bb.svg *License:* Apache License 2.0 *Contributors:* https://code.google.com/p/noto/ *Original artist:* Google

- **File:En_to_my.png** *Source:* https://upload.wikimedia.org/wikipedia/commons/e/ee/En_to_my.png *License:* CC-BY-SA-3.0 *Contributors:* ? *Original artist:* ?

- **File:Factory_USA.svg** *Source:* https://upload.wikimedia.org/wikipedia/commons/8/85/Factory_USA.svg *License:* Public domain *Contributors:* Self made, based on mix of Image:Factory.svg and Image:Flag of the United States.svg *Original artist:* Sagredo

- **File:FasTrak_Orange_County.jpg** *Source:* https://upload.wikimedia.org/wikipedia/commons/2/2e/FasTrak_Orange_County.jpg *License:* CC-BY-SA-3.0 *Contributors:* Transferred from en.wikipedia; transferred to Commons by User:Jay8g using CommonsHelper. *Original artist:* Original uploader was Gary D at en.wikipedia. Later version(s) were uploaded by Ingolfson at en.wikipedia.

- **File:Flag_of_Israel.svg** *Source:* https://upload.wikimedia.org/wikipedia/commons/d/d4/Flag_of_Israel.svg *License:* Public domain *Contributors:* http://www.mfa.gov.il/MFA/History/Modern%20History/Israel%20at%2050/The%20Flag%20and%20the%20Emblem *Original artist:* "The Provisional Council of State Proclamation of the Flag of the State of Israel" of 25 Tishrei 5709 (28 October 1948) provides the official specification for the design of the Israeli flag.

- **File:Folder_Hexagonal_Icon.svg** *Source:* https://upload.wikimedia.org/wikipedia/en/4/48/Folder_Hexagonal_Icon.svg *License:* Cc-by-sa-3.0 *Contributors:* ? *Original artist:* ?

- **File:Free_Software_Portal_Logo.svg** *Source:* https://upload.wikimedia.org/wikipedia/commons/6/67/Nuvola_apps_emacs_vector.svg *License:* LGPL *Contributors:*

- Nuvola_apps_emacs.png *Original artist:* Nuvola_apps_emacs.png: David Vignoni

- **File:FrenchNumberPlates.jpg** *Source:* https://upload.wikimedia.org/wikipedia/commons/0/06/FrenchNumberPlates.jpg *License:* CC-BY-SA-3.0 *Contributors:* ? *Original artist:* ?

- **File:GMP_Vectra.jpg** *Source:* https://upload.wikimedia.org/wikipedia/commons/1/18/GMP_Vectra.jpg *License:* CC BY 2.0 *Contributors:* GMP Vectra *Original artist:* Mikey from Wythenshawe, Manchester, UK

- **File:GNOME_Chess_2D_3.11.92.png** *Source:* https://upload.wikimedia.org/wikipedia/commons/c/c2/GNOME_Chess_2D_3.11.92.png *License:* GPL *Contributors:* Own work *Original artist:* The GNOME Project

- **File:GNOME_Chess_3D_3.11.92.png** *Source:* https://upload.wikimedia.org/wikipedia/commons/6/61/GNOME_Chess_3D_3.11.92.png *License:* GPL *Contributors:* Own work *Original artist:* The GNOME Project

- **File:GNOME_Do_Classic.png** *Source:* https://upload.wikimedia.org/wikipedia/commons/7/71/GNOME_Do_Classic.png *License:* GPL *Contributors:* http://do.davebsd.com/ *Original artist:* David Siegel

- **File:Gnome-chess-icon-glossy.png** *Source:* https://upload.wikimedia.org/wikipedia/commons/b/b0/Gnome-chess-icon-glossy.png *License:* GPL *Contributors:* https://git.gnome.org/browse/gnome-chess/plain/data/icons/256x256/gnome-chess.png *Original artist:* The GNOME Project

- **File:Gnome-mime-sound-openclipart.svg** *Source:* https://upload.wikimedia.org/wikipedia/commons/8/87/Gnome-mime-sound-openclipart.svg *License:* Public domain *Contributors:* Own work. Based on File:Gnome-mime-audio-openclipart.svg, which is public domain. *Original artist:* User:Eubulides

- **File:Gnomelogo.svg** *Source:* https://upload.wikimedia.org/wikipedia/commons/6/68/Gnomelogo.svg *License:* LGPL *Contributors:* http://www.gnome.org/logo-and-trademarks/ *Original artist:* User:Sven and User:Bruce89

- **File:Stephen_Hawking_050506.jpg** *Source:* https://upload.wikimedia.org/wikipedia/commons/3/31/Stephen_Hawking_050506.jpg *License:* Public domain *Contributors:* Photo created by ^{2o1oo}, as documented at Wikipedia fr *Original artist:* ^{2o1oo}

- **File:Swedish_licenseplate.jpg** *Source:* https://upload.wikimedia.org/wikipedia/commons/0/0b/Swedish_licenseplate.jpg *License:* Public domain *Contributors:* Transferred from en.wikipedia to Commons by Unsonique using CommonsHelper. *Original artist:* The original uploader was E70 at English Wikipedia

- **File:Symbol_list_class.svg** *Source:* https://upload.wikimedia.org/wikipedia/en/d/db/Symbol_list_class.svg *License:* Public domain *Contributors:* ? *Original artist:* ?

- **File:Synaptic.png** *Source:* https://upload.wikimedia.org/wikipedia/commons/0/05/Synaptic.png *License:* GPL *Contributors:* [1] *Original artist:* en:User:Burgundavia

- **File:TTS_System.svg** *Source:* https://upload.wikimedia.org/wikipedia/commons/b/b5/TTS_System.svg *License:* Public domain *Contributors:* Transferred from en.wikipedia; transferred to Commons by User:Clusternote using CommonsHelper. *Original artist:* Andy0101 (talk). Original uploader was Andy0101 at en.wikipedia

- **File:Telepass-A9-20060209.ogg** *Source:* https://upload.wikimedia.org/wikipedia/commons/f/fc/Telepass-A9-20060209.ogg *License:* CC BY 2.5 *Contributors:* Own work *Original artist:* Markus Stamm

- **File:Text_document_with_red_question_mark.svg** *Source:* https://upload.wikimedia.org/wikipedia/commons/a/a4/Text_document_with_red_question_mark.svg *License:* Public domain *Contributors:* Created by bdesham with Inkscape; based upon Text-x-generic.svg from the Tango project. *Original artist:* Benjamin D. Esham (bdesham)

- **File:Tripletsnew2012.png** *Source:* https://upload.wikimedia.org/wikipedia/commons/4/43/Tripletsnew2012.png *License:* CC BY 4.0 *Contributors:* Own work *Original artist:* Thinkbig-project

- **File:TuVoxLogo.png** *Source:* https://upload.wikimedia.org/wikipedia/en/f/f4/TuVoxLogo.png *License:* Fair use *Contributors:*
(c) 2006 TuVox. Created by TuVox. Source: http://www.tuvox.com/images/TuVoxLandingLogo.gif *Original artist:* ?

- **File:Unbalanced_scales.svg** *Source:* https://upload.wikimedia.org/wikipedia/commons/f/fe/Unbalanced_scales.svg *License:* Public domain *Contributors:* ? *Original artist:* ?

- **File:VWtinylogo.jpg** *Source:* https://upload.wikimedia.org/wikipedia/en/7/75/VWtinylogo.jpg *License:* Fair use *Contributors:*
The logo may be obtained from VoiceWeb.
Original artist: ?

- **File:Videomaut-A13-Schoenberg.ogg** *Source:* https://upload.wikimedia.org/wikipedia/commons/0/03/Videomaut-A13-Schoenberg.ogg *License:* CC BY 3.0 *Contributors:* Own work *Original artist:* Markus Stamm

- **File:Wiki_letter_w.svg** *Source:* https://upload.wikimedia.org/wikipedia/en/6/6c/Wiki_letter_w.svg *License:* Cc-by-sa-3.0 *Contributors:* ? *Original artist:* ?

- **File:Wiki_letter_w_cropped.svg** *Source:* https://upload.wikimedia.org/wikipedia/commons/1/1c/Wiki_letter_w_cropped.svg *License:* CC-BY-SA-3.0 *Contributors:*

- Wiki_letter_w.svg *Original artist:* Wiki_letter_w.svg: Jarkko Piiroinen

- **File:Wikiversity-logo.svg** *Source:* https://upload.wikimedia.org/wikipedia/commons/9/91/Wikiversity-logo.svg *License:* CC BY-SA 3.0 *Contributors:* Snorky (optimized and cleaned up by verdy_p) *Original artist:* Snorky (optimized and cleaned up by verdy_p)

81.5.3 Content license

- Creative Commons Attribution-Share Alike 3.0

www.ingramcontent.com/pod-product-compliance
Lightning Source LLC
Chambersburg PA
CBHW080551060326
40689CB00021B/4820